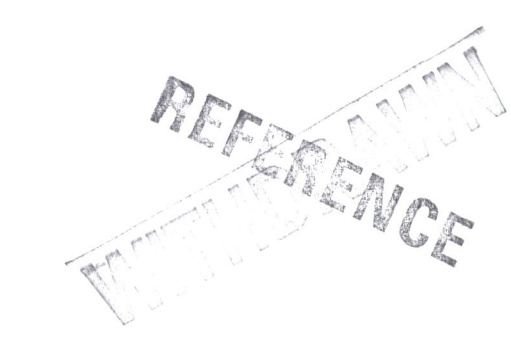

# Political Leaders in Weimar Germany

*A Biographical Study*

Also by Peter D. Stachura

*Nazi Youth in the Weimar Republic*
*The Weimar Era and Hitler 1918–1933. A Critical Bibliography*
*The Shaping of the Nazi State* (Editor)
*The German Youth Movement 1900–1945: An Interpretative and Documentary History*
*Gregor Strasser and the Rise of Nazism*
*The Nazi Machtergreifung* (Editor)
*Unemployment and the Great Depression in Weimar Germany* (Editor)
*The Weimar Republic and the Younger Proletariat. An Economic and Social Analysis*
*Themes of Modern Polish History* (Editor)

# Political Leaders in Weimar Germany
## *A Biographical Study*

*Peter D. Stachura*

**SIMON & SCHUSTER**
New York   London   Toronto   Sydney   Tokyo   Singapore

First published 1993 by
Harvester Wheatsheaf
Campus 400, Maylands Avenue
Hemel Hempstead
Hertfordshire, HP2 7EZ
A division of
Simon & Schuster International Group

and in the USA by
Academic Reference Division
Simon & Schuster
15 Columbus Circle
New York, NY 10023

© 1993 Peter D. Stachura

All rights reserved. No part of this book may be reprinted
or reproduced or utilized in any form or by any electronic,
mechanical, or other means, now known or hereafter
invented, including photocopying and recording, or in any
information storage or retrieval system, without
permission in writing from the publishers.

Library of Congress Cataloging-in-Publication Data

Stachura, Peter D.
    Political leaders in Weimar Germany, a biographical study / Peter D. Stachura.
      p.  cm.
    Includes bibliographical references and index.
    ISBN 0–13–020330–0
    1. Politicians—Germany—Biography.   2. Germany—Politics and government—1818–1933.   I. Title.
DD244.S64   1993
920.043—dc20                                        92–30716
                                                                                   CIP

For Józia,
of Mszana Dolna

# Contents

| | |
|---|---|
| Acknowledgements | vi |
| List of Entries | vii |
| Introduction | 1 |
| Biographies of Political Leaders A–Z | 7 |
| Chronology of the Weimar Republic | 195 |
| Abbreviations and Glossary | 203 |
| Select Bibliography: The Weimar Republic | 207 |
| Index | 219 |

# *Acknowledgements*

The origins of the present study can be traced back to my examination during the late 1970s and early 1980s of the career of Gregor Strasser, the National Socialist Party leader, which awakened my interest in the role of Weimar politicians as a whole. The material that forms the basis for this book has been consequently gathered over a lengthy period and in the course of various other research projects. It gives me pleasure to acknowledge the institutions and their staffs whose willing and expert service facilitated my work, with perhaps particular mention of the Bayerische Staatsbibliothek in Munich, the object of several visits, notably in 1986 and 1991; the libraries of the Universities of Cologne, Hamburg and Munich; the library of the German Historical Institute in London, and the National Library in Edinburgh. Some additional and no less important data were obtained in an occasional way during my many visits to German archives in the 1980s, including the Bundesarchiv in Koblenz, Staatsarchiv Hamburg, the Bayerisches Hauptstaatsarchiv, and the Hauptstaatsarchiv Stuttgart.

The political figures discussed in the book have been the topic of numerous conversations with colleagues at home and abroad over the years, and I would like to thank them collectively for their valuable insights and perspectives.

A special word of thanks is owed to Margaret Dickson who, under pressing circumstances, was primarily responsible for typing my manuscript.

The completion of the final draft of the manuscript this year, especially during the last six months, was helped very substantially by the forbearance and encouragement of my wife, Kay, and children, Gregory and Madeleine. I am most appreciative of their support.

*Peter D. Stachura*
Bridge of Allan
Polish National Election Day, 1991

# List of Entries

Adenauer, Konrad  7
Amann, Max  8
Barth, Emil  9
Bauer, Gustav  10
Bäumer, Gertrud  12
Bernstein, Eduard  13
Bolz, Eugen  15
Bouhler, Philip  16
Braun, Otto  17
Brauns, Heinrich  18
Brecht, Arnold  19
Bredt, Johann  20
Breitscheid, Rudolf  21
Brockdorff-Rantzau, Ulrich Graf von  22
Brüning, Heinrich  23
Crispien, Artur  25
Cuno, Wilhelm  26
Curtius, Julius  27
Dahlem, Franz  28
Darré, Walther  29
Däumig, Ernst  31
David, Eduard  32
Dessauer, Friedrich  33
Dietrich, Hermann  34
Dietrich, Otto  35
Dingeldey, Eduard  35
Dittmann, Wilhelm  37
Dorten, Hans-Adam  38
Drexler, Anton  38
Duesterberg, Theodor  40
Ebert, Friedrich  41
Eisner, Kurt  43
Epp, Franz Ritter von  44
Erkelenz, Anton  45
Erzberger, Matthias  46
Feder, Gottfried  47
Fehrenbach, Konstantin  49
Fischer, Ruth  50

Frick, Wilhelm  51
Frölich, Paul  52
Gayl, Freiherr Wilhelm von  53
Gessler, Otto  54
Goebbels, Joseph  56
Goerdeler, Carl  57
Goering, Hermann  59
Gradnauer, Georg  60
Groener, Wilhelm  62
Grotewohl, Otto  63
Grzesinski, Albert  64
Gürtner, Franz  66
Haase, Hugo  67
Hamm, Eduard  68
Haussmann, Conrad  69
Heilmann, Ernst  70
Heine, Wolfgang  71
Held, Heinrich  72
Helfferich, Karl  74
Hellpach, Willy  75
Hergt, Oskar  76
Hermes, Andreas  77
Hertz, Paul  78
Heuss, Theodor  79
Hilferding, Rudolf  81
Hindenburg, Paul von  83
Hirsch, Paul  84
Hirtsiefer, Heinrich  85
Hitler, Adolf  86
Hoernle, Edwin  88
Hoetzsch, Otto  89
Höpker-Aschoff, Hermann  91
Hörsing, Friedrich Otto  92
Hugenberg, Alfred  93
Jarres, Karl  95
Joos, Joseph  96
Juchacz, Marie  97
Kaas, Ludwig  98

Kahl, Wilhelm  98
Kahr, Gustav Ritter von  100
Kapp, Wolfgang  102
Keil, Wilhelm  103
Koch-Weser, Erich  105
Koenen, Wilhelm  107
Köhler, Heinrich  108
Köster, Adolf  109
Kube, Wilhelm  110
Külz, Wilhelm  111
Landsberg, Otto  113
Ledebour, Georg  114
Levi, Paul  115
Liebknecht, Karl  117
Löbe, Paul  118
Luther, Hans  120
Luxemburg, Rosa  121
Marx, Wilhelm  122
Moldenhauer, Paul  124
Müller, Hermann  125
Neumann, Heinz  126
Noske, Gustav  128
Papen, Franz von  130
Pieck, Wilhelm  131
Popitz, Johannes  133
Preuss, Hugo  134
Pünder, Hermann  136
Radbruch, Gustav  137
Rathenau, Walther  139
Raumer, Hans von  141

Remmele, Hermann  142
Röhm, Ernst  143
Rosenberg, Alfred  145
Schäffer, Fritz  147
Scheidemann, Philipp  149
Schiele, Martin  150
Schiffer, Eugen  152
Schlange-Schöningen, Hans  154
Schleicher, Kurt von  155
Schmidt, Robert  157
Scholz, Ernst  159
Schwerin von Krosigk, Lutz  161
Seeckt, Hans von  162
Seldte, Franz  163
Severing, Carl  164
Sollmann, Wilhelm  166
Stegerwald, Adam  168
Strasser, Gregor  170
Stresemann, Gustav  172
Thalheimer, August  174
Thälmann, Ernst  176
Treviranus, Gottfried  178
Ulbricht, Walter  180
Wels, Otto  181
Westarp, Kuno Graf von  183
Wirth, Joseph  185
Wissell, Rudolf  188
Zeigner, Erich  190
Zetkin, Clara  192

# Introduction

It has often been observed that the Weimar Republic produced a mere handful of political personalities of genuine international stature: the names of Gustav Stresemann, Walther Rathenau and, perhaps, Friedrich Ebert spring most readily to mind. On the other hand, that era is more usually associated with politicians who played a conspicuous role in the destruction of Germany's first parliamentary democracy, most notably Paul von Hindenburg, Alfred Hugenberg, Kurt von Schleicher and, of course, Adolf Hitler. Between these two extremes of the spectrum, however, lay the mass of those who achieved positions of political authority and responsibility, and whose actions in consequence had also much to do with determining Germany's fate before 1933.

The broad historical context in which Weimar's political leaders operated has been the subject of intensive international scholarship over the years, resulting in a voluminous and ever-expanding literature that focuses on institutions, organizations, philosophies, movements, constitutions, as well as personalities. Although everyone's situation is conditioned by historical circumstances, and actions are dictated to an extent by contemporary exigencies, sight must not be lost of the capacity of individuals to exert a vital, sometimes decisive, influence on the course of events. The present work, which is the first English-language biographical study of the most significant politicians of a crucial and dramatic period in modern German and European history, aims to analyze this particular dimension of the Weimar experience.

While the creation of a political culture was the work of a large number of prominent people in many different spheres of activity, including diplomacy, education, the economy, armed forces, trade unions, the Churches, the arts and media, the policies and decisions which ultimately shaped the essential development of the Republic were fashioned by a relatively small circle at the very heart of politics. Members of this circle constituted an informal élite who did more than anyone else to influence the Republic's destiny by virtue of their strategic location at the forefront of governmental, parliamentary and party-political life. The subjects in this study are restricted, therefore, to the most important decision-makers: Reich chancellors, distinguished ministers, party leaders, outstanding parliamentarians, chairmen and high-profile members of principal government agencies, and a number of provincial politicians whose connections extended to the highest echelons of power. A limited group of senior civil servants who are known to have played a major part in government decisions on policy and legislation at a national level are also included, as are the leaders of Weimar's most important non-party paramilitary organization that was responsible for mobilizing substantial numbers on the Right against the democratic system.

The criteria thus employed to adjudicate the inclusion and omission of individuals have been formulated as precisely as possible, but they are not and cannot be absolutely watertight. Inevitably, there will be argument or disagreement about the final choice, but this has ultimately to be accepted as a necessary occupational hazard because a line has to be drawn somewhere. In all, a select list of 135 names is presented, in alphabetical order, in the form of concise biographies, which provide not only salient details of background and career, but also a critical assessment of the subject's significance and contribution to Weimar politics at the top. Some discussion of pre-1918 and post-1933 career is also given, thus to offer a rounded picture.

Those discussed here represent a rich cross-section of German society during the 1918–33 period, emanating from diverse social, educational, denominational and political backgrounds. While figures from all the major parties are listed, the largest contingent is supplied by the two principal pro-republican parties, the Social Democrats and the Centre. Workers and aristocrats form small minorities alongside the majority that was upper or lower middle-class. Only a few did not progress beyond primary school education, while the numbers going on to obtain university undergraduate degrees, doctorates and post-doctoral qualifications were somewhat greater. In confessional terms, approximately 18 per cent of the 135 subjects are Catholic, 15 per cent Jewish or of Jewish origin, and some two-thirds either Protestant or atheist. In other words, whereas Catholics were underrepresented in this political élite in relation to their percentage of the Reich population (about 33 per cent), Jews were considerably overrepresented (1 per cent of the total population). A more striking contrast is apparent in the male/female ratio, for only five women have been found a place in my selection, which is simply a reflection of the fact that Weimar politics was constructed very definitely on a male ethos. In any event, I did not consider that, apart from Gertrud Bäumer, Ruth Fischer, Marie Juchacz, Rosa Luxemburg and Clara Zetkin, there were female politicians who could be classified as top-level decision-makers. This is not to deny the merits of a number of other women who achieved a certain prominence, such as Marie-Elizabeth Lüders, Toni Sender,[1] Christine Teusch and Luise Tietz.

Besides easily recognizable names – for example, those of Heinrich Brüning, Franz von Papen and Carl Severing – are scores of lesser-known but none the less fundamental figures who carried substantial burdens of office. Into this category fall the likes of Paul Löbe, president of the Reichstag for many years; Hermann Dietrich, Vice-Chancellor in the Brüning cabinet and a leader of the German Democratic Party; Martin Schiele, Reich Minister and leading German nationalist; Rudolf Wissell, Reich Minister of Labour in the Müller-led Grand Coalition government (1928–30); and many others. Finally, excluded from my list after much agonizing were Dr Hjalmar Schacht, whose direct political influence as president of the Reichsbank from 1923 to 1930 is difficult to ascertain precisely;[2] Professor Hermann Warmbold, whose tenure of the Reich Economics Ministry 1931–33 was overshadowed by the authority directly wielded in that sphere by the chancellors he served; Walther von Keudall, who made a limited contribution as Reich Minister of the Interior in the fourth Marx cabinet; Johannes Hoffmann, Bavarian Minister-President in 1919–20, who quickly faded from what was for him a strictly regional political scene;[3] and Dr Rudolf Heinze, Vice-Chancellor in the Fehrenbach cabinet in 1920–21 and Reich Minister of Justice in 1922–23 under Chancellor Wilhelm Cuno, who made little impression.

The length of each biographical appraisal naturally varies according to the subject, but a minimum of 400 and a maximum of 1000 words are used. In bibliographies attached to each entry, reference is made to relevant memoirs, diaries, autobiographies, collections of speeches and other works authored by the subject, together with biographies, monographs, articles or other scholarly literature which relate directly and importantly to an individual's political career or activity. In this manner, opportunities for further reading and consultation are intimated. Moreover, a select bibliography is provided at the end, comprising those works that were used for information or reference during the preparation of this study, and which furnish additional sources for understanding major events and developments of the Weimar era.

The book is designed as a reliable and appropriately detailed source of information, reference and critical evaluation, and also as a basic resource tool for further research, directed towards a readership encompassing students and scholars of twentieth-century history, politics and sociology.

## Notes

1. See T. Sender, *The Autobiography of a German Rebel*, New York, 1939.
2. H. Schacht, *Account Settled*, London, 1949; *My First Seventy Six Years. An Autobiography*, London, 1955; *1933. Wie eine Demokratie stirbt*, Düsseldorf, 1968. Critical studies include E.N. Peterson, *Hjalmar Schacht. For and Against Hitler. A Political-Economic Study of Germany, 1923–1945*, Boston, 1954; A.E. Simpson, *Hjalmar Schacht in Perspective*, The Hague, 1969.
3. D. Hennig, *Johannes Hoffmann. Sozialdemokrat und Bayerischer Ministerpräsident. Biographie*, Munich, 1990. Chapters V–XVII inclusive (pp. 85–449) deal with the 1918–20 period, the most critical of his career.

# Biographies of
# Political Leaders

## A–Z

# ADENAUER, Konrad (1876–1967)

Adenauer's primary claim to historical celebrity rests with his leadership, as Chancellor, of the Federal Republic of Germany from 1949 until his retirement in 1963. A cofounder of the Christian Democratic Party in July 1945, the party which dominated government during his 14-year tenure, he provided astute and judicious guidance from the top which allowed West Germany to achieve economic and political stability at home and a certain respectability in the international community following the barbarism of the Third Reich. The hallmarks of his chancellorship were the economic revival (*Wirtschaftswunder*) based on social market principles, rapprochement with General de Gaulle's France and reconciliation with the Jews and Israel. In the age of the 'cold war', he steered his country in a decisively western direction, spurning a Soviet offer of reunification in 1952.

His earlier political career was not quite as dramatic but it did see him emerge as an influential and noteworthy personality in his own right, above all, as Lord Mayor (*Oberbürgermeister*) of his native city of Cologne from 1917 until 1933. Born the son of a Catholic middle-ranking civil servant on 5 January 1876, Adenauer completed his law degree, married and in 1906 was elected an official (*Beigeordneter*) of Cologne city council. Three years later he served as Deputy Mayor. At the end of the First World War it fell to the recently appointed Lord Mayor to cope with the prodigious problems in the city created by political, economic and social upheaval. Adenauer, a member of the left-wing of the Centre Party, and from 1921 until 1933 president of the Prussian State Council (Staatsrat), set about his task with characteristic vigour. He believed that the key to re-establishing order and social peace in his city and in Germany as a whole was the provision of high-standard social and civil amenities. In this enterprise he was conspicuously successful and Cologne's position as one of the foremost cites in Germany was extended – but at the price of a soaring municipal budget which already by 1929 had brought the city to the verge of financial collapse. During the ensuing Depression, he was still reluctant to curtail expansion and fiercely criticized Chancellor Brüning's deflationary policies. Only with the banking crisis in 1931 did Adenauer finally succumb to demands for retrenchment. Throughout this time, he had jealously guarded the fiscal and financial autonomy of local government from what he regarded as unnecessary interference from the Reich and Prussian authorities, and for this stance won much popularity among his fellow citizens. However, Adenauer's Weimar political career also had its failures and controversies. Twice, first in 1921 and then in 1926, he was approached about assuming the office of Reich Chancellor. On the latter occasion, for instance, President von Hindenburg wanted him to take the place of Hans Luther who had been forced to resign, but Adenauer's hopes of moulding a broadly-based cabinet floundered in the face of opposition from the DVP. In any case, he and Gustav Stresemann, that party's leader, were locked in a bitter personal dispute.

The most controversial aspect of his early political involvement, which was to resurface after 1949, was Adenauer's alleged sympathy and support for the Rhenish separatist movement in the early 1920s. When the French invaded the Ruhr in

January 1923 in response to Germany's defaulting on reparations payments, Adenauer was apparently one of a number of leading personalities in the Rhineland who advocated the establishment of an independent Rhenish republic, with its capital in Cologne. Otherwise, he maintained good diplomatic relations with the British army of occupation in the Rhineland until its withdrawal in 1926.

As a vigorous opponent of the NSDAP, it was hardly unexpected that Adenauer should have been dismissed from office in 1933, or that he should have been arrested by the Gestapo a year later and again in 1944. But his impeccable anti-Nazi credentials formed an indispensable basis for his post-war career. He died at the age of 91, in Rhöndorf on the Rhine, on 19 April 1967.

## Further Reading

K. Adenauer, *Erinnerungen*, Stuttgart, 1965–68. The most recent biographies are the best, including P. Koch, *Konrad Adenauer. Eine politische Biographie*, Hamburg, 1985; H.-P. Schwarz, *Adenauer*. Vol. 1, *Der Aufstieg, 1876–1954*, Stuttgart, 1986; Vol. 2, *Der Staatsmann, 1952–1967*, Stuttgart, 1991. W. von Sternburg, *Adenauer. Eine deutsche Legende*, Frankfurt am Main, 1987; S. Thomas, *Konrad Adenauer und die Entstehung der Bundesrepublik Deutschland*, Berlin, 1989. On the separatist controversy, see K.D. Erdmann, *Adenauer in der Rheinlandpolitik nach dem Ersten Weltkrieg*, Stuttgart, 1966. See also H. Stehkämper (ed.), *Konrad Adenauer. Oberbürgermeister von Köln*, Cologne, 1976; J. Foschepoth (ed.), *Adenauer und die deutsche Frage*, Göttingen, 1988, H.P. Mensing (ed.), *Adenauer im Dritten Reich*, Berlin, 1991.

# AMANN, Max (1891–1957)

The later press and publishing magnate of the Third Reich was born into a lower middle-class background in Munich on 24 November 1891. After school, Amann completed a course in business and commercial studies and worked as a clerk in a Munich law practice. He served in a Bavarian infantry regiment throughout the First World War and for a short period was Hitler's company sergeant. Demobilized in 1919, Amann married and found secure employment in a mortgage bank in Munich. His political career commenced in February 1920 when he joined the NSDAP and was persuaded by Hitler to assume the post of party business manager in August 1921, thus at a time when the *Führer* was asserting his dictatorial control and introducing to sensitive positions in the party hierarchy personnel whom he trusted. Quickly becoming recognized as one of Hitler's most loyal associates, Amann also took over the directorship the following year of the Eher Verlag, the NSDAP's official publishing house, and was instrumental in the development and expansion of the *Völkischer Beobachter* into the party's principal daily newspaper in the later 1920s.

For his active participation in the ill-fated Beer Hall putsch in Munich in November 1923, Amann was arrested, imprisoned for a few weeks and charged with 'aiding and abetting high treason'. At his subsequent trial in April 1924, however, he was merely fined a modest amount on a lesser charge. A Hitler loyalist during a period of turbulence in the National Socialist movement, he was elected an NSDAP representative on the Munich city council in 1924 where his brusque, often arrogant and offensive manner brought him frequently into conflict with his colleagues. From 1928 to 1930 he also sat on the local council of Upper Bavaria. He successfully supervised Hitler's private financial and business affairs, including the royalties from *Mein Kampf*, and despite losing his left arm in a hunting accident in 1931, was able to use his considerable organizational talent and business acumen to consolidate firmly the party's publishing activity and prepare it for a vast programme of expansion after 1933. As president of the Reich Association of German Newspaper Publishers and president of the Reich Press Chamber, Amann was well placed to mastermind the construction of a Nazi publishing empire which within a few years left little room for independent publishing. To this extent, his work for the totalitarian state perfectly complemented Goebbels's propaganda system. For this service he was awarded the title of *Reichsleiter* in 1942. An *SS-Obergruppenführer* since the previous year, he also sat in the Reichstag from 1933 to 1945.

Detained by the occupying American forces in summer 1945 at the Seckenheim detention centre near Heidelberg, Amann's attempts at self-justification proved fruitless. In September 1948 he received a two-and-a-half-year sentence from a Munich court for a misdemeanour involving an anti-Nazi newspaper editor, and in December of the same year the Central Denazification Court found him to have been a 'major offender' in the Third Reich, handing out a sentence of ten years' imprisonment in a labour camp and loss of civil rights. It had been revealed at his trial that of all the top leadership of Hitler's regime, he had made the most material gain from his political office. Subsequently stripped also of his wealth, Amann died in his native city on 30 March 1957.

## Further Reading

M. Amann, *Ein Leben für Führer und Volk*, Munich, 1941. See also A. Krebs, *Tendenzen und Gestalten der NSDAP*, Stuttgart, 1959; O.J. Hale, *The Captive Press in the Third Reich*, Princeton, 1964.

## BARTH, Emil (1879–1941)

Barth was one of the most influential and controversial figures during the revolutionary period in Germany at the end of the First World War, emerging as the most radical member of the Council of People's Representatives. He was born in Heidelberg on 23 April 1879, and after completing his apprenticeship as a plumber became an official in the left-wing German Metalworkers' Union and a member of the left wing of the SPD. He served several prison sentences for petty offences and his personal reputation was unsavoury, but he showed courage and tenacity in pursuit of his political ambitions.

While serving in the army he joined illegally the USPD, and on being invalided out in 1918, became leader of the Berlin Revolutionary Shop Stewards' movement, which was the main organizational link between the strike of Berlin workers in January 1918 and the November Revolution. Barth declared his intention in fiery revolutionary rhetoric: 'The objective is proletarian peace, that is, a peace imposed by the proletariat, that is, socialism, that is, the dictatorship of the proleteriat'. He saw himself as the chief of staff of the impending revolution and set about collecting arms and funds. He knew that a rising would have little chance as long as the army remained undefeated, but he did expect its defeat. His active preparations were aided by the Russian Embassy, but Barth kept his distance from the Spartacists whom he regarded as politically immature. Indeed, he was one of the small group of left-wing Independent Socialists who never became a Communist. Barth's impetuous search for the day of revolutionary action in November 1918 was not always reciprocated by his colleagues, and he later claimed that the absence of decisive action at an earlier date caused the failure of the Revolution. In reality, the divisions on the Left were more important. On 10 November he joined the provisional government of the Council of People's Representatives as the delegate of the Revolutionary Shop Stewards and as a left-wing member of the USPD. Although his specific brief was for social and health affairs, Barth sought to play a larger role in developments. Often in conflict with fellow members of the Council, whom he accused of lacking radical zeal, he lost out in the frenetic power game that German politics had become in late 1918. His removal as chairman of the Revolutionary Shop Stewards on 18 December was a serious blow, for his scope for political leadership was then seriously restricted. His support for the rebellion against the Council by the sailors' *Volksmarinedivision* a few days later marked the final break between Barth and his erstwhile colleagues. He rapidly fell into political obscurity, particularly following an abortive attempt to make a comeback through a revived Revolutionary Shop Stewards' movement in 1919. Two years later he rejoined the SPD, and until 1924 was secretary of the Factory Council Department of the socialist trade unions (ADGB). He lived quietly thereafter until his death in Berlin on 15 July 1941.

## Further Reading

E. Barth, *Aus der Werkstatt der deutschen Revolution*, Berlin, 1919. See also C.B. Burdick and R.H. Lutz (eds), *The Political Institutions of the German Revolution 1918–1919*, New York, 1966; E. Kolb and R. Rürup (eds), *Der Zentralrat der deutschen sozialistischen Republik 1918–1919. Quellen zur Geschichte der Rätebewegung in Deutschland 1918/19*, Leiden, 1968; E. Matthias and S. Miller (eds), *Die Regierung der Volksbeauftragten 1918/19*, 2 vols, Düsseldorf, 1969; A.J. Ryder, *The German Revolution of 1918. A Study of German Socialism in War and Revolt*, London, 1967.

# BAUER, Gustav (1870–1944)

Prior to his notable contribution to the development of the Weimar Republic, Bauer had already built up considerable trade unionist and political experience in the *Kaiserreich*. Born in the village of Darkehmen, East Prussia, on 6 January 1870, his lack of formal education above primary school level did not deter an early interest in trade union affairs. While employed as a clerical assistant in a lawyer's practice in Königsberg he founded and shortly thereafter led the Association of Office Employees, which was a stepping stone to his appointment in 1908 as deputy chairman of the General Commission of German Trade Unions, a post he held until 1918. A longstanding member of the SPD, he was elected to the Reichstag following the party's electoral triumph in 1912. During the First World War, while retaining his parliamentary seat, he was involved in various official capacities to do with national defence.

Bauer was prominently engaged in the politically unstable early years of the new state. Along with Philipp Scheidemann, he served, as a Secretary of State in the Reich Labour Office, in the transitional government headed by Prince Max of Baden in October–November 1918; they were the first socialists in German history to serve in central government. In the ensuing Council of People's Representatives in November–December of that year, Bauer was departmental head of the Reich Labour Ministry. Representing the SPD in the National Assembly in 1919–20, he was appointed Reich Labour Minister in the Scheidemann cabinet (February–June 1919), adopting a firmly anti-radical course while at the same time arguing for the workers to be given a formal role in the economy. Consequently, Bauer made a useful contribution to the framing of the Factory Councils Law of 1920. After Scheidemann had resigned in protest at the terms of the Versailles Treaty and the DDP withdrew from government, a new coalition comprising the SPD and Centre Party was established in June 1920 under Bauer's leadership. It was left to his cabinet to accept and sign the Treaty. A few months later it also formally accepted the new Weimar Constitution. Adopting the traditional title of *Reichskanzler*, Bauer continued to lead the government through the subsequent stormy months until it was confronted by the Kapp Putsch in March 1920. Although his government survived, thanks mainly to a general strike called by the trade unions and the refusal of the higher civil service to co-operate with the insurgents, he resigned later that month. He immediately came back into government as Reich Treasury Minister and (from 1 May) as Reich Transport Minister in the Hermann Müller administration. When it fell in June 1920, Bauer did not return to office until appointed Reich Treasury Minister and Vice-Chancellor in Joseph Wirth's coalition cabinets which extended from May 1921 until November 1922. He was generally regarded as a conscientious and reliable minister.

For his indirect involvement in the Barmat financial scandal, Bauer was expelled for a period from the SPD until rehabilitated at the Heidelberg Conference in 1926. He continued to serve in the Reichstag for a further three years before retiring from politics altogether. He died in Berlin on 16 September 1944.

## Further Reading

A. Golecki (ed.), *Akten der Reichskanzlei. Weimarer Republik. Das Kabinett Bauer: 21. Juni 1919 bis 26. März 1920*, Boppard, 1980; S. Miller, *Die Bürde der Macht. Die deutsche Sozialdemokratie 1918–1920*, Düsseldorf, 1978; U. Kluge, *Die deutsche Revolution 1918/19*, Frankfurt am Main, 1985; H.A. Winkler, *Die Sozialdemokratie und die Revolution 1918/19*,

Bonn, 1979; E. Laubach, *Die Politik der Kabinette Wirth 1921–22*, Lübeck, 1968; E. Lucas, *Märzrevolution 1920*, 3 vols, Frankfurt am Main, 1978.

## BÄUMER, Gertrud (1873–1954)

The leader of the liberal middle-class feminist movement before 1914 and throughout the Weimar era, as well as a prominent female member and Reichstag deputy of the DDP, Bäumer was born in Hohenlimburg on 12 September 1873, the daughter of a Protestant pastor and district school inspector. After attending primary and secondary school in Cammin, Pomerania, she completed her teacher training, taught between 1892 and 1898, and went on to study German language and theology in Berlin. In 1900 she qualified as a secondary schoolteacher and four years later took her doctorate with a dissertation on Goethe's work.

Dr Bäumer was strongly influenced by her association with Helene Lange, the women's rights campaigner, whom she helped edit *Die Frau*, the journal of the middle- class League of German Women's Associations (BDF). At the same time, she became a close associate and admirer of Friedrich Naumann and his national-social ideas, and also helped edit *Die Hilfe*, his movement's journal. Bäumer replaced Marie Stritt as BDF president in 1910 and guided the movement towards abandonment of the idea of the equality of the sexes in favour of the view that women were fundamentally different in character and abilities from men. Rather than compete with men, women were to seek out the 'female sphere' in life and develop their own talents accordingly. This doctrine was enshrined in the revised BDF programme of 1919. Its retreat before the war from the emancipatory tenets of feminism was underlined by the BDF's adoption of an increasingly authoritarian Social Darwinist ideology, nationalism, 'racial hygiene' and eugenics. Bäumer's links with the conservative Evangelical Social Congress further influenced the BDF's swing to the right. The entry of other right-wing groups into the BDF with her encouragement, including the German Women's League, boosted membership to almost 250,000 in 1914. In addition to her BDF activities, she found time to teach at the Soziale Frauenschule in Berlin and to establish links with the independent German youth movement. In response to a government request to the BDF in 1914, she set up the Nationaler Frauendienst to mobilize volunteers for welfare work among women adversely affected by the war, and for the making of clothing for the armed forces. In 1917 she became head of the Social Educational Institute in Hamburg.

After the war, Bäumer continued to lead a full political and professional career. From 1920 until 1933 she was a high-ranking official in the Reich Interior Ministry, with special responsibility for educational and youth welfare matters, contributing to the framing of important legislation such as the National Youth Welfare Act in 1922 and the Law for the Protection of Youth from Trashy and Erotic Literature in 1926. That year also, she was the German delegate to the League of Nations Committee on social and humanitarian issues, and, especially in the 1930s, warned of the demoralizing and politically dangerous effects of mass unemployment on the younger generation. She carried the Naumann tradition into the DDP when she joined in 1918, representing the party in the National Assembly and then until 1932 in the Reichstag. A member of the Reichstag's Population Policy Committee, Bäumer also played a leading role in the formation of the German State Party in 1930. Maintaining a leading profile in the BDF, which she represented at international disarmament conferences, she was a prominent campaigner for women's rights, democracy and international peace.

In 1933, being deemed 'politically unreliable' by the National Socialists, Bäumer was dismissed from her government post on a reduced pension, and was barred from publishing her writings from 1935 until 1937. The BDF was dissolved in 1933, but she reached a *modus vivendi* with the regime which allowed her to keep the issue of women's rights at least marginally afloat while she refrained from making any political comment. Indeed, she supported quotas against women university students and she was able to collaborate with the Nazi women's organization (Frauenschaft) on minor concerns. She even refused to speak out publicly against the Lebensborn programme of the SS, for which she forfeited the admiration of many former colleagues. She was allowed to continue publishing *Die Frau* until 1944, and took also to publishing historical novels. At the end of the war, she was forced to flee Silesia, where she had made her second home, and eventually settled in Bad Godesberg. No longer politically active, Bäumer continued to publish as a novelist. She died in Bielefeld-Bethel on 25 March 1954.

## Further Reading

Among Bäumer's most notable writings are: *Grundlagen demokratischer Politik*, Karlsruhe, 1928; *Sinn und Form geistiger Führung*, Berlin, 1930; and *Lebensweg durch eine Zeitenwende*, Tübingen, 1933. See also R.J. Evans, *The Feminist Movement in Germany, 1894–1933*, London, 1976; B. Greven-Aschoff, *Die Bürgerliche Frauenbewegung in Deutschland 1894–1933*, Göttingen, 1981; M.L. Bach, *Gertrud Bäumer. Biographische Daten und Texte zu einem Persönlichkeitsbild*, Weinheim, 1989.

## BERNSTEIN, Eduard (1856–1932)

Although he is most immediately identified as the leading ideological force behind the revisionist controversy in the SPD before 1914, Bernstein also made an important contribution to the party's development in the early years of the Weimar Republic. Coming from an assimilated Jewish family which had produced rabbis, doctors, mathematicians as well as the religious reformer and liberal newspaper publisher, Aaron Bernstein, Eduard was born the son of a train driver in Berlin on 6 January 1856. He worked as a bank clerk, and renounced Judaism in favour of Marxist atheism some time before entering politics. An active participant in the Gotha unity congress in 1875, he was appointed private secretary three years later to the neo-Kantian philanthropist Karl Höchberg, accompanying him to Switzerland. With his patron's financial support he helped found, in 1879, an illegal *émigré* newspaper, *Der Sozialdemokrat*, henceforth the official organ of the SPD. Bernstein became its chief editor in 1881. Enjoying the confidence of Marx and Engels – the latter designating him, jointly with August Bebel, executor of his literary estate – he was one of those principally responsible for the acceptance of Marxism as the party's official ideology during the years of persecution and repression by the Reich government. When Bismarck's anti-socialist law lapsed in 1890, he and Karl Kautsky together drafted the Erfurt Programme, the first self-consciously Marxist programme of the SPD which remained in force until shortly after the First World War. While the party was free after 1890 to operate openly, Bernstein was not: the warrants for his arrest were renewed annually until 1900, and Prussian pressure on the Swiss authorities compelled him to leave Switzerland in 1887.

From his base in London from 1888 to 1901 he contributed to the central party newspaper *Vorwärts* and to Kautsky's theoretical journal *Die Neue Zeit*, and formulated a series of theoretical positions which were soon to feed into the debate on 'revisionism'. Allowed to return to Germany by Chancellor von Bülow, Bernstein was elected to represent the constituency of Breslau in the Reichstag between 1902 and 1906, and again from 1912 until 1918. Later, from 1920 to 1928 he was a representative of a Berlin electoral district. The sequence was broken by his membership of the USPD in 1917–1919.

At the outbreak of war in August 1914, Bernstein was carried away by his patriotic russophobia and voted in favour of war credits. But by early the following year he had changed his mind in view of what he now saw as a war of annexationism by Germany, and he became an anti-war activist. In June 1915, he published with Hugo Haase and Karl Kautsky a ringing denunciation of the war entitled '*Das Gebot der Stunde* (*The Demand of the Hour*). As his commitment to pacifism and internationalism increased, he moved to the left of the SPD and then, in 1917, to the USPD. During the Revolution of 1918–19 he served as a *Beirat* (supernumerary official) in the Reich Treasury Office, and otherwise campaigned against the vision of a proletarian Soviet Germany offered by the radical Left. He fully supported moves to establish the National Assembly as an interim parliamentary body, and defended the tough, controversial measures taken by Gustav Noske, the Reich Defence Minister, to protect the Republic from left-wing extremists. Despite being afflicted by poor health and family tragedy, Bernstein re-emerged as a provocative thinker and debater in party circles, commencing with a major paper at the SPD's first post-war annual congress in Weimar in 1919 on Germany's responsibility for the First World War. Here, and in subsequent speeches and writings, he opposed the prevailing nationalist thesis, which was broadly accepted in his own party, that encircled Germany had been forced into fighting a defensive war. His creative intellectual energy was also channelled into the drafting of the Görlitz Programme of 1921, which committed the SPD as 'the party of working people in town and country' to socialism within the context of the democratic Republic. He championed the cause of coalition with bourgeois parties, including the right-of-centre DVP. While continuing to be concerned with party affairs, he broadened his interests during the 1920s to encompass Zionism and internationalism, bringing to these subjects the same intellectual honesty and moral probity as to others.

Bernstein's death in Berlin on 18 December 1932, thus a few weeks before his entire human and political philosophy was brutally swept aside in Germany, passed almost unnoticed, even in the SPD.

## Further Reading

E. Bernstein, *Die Voraussetzungen des Sozialismus und die Aufgaben der Sozialdemokratie*, Stuttgart, 1899; *Zur Theorie und Geschichte des Sozialismus*, Berlin, 1901; *Die Arbeiterbewegung*, Frankfurt am Maine, 1910; *Sozialdemokratie und Völkerpolitik*, Leipzig, 1917; *Die deutsche Revolution. Ihr Ursprung, ihr Verlauf und ihr Werk*, Berlin, 1921; *Entwicklungsgang eines Sozialisten*, Leipzig, 1930. See also P. Gay, *The Dilemma of Democratic Socialism. Eduard Bernstein's Challenge to Marx*, New York, 1952; H. Grebing, *Der Revisionismus. Von Bernstein bis zum 'Prager Frühling'*, Munich, 1977; H. Heimann and T. Meyer (eds), *Bernstein und der Demokratische Sozialismus*, Berlin and Bonn, 1978; R. Fletcher (ed.), *Bernstein to Brandt. A Short History of German Social Democracy*, London, 1987.

# BOLZ, Eugen (1881–1945)

The leading Centre Party politician in Württemberg in the Weimar era, Bolz remained a constantly firm supporter of the parliamentary democratic order even when his own party moved perceptibly to the right from the late 1920s onwards. He was born into a pious Catholic family in Rottenburg am Neckar on 15 December 1881, joining the Centre Party while still studying law at university, and elected to represent it in the Reichstag in 1912 as well as in the Württemberg Landtag the following year; he gave uninterrupted service in both houses until 1933.

In successive post-war coalition governments in his home state he served as Minister of Justice in 1919–24, and Minister of the Interior in 1924–28, before being elected State President in 1928. He combined this office with his Interior Ministry portfolio until 1933. In all of these posts, but particularly as State President, Bolz exhibited a commendable degree of integrity, diligence and loyalty to the Republic, qualities that were frequently absent in his fellow politicians of the period. He strongly favoured constitutional reform that would curtail the powers of central government, believing that federalism was the most efficacious model for running the country. In these respects, and taking account of his Christian commitment, Bolz emerged as a prime example of political Catholicism at its most positive in the Weimar period.

For a few months following the National Socialist advent to power, Bolz led an interim administration in Württemberg, and one of his last political acts was to vote, against his better judgement but in deference to party discipline, for the Enabling Bill in the Reichstag in March 1933. Held briefly in a concentration camp that year, he then withdrew from politics to pursue a business career. In 1941–42, however, he was drawn into the conservative resistance around Carl Goerdeler, and in the last cabinet list drawn up by the conspirators of July 1944 he was earmarked to head the Ministry of Culture. For his involvement in the plot, he was hanged in Berlin's Plötzensee prison on 23 January 1945.

*Further Reading*

M. Miller, *Eugen Bolz. Staatsmann und Bekenner*, Stuttgart, 1951; W. Besson, *Württemberg und die deutsche Staatskrise, 1928–1933*, Stuttgart, 1959; L. Biewer, *Reichsreformbestrebungen in der Weimarer Republik*, Frankfurt am Main, 1980; G. Schulz, *Zwischen Demokratie und Diktatur. Verfassungspolitik und Reichsreform in der Weimarer Republik*, Vols I and II, Berlin, 1987; T. Schnabel (ed.), *Die Machtergreifung in Südwestdeutschland. Das Ende der Weimarer Republik in Baden und Württemberg, 1928–1933*, Stuttgart, 1982; T. Schnabel, *Württemberg zwischen Weimar und Bonn, 1928–1945/54*, Berlin, 1986.

## BOUHLER, Philip (1899–1945)

Although uninvolved in the decision-making machinery of the NSDAP and virtually unknown to the general public, Bouhler, in his capacity as executive secretary of the party from 1925 until the end of the *Kampfzeit*, was one of the most significant backstage influences in Weimar politics. Born in Munich on 2 September 1899, the son of a retired colonel, he joined the Royal Bavarian Cadet Corps and was wounded in action as a lieutenant in the First Bavarian Foot Artillery during the First World War.

He worked for various publishers after 1918 and matriculated as a philosophy student at the University of Munich, joining the NSDAP in 1921. The following year he abandoned his studies to help edit the *Völkischer Beobachter*. When the party broke up after the Beer Hall putsch, he was appointed business manager of one of the cover organizations that temporarily replaced it in southern Germany, the Grossdeutsche Volksgemeinschaft (Greater German People's Community). As executive secretary (*Reichsgeschäftsführer*) of the recreated NSDAP, Bouhler played a key role in extending the authority of the party's central office (*Reichsleitung*) over local branches and leaders, and in imposing unitary party discipline. He asserted, most importantly, the exclusive right of central office to issue membership cards, thus allowing it to maintain accurate records of party membership in each locality and of local party finances. Bouhler had many of the qualities of a traditionally-minded bureaucrat; he was diligent, efficient, punctilious, self-effacing, devoid of personal or political ambition, and completely loyal to his superior, Hitler. As Bouhler supervised the progressive centralization of the party's organizational apparatus and its development into the most effective in contemporary German politics, Hitler was free to concentrate on long-term political strategy and objectives.

In 1933, Bouhler was rewarded for his vital services with the title and status of *Reichsleiter* of the NSDAP and a seat in the Reichstag for the district of Westphalia. A number of other offices came his way, including those of police president of Munich, chief of the *Führer's* Chancellery, and head of the party's Censorship Committee for the Protection of National Socialist Literature, as well as of the Study Group for German History Books and Educational Material, without ever entering the élite leadership of the Third Reich. Subsequently appointed a *Gruppenführer* in the SS and director of the abortive euthanasia programme, Bouhler committed suicide at Goering's headquarters at Zell-am-See in early May 1945.

## Further Reading

P. Bouhler, *Adolf Hitler. Das Werden einer Volksbewegung*, Lübeck, 1932. See also D. Orlow, *The History of the Nazi Party, Volume I, 1919–1933*, Pittsburgh, 1969; *Volume 2, 1933–1945*, Pittsburgh, 1973.

## BRAUN, Otto (1872–1955)

As Minister-President of Germany's largest and most important state, Prussia, from 1920 to 1933 (with very brief interruptions in 1921 and 1925), Braun emerged as one of the most capable politicians in the ranks of the SPD, who was resolutely dedicated to the preservation and defence of the democratic Republic. Presiding over coalition governments comprising the SPD, Centre Party and DDP – occasionally also the DVP – he sought to organize Prussia as a model republican *Volksstaat*, to be extended in time to the rest of the country. Supported by able party colleagues, such as Carl Severing, Braun gave Prussia efficient, orderly government, which took a vigorous attitude towards both left- and right-wing enemies of the Republic. In consequence, 'Red Prussia' was widely perceived as a republican bastion under the stewardship of the 'Red Tsar', Braun. Although lacking charisma and regarded by some as a party-machine man with no particular interest in the ideas and theories of social democracy, his organizational abilities and talent for arranging compromises marked him as the quintessential pragmatist who was able to be on good terms with most of the major factions in the SPD. Indeed, it was his private lifestyle which attracted most criticism from party comrades, on account of the rather grand manner in which he pursued his love of hunting.

Braun was born the son of a shoemaker in Königsberg, East Prussia, on 28 January 1872 and completed his apprenticeship as a lithographer. He joined the SPD at the age of 17 and soon became chairman of the Königsberg branch. From 1893 he both printed and edited the local party newspaper. A leading official of the German Agricultural Workers' Union from 1909 to 1920, he was elected to the SPD's national executive in 1911, and two years later began to represent the party in the Prussian House of Deputies. With this strong personal and political background in East Prussia, it is perhaps not surprising that Braun possessed the traditional reserve of inhabitants of that part of Germany, or that he was militantly anti-Polish.

Braun was elected by the radical Berlin metalworkers to their strike committee in January 1918, and during the November Revolution sat on the Berlin Workers' and Soldiers' Council. He was a member of the National Assembly in 1919, then the Reichstag, and from 1921 also of the Prussian Landtag. From 1919 to 1921 he was

Minister of Agriculture in the Prussian government. He regarded the SPD's Görlitz Programme (1921) as a fundamental turning-point in the party's history, in that it was now prepared to move out of agitation and opposition to accept governmental responsibility at all levels. In the 1925 Reich presidential election he was the SPD's candidate in the first ballot, attracting nearly 8 million votes; he dropped out of the second round of voting in favour of the SPD–Centre–DDP joint candidate, Wilhelm Marx.

Following the NSDAP's success at the Reichstag elections in September 1930, Braun called for a 'great coalition of men of good sense' in preference to a presidential cabinet, but his proposal received little support, even from his own party. His steadfastness in the face of political adversity in the early 1930s when anti-democratic extremists inexorably gained ground was highly commendable, but when the coalition parties lost their majority in the Prussian Landtag elections in April 1932 he never recovered from the blow. Thus, when Chancellor von Papen deposed the Prussian cabinet in July 1932, Braun was on sick leave, determined never to return to office. In March 1933 he abandoned politics and emigrated, finally settling in Switzerland, where he died on 15 December 1955.

## Further Reading

O. Braun, *Deutscher Einheitsstaat oder Föderativsystem?*, Berlin, 1927; *Von Weimar zu Hitler*, New York, 1940. See also H. Schulze, *Otto Braun oder Preussens demokratische Sendung. Eine Biographie*, Frankfurt am Maine, 1977; H.-P. Ehni, *Bollwerk Preussen? Preussen-Regierung, Reich-Länder-Problem und Sozialdemokratie 1928–1932*, Bonn, 1975; S. Höner, *Der nationalsozialistische Zugriff auf Preussen. Preussischer Staat und nationalsozialistische Machteroberungsstrategie, 1928–1934*, Bochum, 1984; H. Möller, *Parlamentarismus in Preussen 1919–1932. Handbuch der Geschichte des deutschen Parlamentarismus*, Düsseldorf, 1985; D. Orlow, *Weimar Prussia 1918–1925. The Unlikely Rock of Democracy*, Pittsburgh, 1986.

## BRAUNS, Heinrich (1868–1939)

Born into a working-class family in Cologne on 3 January 1868, Brauns was ordained a Catholic priest before becoming prominently involved before the war in the Christian trade union movement and the social welfare organization, Volksverein für das Katholische Deutschland. Taking a doctorate in 1905, Brauns actively promoted co-operation between both sides of industry on a Christian basis that was heavily influenced by the example of Bishop Ketteler in the mid-nineteenth century. A member of the National Assembly in 1919, he went on to represent the electoral district of Cologne-Aachen as a Centre Party deputy in the Reichstag until 1933.

His expertise in social and labour affairs was recognized by Reich Chancellor Fehrenbach in 1920 when Brauns was appointed Reich Labour Minister, a post he held until 1928. During his tenure he made an outstanding contribution to the creation and development of the public welfare system (*Sozialstaat*). He played a major role in the formulation of legislation on many varied aspects of welfare, including trade union and workers' rights, applying Catholic concepts of social justice. He emphasized the importance of social corporatism and the 'just wage' as prerequisites of social stability. It was perhaps inevitable, therefore, that he was seen by the Right as pro-labour and anti-capitalist. For industrialists he epitomized all that was wrong with the public welfare system, particularly its considerable cost. After leaving office, Brauns continued to be active in social and labour matters as a member of Reichstag committees and as leader of the German delegations to the International Labour Conference held in Geneva in 1929–31. In January 1931 Chancellor Brüning appointed him to head the Commission for the Investigation of the World Economic Crisis and its Consequences, the so-called Brauns Commission. It recommended as the principal solution to Germany's economic problems a state-encouraged increase in capital imports from abroad.

With Hitler's advent to power, Brauns did not stand in the 1933 Reichstag election, and retired to Lindenberg in the Allgäu, where he died on 19 October 1939.

## Further Reading

H. Brauns, *Christliche Gewerkschaften oder Fachabteilungen in katholischen Arbeitervereinen*, Cologne, 1904; and *Die christlichen Gewerkschaften*, Mönchengladbach, 1908; *Katholische Sozialpolitik im 20. Jahrhundert. Ausgewählte Aufsätze und Reden von Heinrich Brauns* (edited by H. Mockenhaupt), Mainz, 1976. See also E. Deuerlein, 'Heinrich Brauns – Schattenriss eines Sozialpolitikers', in F.A. Hermens and T. Schieder (eds), *Staat, Wirtschaft und Politik in der Weimarer Republik. Festschrift für Heinrich Brüning*, Berlin, 1967, pp. 41–96; W. Abelshauser (ed.), *Die Weimarer Republik als Wohlfahrtsstaat. Zum Verhältnis von Wirtschafts- und Sozialpolitik in der Industriegesellschaft*, Stuttgart, 1987; A. Baumgartner, *Sehnsucht nach Gemeinschaft. Ideen und Strömungen im Sozialkatholizismus der Weimarer Republik*, Munich, 1977; G.A. Ritter, *Der Sozialstaat. Entstehung und Entwicklung im internationalen Vergleich*, supplement to *Historische Zeitschrift*, 1989; C. Sachsse, *Fürsorge und Wohlfahrtspflege 1871–1929. Geschichte der Armenfürsorge in Deutschland*, Stuttgart, 1988.

# BRECHT, Arnold (1884–1977)

As a high-ranking civil servant of strong pro-republican sympathies who served under seven Reich chancellors and many more Reich and Prussian ministers, Brecht was uniquely placed both as a witness and frequently as an active participant in Weimar politics. He made a major contribution to the drafting of important legislation, including the Law for the Protection of the Republic (1922), took a leading role in discussion of constitutional and electoral reform, advised government on the most momentous events of that period, and defended the deposed Prussian government of July 1932 in the Staatsgerichtshof. He was born into a comfortable and well-connected upper middle-class Protestant family in Lübeck on 26 January 1884, growing up in a National Liberal environment that was patriotic, conservative and anti-socialist, while devoid of party affiliation. After completing his law degree at the University of Leipzig, he served in the Reich Justice Office from 1910 to 1918.

In October 1918 Chancellor Prince Max of Baden appointed him secretary to his cabinet, followed in 1921 by an appointment as a departmental head in the Reich Interior Ministry. After six eventful years in that office he was dismissed on political grounds by the new Reich Interior Minister, Walther von Keudall, a member of the DNVP, but was almost immediately brought into Prussian government service by Minister-President Otto Braun. As Prussia's representative, on 2 February 1933 Brecht made the last free speech in the Reichsrat. A few days later he was dismissed from office by Hitler's regime and took up an academic post at the New School for Social Research in New York. He remained in the United States for many years, took American citizenship and did not return to Germany until 1948 for a temporary visit. He died in Eutin, in Schleswig-Holstein, on 11 September 1977.

## Further Reading

A. Brecht, *Die Geschäftsordnung der Reichsministerien*, Berlin, 1927; *Reichsreform. Warum und Wie?*, Berlin, 1931; *The Art and Technique of Administration in German Ministries*, Cambridge, Massachusetts, 1940; *Prelude to Silence. The End of the German Republic*, London, 1944; *Federalism and Regionalism in Germany. The Division of Prussia*, New York, 1945; *Walther Rathenau und das deutsche Volk*, Munich, 1950; *Politische Theorie. Die Grundlagen politischen Denkens im 20. Jahrhundert*, Tübingen, 1961; *Aus nächster Nähe. Lebenserinnerungen 1884–1927*, Stuttgart, 1966; *Mit der Kraft des Geistes. Lebenserinnerungen 1927–1967*, Stuttgart, 1967. An abridged English version of the latter two volumes of memoirs was published as *The Political Education of Arnold Brecht. An Autobiography, 1884–1970*, Princeton, 1970.

# BREDT, Johann Victor (1879–1940)

A specialist in constitutional law, university professor and politician, Bredt was born in Barmen on 2 March 1879 into a wealthy manufacturing family, and on completing his academic studies in law and political economy, including his *Habilitationsschrift* in 1909, he took up an appointment at the University of Marburg. He joined the Free Conservative Party and represented it in the Prussian House of Deputies from 1911 to 1918. In November 1918 he was a co-founder of the DNVP, though he resigned to join the Economic Party, a right-wing middle-class interest group, in the wake of the Kapp Putsch. He represented his new party, renamed at his suggestion in 1925 the Reichspartei des deutschen Mittelstands, from 1924 to 1933 in the Reichstag.

Bredt carved out a prominent niche for himself by his critical views on constitutional reform. In 1919, for instance, he produced his own draft Reich constitution which was more heavily influenced by the American presidential ethos than the version drawn up by Theodor Heuss. He was a member of various parliamentary committees, among them the Committee of Investigation into the Causes of the German Collapse in 1918. At the same time, he developed a keen interest in the affairs and ecclesiastical law of the Protestant churches. As leader of his party, Bredt was brought into Chancellor Brüning's first cabinet in March 1930 as Minister of Justice. In November of the same year, however, he was withdrawn from government by his party in protest at Brüning's allegedly pro-socialist attitudes. His party's increasingly accentuated right-wing, capitalist and nationalist views could not prevent a mass exodus of its followers to the NSDAP in the early 1930s, so much so that after the Reichstag elections in November 1932 he remained its lone representative in parliament. Bredt was not sorry to see the parliamentary state disintegrate but, on the other hand, he at no time endorsed the NSDAP. Having been promoted to a full professorship in public law at Marburg in 1931, he returned there after Hitler's advent to power to pursue his academic career. He died in Marburg on 1 December 1940.

## Further Reading

J. Bredt, *Neues evangelisches Kirchenrecht für Preussen*, 3 vols, Berlin, 1921–27; *Der Geist der deutschen Reichsverfassung*, Berlin, 1924. See also M. Schumacher (ed.), *Johann Victor Bredt. Erinnerungen und Dokumente, 1914 bis 1933*, Düsseldorf, 1970; M. Schumacher, *Mittelstandsfront und Republik. Die Wirtschaftspartei – Reichspartei des deutschen Mittelstandes*, Düsseldorf, 1972.

## BREITSCHEID, Rudolf (1874–1944)

A major personality and source of influence in the SPD before 1933, Breitscheid cut an elegant, urbane figure in a party where leaders rarely rose above the ordinary and pedestrian. He was the party's best speaker, well known for his diplomatic skill, articulate and possessing a first-rate political intelligence. A radical democrat rather than a Marxist, he regarded the left-wing Liberal Theodor Barth, not Karl Marx, as his political mentor. Born the son of a bookshop assistant in Cologne on 2 November 1874 and educated at the universities of Munich and Marburg, Breitscheid took his doctorate in economics in 1898 and went into journalism, writing and editing for liberal publications of various types. His early political activity in Liberal-Democratic circles removed the heady nationalistic views of his student days, and in 1912 he joined the SPD. A member of the Berlin-Wilmersdorf city council from 1914 to 1920, he broke with the SPD to join the USPD in 1917, largely because of his strong pacifism, and edited the weekly journal, *Der Sozialist*.

Immediately after the November Revolution, Breitscheid was a member of the Prussian revolutionary government as Minister of the Interior and played a useful role in reducing separatist tensions in the Rhineland. Elected to represent the USPD in the Reichstag in 1920, he rejoined the SPD in 1922 and served it in that forum, latterly as co-chairman of its faction, until 1933. During the 1920s he was the party's leading spokesman on foreign affairs and as a firm believer in international reconciliation gave not inconsiderable support to many of Gustav Stresemann's policies. Indeed, from 1926 to 1930 he served, at the foreign minister's invitation, on the German League of Nations Commission. An architect of the SPD's policy of toleration towards the Brüning administration and a member of the party executive from 1931, Breitscheid can be criticized for a rather complacent interpretation of the Nazi threat. As one of the leading theorists in the party, he was instrumental in propagating the mistaken view that the NSDAP was merely a phenomenon of the Depression which would decline into relative political obscurity once the economy revived. In January 1933 he forcefully made clear the SPD's refusal to collaborate in any way with Chancellor von Schleicher's attempts to create a broadly-based national government, which was to include the socialist trade unions, and his intervention persuaded the latter to remain aloof.

In spring 1933, in the face of Nazi terror tactics against the Left, Breitscheid fled to Switzerland and then to Paris, where he spent the years until the German invasion writing for the exiled SPD press. Arrested by the French authorities in late 1940 and delivered to the Gestapo in February 1941, he was charged with high treason and sent to Sachsenhausen, and later, Buchenwald concentration camps. He died as a result of an allied air attack on Buchenwald on 24 August 1944.

## Further Reading

G. Zwoch (ed.), *Rudolf Breitscheid. Reichstagsreden*, Bonn, 1974; D. Lange (introd.), *Rudolf Breitscheid. Antifaschistische Beiträge 1933–1939*, Frankfurt am Main, 1977; W.H. Maehl, *The German Socialist Party. Champion of the First Republic, 1918–1933*, Philadelphia, 1986; W. Pyta, *Gegen Hitler und für die Republik. Die Auseinandersetzung der deutschen Sozialdemokratie mit der NSDAP in der Weimarer Republik*, Düsseldorf, 1989; R. Schaefer, *SPD in der Ära Brüning. Tolerierung oder Mobilisierung? Handlungsspielräume und Strategien sozialdemokratischer Politik 1930–1932*, Frankfurt am Main, 1990.

# BROCKDORFF-RANTZAU, Ulrich Graf von (1869–1928)

Before playing a leading role in the diplomatic and political history of the Weimar Republic in the early and mid-1920s, Brockdorff-Rantzau had built up a formidable set of credentials from 1894 when he joined the diplomatic service and which included an appointment as ambassador to Denmark from 1912 until 1918. A scion of an old aristocratic family in Holstein, he was born in the town of Schleswig on 29 May 1869 and took his doctorate in law at the University of Leipzig in 1891. Towards the end of the First World War he was being spoken of as a serious candidate for the Foreign Ministry, and had emerged as an unconventional thinker of Germany's relations with Russia. Believing that the collapse of Tsarism would be to Germany's great advantage, he was one of a small number of influential political and military figures who advocated moral and material support for the Bolshevik revolutionaries. He was also beginning to earn a certain notoriety in domestic conservative circles for his liberal and reformist views – hence the sobriquet, 'Red Count', pertained for the remainder of his career. That reputation was enhanced by his appointment in December 1918 as Secretary for Foreign Affairs in the Council of People's Representatives. He was, and remained, without party affiliation. He found it easier than the vast majority of those of his milieu to accept and adapt to the new political situation in Germany at the end of the lost war, and he continued to be a firm supporter of the

Republic to the end. Initially, in 1918–19, he favoured the council system as the basis of post-war economic reconstruction and saw no incompatibility between it and the imperatives of parliamentary democracy.

As Foreign Minister in the Scheidemann cabinet (February–June 1919), Brockdorff-Rantzau was the chief plenipotentiary of Germany to the Paris peace talks, and was convinced his country would be able to negotiate a fair and just settlement on the basis of the Armistice terms, as he indicated in an important speech to the National Assembly in February 1919. The draft peace terms that were presented to him in May came as a rude shock, and in cabinet he appealed unsuccessfully for their rejection. His peace strategy in ruins, he was not a candidate for office in the new Bauer administration.

At the end of 1922 he was sent by Foreign Minister Walther Rathenau to Moscow as German ambassador, with the task of consolidating relations between the two countries that had been set on a new course by the Treaty of Rapallo earlier that year. In this delicate and important mission, the polished and skilful Brockdorff-Rantzau was an outstanding success. He believed as passionately in a Russo-German rapprochement as he did about rejecting Stresemann's policy of fulfilment and reconciliation with France in the West. Thus, while he regarded the Treaty of Berlin in 1926 as a triumph, he could only see Germany's entry to the League of Nations as a disaster. Unfortunately, he was unable to realize his full potential in international affairs, dying suddenly at the early age of 59 years, in Berlin, on 8 September 1928.

## Further Reading

U. Graf von Brockdorff-Rantzau, *Dokumente und Gedanken um Versailles*, Berlin, 1920. See also E. Stern-Rubarth, *Graf Brockdorff-Rantzau. Wanderer zwischen zwei Welten. Ein Lebensbild*, Berlin, 1929; U. Wengst, *Graf Brockdorff-Rantzau und die aussenpolitischen Anfänge der Weimarer Republik*, Frankfurt am Main, 1973. For what is essentially a biography, see K. Rosenbaum, *Community of Fate. German–Soviet Diplomatic Relations 1922–1928*, Syracuse, 1965.

## BRÜNING, Heinrich (1885–1970)

The most controversial Reich Chancellor in Weimar's short history was born the son of a Catholic vinegar manufacturer and wine merchant in Münster, Westphalia, on 26 November 1885. He took a university degree in philology and qualified as a secondary schoolteacher in 1911, went on to complete his doctorate in political economy at the University of Bonn three years later, and promptly volunteered for army service. His experience as an infantry officer on the Western Front in 1915–18 deepened his firmly Catholic, nationalist and monarchist outlook. Embarking on a political career with the Centre Party in 1919, Brüning served on the small advisory staffs of the prominent Catholic politicians, Carl Sonnenschein and then Adam Stegerwald, who appointed him business manager in 1920 of the Association of Christian Trade Unions – a post he held until 1930. A co-founder of the daily newspaper, *Der*

*Deutsche*, he was elected to the Reichstag in 1924 as a representative of Breslau, retaining the seat until 1933, and became one of the Centre Party's leading financial experts. Always identified with the right wing of his party, he was an obvious choice to head its Reichstag faction in 1929–30 during the era of Monsignor Kaas's conservative leadership.

Appointed Reich Chancellor in March 1930 following the collapse of the 'Grand Coalition' administration, Brüning was a rather ascetic, aloof figure, whose period of office in Depression-hit Germany could hardly have been more challenging. Lacking a parliamentary majority, he dissolved the Reichstag in July 1930 when it failed to support his tough fiscal policy, and called new elections. The result of that election in September 1930, particularly the successes of the NSDAP and KPD, left him to govern by emergency decree on the basis of the special powers accorded the Reich President by Article 48 of the Constitution. In practice, henceforth, the Chancellor was dependent on von Hindenburg's goodwill and support, though his position was slightly eased by the temporary, cautious backing of the army, and the policy of toleration adopted by the SPD. To confront the deepening economic crisis, Brüning devised a severe deflationary strategy aimed at reducing the Reich's deficit and balancing the budget: wholesale public expenditure cuts, wage and salary reductions, tax and social insurance payment increases, and savage curtailment of welfare provision, including unemployment benefit, were swiftly introduced. This domestic objective was intimately linked, even subordinated, to his foreign policy goal of having reparations cancelled by the Allies and securing other concessions from the Versailles Treaty.

The rigour with which these policies were executed resulted not only in an increase in social misery and mass unemployment, but also the rapid erosion of public confidence in the democratic system and the concomitant advance of political radicalism. The so-called 'Hunger Chancellor' would not be deflected from his course, convinced as he was that the economy could be revived by private enterprise alone and not by direct state intervention. While his widespread unpopularity was an important factor in Brüning's eventual downfall, just as telling was the loss of the army's support and the hostility he aroused among the powerful landed interest who denounced his plans for tackling the bankrupt estates east of the Elbe as 'agrarian Bolshevism'. That was enough for President von Hindenburg to dismiss his Chancellor abruptly on 30 May 1932. By that date, the cause of democracy was irretrievably lost, the economy was on the verge of total collapse and Hitler was already demanding power. It was bitter consolation to Brüning that a few weeks after being ousted from office, the Lausanne Conference did cancel reparations and that further concessions followed on the Versailles settlement.

Brüning's political career ended in July 1933 with the dissolution of the Centre Party whose chairman he had been elected two months previously. The following summer he left for Holland, Switzerland, Britain and then finally emigrated to the United States where, from 1937 to 1952, he held a professorship in political science at Harvard. He returned to Cologne for a short period in 1948 to visit his sister, and in 1951 was appointed to a Chair in political science at the University of Cologne, but returned after a few years to permanent residence in the United States. He died in

Norwich, Vermont, on 30 March 1970, exactly 40 years since assuming the Reich Chancellorship. His memoirs, which were posthumously published later the same year, indicated a monarchist and essentially anti-parliamentary figure, which deeply disappointed his admirers who had defended him from accusations of having helped prepare the way for Nazism.

## Further Reading

H. Brüning, *Memoiren 1918–1934*, 2 vols, Stuttgart, 1970; C. Nix (ed.), *Heinrich Brüning. Briefe und Gespräche 1934–1945*, Stuttgart, 1974; C. Nix (ed.), *Heinrich Brüning. Briefe 1946–1960*, Stuttgart, 1974. See also W. Vernekohl (ed.), *Heinrich Brüning. Ein deutscher Staatsmann im Urteil der Zeit*, Münster, 1961; F. Hermens and T. Schieder (eds), *Staat, Wirtschaft und Politik in der Weimarer Republik. Festschrift für Heinrich Brüning*, Berlin, 1967; W. Vernekohl and R. Morsey (eds), *Heinrich Brüning. Reden und Aufsätze eines deutschen Staatsmanns*, Münster, 1968; G.R. Treviranus, *Das Ende von Weimar. Heinrich Brüning und seine Zeit*, Düsseldorf, 1968; I. Maurer and U. Wengst (eds), *Staat und NSDAP 1930–1932. Quellen zur Ära Brüning*, Düsseldorf, 1977; T. Koops (ed.), *Akten der Reichskanzlei. Weimarer Republik. Die Kabinette Brüning I und II*, Boppard, 1990.

## CRISPIEN, Artur (1875–1946)

The prominent USPD and later SPD leader was born into a working-class family in Königsberg, East Prussia, on 4 November 1875, and spent most of his early political activity editing the Social Democratic newspapers *Freie Volkszeitung*, in his home town, and then the *Schwäbischer Tagwacht* in Stuttgart. His strong pacifist and anti-militarist views brought him into conflict with the party leadership over the question of supporting war credits in the Reichstag, resulting in his dismissal in November 1914 from the *Tagwacht*. He joined up with radical oppositional elements in the Stuttgart SPD but his call-up to military service in 1916 ended this first phase of his political agitation.

On discharge from the army, he resumed his career in the USPD, representing it as Minister of the Interior and Deputy Minister-President in the revolutionary government in Württemberg from November 1918 until January 1919. At the first post-war congress of his party in March of that year he was elected co-chairman (with Hugo Haase), a position he held for the next three years. Although a self-styled proletarian internationalist, Crispien was unimpressed by the Bolshevik experiment in Russia and at the USPD congress in Halle in 1920 argued against the party affiliating to the Communist International. That controversial issue provoked a schism, of course, but he cleverly took steps to ensure that the moderate right-wing grouping he led continued to enjoy ownership of the party's name, property and press. At the USPD's congress in Gera two years later, he successfully advocated, with others, that it unite with the SPD. Crispien was one of seven former USPD leaders then admitted to the SPD's all-powerful party executive. At the same time, he was nominated to be one of the three co-chairmen of the party, with equal rights, and a Reichstag deputy. He was always associated with the SPD's left wing, but until 1933 he found little difficulty in supporting mainstream party policy, including rejection of co-operation with the KPD, that was formulated by the dominant moderate faction.

Crispien had little choice but to leave Germany in early 1933, eventually settling in Switzerland. He continued to be active on behalf of the SPD in exile for a long period. He died in Berne on 29 November 1946.

## Further Reading

A. Crispien, *Die Internationale. Vom Bund der Kommunisten bis zur Internationale der Weltrevolution*, Berlin, 1920; and *Nie wieder Krieg*, Berlin, 1928. See also H. Krause, *USPD. Zur Geschichte der Unabhängigen Sozialdemokratischen Partei Deutschlands*, Frankfurt am Main, 1975; D.M. Morgan, *The Socialist Left and the German Revolution. A History of the German Independent Social Democratic Party 1917–1922*, London, 1975; H.A. Winkler, *Von der Revolution zur Stabilisierung. Arbeiter und Arbeiterbewegung in der Weimarer Republik 1918 bis 1924*, Berlin and Bonn, 1984.

## CUNO, Wilhelm (1876–1933)

Cuno's prominence in Weimar politics is due almost entirely to the period from November 1922 until August 1923 when, as Reich Chancellor, he headed a cabinet of non-party economic experts and several right-wing politicians drawn mainly from the Centre Party and the DVP during a period of acute economic and political crisis. Enjoying high personal esteem as an industrialist – he was appointed managing director of the Hamburg-American shipping line in succession to Albert Ballin in 1918 – and the confidant of leading personalities, including the Reichswehr supremo, General Hans von Seeckt, Cuno saw his task as continuing to press for a revision of the Treaty of Versailles and to convince the Allies that reparations had to be adjusted to correspond to Germany's capacity to pay. Both objectives quickly floundered in the face of French intransigence, which was vividly displayed in January 1923 when Prime Minister Poincaré ordered his troops into the Ruhr district in response to a technical but petty default on reparations by Germany. Cuno's cabinet immediately ordered a campaign of passive resistance, but the consequent standstill of industry had to be subsidized by the unlimited inflation of Germany's note issue. The results were not only the eventual failure of passive resistance to defeat the French occupation, but also the destruction of the currency, exemplified by its stunning depreciation against the dollar, and widespread social misery. The cabinet was compelled to resign following a no-confidence vote in the Reichstag and a Communist-inspired general strike in Berlin.

Born in Suhl, Thuringia, on 2 July 1876, Cuno completed his university studies with a doctorate in law in 1907 and was employed before the war in the Reich Treasury Office. During the conflict his key role in helping to organize the war economy kept him from military service. After 1918, in addition to his post in shipping, he represented the Reich government as an economic expert at the peace and reparations negotiations, and was a member of the Reich Economic Council. It was very much for his professional expertise, therefore, that Reich President Friedrich Ebert persuaded him to accept appointment as Reich Chancellor. Cuno's non-party political background (though he was regarded as being close to the DVP) was an added recommendation in the fraught circumstances in Germany at that time. The nature of his cabinet is sometimes seen as proof of a certain breakdown in the party system and a forerunner of the presidential cabinets of the early 1930s.

On leaving office in August 1923, Cuno returned to his shipping interests and became chairman of the Hamburg-American line three years later. He never returned to active politics, and died in Hamburg (Aumühle) on 3 January 1933.

## Further Reading

A.E. Cornebise, *The Weimar Republic in Crisis. Cuno's Government and the Ruhr Occupation*, Washington, DC, 1980; H.-J. Rupieper, *The Cuno Government and Reparations 1922–1923*, The Hague, 1979; K. Harbeck (ed.), *Akten der Reichskanzlei. Weimarer Republik. Das Kabinett Cuno, 22. November 1922 – 12. August 1923*, Boppard, 1968.

## CURTIUS, Julius (1877–1948)

Curtius was born into a rich and nationalist upper middle-class home in Duisburg on 7 February 1877 and practised law there after graduating from university. From 1910 to the outbreak of war he continued his law studies in Heidelberg and taught international law on a part-time basis at the university. He then served for four years as an artillery officer on the Western Front and immediately afterwards went into politics. In 1919 he helped found the German Liberal People's Party in Heidelberg, representing it on the town council until 1921. In 1919 also, he joined the DVP, taking up and retaining until 1932 a position on the party's main executive and management committee, while throughout the same period (until February 1932) representing it in the Reichstag. Expelled from the parliamentary faction for failing to support a no-confidence motion against the Brüning government, Curtius crossed to the German State Party, which he represented until 1933. Like most of the DVP, he welcomed the Kapp Putsch, but thereafter developed into a responsible backer of the Republic, while remaining an implacable opponent of the Treaty of Versailles and a staunch patriot.

Curtius moved to Berlin in 1921, where alongside his political career he built up a very successful law practice, particularly with wealthy industrial clients, thus allowing him to extend long-standing family links with a number of firms, notably the Gutehoffnungshütte, one of Germany's largest mining, iron-producing and manufacturing combines. In the Reichstag he became noted as a spokesman for big business and as a vehement anti-socialist, and when appointed to the Luther cabinet as Reich Economics Minister in January 1926, industrialists looked to him for unqualified support of their interests. As it turned out, however, Curtius adopted a fairly even-handed approach: although he took steps in early 1928 that would prevent the restoration of the eight-hour day in certain areas of heavy industry, he incurred the wrath of businessmen when he gave priority to the general interest, as when he vetoed proposed increases in the price of coal. Though an able administrator, by the time he left the Ministry in November 1929 he had come to be regarded with suspicion and antipathy by many large-scale businessmen. On another level, his attempts to restore balance to the Reich budget were unsuccessful and the short-term deficit increased during his tenure.

When he took over as Foreign Minister in October 1929, Curtius was widely seen as the principal heir to the liberal legacy that Stresemann had bequeathed to the DVP and to the policy of international reconciliation in European affairs. But the radicalization of German politics after 1929, and its concomitant surge of ultra-nationalism, generated new pressures which clashed with the cautious, moderate approach adopted, initially at least, by him. He is best remembered as the principal architect, then victim, of the abortive German–Austrian Customs Union, which was designed to enhance the nationalist image of the government in the face of concerted assaults on it by the DNVP and NSDAP. The intransigence of the French, whom Curtius had deliberately excluded from negotiations, caused the proposal to be abandoned in autumn 1931. He was consequently forced to resign – Reich President von Hindenburg demanded that he be dismissed – though it must also be recorded that his overall performance as Foreign Minister had been lacklustre. One of the few successes for which he could claim some credit was the securing of the Hoover Moratorium on reparations payments in June 1931.

After 1933, Curtius retired to Mecklenburg to farm his estate and to practise law for the duration of the Third Reich. In 1945 he chose to return to the place of his early political activity, Heidelberg, where he died on 10 November 1948.

## Further Reading

J. Curtius, *Innere Konsolidierung und aussenpolitische Aktionsfähigkeit*, Berlin, 1930; *Sechs Jahre Minister der deutschen Republik*, Heidelberg, 1948; *Bemühung um Österreich. Das Scheitern des Zollunionplans von 1931*, Heidelberg, 1947. See also W.G. Ratliff, *Faithful to the Fatherland. Julius Curtius and Weimar Foreign Policy*, New York, 1990.

## DAHLEM, Franz (1892–1981)

Beginning with his promotion to the Politburo and election to the Reichstag faction of the KPD in 1928, Dahlem emerged as a figure of considerable significance in the organization and leadership of the party, achieving national prominence in 1931 when he succeeded Paul Merker as *Reichsleiter* of the Revolutionary Trade Union Opposition (RGO). From a Catholic working-class background in Rohrbach, where he was born on 14 January 1892, he was a white-collar employee when he joined the SPD in 1913. But he did not become politically active until after he had spent the war years in the army. Crossing over to the USPD, he was a member of the Workers' and Soldiers' Council in Allenstein in November 1918 before moving to Cologne the following year to edit the USPD newspaper, *Sozialistische Republik*. His political radicalism led him to the KPD in 1920, and he spent a number of years gaining experience of party organizational work before having the opportunity to advance to the upper echelons of the party in the wake of its adoption of the ultra-leftist strategy in 1928. From 1920 to 1924 he represented the KPD in the Prussian Landtag. A bitter opponent of the SPD, Dahlem was able to achieve a degree of success with the RGO without managing to finally attract workers in the mass numbers he had aimed for. Nevertheless, the RGO's expanding presence in the factories gave the KPD an extra dimension to its revolutionary agitation against the democratic Republic and the ever-threatening challenge of the NSDAP.

After 1933 Dahlem went underground and made a notable contribution to the organization of Communist resistance in Germany and then abroad. In 1937 he was political leader of the International Brigade in Spain. Arrested in France in 1941, he spent the rest of the war in Mauthausen concentration camp. From 1945 to 1953 he was a member of the Socialist Unity Party's central committee and Politburo, but was dismissed from all posts at the insistence of Walter Ulbricht, a long-standing personal enemy. Dahlem was rehabilitated in 1958 and rejoined the party's central committee and went on to become Deputy Higher Education Minister of the German Democratic Republic. He died in East Berlin on 17 December 1981.

## Further Reading

F. Dahlem, *Am Vorabend des Zweiten Weltkrieges. Erinnerungen. 1938 bis August 1939*, 2 vols, East Berlin, 1977, 1979; *Ausgewählte Reden und Aufsätze 1919–1979. Zur Geschichte der Arbeiterbewegung*, East Berlin, 1980; *Jugendjahre. Vom katholischen Arbeiterjungen zum proletarischen Revolutionär*, East Berlin, 1982. See also E.C. Schöck, *Arbeitslosigkeit und Rationalisierung. Die Lage der Arbeiter und die kommunistische Gewerkschaftspolitik 1920–1928*, Frankfurt am Main, 1977; F. Eisner, *Das Verhältnis der KPD zu den Gewerkschaften in der Weimarer Republik*, Cologne, 1977; W. Müller, *Lohnkampf, Massenstreik, Sowjetmacht. Ziele und Grenzen der 'Revolutionären Gewerkschafts-Opposition (RGO) in Deutschland 1928 bis 1933*, Cologne, 1988.

## DARRÉ, Richard Walther (1895–1953)

A relatively late recruit to the NSDAP in 1930, Darré nevertheless made an immediate impact when put in charge of the party's fledgling Agrarian Office. Over the next three years he made a crucial contribution to the party's success in attracting the disgruntled peasant vote in the countryside. Skilfully exploiting the implications of the agricultural depression which had hit Germany as early as 1926, he fed the farmers' anger and feeling of betrayal by the Republic and their growing disillusionment with their existing representative organizations through a vigorous propaganda campaign centred around the notion of *Blut und Boden*. At the same time, he masterminded a strategy of systematic infiltration of the Landbund and other peasant bodies, resulting by 1932 in the NSDAP's domination of this sector of agrarian life. Darré's impressive powers of organization and ideological persuasion helped to ensure that millions of small farmers, particularly in Protestant regions of northern, central and eastern Germany, came to regard Hitler as their saviour from Marxism, the Jews and the 'red' Republic.

Darré was an *Auslandsdeutscher*, born on 14 July 1895 near Buenos Aires, Argentina, educated in Germany, and for a year at King's College in Wimbledon, who fought as an artillery officer on the Western Front in the First World War. A member of a *Freikorps* unit for a short time after being demobbed in 1918, he completed his training as an agronomist in 1922, describing himself as a strict Mendelian and specialist in animal breeding. During most of the 1920s he followed a rather haphazard professional and political career, representing several agricultural bodies abroad, working in 1928–29 at the German embassy in Riga, and flirting with a number of *völkisch* groups, including the Saalecker Circle, the Nordic Ring, and the back-to-the-land romanticist Artamanen movement, where he met fellow agricultural expert, Heinrich Himmler. Darré was also apparently a member of the Stahlhelm in 1922. His first contacts with the NSDAP were made informally in Wiesbaden in 1928, but it took a further two years for him to enrol as a member. He had come to Hitler's notice as the author of a few works extolling the virtues of racial breeding and of the peasantry, and denouncing the corrupting influence of Jews and Marxists in the German community. A further recommendation may have been his pronounced anti-Christian views (despite a Lutheran background) and a suggestion of an inclination towards neo-paganism. The NSDAP had been alerted to the possibilities of winning support among the peasantry as early as 1927 and had made some gains prior to Darré's appointment in July 1930 as head of the party's newly created Agrarian Office in the central executive (*Reichsleitung*). But it was primarily due to his efforts that this peasant support increased dramatically in the years to 1933.

After 1933 Darré consolidated his status as the dominant authority in German agriculture. As *Reichsbauernführer* (National Farmers' Leader), Reich Minister for Food and Agriculture and a Reichstag Deputy from 1933, he pushed through important legislation, such as the Law of Hereditary Entailment (*Reichserbhofgesetz*), and set up new bodies, including the *Reichsnährstand*, to co-ordinate the production, pricing and marketing of farm products. His policies enjoyed initial success and pleased the farmers, but from the mid-1930s began to run into difficulties in the face of competing demands in the economy generated above all by the Four Year Plan and rearmament. By 1939 his standing with Hitler had been considerably diminished as a result of these setbacks, and during the Second World War he was ousted more and more from his ostensible sphere of responsibility. Finally, in May 1942, he was dismissed for failing to organize Germany's food supply efficiently. Captured in 1945, Darré was later imprisoned for five years following a conviction for crimes against Polish and Jewish farmers before an American military tribunal. He was released in 1950, settled in Bad Harzburg and died in a Munich hospital on 8 September 1953.

## Further Reading

R. Walther Darré, *Das Schwein als Kriterium für nordische Völker und Semiten*, Munich, 1927; *Das Bauerntum als Lebensquell der nordischen Rasse*, Munich, 1929; *Neuadel aus Blut und Boden*,

Munich, 1930; *Erkenntnisse und Werden. Aufsätze aus der Zeit vor der Machtergreifung* (edited by M.A. Reuss zur Lippe), Goslar, 1940; *Um Blut und Boden. Reden und Aufsätze*, Munich, 1941. See also J.E. Farquharson, *The Plough and the Swastika. The NSDAP and Agriculture in Germany, 1928–45*, London, 1976; H. Gies, 'NSDAP und landwirtschaftliche Organisationen in der Endphase der Weimarer Republik', *Vierteljahrshefte für Zeitgeschichte*, 15 (1967), pp. 341–76; T.A. Tilton, *Nazism, Neo-Nazism and the Peasantry*, Bloomingdale, 1975; Z. Zofka, *Die Ausbreitung des Nationalsozialismus auf dem Lande. Eine regionale Fallstudie zur politischen Einstellung der Landbevölkerung in der Zeit des Aufstiegs und der Machtergreifung der NSDAP, 1928–1936*, Munich, 1979; A. Bramwell, *Blood and Soil. Walther Darré and Hitler's Green Party*, Abbotsbrook, 1985; G. Corni: *Hitler and the Peasants. The Agrarian Policy of the Third Reich, 1930–1939*, Oxford, 1990.

## DÄUMIG, Ernst (1866–1922)

During the November Revolution in 1918 and the early years of the Weimar Republic, Däumig emerged as one of the most actively radical personalities on the far Left, moving from the USPD to the KPD, and back, with arresting rapidity. From a middle-class background in Merseburg, where he was born on 25 November 1866, he completed his secondary school education and studied theology at university before embarking on a military career, first in the French Foreign Legion, and then from 1893 to 1898 in the officer corps of the Prussian army. On leaving the army, he immediately became active in the SPD, particularly in its press empire, including from 1911 to 1916 a spell on the editorial staff of *Vorwärts*. That role ended when he joined the party's leftist opposition and in 1917 he helped set up the USPD in which he was subsequently to make his name as an outspoken leader of its radical wing.

A leader of the Revolutionary Shop Stewards' movement in Berlin during the November Revolution, he advocated that the Workers' and Soldiers' Councils should form the constitutional basis of the new German state. A proposal to this effect which he put forward at the General Congress of Workers' and Soldiers' Councils in Berlin in December 1918, however, was rejected in favour of having a National Assembly elected by universal suffrage. His assessment of political opportunities was not entirely reliable. Thus, when he was selected by the USPD as its representative in the Prussian Ministry of Defence in late 1918, he refused to accept the appointment and his party was unable to find a replacement. Had he gone he might well have been able to effect substantial change in a crucial sphere of government which at that time was rather vulnerable. During the course of 1919 he continued to plead the Shop Stewards' case for a comprehensive socialization of industry and government, and to argue that the USPD should join the Communist International. Appointed chairman of the USPD in December 1919, he opened negotiations with the Comintern and put the case for the party joining it at the party's Congress in Halle the following year. When the USPD split on this controversial issue, he led the Shop Stewards' wing to a merger in December 1920 with the Spartacists in the United Communist Party, of which he soon shared the chairmanship with Paul Levi. He and his cohorts continued to oppose the theory and practice of putschism, however, and after the failure of yet another insurrection, the 'March Action', in 1921, most of them followed Levi's departure from the KPD. Däumig founded with Levi in September 1921 the Communist *Arbeitsgemeinschaft*, which lasted only six months. In February 1922 its members returned to the USPD. Throughout the turbulent events of these last few years, Däumig was a USPD member of the Reichstag. He died suddenly in Berlin on 4 July 1922, having conspicuously failed to realize any of his major political aims.

*Further Reading*

R.F. Wheeler, *USPD und Internationale*, Frankfurt am Main, 1975; H. Krause, *USPD. Zur Geschichte der Unabhängigen Sozialdemokratischen Partei Deutschlands*, Frankfurt am Maine, 1975; D.W. Morgan, *The Socialist Left and the German Revolution. A History of the German Independent Social Democratic Party 1917–1922*, London, 1975; H.A. Winkler, *Von der Revolution zur Stabilisierung. Arbeiter und Arbeiterbewegung in der Weimarer Republik 1918 bis 1924*, Berlin and Bonn, 1984; T. Bergmann: '*Gegen den Strom'. Geschichte der Kommunistischen-Partei-Opposition*, Hamburg, 1988.

# DAVID, Eduard (1863–1930)

A leading revisionist thinker and official of the SPD before 1914, committed to a moderate patriotism and the parliamentary road to power, David was involved at the heart of controversial debates relating to the party's attitude to colonialism, armaments and agrarian reform. Born into the middle-class home of a Prussian civil servant in Ediger in the Mosel valley on 11 June 1863, he taught as a secondary schoolteacher in Giessen until 1894. Before then he had already begun to make a mark in politics by representing the SPD in the Hesse Landtag from 1886 (to 1908), and furthered his position through considerable publishing activity, which included his ownership and editing of the *Mitteldeutsche Sonntagszeitung*. A member of the Reichstag from 1903 to 1930, he was a principal advocate in 1914 for the SPD's support of the government's war policy, while at the same time trying to extract a commitment to the introduction of universal suffrage in Prussia and a package of trade union and social reform. By autumn 1918 he could claim some success in this respect and, having advised his party to enter government, accepted a position as Under-Secretary of State in the Foreign Affairs Office in Prince Max von Baden's administration.

A stout opponent of left-wing radicalism in the November Revolution, David pressed for early parliamentary elections to head off the challenge from both Spartacists and councillor extremists, and for a coalition government of SPD, DDP and the Centre Party. For a few days, he was president of the National Assembly, and his high profile in that crisis-torn period in Germany continued in spring 1919 when he argued in favour of accepting the draft terms of the Versailles peace settlement because there was no realistic alternative. In the Bauer government that accepted the Treaty, David served for a time (June–October 1919) as Reich Interior Minister, and in the succeeding Müller cabinet he was Reich Minister for Reconstruction. During the course of the 1920s, he continued to be active in the party and Reichstag, but was better known for his work as the Reich government's representative in Darmstadt, the capital of Hesse. His informed reports during his period of office from 1921 to 1927 are an important source for understanding the diplomatic and constitutional complexities of relations between the Reich and the *Länder*. David died in Berlin on 24 December 1930.

*Further Reading*

E. David, *Sozialismus und Landwirtschaft*, Berlin, 1903; *Das Kriegstagebuch des Reichstagsabgeordneten Eduard David 1914 bis 1918* (edited by S. Miller), Düsseldorf, 1966; F. Kahlenberg (ed.), *Die Berichte Eduard Davids als Reichsvertreter in Hessen 1921–1927*, Wiesbaden, 1970.

## DESSAUER, Friedrich (1881–1963)

Born into a wealthy Catholic industrialist family of distant Jewish origin in Aschaffenburg on 19 July 1881, Dessauer was already successful in business in his own right before embarking on a political career in the Centre Party following the end of the First World War. At the same time, he was a highly respected academic, taking his doctorate in 1917 at the University of Frankfurt and earning a full professorship there five years later for his pioneering work in quantum biology. He represented the Centre Party in the Frankfurt Bürgerrat and played a vigorous role in shaping the party's social ideology. When elected to the Reichstag in 1924 he became at once a prominent member of the party's left wing alongside Joseph Wirth and Joseph Joos, advocating a series of socially progressive concepts in the economy, industrial relations and political life. Dessauer firmly subscribed to the view that the time had come for the Catholic community to cast off its ghetto mentality and become more fully integrated into the mainstream of German life, and by the end of the 1920s there were signs that his ambition was being realized. During Brüning's chancellorship, Dessauer lent support in a direct way by acting as a major adviser on economic, financial and foreign policy matters. In mid-1932, he was a go-between in the attempts by Gregor Strasser of the NSDAP to establish links with trade union circles.

In 1933, on the collapse of the Centre Party, Dessauer was arrested and made to stand trial. Although freed, he had to forfeit his private possessions and finances, and was deprived of his university position. He emigrated to Turkey in 1934 and from there in 1937 to Switzerland, where he taught at the University of Freiburg. He returned to the University of Frankfurt in 1953. He died in that city on 16 February 1963.

*Further Reading*

F. Dessauer, *Zeit der Wende*, Frankfurt am Main, 1924; *Kooperative Wirtschaft*, Bonn, 1929; *Recht, Richtertum und Ministerialbürokratie*, Mannheim, 1928; *Kontrapunkte eines Forscherlebens. Erinnerungen*, Frankfurt am Main, 1962.

## DIETRICH, Hermann (1879–1954)

A leading democratic politician and important member of Chancellor Brüning's cabinet, Dietrich was born on 14 December 1879 in Oberprechtal, Baden, and was a lawyer by profession. He began his political career as a National Liberal in the Baden Landtag from 1911 to 1918 and as Lord Mayor of Konstanz in 1914. In November 1918 he was appointed Baden Minister for Foreign Affairs and the following year sat in the National Assembly of that state. More importantly, he was a co-founder and executive member of the DDP in 1918, represented it in the National Assembly and then in the Reichstag until 1930. From 1930 to 1933 he sat for the German State Party in that forum. A convinced devolutionist, Dietrich enjoyed a sound reputation as a spokesman for the right wing of his party in the 1920s. Appointed Reich Minister of Agriculture in the 'Grand Coalition' under Hermann Müller from 1928 to 1930, he became widely recognized as an articulate defender of the small rural middle class and peasantry whom he thought were threatened by the growing power of big business and organized labour. He wanted to engineer their economic rehabilitation, partly as a means of tying them to the parliamentary Republic. Wearing his party hat, he called on the broad spectrum of the middle classes to unite behind the DDP in defence of their social and economic interests. As Minister of Agriculture, his policies were usually regarded as favouring this bourgeois constituency to which he appealed for support.

In the first Brüning cabinet, Dietrich was given both the vice-chancellorship and the Ministry of Economics (April–June 1930 only), while in the second cabinet under the Centre Party leader he added the Finance Ministry to the vice-chancellorship. He was a firm believer in the deflationary strategy that was adopted, though grew increasingly alarmed at the currency implications. In the party sphere, in the meantime, he had exerted a major influence in the founding of the German State Party, whose leader he became in November 1930. Under his direction, the new party moved perceptibly to the right on a range of key issues, but this could not prevent large-scale defections of voters, including many from the Jewish community, thus consigning the party to the periphery of Weimar politics. As a result of the Reichstag elections in November 1932, only Dietrich and one other colleague remained in parliament. In 1933, he set aside his antipathy to the NSDAP to declare his support for the Enabling Bill in the national interest, and on the dissolution of his party retired to practise law for the duration of the Third Reich. Active for a few years after 1945 on behalf of the Free Democratic Party, he died in Stuttgart on 6 March 1954.

### Further Reading

H. Dietrich, *Ein Jahr Agrarpolitik*, Berlin, 1929; *Auf dem Wege zum neuen Staat. Die deutsche Aufgabe*, Stuttgart, 1951. See also A. von Saldern, *Hermann Dietrich. Ein Staatsmann der Weimarer Republik*, Boppard, 1966; W. Stephan, *Aufstieg und Verfall des Linksliberalismus 1918–1933. Geschichte der Deutschen Demokratischen Partei*, Göttingen, 1973; L.E. Jones, *German Liberalism and the Dissolution of the Weimar Party System, 1918–1933*, Chapel Hill, 1988; K. Jarausch and L.E. Jones (eds), *In Search of a Liberal Germany*, Oxford, 1990; P. Brandt and R. Rürup, *Volksbewegung und demokratische Neuordnung in Baden 1918/19*, Sigmaringen, 1991.

## DIETRICH, Otto (1897–1952)

From his appointment as Reich press chief of the NSDAP in August 1931, Dietrich played a vital part in the organization of the party's propaganda and publicity activity in the drive for power. He enjoyed Hitler's complete confidence and was a constant companion during the *Führer*'s endless travels from one end of Germany to another. He also used his important contacts with heavy industrial circles in the Ruhr, where he had once been a legal adviser to a large steel combine, to the party's political advantage: Emil Kirdorf and Fritz Thyssen were among his associates.

Dietrich was born in Essen on 31 August 1897, fought as an army volunteer on the Western Front, winning the Iron Cross (First Class), and graduated from the University of Freiburg in 1921 with a doctorate in political science. He pursued a varied career in business during the 1920s, being employed briefly as a research assistant in the Essen Chamber of Commerce, a deputy editor of the *Nationalzeitung*, also in Essen, and business manager of the right-wing *Augsburger Zeitung*. He had been a party member for several years before his appointment to its hierarchy in 1931.

After 1933 Dietrich extended his power base as the NSDAP's press chief, despite numerous conflicts with Max Amann and Joseph Goebbels, becoming president of the Reich Association of the German Press (RVDP) and Reich Leader of the Press (1937–45). In these offices, he decisively helped to purge the press of those deemed to be racially and politically unreliable, to reorganize it to serve the interests of the regime, and to assert National Socialist domination of the publishing world in general. Implementation of the Editors' Law of 3 October 1933, which formed the legal basis for the destruction of newspapers' independence, was his single most important contribution. During the Second World War, Dietrich prepared daily directives for the press in a tightly controlled fashion, especially after Stalingrad. But Hitler sacked him in March 1945. Captured in 1945, he spent a short period in jail following a conviction for crimes against humanity, wrote his memoirs, and died in Düsseldorf on 22 November 1952.

### Further Reading
O. Dietrich, *With Hitler on the Road to Power*, London, 1934; *12 Jahre mit Hitler*, Munich, 1955. See also O.J. Hale, *The Captive Press in the Third Reich*, Princeton, 1964.

## DINGELDEY, Eduard (1886–1942)

A lawyer, born in Giessen on 27 June 1886, and employed by the Hesse state government until 1918, Dingeldey began his active political career at the age of 29. In 1919, having moved to Darmstadt to practise law, he was elected chairman of the DVP in south Hesse and sat in the Landtag. From the early 1920s, he also chaired the South-West German Group of Regional Branches of the DVP, a position which allowed him to exert considerable influence in the party's national executive, to which he had been elected in 1922. During the 1920s he became a leading figure of the party's left wing, giving full support to Stresemann's policies at home and abroad.

Elected to serve in the Reichstag in May 1928, Dingeldey very quickly established a reputation as a sound parliamentarian, and emerged as a firm advocate of bourgeois political unity, which appealed above all to the reformists elements of the party's left wing. Having been appointed deputy party chairman in early November 1930, he succeeded Ernst Scholz a few weeks later, at a time when the German liberal tradition was experiencing a profound crisis. Initial indications that he would lead the DVP into a more promising future as a party of bourgeois concentration and of fundamental social and political reform proved unfounded. He repeatedly sabotaged any moves towards an accommodation with the German State Party and tried instead to find common ground with the forces of 'national opposition', including the DNVP and even, in a more limited way, the NSDAP.

The DVP's clear swing to the right under his direction, particularly following his withdrawal of support from the Brüning government in autumn 1931, dismayed his former leftist colleagues in the party, many of whom seceded. Even so, Dingeldey was not in full control of the party's right wing, who demanded a closer and more definite connection with the nationalist Right. His vacillating leadership and his inflated view of the party's capacity for independent political action contributed to the drastic fall in the number of the DVP's Reichstag seats, from 30 in September 1930 to seven in July 1932. A slight revival in the November 1932 elections could not disguise the fundamental crisis and poverty of leadership in the political middle and moderate Right as the Republic neared its end. Dingeldey's room for manoeuvre was severely restricted but, more importantly, the DVP could no longer be counted a supporter of the parliamentary order. This was underlined in 1933 when he made a series of rather pathetic attempts to link his party to the 'national revolution'. Reduced to two seats in the Reichstag following the March elections, the final political act of Dingeldey and a colleague was to vote for the Enabling Bill, a fitting commentary on the party's swing to the right during the previous three years. With the inevitable dissolution of the DVP in July 1933, Dingeldey returned to his profession. He died in Heidelberg on 19 July 1942.

## Further Reading

E. Dingeldey, *Kampf und Politik der Deutschen Volkspartei. Rede des Parteiführers Dingeldey in der Sitzung des Zentralvorstandes der Deutschen Volkspartei am 19. April 1931*, Berlin, 1931; *Botschaft an das nationale Deutschland. Rede vor dem Zentralvorstand der Deutschen Volkspartei in Erfurt am 9. Oktober 1932*, Berlin, 1932; *Klarer nationaler Kurs in stürmischer Zeit. Rede gehalten in Darmstadt an 19. Februar 1933*, Berlin, 1933. See also W. Hartenstein, *Die Anfänge der Deutschen Volkspartei 1918–1920*, Düsseldorf, 1962; L. Döhn, *Politik und Interesse. Die Interessenstruktur der Deutschen Volkspartei*, Meisenheim, 1970; L. Albertin (ed.), *Linksliberalismus in der Weimarer Republik. Die Führungsgremien der deutschen Demokratischen Partei und der Deutschen Volkspartei 1918–1933*, Düsseldorf, 1980; L.E. Jones, *German Liberalism and the Dissolution of the Weimar Party System, 1918–1933*, Chapel Hill, 1988; K. Jarausch and L.E. Jones (eds), *In Search of a Liberal Germany*, Oxford, 1990.

## DITTMANN, Wilhelm (1874–1954)

The subsequent USPD and SPD leader was born into a working-class family in Eutin, Schleswig-Holstein, on 13 November 1874, and completed his apprenticeship as a joiner/carpenter before joining the SPD and the Woodworkers' Union. His early party activity centred on the press and he edited the *Norddeutsche Volksstimme* in Bremerhaven, then the *Bergische Arbeiterstimme* in Solingen. Party secretary and district chairman of the SPD in Frankfurt am Main from 1904 to 1909 and member of the local assembly (Stadtverordnetenversammlung) in that city, Dittmann was elected to the Reichstag in 1912, remaining a deputy until 1918. He served in the armed forces for a short period after 1914 but as a member of various parliamentary commissions spent most of the war in a political capacity. Regarded as a left-winger in the pre-war SPD, his vote against war credits in the Reichstag in 1915 signalled a withdrawal from the mainstream party which led to his joining the left-centre 'Eisenacher' group and to his role in helping to found the USPD in 1917. He became the new party's secretary. For his involvement in the armaments workers' strike in January 1918, Dittmann received a five-year sentence from which, however, he was amnestized nine months later.

His active role in the November Revolution was forged around his membership of the Council of People's Representatives and of the USPD's central committee, but while opposed to the moderate course adopted by the Majority Socialists, he was equally resolved not to allow his party to coalesce with the KPD. At the USPD Congress in Gera in 1922, he came out in favour of uniting with the SPD as the best means of defending the democratic Republic, and he was one of a handful of former USPD leaders elected to the SPD's executive committee, on which he served as secretary from 1922 to 1933. Dittmann had been re-elected to the Reichstag in 1920, representing the USPD until 1922, and from then until 1933, the SPD. His organizational skills and capacity for hard work were recognized by his election to the position of Reichstag vice-president for a number of years in the mid-1920s. From 1921 to 1925 he was also a city councillor in Berlin.

Emigrating in 1933 to Austria and then Switzerland, where he remained until 1951, Dittmann was no longer actively involved in party politics at the top level, and died in Bonn, where he worked in the SPD archives, on 7 August 1954. His had been a considerable contribution to the development of the SPD before Hitler.

## Further Reading

W. Dittmann, *Die Marine-Justizmörde von 1917 und die Admiralsrebellion vom 1918*, Berlin, 1926; and *Das politische Deutschland vor Hitler. Nach dem amtlichen Material des Statistischen Reichsamtes in Berlin*, Zurich, 1945. See also D.W. Morgan, *The Socialist Left and the German Revolution. A History of the German Independent Social Democratic Party 1917–1922*, London, 1975; H. Krause, *USPD. Zur Geschichte der Unabhängigen Sozialdemokratischen Partei Deutschlands*, Frankfurt am Main, 1975.

## DORTEN, Hans Adam (1880–1963)

The leader of the separatist movement in the Rhineland during the early 1920s and one-time provisional head of the so-called Rhenish Republic, Dorten emerged as a significant if disruptive personality in the difficult, often chaotic sphere of foreign affairs for the Weimar Republic following the end of the First World War. With no record of political activity before 1918, he returned from army service determined to play a part in the political reorganization of Germany. He claimed backing from certain influential industrial circles and from elements of the Centre Party in the Rhineland for his separatist ideas, and with the additional encouragement of the French occupation authorities proclaimed in Wiesbaden on 1 June 1919 an independent Rhenish Republic. However, his hastily constructed government collapsed just as rapidly for want of popular and official support. In June 1920 he established the Rheinische Volksvereinigung to pursue the aim of separatism. By 1923 the organization had 20,000 members, its own press organs in the shape of the *Rheinischer Herold* and the *Rheinische Warte*, and backing from the French, particularly after their invasion of the Ruhr at the beginning of that year. During the catastrophic economic and political crisis which engulfed the Republic in 1923, Dorten spearheaded the *Rheinisch-Republikanische Volkspartei*'s drive for an independent Rhineland state and as such posed a most serious threat to the integrity of the Reich. But against a background of the invasion fiasco and popular hostility, Dorten's initiative finally had to be abandoned once and for all. His own leadership qualities and political skills had not been equal in any case to the objective he had set out to achieve.

Dorten, who was born in Bonn-Endenich on 10 February 1880 and who had a doctorate in law, had been appointed *Staatsanwalt* (public prosecutor) in Düsseldorf in 1914 and had fought as an army captain in the war. His political activity abruptly terminated in late 1923, he fled Germany, eventually took French citizenship and worked as an industrial consultant. He died in Nice in April 1963.

### Further Reading

H.A. Dorten, *La Tragédie rhénane*, Paris, 1945. See also E. Bischof, *Separatismus 1918–1924. Hans Adam Dortens Rheinstaatsbestrebungen*, Frankfurt am Main, 1969; H. Köhler, *Autonomiebewegung oder Separatismus? Die Politik der 'Kölnischen Volkszeitung' 1918–1919*, Berlin, 1974; W.A. McDougall, *France's Rhineland Diplomacy*, Princeton, 1978; K. Reimer, *Rheinlandfrage und Rheinlandbewegung (1918–1933)*, Frankfurt am Main, 1979; H.E. Nadler, *The Rhenish Separatist Movements During the Early Weimar Period*, New York, 1989.

## DREXLER, Anton (1884–1942)

One of the earliest and most prominent associates of Hitler in the nascent National Socialist movement and co-founder of the German Workers' Party, the immediate forerunner of the NSDAP, Drexler was born into a working-class household in Munich on 13 June 1884. After an apprenticeship as a machine-fitter and locksmith, he was employed in various firms in his home city and for a brief period, in 1901–02, in Berlin, where he later claimed to have become an anti-Semite and an anti-Marxist. He returned to Munich in October 1902 and took up a post with the Reichsbahn main repair works, where he remained until 1923. Unable to be accepted as a volunteer for military service because the Reichsbahn regarded him as an essential worker, Drexler developed his right-wing sympathies to the point where in summer 1917 he briefly joined the ultra-nationalist and annexationist German Fatherland Party. On 7 March 1918 he founded the Free Workers' Committee for a Good Peace, which aimed to unite the working classes behind the war effort and to combat usury. Linked to a similarly named main group in Bremen, Drexler's Munich organization took part in a national conference which resulted in him being elected to a newly created Reichsausschuss (national committee) in spring 1918. The quiet, sober and somewhat naively idealistic Drexler joined forces with a journalist, Karl Harrer, six months later to found a new grouping, the Political Workers' Circle, which tried to act as a bridge between the popular masses and the organized nationalist Right.

The activity of this small group formed the basis in January 1919 of the German Workers' Party, of which Drexter became chairman. Initially lacking a programme, an organizational structure and funding, the new party was able nevertheless to make certain advances during its first year which gave it a rather more definite profile and base: it was nationalist, anti-Semitic, anti-Marxist and anti-capitalist, attracting a small membership from Munich's lower middle and working classes. In September 1919 Adolf Hitler joined the party.

By December 1919 Drexler and Hitler co-operated to complete the draft of a new party programme comprising 25 Points, which was approved by a party meeting the following February. In July 1921, when Hitler succeeded in asserting his dictatorial control over what was now the NSDAP, Drexler was appointed honorary chairman (a post he retained until the party's dissolution in November 1923), with not unimportant residual powers as head of the sub-committee on internal mediation. However, from that time onwards, it was Hitler who directed the fortunes of the NSDAP, and not Drexler. In early November 1923, he was part of the entourage that accompanied the *Führer* to the Bürgerbräukeller, was arrested at the Feldherrnhalle and was imprisoned for a short time in Landsberg jail, pending trial for his participation in the abortive putsch. He later claimed the dubious credit for talking Hitler out of a scheme to starve himself to death in a hunger strike. In 1924 Drexler was a leading member of the Völkischer Block in Bavaria and went on to represent it in the Landtag until 1928. Meanwhile, he seceded from the NSDAP in 1925 when Hitler insisted on retaining Hermann Esser, a notorious reprobate, in the re-established party. Drexler co-founded the National Social People's League (Volksbund), which was affiliated as its Bavarian branch to the anti-Hitler Deutschvölkische Freiheitspartei until bludgeoned out of existence by NSDAP thugs. From 1928 to 1933 Drexler was politically inactive.

In 1933 the new political circumstances allowed Drexler to make a small-time comeback in the NSDAP and to regain a position with the Reichsbahn, from which he had been forced to resign in 1923 after receiving a severe beating from fellow workers of a different political persuasion. He was appointed an *Oberinspektor* and rejoined the party that year, with his old membership number 526 reinstated. In 1934, his rehabilitation was completed when he was awarded the highly coveted *Blutorden* by his party. Subsequently, he provided the Hauptarchiv of the NSDAP with valuable information and documents relating to the party's early development, and occasionally exchanged letters with the *Führer*. Drexler died in Munich on 25 February 1942.

## Further Reading

A. Drexler, *Mein Politisches Erwachen. Aus dem Tagebuch eines deutschen sozialistischen Arbeiters*, Munich, 1919. See also A. Tyrell, *Vom 'Trommler' zum 'Führer'. Der Wandel von Hitlers Selbstverständnis zwischen 1919 und 1924 und die Entwicklung der NSDAP*, Munich, 1975; W. Maser, *Der Sturm auf der Republik. Frühgeschichte der NSDAP*, Stuttgart, 1973; G. Franz-Willing, *Ursprung der Hitlerbewegung, 1919–1922*, 2nd edn, Preussisch Oldendorf, 1974.

# DUESTERBERG, Theodor (1875–1950)

Born in Darmstadt on 19 October 1875, the son of an army major in the medical corps, Duesterberg served his military cadetship in Potsdam before joining an infantry regiment in 1893. He was involved in the China expedition of 1900–01 during the Boxer rebellion. In 1908 he was given command of an infantry company and at the beginning of the First World War saw action as a battalion commander on the Western Front. He ended the war with the rank of lieutenant-colonel.

After leaving the army in protest at Germany's acceptance of the Treaty of Versailles, he started up a small manufacturing business and entered politics, first, as secretary of the DNVP's branch in Halle and then, more significantly, after this brief period of office, as co-founder of the right-wing veterans' association, the Stahlhelm. Appointed *Gauleiter* of its Halle branch in April 1923, Duesterberg organized around him a radical, *völkisch* faction which extended its influence during the mid-1920s in the organization at the expense of the relatively moderate conservative-bourgeois elements headed by Franz Seldte. Indeed, rivalry between the two factions became endemic in the Stahlhelm. Duesterberg actively developed it as a radical anti-republican movement with a profile that was as much political as it was paramilitary: ultra-nationalism, anti-Marxism and anti-Semitism characterized its outlook. Deputy leader since 1924, his growing personal stature was underlined in 1927 when he was appointed the Stahlhelm's representative on the Presidium of the Union of Patriotic German Associations (VVVD), a confederation of right-wing groups, and also equal co-leader of the veterans' organization. He fully supported the Stahlhelm's alliance with the DNVP and NSDAP in the campaign against the Young Plan in 1929, and in the Harzburg Front two years later, believing that as one of the largest extraparliamentary forces in Germany it had as vital a part to play as anyone in bringing down the democratic Republic. As his memoirs reveal, however, this was a rather naive view, given the ruthless tactics and mounting strength of the NSDAP, whose totalitarian aspirations spared no one, including fellow-travellers on the radical Right. This point was made in callous fashion by the NSDAP during the Reich presidential election campaign in spring 1932 when it disclosed that Duesterberg, the candidate of the Stahlhelm and DNVP, was of partly Jewish origin. His paternal grandfather, Abraham Selig Duesterberg, had been a Jew. That he had been awarded the Iron Cross in 1813 for valour during the War of Liberation, apparently counted for nothing. The Stahlhelm leader, who polled very modestly in any case, withdrew from the second ballot, with his reputation in his own extremist milieu considerably diminished. Surprisingly, von Papen sounded him out a few days before Hitler's appointment as Reich Chancellor about a post in the new cabinet, but Duesterberg rejected the idea out of hand. His political career as a vociferous paramilitary leader was at an end.

In the immediate aftermath of the Röhm putsch in June 1934, Duesterberg was arrested for criticizing the regime and sent for a short period to a concentration camp. Thereafter he retired from public life. After 1945 he made an unsuccessful attempt to revive the Stahlhelm, and died on 4 November 1950 in Hameln.

## Further Reading

T. Duesterberg, *Der Stahlhelm und Hitler*, Wolfenbüttel, 1949. See also V.R. Berghahn, *Der Stahlhelm. Bund der Frontsoldaten 1918–1935*, Düsseldorf, 1966; J.M. Diehl, *Paramilitary Politics in Weimar Germany*, Bloomington, 1977; H.J. Mauch, *Nationalistische Wehrorganisationen in der Weimarer Republik. Zur Entwicklung und Ideologie des 'Paramilitarismus'*, Frankfurt am Main, 1982.

## EBERT, Friedrich (1871–1925)

The former saddler of working-class background and limited formal education was one of the most important political figures, as Reich Chancellor during the November Revolution, co-chairman of the Council of People's Representatives and Reich President, during the turbulent early history of the Weimar Republic. His precise role at that time is still the subject of considerable historical controversy. He is seen by some as a failed socialist who betrayed the working class, by others as a staunch patriot, even nationalist, who saved Germany from the extremism of both the Left and the Right, and laid the foundations of a social democratic, modern state.

Ebert's earlier career was relatively straightforward in political terms. Although born in Heidelberg on 4 February 1871, he had made Bremen his base by the early 1890s. In 1893 he joined the editorial staff of the SPD newspaper *Bremer Bürgerzeitung*, and between 1891 and 1905 he served intermittently as chairman of the party in that city. In 1900 he was elected a local councillor. Meanwhile, the party activist who was building a reputation as an outstanding administrator and skilled public speaker, owned and ran a tavern. He was also developing as a man of some bourgeois pretension, as revealed by his sober sartorial habits and his love of sailing and hunting. Although his public statements frequently carried a radical, if not revolutionary animus, he was more comfortable with the revisionist right wing of his party. In 1905 he was appointed party treasurer and national organizer, and in 1913 entered the Reichstag. The same year, he succeeded August Bebel as chairman (with Hugo Haase) of the party. Ebert did not serve in the armed forces during the First World War. In 1916 he was elected chairman of the SPD's parliamentary faction. Although he supported the war in 1914 and found no difficulty in voting for the necessary war credits in the Reichstag, he grew increasingly concerned at the chauvinistic annexationalist policy of the government and the accelerating power of the army high command. In February 1917 he gave his full backing to the Peace Resolution that was then introduced by the left-wing and centre parties into the Reichstag. A year later he was controversially involved in the Berlin armaments workers' strike. By the end of the war, Ebert had firmly anchored his presence as the most authoritative leader of his party. He had contributed a great deal to its development during the previous 25 years, and in particular had managed to stamp his personal sense of moderation and responsibility on it.

During the revolutionary period of 1918–19, he was determined to defend and preserve the newly established parliamentary Republic from all extremist threats, and towards this end the one-time anti-militarist joined forces with the conservative-monarchist army to defeat the Spartacists in 1919 and subsequently Communist insurrections in various parts of Germany. He was also very influential in blocking any attempts to bring about radical changes to the social and economic structure of the country. Following his election as Reich President in February 1919, he emerged as a stout defender of what he regarded as a significant change in the political complexion of the state. In the crisis years of 1922–23 he often employed the emergency powers accorded the President under Article 48 of the Constitution to introduce protective legislation and other measures. Ebert's personal popularity, however, remained consistently low. He was the target of abuse and vilification from the Right, which often resulted in widely publicized, unpleasant litigation, and he was never forgiven by sections of the working class and the far Left for his counterrevolutionary strategy in 1918–19. The culmination of this hate campaign was the decision of a Magdeburg court in December 1924 to uphold an accusation brought against him by a newspaper editor that his role in the Berlin armament workers' strike in 1918 amounted to high treason. A shattered Ebert died of a sudden illness in Berlin on 28 February 1925.

## Further Reading

F. Ebert, *Schriften, Aufzeichnungen, Reden. Mit unveröffentlichten Erinnerungen aus dem Nachlass*, 2 vols, Dresden, 1926; G. Kotowski, *Friedrich Ebert. Eine politische Biographie*, Volume I, *Der Aufstieg eines deutschen Arbeiterführers 1871 bis 1917*, Wiesbaden, 1963; W. Besson, *Friedrich Ebert. Verdienst und Grenze*, Göttingen, 1963; P.-C. Witt, *Friedrich Ebert. Parteiführer, Reichskanzler, Volksbeauftragter, Reichspräsident*, Bonn, 1987, first published 1971; R. König, H. Soell and H. Weber (eds), *Friedrich Ebert und seine Zeit. Bilanzen und Perspektiven der Forschung*, Munich, 1990; R. Münch, *Von Heidelberg nach Berlin. Friedrich Ebert 1871–1905*, Munich, 1991. See also H.-O. Meissner, *Junge Jahre im Reichspräsidentenpalais. Erinnerungen an Ebert und Hindenburg 1919–1934*, Esslingen, 1988.

## EISNER, Kurt (1867–1919)

The leader of the revolution in Bavaria in 1918 was a Berlin Jew, born on 14 May 1867, who before the war had earned a considerable reputation as a literary critic, essayist and journalist. He was editor of various newspapers, including the *Frankfurter Zeitung* and *Vorwärts*, and his caustic pen landed him in jail on one occasion for lese-majesty. In 1907 he was appointed chief editor of the *Fränkischer Tagespost*, took Bavarian citizenship and settled in Munich. By 1914 he identified with the revisionist wing of the SPD but was a committed internationalist, pacifist and anti-militarist. Though he initially accepted the validity of a defensive war by Germany in 1914, his sympathies moved increasingly to the left as the war dragged on, causing him to join the oppositional *Arbeitsgemeinschaft* in the SPD. In early 1917 he helped found the USPD and established a public profile as an anti-war campaigner through passionate agitation and involvement in the Berlin munitions strike in January 1918. But it was his important role in Bavarian politics at the end of the war which has given Eisner his place in history.

A utopian independent socialist rather than a Marxist, he was idealistic, energetic and creative, and undoubtedly possessed a flair for revolutionary leadership. But he lacked a proper sense of realism. He believed that a completely new Germany had to arise from defeat, in which concepts of justice, peace and reason would predominate, and that this new Germany could take her place in a new era of international reconciliation. The war-weariness of the Bavarian population in November 1918, widespread anti-Prussianism and a fear of Allied invasion created a situation that was receptive to Eisner's radical oratory and promises of a better future. He led the demand for the abolition of the Bavarian monarchy and the creation of a socialist republic, of which he became Minister-President. On a national level, he sought to retain the workers' and soldiers' Councils that had sprung up so as to provide a proletarian balance to the emerging bourgeois democracy of parliament, and to combine both in some form of dual control. This idea, and others, were shattered by the poor showing of the USPD in elections for the new Bavarian parliament in January 1919. But he lingered in office and somewhat unwisely went off to Berne to take part in the first post-war conference of the Socialist International, when he acted as the honest broker between Left and Right factions. Shortly after his return, on 21 February 1919, he was assassinated by a radical nationalist on his way to the Bavarian Landtag, where he was reputedly to announce his resignation. In the political turmoil that ensued, more extremist elements gained control and proceeded to establish a Soviet dictatorship which, in turn, was destroyed by the far Right. Eisner's own radicalism was a significant factor in the subsequent development of the state he sought to lead in a new direction as an anti-Communist and nationalist bastion.

## *Further Reading*

K. Eisner, *Schuld und Sühne*, Berlin, 1919, which purports to show documentary evidence for Germany's war guilt; *Gesammelte Schriften*, 2 vols, Berlin, 1919. See also R. Schmolze and G. Schmolze (eds), *Kurt Eisner. Die halbe Macht den Räten. Ausgewählte Aufsätze und Reden*,

Cologne, 1969; A. Mitchell, *Revolution in Bavaria 1918–1919. The Eisner Regime and the Soviet Republic*, Princeton, 1965; F. Eisner, *Kurt Eisner. Die Politik des libertären Sozialismus*, Frankfurt am Main, 1979; F.J. Bauer (ed.), *Die Regierung Eisner 1918/19. Ministerratsprotokolle und Dokumente*, Düsseldorf, 1987; F. Hitzer, *Anton Graf Arco. Das Attentat auf Kurt Eisner und die Schüsse im Landtag*, Munich, 1988; H. Beyer, *Die Revolution in Bayern 1918/19*, 2nd edn, Berlin, 1988.

## EPP, Franz Xaver Ritter von (1868–1947)

A distinguished professional soldier and influential figure in right-wing political circles before joining the NSDAP, Epp was born the son of an artist in Munich on 16 October 1868, attended the War School and War Academy in that city and entered the service of the Royal Bavarian Ninth Infantry Regiment in 1887. He saw active service in various parts of the world before 1914, including China and South West Africa. During the First World War, when he commanded the Bavarian Infantry Guard Regiment, he was highly decorated for bravery: the *Pour le Mérite*, Iron Cross (First and Second Classes), and the Bavarian Military Max-Joseph Order, which carried with it the right to aristocratic status. During the revolutionary period after the end of the war, he set up under his command, while still an officer in the Reichswehr, the Epp *Freikorps*, which in spring 1919 played a crucial part in the liberation of Munich from the grip of the Soviet Republic. For a brief period thereafter he was military dictator of Bavaria and emerged as a well-known personality in the radical rightist camp. He had links with the Kapp putschists, helped secure funding for the NSDAP's purchase of the *Völkischer Beobachter*, and led his *Freikorps* into action against Communist insurrections in the Ruhr and Hamburg. In 1923 he was promoted to General-Major and given command of the Seventh (Bavarian) Reichswehr Division – a post he was quickly forced to renounce because of a possible conflict with his extremist political views.

Epp's formal involvement with the National Socialist movement began in 1926 when he was made commander of the SA in Bavaria, and before joining the party in 1928, represented the BVP in the Bavarian parliament. He was also leader of the Deutscher Notbann, which the Bavarian government set up to carry out illegal military training. His rise in the NSDAP was swift. Elected to the Reichstag in 1928, he became a *Reichsleiter* in charge of the party's Defence Policy Department in 1932, and frequently advised Hitler on important affairs. After 1933, he held several top posts on behalf of the regime, most notably, that of Governor (*Reichstatthalter*) until 1945. An old-fashioned authoritarian conservative-nationalist and monarchist rather than a quintessential Nazi, he died in an American internment camp in Munich on 31 January 1947.

### Further Reading

F. von Epp, *Die heutige Bedeutung von Raum und Rohstoffen*, Munich, 1937; and *Deutschlands koloniale Forderungen*, Munich, 1939. See also W. Frank, *Franz Ritter von Epp. Der Weg eines deutschen Soldaten*, Hamburg, 1934; H. Fenske, *Konservatismus und Rechtradikalismus in Bayern nach 1918*, Bad Homburg, 1969; H. Schulze, *Freikorps und Republik 1918–1920*, Boppard, 1969.

## ERKELENZ, Anton (1878–1945)

Unusually for an important DDP leader, Erkelenz came from a working-class Catholic background in Neuss, where he was born on 10 October 1878. After completing his apprenticeship as a locksmith and turner, he became involved in the liberal Hirsch–Duncker trade union movement, joining its governing committee in 1907, and also in liberal politics, developing as a disciple of Friedrich Naumann.

Active in the Workers' and Soldiers' Council in Neuss in 1918–19, he joined the DDP and was elected as one of its representatives in the National Assembly. A year later, he entered the Reichstag, where he sat until his resignation from the party in 1930. From the outset, Erkelenz was regarded as one of the principal exponents of the National Social tradition in the DDP and was co-editor of that faction's mouthpiece, *Die Hilfe*. He quickly established his credentials as a left-wing member of the party, advocating socialization of designated key sectors of the economy, labour law reform, and a comprehensive programme of social and economic reconstruction designed to attract the working class to the DDP. As chairman of the party Executive Committee from 1921 until 1929, he sought to promote a democratic-progressive course which frequently brought him into conflict with the DDP's business wing and its right-wing Reichstag delegation. Indeed, several times during the 1920s he raised the spectre of a left-wing secession from the DDP, which seems a clear signal that Erkelenz sat uncomfortably in its ranks for much of this period. It is not too surprising to discover, therefore, that in 1920 he had proposed the creation of a new Republican Democratic People's Party, thus to the left of the DDP, which would attempt to unite working-class and bourgeois supporters of the Republic. He remained an implacable opponent of the linking of the DDP with the DVP to form a single liberal party. His concern to make the DDP appealing to the working class was expressed further not only in his continuing trade union activity, but also in his establishment in 1920 of the National Workers' Council in the party (Reichsarbeitnehmerausschuss der DDP). Under his chairmanship, however, the 11,000-strong body achieved very limited success. In 1924 Erkelenz was among a number of prominent non-socialist politicians who lent their support to the founding of the Reichsbanner Schwarz-Rot-Gold, the paramilitary organization designed to defend the democratic Republic.

As leader of the Hirsch–Duncker trade union during the 1920s, he sought to extend its relations with other unions, with the ultimate aim of creating a united German trade union. But only under the pressures generated by Hitler's advent to power did this initiative display any real life. In April 1933 Erkelenz, who had disappeared from the centre ground of politics after his resignation in 1930 in protest at the DDP's merger with the Jungdeutsche Orden to form the German State Party, was a member of a trade union *Führerkreis* which belatedly tried to arrange for a unitary organization to emerge. The National Socialist regime's destruction of the trade unions in May 1933 and the setting up of the German Labour Front aborted this endeavour. A member of the SPD from 1930, Erkelenz withdrew from politics altogether during the Third Reich. He died at the hands of the Russians in Berlin on 25 April 1945.

## Further Reading

A. Erkelenz, *Unternehmer und Arbeitnehmer in der neuen Wirtschaft*, Berlin, 1922. He also published *Demokratie und Parteiorganisation. Dem Andenken an Friedrich Naumann und Wilhelm Ohr*, Berlin, 1925; *Junge Demokratie. Reden und Schriften politischen Inhalts*, Berlin, 1925; and edited *Zehn Jahre Deutsche Republik. Ein Handbuch für republikanische Politik*, Berlin, 1928. See also R.W. Brantz, 'Anton Erkelenz, the Hirsch–Duncker Trade Unions, and the German Democratic Party', doctoral dissertation, Ohio State University, 1973; R. Pois, *The Bourgeois Democrats of Weimar Germany*, Philadelphia, 1976; L.E. Jones, *German Liberalism and the Dissolution of the Weimar Party System, 1918–1933*, Chapel Hill, 1988.

# ERZBERGER, Matthias (1875–1921)

One of the most influential political leaders of the early post-war years in Germany and an anathema to the nationalist Right, Erzberger was born in Buttenhausen on 20 September 1875 into a working-class Catholic family. Trained as a primary schoolteacher, he was a journalist and editor before beginning to represent the Centre Party in the Reichstag in 1903. Before the war he had become a leading member of his party caucus and developed a considerable expertise in financial and tax matters. After 1914 he moved from a pro-annexationist position to advocacy of a just peace and international reconciliation, incurring the wrath of the nationalist camp when he proposed the famous Peace Resolution in the Reichstag in July 1917. He held office as *Staatssekretär* in Prince Max of Baden's cabinet, and in November 1918 led, by agreement with the army high command, the German delegation to the Armistice talks. He signed the Armistice for Germany on 11 November. As Minister without Portfolio in the Scheidemann cabinet that took office in February 1919, he emerged as the principal advocate of accepting the harsh terms of the Treaty of Versailles, which was yet another reason for his extreme unpopularity among nationalists. Appointed Vice-Chancellor and Reich Finance Minister in the new government led by Gustav Bauer, Erzberger undertook a comprehensive reform of Germany's financial structure which, in implementing sections of the Weimar Constitution, asserted the authority of central government over the regional state governments in a relationship aimed at fiscal equilibrium.

Erzberger was seen very much as the dominant political figure in government in 1919–20, the veritable linchpin of the Centre–SPD coalition that constituted its base. For many nationalists he was the personification of the hated Republic and had to endure, in the first instance, a torrent of abuse and vilification, which culminated in a well-publicized libel action he brought against one of his tormentors, Karl Helfferich of the DNVP, in 1920. The verdict of the court in March of that year partly upheld Helfferich's accusation that Erzberger had used his political office for dishonest financial transactions. His decision to resign immediately was greeted with euphoria on the Right. The verdict was a clear instance of the nature of 'political' justice in the Weimar era: leniency towards the Right and hostility to the Left and the Republic's supporters. Erzberger was determined, however, that his career should not end in such controversial circumstances and took steps to rehabilitate his private reputation. He was re-elected to the Reichstag in June 1920 and there seemed no reason why in the longer term he should not emerge once again as a formidable figure in party and national politics. His assassination on 26 August 1921, while walking in the Black Forest near Bad Griesbach, ended that prospect. His was but one of a series of murders carried out by members of the fanatical right-wing Organisation Consul at that time.

## Further Reading

M. Erzberger, *Der Verständigungsfriede*, Stuttgart, 1917; *Reden zur Neuordnung des deutschen Finanzwesens*, Berlin, 1919; *Erlebnisse im Weltkrieg*, Stuttgart, 1920; and *Der Völkerbund als Friedensfrage*, Berlin, 1919. See also K. Epstein, *Matthias Erzberger and the Dilemma of German Democracy*, Princeton, 1959; R. Morsey and K. Ruppert (eds), *Die Protokolle der Reichstagsfraktion der Deutschen Zentrumspartei, 1920–1925*, Mainz, 1981.

## FEDER, Gottfried (1883–1941)

An important influence on the early NSDAP's economic and financial policy without ever succeeding in establishing himself as the official party spokesman in this sphere, Feder developed an active interest in politics only after the end of the First World War. Born in Würzburg into a comfortable middle-class family of civil service tradition on 27 January 1883, he studied civil engineering, specializing in the technique of reinforced concrete, and in 1908 joined a Munich construction firm as a partner and manager. Before and during the war, for which he was not called up for medical reasons, he continued his professional career at home and abroad with limited success. By 1917–18 he was already developing an economic and financial theory which established his reputation as a theorist in the post-war era: the 'breaking of interest slavery', which he expounded in a brochure published in 1919, *Manifesto for the Breaking of Interest Slavery*, and in subsequent works. Unoriginal, collated from various reformist and *völkisch* economic theorists, and thoroughly unconventional, his theory was essentially the demand to break the cycle of interest in capitalist-industrial society through the abolition of all interest payments and the nationalization of banks and the stock exchange. Feder did not oppose capital and private ownership as such, but wanted to link both to individual achievement and social obligation, with priority to be given to the state where the public interest required it. He distinguished between 'rapacious' and 'productive' capital, which carried an explicit anti-Semitic message: the former was identified as the allegedly Jewish-dominated international commercial and finance capital.

After 1918, Feder abandoned his business interests to devote his time to propagating his views among the multitude of extreme nationalist and *völkisch* groups in Munich and other parts of Germany, largely through public lectures, but also by writing articles for a number of right-wing newspapers and magazines. He even helped prepare information courses for members of the Bavarian *Reichswehr* at the invitation of Captain Karl Mayr. In September 1919 he joined the DAP, thus at the same time as Hitler, who was subsequently most impressed by his colleague's theories. In the NSDAP party programme published in February 1920, they found a conspicuous place, most notably in Points 10 and 11, even though Feder himself did not author or co-author a work for which Hitler and Drexler were responsible. His further contacts with the NSDAP in 1920 and 1921 were restricted to occasional speeches at party meetings in Munich, while at the same time he sought to develop his Deutscher Kampfbund zur Brechung der Zinsknechtschaft, which he founded in January 1920. Nevertheless, he regarded himself as a pioneer of the NSDAP who had made a crucial contribution to its ideology. Envisaged by Hitler as his finance minister in the provisional government that was to come into place as a result of the Beer Hall putsch in November 1923, Feder marched to the Feldherrnhalle, and later fled to Czechoslovakia. In May 1924 he was elected to the Reichstag as a representative of the Grossdeutsche Freiheitsbewegung and in February 1925 rejoined the born-again NSDAP, electing to be one of its three parliamentary deputies. It was at his initiative that Hitler convened the famous meeting with northern NSDAP leaders in Bamberg in February 1926, during which he put Feder in charge of the maintenance of the party programme's integrity. Henceforth, he called himself the 'ideologist of the movement', a description also employed by the party press. He was also appointed editor in 1926 of the Nationalsozialistische Bibliothek, in which official party publications appeared. In 1928 he secured a foothold in the party's press by acquiring the Fränkischer Volksverlag, which produced a number of newspapers in Hesse and southern Germany. The venture was not a success and he withdrew with heavy losses in 1932.

The early 1930s witnessed a definite decline in Feder's status in the party, particularly as it came more into contact with sections of big industry where his economic theories were dismissed out of hand. Despite his appointment in November 1931 as head of the NSDAP's Reich Economic Council, he exercised less and less influence in leading party circles. His friendship with Gregor Strasser proved to be a distinct liability when the latter resigned his party offices in December 1932. In the Third Reich, Feder was a figure of secondary importance, despite accumulating a series of posts: State Secretary in the Reich Ministry of Economics (1933), and in March also Reich Commissioner for Settlement Policy; he was also chairman of the Reich Association of German Technology. By the mid-1930s he had lost most of his posts, the last in 1936 when he was dismissed from his Reichstag seat. The fundamental reason for his political demise must lie in his failure to keep up with the imperatives of power politics in Hitler's Germany. Until his death in Murnau, Upper Bavaria, on 29 September 1941, Feder lived out a quiet existence as professor of land economics at Berlin's Technical Academy, where he had been a student before the First World War. The NSDAP did not acknowledge his passing.

## Further Reading

Among Feder's publications were: *Das Manifest zur Brechung der Zinsknechtschaft des Geldes*, Diessen, 1919; *Der Staatsbankrott – Die Rettung*, Diessen, 1919; *Der Deutsche Staat auf nationaler und sozialer Grundlage. Neue Wege in Staat, Finanz und Wirtschaft*, Munich, 1923; *Das Programm der NSDAP und seine weltanschaulichen Grundgedanken*, Munich, 1927; *Kampf gegen die Hochfinanz*, Munich, 1933. In the absence of a full-length biography, see A. Tyrell: 'Gottfried Feder and the NSDAP', in P.D. Stachura (ed.), *The Shaping of the Nazi State*, London, 1978, pp. 48–87; Manfred Riebe, 'Gottfried Feder: Wirtschaftsprogrammatiker Hitlers. Ein biographischer Beitrag zur Vor- und Frühgeschichte des Nationalsozialismus', M.A. Dissertation, University of Erlangen, 1971.

Other aspects of Feder's career are touched on by A. Barkai, *Das Wirtschaftssystem des Nationalsozialismus. Der historische und ideologische Hintergrund 1933–1936*, Cologne, 1977; K.-H. Ludwig, *Technik und Ingenieure im Dritten Reich*, Düsseldorf, 1974; E. Forndran, *Die Stadt- und Industriegründungen Wolfsburg und Salzgitter*, Frankfurt am Maine, 1984.

## FEHRENBACH, Konstantin (1852–1926)

As Reich Chancellor from June 1920 until May 1921, Fehrenbach enjoyed the status of elderly statesman, having spent most of his successful professional and political career in the Kaiser's Germany. Born into a lower middle-class Catholic family in the small village of Wellendingen in Baden on 11 January 1852, he came to personify the south German type of democratic yet rather conservative Centre Party politician. After completing his university studies in theology and law, which earned him a doctorate, he built up a flourishing practice in Freiburg im Breisgau before embarking on a career in the Baden Landtag, whose president he later became, and in the Reichstag, to which he was elected in 1903.

During the First World War he emerged as an outstanding parliamentarian: chairman of the Main Committee of the Reichstag in 1917, he supported the Peace Resolution in July 1917; in the following year he was appointed chairman of the Budget Committee, and in July was elected president of the Reichstag. In 1919 he assumed this office in the National Assembly, which was a tribute to the broad cross-party respect he enjoyed as a sober, fair-minded colleague of considerable dignity. However, his period as Reich Chancellor was less successful, partly because of the very formidable problems confronting his cabinet at home and in foreign affairs to which there were no easy answers, and partly also because Fehrenbach never felt comfortable in this position. Lacking a sense of dynamism and creative political skill, he returned empty-handed from discussions concerning reparations at the Spa Conference in July 1920 and the London Conference the following year. Nor did he come up with any substantive policies for dealing with internal issues relating to the economy or political stability. Indeed, he was anxious to resign because of old age and the onerous burden of office sometime prior to the DNVP's withdrawal of support from his minority cabinet in May 1921, which finally compelled his resignation. In a wider perspective, his chancellorship amounted to little more than a disappointing holding operation.

Fehrenbach's career, however, was not quite over, for during the next few years he maintained a conspicuous profile as a member of the special Court for the Protection of the Republic, before which the most important infringements of the Act of that title (July 1922) were examined, as chairman of the Centre Party delegation in the Reichstag (1923–26), and as deputy chairman of the association dedicated to combating anti-Semitism (Verein zur Abwehr des Antisemitismus). He died in Freiburg on 26 March 1926, leaving no historical records of his career.

## Further Reading

P. Wulf (ed.), *Akten der Reichskanzlei. Weimarer Republik. Das Kabinett Fehrenbach. 25. Juni 1920 bis 4. Mai 1921*, Boppard, 1971; R. Morsey, *Die deutsche Zentrumspartei 1917–1923*, Düsseldorf, 1966; E.L. Evans, *The German Center Party, 1870–1933. A Study in Political Catholicism*, Carbondale, 1981.

## FISCHER, Ruth (1895–1961)

Born Elfriede Eisler into a Jewish family in Leipzig on 11 December 1895, Fischer's childhood was spent in Vienna where her father taught philosophy at the university. Before moving back to Germany in 1919 she had been active in the Austrian Socialist and Communist parties and already had a reputation for radical, uncompromising commitment, which was carried over to the KPD, whose Berlin branch she led from 1921. A firm advocate of revolutionary violence to attain the dictatorship of the proletariat, she emerged as a prominent member and then leader (with Arkady Maslow and Ernst Friesland) of the so-called 'ultra-leftist' faction in the party which was at the heart of the vicious internecine squabbling that characterized the KPD during most of the 1920s.

A persistent critic of the KPD leadership's alleged passivity, opportunism and 'revisionism', and an opponent of Stalin's theory of 'socialism in one country', Fischer and her colleagues constituted a vigorous intellectual force in the party, though from a wider political point of view it was ultimately destructive and unsuccessful. This was clearly revealed during Fischer's leadership of the party in 1924–25 when her confident, almost abrasive, and ambitious approach brought the KPD no obvious gains. Ongoing conflicts with the Comintern exacerbated her situation. Having subsequently turned against her ultra-leftist friends, as exemplified by her behaviour at the tenth party congress in Berlin in July 1925, she was forced into publicly admitting in an open letter two months later that grave errors had been made in her leadership of the party. This was the prelude to her removal from that post in November 1925 and to her expulsion altogether from the party in 1926. Fischer was no more successful as a member of the Reichstag, where she sat from 1924 until 1928. Acerbic, outspoken, contemptuous of the 'bourgeois' conventions of the chamber, she cut a distinctive if unprepossessing figure, ending up as something of an embarrassment.

From 1928 until 1933, Fischer, who had remarried and sported the name 'Golke', worked in social welfare in Berlin. In no way further involved in active politics, she emigrated in 1933, finally to the United States, where she worked in publishing. She returned to Europe after the war, dying in Paris on 13 March 1961.

## Further Reading

R. Fischer, *Stalin and German Communism. A Study in the Origins of the State Party*, Cambridge, Massachusetts, 1948. See also W.T. Angress, *Die Kampfzeit der KPD 1921–1923*, Düsseldorf, 1973; O.K. Flechtheim, *Die Kommunistische Partei Deutschlands in der Weimarer Republik*, new edn, Frankfurt am Main, 1969; B. Fowkes, *Communism in Germany under the Weimar Republic*, London, 1984; H. Weber, *Die Wandlung des deutschen Kommunismus. Die Stalinisierung der KPD in der Weimarer Republik*, 2 vols, Frankfurt am Main, 1969.

## FRICK, Wilhelm (1877–1946)

One of the most prominent members of the Third Reich's hierarchy as Reich Minister of the Interior (1933–43), Prussian Minister of the Interior (1934–43) and as Reich Minister without Portfolio and Reich Protector of Bohemia and Moravia (1943–45), Frick also played an important role as a close associate of Hitler during the *Kampfzeit*. Born on 12 March 1877 in Alsenz, in the Palatinate, the son of a Protestant secondary schoolteacher, he completed a doctorate in law at the University of Heidelberg in 1901. He practised as a lawyer in Kaiserslautern before entering the Royal Bavarian civil service in 1904. A weak chest prevented him from taking part in the First World War. He continued his career as a civil servant, heading the political police section after 1919, and in this capacity was a source of considerable help to the broad rightwing cause in Munich, including the NSDAP, which he joined in 1920. For his involvement in the Beer Hall putsch in November 1923 he was sentenced to 15 months' imprisonment, which he did not actually serve. In 1924, when he left the civil service, he was elected to represent the National Socialist Freedom Party in the Reichstag, crossing to the NSDAP when it was refounded the following year. Appointed chairman of the party's parliamentary delegation in 1928, retaining the position until 1945, he introduced a Bill designed to exclude Jews from all public offices and to limit their participation in the economy.

Frick came into national politics in January 1930 when he became the first member of his party to be appointed to a ministerial post in state government. Following the NSDAP's success in Landtag elections in Thuringia, he was appointed that state's Minister of the Interior and Education, where he remained until forced out by a noconfidence vote in April 1931. He made full use of his powers to demonstrate how his party went about the business of government: political opponents were purged from office, school textbooks were rewritten to reflect the Nazi *Weltanschauung*, nationalist and anti-Semitic propaganda was disseminated in schools, universities and government, and Nazi supporters were brought into positions of responsibility. A Chair was established in the University of Jena for the racist ideologue, Hans Günther. It was a practice which created the model for the *Gleichschaltung* programme instituted by

Hitler's regime in 1933. By his actions in Thuringia and his fanatically anti-democratic and anti-Marxist diatribes in the Reichstag, Frick revealed himself as a loyal, reliable and highly competent NSDAP leader. At the same time, he was on close terms with Gregor Strasser in the early 1930s and seemed for a period to be sympathetic to his more flexible methods of attaining power.

Frick's career was brought to an ignominious end in 1946 when he was convicted by the Nuremberg Military Tribunal of war crimes and crimes against humanity. He was consequently hanged in Nuremberg on 16 October 1946.

## Further Reading

W. Frick, *Die Nationalsozialisten im Reichstag 1924–1928*, Munich, 1928; *Die Nationalsozialisten im Reichstag 1928–1931*, Munich, 1932; *Erziehung zum lebendigen Volke*, Berlin, 1933; *Wir bauen das Dritte Reich*, Oldenburg, 1934; *Der Neuaufbau des Reichs*, Berlin, 1934; *Freiheit und Bindung der Selbstverwaltung*, Munich 1937. See also H. Fabricius, *Dr. Frick. Der revolutionäre Staatsmann*, Berlin, 1934.

Also of interest are E.N. Petersen, *The Limits of Hitler's Power*, Princeton, 1969; H. Mommsen, *Beamtentum im Dritten Reich*, Stuttgart, 1966; D.R. Tracey, 'The Development of the National Socialist Party in Thuringia 1924–1930', *Central European History*, 8, 1975, pp. 23–50; J. Caplan, *Government without Administration. State and Civil Service in Weimar and Nazi Germany*, Oxford, 1988.

# FRÖLICH, Paul (1884–1953)

The leading member and publicist of the KPD in the 1920s was born into a working-class family in Leipzig on 7 August 1884 and completed a commercial-vocational training before joining the SPD in 1902. He became mainly involved in the party's press empire and progressed to the editorship of the *Hamburger Echo* (1910–12) and the *Bremer Bürgerzeitung* (1912–16). Shortly before the end of the First World War he was a patient in a psychiatric hospital, and when he resumed his political career it was as managing editor of the principal KPD newspaper, *Die Rote Fahne*.

He played a part in the government of the Soviet Republic in Munich in spring 1919, adding to a growing profile in Communist circles, including the Comintern. In 1921–24 and 1928–30, he was a KPD deputy in the Reichstag, and he emerged as a figure of influence in the interminable and often bewildering faction fighting in the party, being at one time identified with the leftist opposition and another with the right. Frölich was a thoughtful man of ideas rather than a man of decisive political or organizational action, but apart from a long-standing admiration for Rosa Luxemburg, whose biographer be became, he vacillated too frequently between different ideological postures to have any real chance of constructing a stable political base in the KPD. He broke with it in December 1928 and co-founded a splinter group, the KPD (Opposition), which was ephemeral and insignificant in wider political terms. Frölich left it in early 1932 and in March joined the Socialist Workers' Party (SAP), which had been created by an assortment of left-wingers the previous

October. At the Reichstag elections in July 1932, the SAP, of whose executive committee Frölich was now a member, polled a derisory 72,630 votes, or 0.2 per cent of the total. Even worse was to follow at the Reichstag elections in November 1932 when the party fell to 45,201 votes, or 0.1 per cent of the total. Frölich thus joined that large group of radical leftists whose political career had ended sometime before the advent of National Socialism, and whose particular contribution had been rendered virtually meaningless by the turn of events in the late Weimar era.

Arrested while trying to flee the country in 1933, he spent some months in a concentration camp, then made his way into exile, first to Prague, later to Paris and the United States. Frölich returned to West Germany after the war and took up modest activity on behalf of the SPD until his death in Frankfurt am Main on 16 March 1953.

## Further Reading

P. Frölich (using pseud. Paul Werner), *Die Bayerische Räterepublik. Tatsachen und Kritik*, Leipzig, 1920; and by the same author (using his real name), *Zehn Jahre Krieg und Bürgerkrieg*, Berlin, 1924; *Keinen Pfennig den Fürsten!*, Berlin, 1926; *Rosa Luxemburg. Gedanke und Tat*, Frankfurt am Main, 1967 (first published 1939). See also W.T. Angress, *Die Kampfzeit der KPD 1921–1923*, Düsseldorf, 1973; O.K. Flechtheim, *Die KPD in der Weimarer Republik*, Frankfurt am Main, 1969; K.H. Tjaden, *Struktur und Funktion der 'KPD-Opposition' (KPO). Eine organisationssoziologische Untersuchung zur 'Rechts'-Opposition im deutschen Kommunismus zur Zeit der Weimarer Republik*, Meisenheim, 1964; H. Drechsler, *Die Sozialistische Arbeiterpartei Deutschlands (SAPD). Ein Beitrag zur Geschichte der deutschen Arbeiterbewegung am Ende der Weimarer Republik*, Meisenheim, 1965.

# GAYL, Freiherr Wilhelm von (1879–1945)

One of the most influential and perhaps the most loyal member, as Reich Minister of the Interior, of Franz von Papen's cabinet in 1932, Gayl was the scion of a long-established East Prussian aristocratic family. Born in Königsberg on 4 February 1879, he qualified as a lawyer and joined the Prussian civil service in 1904, where he was employed, eventually as a director, in the East Prussian Settlement Bank, until 1932. East Prussian agrarian interests remained a primary consideration throughout his political career through the agency of the DNVP, for he was convinced that the landowning élite constituted the backbone of the German nation and its defence against Polish incursion. In the First World War he served in a Prussian Guards regiment, which enjoyed élite status, and attained the rank of lieutenant-colonel while serving under Field Marshal von Hindenburg in the military high command. This wartime connection with the man who later became Reich President proved to be of some importance in the political sphere in 1932. In 1918 Gayl was appointed *Landeshauptmann* to represent the German military authorities in Lithuania. Although vehemently opposed to the November Revolution, he allowed his election to the Soldiers' Council in Kowno, Lithuania, so that he could help divert the revolutionary impulse into moderate channels. In 1919, having joined the DNVP, Gayl was the East Prussian delegate at the Paris Peace Conference, and the following year was appointed Reich Commissioner to supervise the plebiscite in Allenstein. From 1920 until the end of the Weimar period he played a prominent role as East Prussia's representative in the Prussian State Council and in the Reichsrat.

This intelligent and highly capable Junker became a leading member of the DNVP's right wing and had a strong personal friendship with Alfred Hugenberg. In the early 1930s he vigorously opposed Chancellor Brüning's plans for reforming agriculture east of the Elbe, and was not averse to exploiting his ties to President von Hindenburg to aid his cause. On Brüning's fall from office, he was one of several candidates considered by the President to take over the Chancellorship before von Papen was finally chosen. Accepting the Interior portfolio somewhat reluctantly, and only after a personal appeal to his soldierly sense of duty by Hindenburg, Gayl nevertheless devoted considerable energy to his task. He was instrumental in convincing von Papen to adopt a tough attitude towards the Prussian government in July 1932, resulting in the infamous *Preussenschlag*, and he was an outspoken critic of the Weimar Constitution, proposing a series of significant reforms in August 1932, none of which were actually implemented. In late November, when Papen's cabinet deserted him, Gayl was the only minister to support the Chancellor; they both resigned together. Gayl thereafter withdrew entirely from public life and died in Potsdam on 7 November 1945.

## Further Reading

Freiherr W. von Gayl, *Der politische und wirtschaftliche Kampf um Ostpreussen*, Münster, 1934; *Ostpreussen unter fremden Flaggen. Ein Erinnerungsbuch an die ostpreussische Volksabstimmung vom 11. Juli 1920*, Königsberg, 1940. See also L. Hertzman, *DNVP. Right-Wing Opposition in the Weimar Republic 1918-1924*, Lincoln, Nebraska, 1963; G. Schwerin, *Wilhelm Freiherr von Gayl, der Innenminister im Kabinett 1932*, Erlangen, 1972; H. Holbach, *Das 'System Hugenberg'. Die Organisation bürgerlicher Sammlungspolitik vor dem Aufstieg der NSDAP 1918–1928*, Stuttgart, 1980; U. Hörster-Philipps, *Konservative Politik in der Endphase der Weimarer Republik. Die Regierung Franz von Papen*, Cologne, 1982.

# GESSLER, Otto (1875–1955)

The prominent DDP politician, best known for his extended period in office as Reich Minister of Defence (1920–1928), was born into a Catholic peasant family in Ludwigsburg, Württemberg, on 6 February 1875. Completing his legal studies with a doctorate, he followed a legal and administrative career in the Bavarian state government before becoming involved in local affairs. In 1913 he was appointed Lord Mayor of Nuremberg, bringing to bear a decided liberal influence in the Friedrich Naumann tradition in a city closely associated with a Protestant-based, right-wing nationalism.

A co-founder of the DDP in Nuremberg in 1918, he was appointed Minister for Reconstruction in the Bauer government (1919–20). In March 1920 Gessler succeeded Gustav Noske in the highly sensitive Ministry of Defence. But he never commanded the personal authority of his forceful predecessor and was overshadowed until 1926 by the chief of the army command, General von Seeckt, who successfully resisted attempts to assert predominant civilian control over the Reichswehr. While Gessler was the public face of the military in the Reichstag, it was Seeckt who did the important negotiating behind the scenes with party and other leaders. Thus, Gessler's aim of rebuilding the army on a thoroughly democratic and pro-republican basis, which he had declared to the National Assembly on his appointment, never actually materialized. In practice, he loyally co-operated with Seeckt in virtually all significant matters, but in doing so considerably demeaned his office. Personal indecisiveness and inexperience, an exaggerated respect for Seeckt and possibly also a somewhat misplaced sense of patriotism may explain Gessler's timidity. During the crisis created by the Beer Hall putsch in November 1923, for example, President Ebert reacted by transferring executive powers to Seeckt and giving him supreme command over the entire Wehrmacht. Gessler's subordination could not have been more blatantly demonstrated. Ultimately, even he grew resentful of being Seeckt's puppet and played a part in the latter's dismissal in October 1926. Gessler then became more assertive in defending the interests of the Republic *vis-à-vis* the army, as shown by his decree regarding the display of national colours in 1926, but he ran into serious difficulties on other issues. When it was disclosed in the Reichstag in December 1926 that the army had committed a long list of violations of the Treaty of Versailles, he had to resign from his party in January 1927 to save it embarrassment. In early 1928 his clumsy involvement in the Lohmann army financial scandal brought about his ministerial resignation.

Gessler's career in the DDP was also not free of drama. In 1924 he was one of a number of party leaders who tried to form a new liberal party on the basis of the Bavarian DDP, and the same year he gained much publicity by advocating a fundamental reform of the Weimar Constitution in such a way as to allow the formation of a government capable of commanding a parliamentary majority. Without such reform, he argued, the state's authority faced complete paralysis. His was an astute analysis of the political impasse Germany had reached by the mid-1920s. In 1925 he was for a time considered by the DDP and the Centre Party a worthwhile presidential candidate, but Gustav Stresemann had an important hand in having his nomination rejected.

For the remainder of the Weimar period, Gessler took on numerous honorary offices that had little direct connection with politics, including the chairmanship of the Association for Germandom Abroad (Verein für das Deutschtum im Ausland). After 1933 he withdrew to private life, though he was arrested and imprisoned for a time in Ravensbrück concentration camp in relation to the July Plot of 1944; there is no evidence to suggest that he was implicated as a plotter. After the Second World War he served as president of the German Red Cross (1950–52). He died in Lindenberg, Allgäu, on 24 March 1955.

## Further Reading

O. Gessler, *Reichswehrpolitik in der Weimarer Zeit* (edited by Kurt Sendter), Stuttgart, 1958. Gessler also authored *Die Träger der Reichsgewalt*, Hamburg, 1931. See also F.L. Carsten, *The Reichswehr and Politics, 1918–1933*, Oxford, 1966; J. Schmädeke, *Militärische Kommandogewalt und parlamentarische Demokratie. Zum Problem der Verantwortlichkeit des Reichswehrministers in der Weimarer Republik*, Lübeck, 1967; M. Geyer, *Aufrüstung oder Sicherheit. Die Reichswehr in der Krise der Machtpolitik, 1924–1936*, Wiesbaden, 1980.

## GOEBBELS, Joseph (1897–1945)

The brilliant if completely cynical propagandist of the NSDAP, who more than anyone else cultivated to devastating effect the quasi-religious *Führerkult* around Adolf Hitler, and who, as *Gauleiter* of Berlin-Brandenburg from 1926 onwards, turned Germany's capital city into the decisive flashpoint of late Weimar politics, Goebbels rendered invaluable service to the National Socialist cause. Born the son of a devout Catholic bookkeeper in Rheydt, in the Rhineland, on 29 October 1897, his contraction of polio as a child left him with a club-foot which, besides disqualifying him for military service in 1914, left deep psychological scars which contributed to a somewhat unstable, radical and self-destructive outlook and personality. The intrinsically anti-intellectual and vehemently anti-bourgeois Goebbels received a sound grammar school education before proceeding to university to study history and literature. He took his doctorate from the University of Heidelberg in 1922, the same year that he joined the NSDAP, an appropriate vehicle for his anger at the world which he saw as dominated by Marxists and Jews. With his literary endeavours, including a mediocre expressionist novel entitled *Michael. Ein deutsches Schicksal in Tagebuchblättern*, ending in failure, he was forced to channel his resentments into his political career.

Rejoining the NSDAP in 1925, his first notable position was that of business manager of Gau Rhineland-North, where he became closely associated with the Strasser brothers and their peculiar brand of anti-capitalist *völkisch* nationalism. As a member of the so-called 'Nazi Left', or the social revolutionary wing of the party in northern Germany in the mid-1920s, Goebbels founded and edited the *Nationalsozialistische Briefe*, which sought to carry the ideological debate into the party as a whole and further into the industrial working class. His *Early Diary* reveals him as something of a National Bolshevik, bitterly anti-Western and pro-Soviet. He helped Gregor Strasser compose an alternative draft programme for the NSDAP in 1925 which put more emphasis than the official version of 1920 on 'socialism'. A critic of Hitler's style of leadership, Goebbels showed remarkable opportunism after the Bamberg Conference in February 1926 in deserting his erstwhile colleagues in favour of the *Führer*: the Strassers never forgave him this 'treachery'.

Posted as *Gauleiter* to Berlin in November 1926, he set about transforming a moribund party organization with relish. Developing his gift for eye-catching, sensationalist and radical publicity, in which the use of physical violence in the streets against the Left formed an indispensable part, he brought the NSDAP to the forefront of the political fight in an environment that was intrinsically alien and unsympathetic to the Nazi message of chauvinism, racism and anti-Semitism. His sharp intelligence, shrewd political instincts, flair for theatrical effects and superb organizational and oratorical skills were deployed to telling purpose, particularly during the Depression. The truth was never allowed to inhibit agitation and hectoring of opponents: marches, parades, brawls, murder and intimidation were brought together to produce a frightening dynamism. *Der Angriff*, the party newspaper founded by Goebbels in 1927, became notorious for the venom of its crusading zeal as well as for its catchy headlines and slogans. A member of the Reichstag from 1928, he shamelessly exploited its privileges for the benefit of the party, swearing to destroy the democratic Republic from within. As Reich Propaganda Leader of the NSDAP from April 1930, he was well equipped to provide nation-wide propaganda support as the party strove for power, and as one of Hitler's inner circle played a crucial advisory role.

In the Third Reich, Goebbels was Reich Minister of Propaganda 1933 to 1945, which gave him absolute control of all branches of the media and the arts, and a unique opportunity to mobilize the masses behind the *Führer* and the regime. In the later stages of the war his influence became even more important as he sought to prepare Germany for supreme sacrifice. Appointed General Plenipotentiary for Total War in July 1944, Goebbels could not prevent the disintegration of the Third Reich and the devastation of his dreams, yet he remained fanatically loyal to Hitler right to the end. He died with his wife and family in the Berlin *Führerbunker* on 1 May 1945.

## Further Reading

J. Goebbels, *The Early Diaries: The Journal of Joseph Goebbels, 1925-1926.* (edited by H. Heiber), London, 1962; *Die zweite Revolution. Briefe an Zeitgenossen*, Zwickau, 1926; *Lenin oder Hitler? Eine Rede*, Zwickau, 1926; *Signal zum Aufbruch*, Munich, 1931; *Wege ins Dritte Reich. Briefe und Aufsätze für Zeitgenossen*, Munich, 1927; *Vom Kaiserhof zur Reichskanzlei. Eine historische Darstellung in Tagebuchblättern*, Munich, 1934 (English edition entitled *My Part in Germany's Fight*, London, 1935; new edition 1979); *Wetterleuchten. Aufsätze aus der Kampfzeit* (edited by Georg-Wilhelm Müller), Munich, 1939. See also E.K. Bramsted, *Goebbels and National Socialist Propaganda 1925–1945*, East Lansing, Michigan, 1965; H. Heiber, *Joseph Goebbels*, Berlin, 1962 (new edn, 1988); H. Heiber (ed.), *Goebbels-Reden, Vol I. 1932–1939*, Düsseldorf, 1971; E. Frölich (ed.), *Joseph Goebbels. Die Tagebücher. Sämtliche Fragmente. Teil I. Aufzeichnungen von 1924 bis 1941*, 4 vols, Munich, 1987; W. von Oven, *Wer war Goebbels? Biographie aus der Nähe*, Munich, 1987; R.G. Reuth, *Goebbels*, Munich, 1990.

# GOERDELER, Carl (1884–1945)

Best remembered perhaps as the leading civilian figure in the conservative, nationalist resistance to Hitler in Germany, Goerdeler was none the less a substantial politician in his own right during the last years of the Weimar Republic. He was born into a well-established Protestant and nationalist family of civil service tradition on 31 July 1884 in Schneidemühl. He read law at the universities of Tübingen and Königsberg and entered local government service in 1911. Appointed Chief Overseer (*Beigeordneter*) in Solingen in 1912, he spent the war years in an administrative capacity, and from 1920 until 1930 served as Deputy Mayor of Königsberg. His political sympathies were firmly on the Right. He believed in a strong national state that was conservative politically but liberal economically, in which the rule of law was sacrosanct, and was committed to a restoration of Germany as a major force in international affairs.

After appointment as Lord Mayor of Leipzig in 1930, Goerdeler had a solid platform for expressing his political views. But despite being highly critical of the party system and of the obvious weaknesses of Weimar parliamentarianism, he advocated an all-party coalition government as the way out of Germany's economic and political crisis in 1932. He himself was mentioned several times in influential circles as a candidate for the Reich chancellorship. He was one of the few figures in public life who thought seriously about ways of overcoming mass unemployment, but his only official post came in December 1931 when Brüning brought him into government as Reich Prices Commissioner, specifically to supervise the implementation of the Emergency Decree for the Protection of the German Economy and Finances. This extraordinarily radical measure was primarily designed to lower prices or, as the Chancellor expressed it, 'to prevent the sinking of real purchasing power'. Price decreases and maxima were ordered, and during his six months in office Goerdeler had some success.

In the Third Reich, he continued as Lord Mayor of Leipzig until April 1937, when he resigned over the regime's decision to remove the bust of the Jewish composer Felix Mendelssohn from its place in front of City Hall, and acted also as an economics adviser before accepting once again, in January 1934, the position of Reich Prices Commissioner; he resigned from this post in July 1935 in protest at government policies, which rejected his economic liberalism and plans for local administrative reform. Never an NSDAP member, Goerdeler could not accept the racial anti-Semitism and rearmament policies of the regime, though it must be said that he did not wholly disapprove of the Nuremberg Race Laws (1935) and remained a stout admirer of the German army and its traditions. Joining the Stuttgart engineering and car manufacturing firm of Robert Bosch in 1937, Goerdeler's anti-Nazi convictions quickly led him into resistance activity that culminated in his principal role in the July Plot of 1944. Designated Chancellor of a post-Hitler Germany, he was arrested by the Gestapo, sentenced to death by the People's Court, and executed on 2 February 1945 in Plötzensee prison, Berlin.

## Further Reading

W. Ritter von Schramm (ed.), *Beck und Goerdeler. Gemeinschaftsdokumente für den Frieden*, Munich, 1965; G. Ritter, *Carl Goerdeler und die deutsche Widerstandsbewegung*, Stuttgart, 1954; P. Hoffmann, *Widerstand. Staatsstreich. Attentat. Der Kampf der Opposition gegen Hitler*, Munich, 1969; M. Meyer-Krahmer, *Carl Goerdeler und sein Weg in den Widerstand. Eine Reise in die Welt meines Vaters*, Freiburg im Breisgau, 1989.

# GOERING, Hermann (1893–1946)

The most important leader in the Third Reich after Hitler, and the *Führer*'s designated successor, Goering exercised influence through a formidable array of official positions during a 25-year career in German politics. During the *Kampfzeit* of the NSDAP, he finally emerged as a crucial factor in the developments that led to Hitler's appointment as Chancellor. He was born a Protestant in Rosenheim, Bavaria, on 12 January 1893, the descendant of a long line of bureaucrats and jurists with aristocratic and royal connections in Prussia. His father fought in Bismarck's wars, qualified as a jurist, then joined the Reich Consular Service, serving as consul-general in Haiti and subsequently as the first Resident Minister Plenipotentiary in South West Africa. Due to marital complications which resulted in his mother becoming the mistress of a wealthy Jew who lived in a castle at Veldenstein near Nuremberg, Goering's childhood was materially secure if emotionally somewhat disturbed. He had already developed an emotional-romantic sense of nationalism when he attended the military cadets' college at Karlsruhe and then at Berlin-Lichterfelde. Completing his training with distinction, he joined the army in 1914 as an infantry lieutenant, before being transferred to the air force as a combat pilot. The last commander in 1918 of the famous Richthofen Fighter Squadron, Goering emerged as an ace pilot and war hero, earning not only the Iron Cross (First Class) but also the much-coveted *Pour le Mérite* for repeated and exceptional acts of bravery in the field.

The early post-war era was one of profound disappointment and disillusion for Goering, as it was for most of the upper classes. The collapse of the old imperial order and its replacement by the despised Republic engendered resentments and feelings of revenge which shaped his political outlook. He read right-wing nationalist literature and attended *Freikorps* meetings, while earning a living as a showflier at home and, for a period, in Denmark and Sweden. In 1921 he settled in Munich with his first wife, and met Hitler for the first time the following year. Eager to attract a man of Goering's social and military pedigree to the struggling, predominantly lower middle-class NSDAP, Hitler offered him the leadership of the SA. The offer was accepted and from then (December 1922) until the Beer Hall putsch, Goering was successful in expanding and instilling some sense of discipline into the party's paramilitary outfit. Goering was seriously wounded during the putsch, but escaped to Austria, Italy and finally Sweden, where he became a morphine addict during his medical recovery programme. Not until a general amnesty was declared in 1927 did he return to Germany. He rejoined the NSDAP, became a salesman for Bayerische Motorenwerke (BMW) in Berlin, and entered the Reichstag the following year as one of the 12-man Nazi delegation. From that point onwards, his significance for the party's cause grew substantially, for although he did not hold formal office, he was Hitler's roving ambassador in conservative upper-class society, among leading bankers and industrialists, aristocrats and financiers, and prominent right-wing political circles. He was able to promote Hitler and National Socialism in the most influential sections of social and political life, soliciting support, sympathy and some funding. His was the respectable, almost debonair face of Nazism. A new power base was created for his activity when, following the party's spectacular triumph at the national elections in July 1932, he was elected president of the Reichstag. In the last week before Hitler's appointment as Chancellor, Goering played a vital role in the negotiations with the traditional, conservative élites, whose last-minute support had to be secured.

In 1933, as Prussian Minister of the Interior and chief of the Prussian police, Goering played yet another indispensable role, this time in rapidly destroying oppositional elements and clearing the way for a total Nazi takeover of power. He acted ruthlessly against Röhm and his group in the SA in summer 1934. Having done so much to consolidate the regime, Goering moved on to extend its power throughout Germany. In March 1935, he was appointed commander-in-chief of the Luftwaffe, and the following year plenipotentiary for the implementation of the Four Year Plan, which allowed him to construct an economic empire on behalf of the state and at the expense of the independence of private capital. Throughout this activity Goering revealed a multifaceted personality, but the political success of his efforts was undeniable. A committed supporter of an expansionist foreign policy, a passionate anti-Semite and anti-Communist, he was appointed chairman of the Reich Council for National Defence in August 1939. In June 1940 he was promoted to Reich Marshal and saw the zenith of his power and popularity in 1942. Thereafter, against a background of Luftwaffe failures and inefficiencies in the war economy, not to mention a deterioration in his health and powers of judgement, Goering's star waned, until in 1945 Hitler stripped him of all posts, expelled him from the party and had him arrested. Notwithstanding a stylish and clever performance at his trial before the Nuremberg Military Tribunal, he was condemned to death by hanging. He committed suicide in his prison cell shortly afterwards, on 15 October 1946.

## Further Reading

H. Goering, *Aufbau einer Nation*, Berlin, 1934 (English version published as *Germany Reborn*, London, 1934; E. Goering (his second wife), *An der Seite meines Mannes. Begebenheiten und Bekenntnisse*, Göttingen, 1967. See also S. Martens, *Hermann Göring. 'Erster Paladin des Führers' und 'Zweiter Mann im Reich'*, Paderborn, 1985; A. Kube, *Hermann Göring im Dritten Reich. Pour le Mérite und Hakenkreuz*. Munich, 1986; R.J. Overy, *Goering. The 'Iron Man'*, London, 1984; D. Irving, *Göring*, London, 1990.

# GRADNAUER, Georg (1866–1946)

One of the leading provincial politicians of the early Weimar period, Gradnauer used his base in Saxony to exert considerable influence at the centre of government in Berlin, particularly when directly involved as a Reich Minister and member of the Reichstag and Reichsrat. Born into a lower middle-class Jewish family in Magdeburg on 16 November 1866, he studied history, literature and philosophy before earning a doctorate from the University of Halle in 1889. His pre-war career in the SPD was built around his membership of the Reichstag from 1898 to 1907, and journalistic and editorial activity on a number of socialist newspapers, including the *Sächsische Arbeiterzeitung, Vorwärts* and the *Dresdner Volkszeitung*. Returning to the Reichstag in 1912, he forcefully argued the case for the SPD's co-operation with the government on the outbreak of war and during the conflict, notably at the party's *Reichskonferenz* in September 1916, when he warned that failure to lend support might help lead to the establishment of a military dictatorship. The following month he intimated in the Reichstag that the SPD, extending this co-operation, might be prepared to work with the bourgeois parties on the basis of parliamentarianism and equal suffrage. Here Gradnauer was articulating a reinvigorated desire for power by the party.

In November 1918, he joined the Workers' and Soldiers' Council in Dresden as a moderating voice, and then served in the Saxon revolutionary government as Minister of Justice. When this SPD–USPD coalition collapsed in January 1919, he took over as Minister President, as well as the Minister of External Affairs and of the Interior. When confronted by a breakdown of law and order from the radical Left, he had little hesitation in summoning the assistance of the Reichswehr and some *Freikorps* units, which was never forgotten or forgiven by his opponents. Indeed, he was forced out of office in May 1920. When once again elected to the Reichstag in June 1920, where he remained until 1924, he emerged as a respected speaker on legal and constitutional matters. His brief experience as Reich Minister of the Interior in the Wirth cabinet (May–October 1921), a post to which he was apparently appointed as President Ebert's personal choice, taught him that the new democratic system had to be vigorously defended against all shades of extremism, but that action had also to be tempered with caution. Thus, when the League of Nations committee announced its decision on the partition of Upper Silesia between Germany and Poland, Gradnauer's advice to his cabinet colleagues not to resign, as suggested by Walther Rathenau and others, prevailed. However unpleasant the decision, he was certain that the resignation of the government would be a futile gesture. His service as envoy of the Saxon government to the Reich from 1921 to 1931 and as the Saxon plenipotentiary to the Reichsrat gave him additional means of influencing central government, and also strengthened his support for a properly balanced relationship between Berlin and the *Länder* within a federal framework. His involvement in the difficult governmental situation in Saxony in autumn 1923 was primarily motivated by this concern.

Gradnauer withdrew from politics after 1933, but was arrested and dispatched to Theresienstadt concentration camp in 1944. He survived his liberation from there for only a short time, dying in Berlin on 18 November 1946.

## Further Reading

G. Gradnauer, *Das Elend des Strafvollzugs*, Berlin, 1905; *Die deutsche Volkswirtschaft*, Berlin, 1921. See also K. Hohlfeld, *Die Reichsexekution gegen Sachsen im Jahre 1923. Ihre Vorgeschichte und politische Bedeutung*, Erlangen, 1964; H.J. Gordon, *The Reichswehr and the German Republic 1919–1926*, Princeton, 1957; H. Weiler, *Die Reichsexekution gegen den Freistaat Sachsen unter Reichskanzler Dr. Stresemann im Oktober 1923*, Frankfurt am Main, 1987.

## GROENER, Wilhelm (1867–1939)

The top army general who became a decisive political influence at crucial moments during the lifespan of the Weimar Republic was born the son of a professional soldier in the Württemberg army on 22 November 1867 in Ludwigsburg. Although seen by some later observers as a south German democrat, he was in reality moulded by education and training by Prussian ideas and traditions that had nothing to do with reactionary conservatism or narrow-minded chauvinism. He joined the General Staff of the Kaiser's army in 1899, advanced to the rank of lieutenant-colonel, and as chief of the Transport Division of the High Command ensured the efficient dispatch of troops to the Front in 1914. In 1916 he was appointed head of the War Office in the Prussian War Ministry, a post somewhat approaching that of a Minister of Munitions. From here he organized war production and the direction of labour, in friendly collaboration with the leadership of the trade unions and the SPD. In October 1918 he succeeded General Erich Ludendorff as First Quartermaster-General and was, therefore, to all intents and purposes Chief of the General Staff, second-in-command to Field Marshal von Hindenburg. As a sober realist in November 1918 who saw that the war could not be won, it was he who advised Kaiser Wilhelm to abdicate, an action for which the monarchist officer corps never forgave him.

On 10 November 1918 Groener made by telephone the infamous pact between the army high command and the socialist Chancellor, Friedrich Ebert, by which he offered to put the army at the government's disposal to ensure law and order and the defeat of the perceived threat from Bolshevism. This agreement had important and far-reaching implications for the Republic. It immediately laid the foundations for a moderate outcome of the Revolution and the army's retention of a privileged and largely independent status in the new democratic state. Groener's aim to make the army a significant factor of power was triumphantly realized and over the difficult early years of the Republic it was instrumental in eradicating the threat from the radical Left in various parts of the Reich. The officer corps emerged from this period still as a bastion of monarchist and anti-democratic sentiment. Groener was also responsible for the orderly return and demobilization of troops from the Front, for the authorization to create volunteer units to defend the eastern frontier, and for the army's acceptance of the Treaty of Versailles. Groener was a non-aligned political moderate, anti-Communist and nationalist to be sure, but contemptuous of the far Right and its extravagant antics. His concern also in 1918–19 was to re-establish the authority of a unitary German state and soon came to believe that it should and could exist within a parliamentary framework.

From 1920 to 1923 Groener served as Reich Transport Minister in a thoroughly competent fashion and then retired from politics. He was brought back at the express wish of President von Hindenburg in January 1928 to succeed Otto Gessler as Minister of Defence, a post he retained until May 1932. He was seen as a reliable and astute defender of the army's interests which demanded, as far as he was concerned, making it entirely non-political and loyal to the state. He publicly defended the Republic and warned against right-wing groups, particularly the NSDAP, trying to infiltrate and use the army for political ends. This stance made him anathema to the Right. But he used political influence outside the mere scope of army affairs, and when also appointed Reich Minister of the Interior in October 1931 his position as the 'hard man' of the Brüning government allowed him to extend that influence even further. His undoing resulted from the weakening of the government amidst the economic and political crisis brought on by the Depression, and equally by the intrigues of his protégé, General Kurt von Schleicher, and right-wing circles. Groener ran into trouble over his prohibition of the SA in April 1932, and when he failed miserably to defend his action in the Reichstag on 10 May the pressure on him to resign was irresistible. His departure further undermined the Brüning cabinet and the republican cause as a whole. Retiring finally to private life, his death in Bornstedt, near Potsdam, on 3 May 1939 passed without note from the National Socialist regime. His memoirs were published posthumously.

## Further Reading

W. Groener, *Lebenserinnerungen. Jugend, Generalstab, Weltkrieg* (edited by F.H. von Gaertringen), Göttingen, 1957. See also D. Groener-Geyer, *General Groener. Soldat und Staatsmann*, Frankfurt am Maine, 1954; G.W. Rakenius, *Wilhelm Groener als Erster Generalquartiermeister. Die Politik der Obersten Heeresleitung 1918/19*, Boppard, 1977; F.L. Carsten, *The Reichswehr and Politics, 1918–1933*, Oxford, 1966; M. Geyer, *Aufrüstung oder Sicherheit. Die Reichswehr in der Krise der Machtpolitik 1924–1936*, Wiesbaden, 1980; K.-H. Müller and E. Opitz (eds), *Militär und Militarismus in der Weimarer Republik*, Düsseldorf, 1978.

# GROTEWOHL, Otto (1894–1964)

An active and influential figure in the higher echelons of the SPD during the later Weimar period and Prime Minister of the German Democratic Republic from 1949 until his death, Grotewohl's early career was centred in Brunswick, where he was born into a working-class home on 11 March 1894. A printer by trade, he became a member of the newly-created socialist youth movement in 1908 and joined the SPD four years later. After army service in the First World War, he was involved in the Brunswick Workers' and Soldiers' Council in 1919, having switched to the USPD at the outbreak of revolution. His ability to move between established party lines emerged as a salient feature of his political career as a whole, so that when his party split at the beginning of the 1920s he returned to the SPD. A deputy in the Brunswick Landtag from 1920 until 1925, he held several posts in that state's government, including Minister of the Interior and Education in 1921–22, and Minister of Justice in 1923–24. This experience was valuable following his election to the Reichstag in 1925, where he served until 1933. During the pre-Hitler era he was a prominent personality in the SPD press and in various publications of the trade union movement, as well as a reliable source of counsel in the party leadership.

After 1933 Grotewohl continued party work underground while pursuing a civilian existence in Hamburg. There are no indications that he was a major focal point of resistance, despite his arrest on several occasions by the Gestapo. During the war years he was business manager of a sales company in Berlin. Immediately active in the reconstituted post-war SPD, as chairman of the party's Central Committee in Berlin, he declared his intention of helping to forge the organizational unity of the working class, which meant friendly co-operation in the first instance with the Communists. When they clearly set out to achieve unity on their terms, with overt backing from the Soviet occupation authorities, Grotewohl clashed repeatedly with the tough-minded Kurt Schumacher, head of the SPD in the western zone. Nevertheless, Grotewohl proceeded with unity negotiations and fully supported the establishment of the Socialist Unity Party (SED) in Berlin in 1946. Until his death there on 21 September 1964, he was at the forefront of politics in his capacity as the GDR's first Prime Minister.

*Further reading*
O. Grotewohl, *Dreissig Jahre später. Die Novemberrevolution und die Lehren der Geschichte der deutschen Arbeiterbewegung*, East Berlin, 1952; *Im Kampf um die einige Deutsche Demokratische Republik. Reden und Aufsätze*, 6 vols, East Berlin, 1959–64. See also E.-A. Roloff, *Braunschweig und der Staat von Weimar*, Brunswick, 1964; H. Vosske, *Otto Grotewohl. Ein biographischer Abriss*, East Berlin, 1979; B. Rother, *Die Sozialdemokratie im Land Braunschweig 1918 bis 1933*, Bonn, 1990.

# GRZESINSKI, Albert (1879–1947)

This politically gifted, ambitious and somewhat abrasive Social Democrat gained prominence as a vigorous defender of the Republic and as an equally tough-minded opponent of anti-republican extremists on the Left and Right, particularly during his tenure as Prussian Minister of the Interior in 1926–30 and as commissioner of the Berlin police from late 1930 until the von Papen coup in July 1932. From a working-class background in Treptow, Prussia, where he was born on 28 July 1879, Grzesinski made his early mark in the trade union movement, being appointed secretary of the Metalworkers' Union in 1907 and president of the Trade Unions' Cartel in Kassel in 1913. He did not see military service in the First World War, continuing his political career in the SPD.

While chairman of the Workers' and Soldiers' Council in Kassel in 1918–19, he was appointed to a special committee for Prussian affairs of the Central Committee, the executive organ of the revolutionary socialist republic, and also in 1919 served as his party's supervisor in the Prussian Ministry of Defence. Because of his further experience in 1919–20 as head of the national bureau for completing the final details of the demobilization programme (Reichsabwicklungsamt), he was briefly considered in some circles as a candidate for the Reich Ministry of Defence portfolio. A local councillor in Kassel from 1919 to 1924, he turned down an opportunity to become Lord Mayor, preferring to concentrate his political ambitions on a higher level. After a short period as an adviser in the Reich Ministry of Labour, he secured his first really significant appointment in 1922, when he took over as chief of the Prussian police office. On its dissolution three years later, he served as police president of Berlin in 1925–26. In 1924 he was co-chairman of the highly successful Select Committee established by the Prussian Landtag to oversee the implementation of personnel reductions in the Prussian government administration: he was a Landtag deputy from 1919 to 1933.

On his appointment in October 1926 as Prussian Minister of the Interior, in succession to Carl Severing, Grzesinski let it be known that his highest priority was to defeat the Republic's enemies. He set a series of specific objectives, including the strengthening of state authority, especially through the police, the dismissal of reactionary officials, the elimination of the remaining legal privileges of large estate owners, and thoroughgoing administrative reform. In his campaign to increase the authority of Prussia, he suggested that in the past the SPD had overemphasized the legislative aspect of democracy. The execution of law, he maintained, was more important than legislation. A democracy had to be fleshed out in practical, substantive terms, in other words. Accordingly, he overrode objections to the dissolution of the estate districts (*Gutsbezirke*), where estate owners had preserved total control of local government, and sought with some success to restrict the activities of the right-wing paramilitary groups, making effective use of the Disarmament Law of 1921, which curbed the use of weapons and training, and the Law for the Protection of the Republic. When the latter lapsed in July 1929, he successfully fought for a new law of the same type. For all this, Grzesinski became a favourite hate-object of the Right, including the NSDAP and Stahlhelm, whose Rhenish-Westphalian branch he had banned for a year in 1929. On the other hand, his efforts went a long way towards securing 'Red Prussia' as a bastion of the Republic. However, marital problems which made political complications for his party in the Prussian coalition government, especially with the Centre Party, caused his resignation in 1930.

Nevertheless, Grzesinski remained actively involved in politics within his party and continued to warn against the threat from the far Right and Left. In late 1930 he came back into public view when appointed, for the second time in his career, commissioner of the Berlin police. He advocated a ban on both the NSDAP and KPD, and in December 1931 advised Otto Braun, the Prussian Prime Minister, to have Hitler imprisoned or exiled. Before being ousted from office in July 1932, he had become rather critical of what he considered to be Interior Minister Severing's weak attitude towards the Republic's extremist opponents.

In 1933, Grzesinski went into exile, first in France and from 1937 in New York. He was among a number of Social Democratic political refugees who in March 1939 set up the German Labour Delegation as an auxiliary body of the SPD's executive committee, with the task of organizing relief and rescue operations for victims of Nazi-dominated Europe. He died in New York on 31 December 1947.

## *Further Reading*

A.C. Grzesinski, *Inside Germany*, New York, 1939. See also H.-P. Ehni, *Bollwerk Preussen? Preussenregierung, Reich-Länder-Problem und Sozialdemokratie 1918–1932*, Stuttgart, 1975; A.

Glees, 'Albert C. Grzesinski and the Politics of Prussia 1926–1930', *English Historical Review*, 89, 1974, pp. 814–34; H. Möller, *Parlamentarismus in Preussen 1919–1932. Handbuch der Geschichte des deutschen Parlamentarismus*, Düsseldorf, 1985.

## GÜRTNER, Franz (1881–1941)

Unusually for a civil service lawyer, this Minister of Justice in Bavaria from August 1922 until June 1932, when appointed to Chancellor von Papen's cabinet as Reich Minister of Justice – a post he held continuously until his death in 1941 – was intimately connected with a series of political developments which had a material bearing on the development of National Socialism. Born into a working-class home in Regensburg on 26 August 1881, Gürtner took a law degree from the University of Munich in 1903 and immediately joined the legal services department of the Bavarian state government. An army captain during the First World War, he served on the Western Front and latterly as a battalion commander in Palestine, where he made friends with Franz von Papen. Gürtner was decorated with the Iron Cross (First and Second Class).

Rejoining the Bavarian Justice Ministry in 1920, he began to make a name for himself in legal circles and on the nomination of his party, the Bavarian Middle Party, which was German-nationalist in outlook, was appointed Bavarian Minister of Justice. In this post he was able to exercise considerable influence on the political ambience in Munich in a manner favourable to right-wing paramilitarism and *völkisch* nationalism. A major beneficiary was the NSDAP, for, thanks to Gürtner, Hitler was treated with leniency at his trial for high treason in spring 1924, released prematurely from a five-year sentence in December 1924, allowed to reconstitute his party as a legal organization, and to speak in public again. For the remainder of the *Kampfzeit*, the NSDAP in Bavaria was able to operate under a certain and not insignificant degree of sympathy and protection. This did nothing to diminish Gürtner's professional reputation. On the contrary, by the time he joined von Papen's cabinet in 1932, he was a highly respected lawyer, admired for his personal integrity and character. As Reich Minister of Justice in the von Papen and von Schleicher cabinets he executed his difficult responsibilities with some astuteness and efficiency, and above all, in a manner that commended him to the leader of the NSDAP, despite the fact that he was not, and would never be, a party member.

After 1933 Gürtner's services to the regime were considerable. He provided the legal framework for the 'co-ordination' (*Gleichschaltung*) of legal bodies and practitioners into the National Socialist Lawyers' Association, for the murderous activity of the Röhm affair in 1934, and for numerous other arbitrary acts by Hitler and his henchmen. Through all this nefarious activity he did seek to maintain, up to a point, the coherence and meaning of the law, and he objected to the illegal barbarity of concentration camp procedures. But as time wore on, his position and authority were progressively undermined by more powerful and ruthless agencies, especially the secret police and the SS. He claimed that he stayed in his post to try to moderate the excesses, but this is hardly convincing. Overcome by a sense of fatalism rather than conviction, Gürtner, like so many others in Germany at that time, continued to serve a political system that had been morally bankrupt from the very beginning, and during the war provided legal cover for the most heinous crimes. He died in Berlin on 29 January 1941.

*Further Reading*
F. Gürtner, *Der Gedanke der Gerechtigkeit in der deutschen Strafrechtserneuerung*, Berlin, 1936. See also E. Reitter, *Franz Gürtner: Politische Biographie eines deutschen Juristen 1881–1941*, Berlin, 1976; L. Gruchmann, *Justiz im Dritten Reich 1933–1940. Anpassung und Unterwerfung in der Ära Gürtner*, Munich, 1988.

## HAASE, Hugo (1863–1919)

A major figure of leadership and influence in the socialist movement for many years before his life was prematurely ended, Haase was born the son of a Jewish shoemaker in Allenstein, East Prussia, on 29 September 1863. After obtaining a law degree from the University of Königsberg, he quickly earned a considerable reputation and popularity for defending less privileged members of society and socialists, including the later Minister President of Prussia, Otto Braun, and a group of German socialists in Russia who had been accused of involvement in the 1905 Revolution. Haase's political career also proceeded with notable success. Having been elected in 1894 the first ever Social Democratic town councillor in Königsberg, he was elevated to the Reichstag three years later, where his first term of service lasted until 1907. A second term extended from 1912 until 1919, latterly as a USPD deputy. Known as a left-of-centre SPD politician, he became co-chairman (with August Bebel) of the party in 1911, and, from the beginning of the war, chairman of both the party and its parliamentary delegation. When the latter met on 3 August 1914 to discuss the threatening international situation, Haase was one of a minority of deputies who voted to oppose giving approval to the government's war credits Bill. For the sake of party unity, however, he joined with every other SPD deputy in supporting the measure when it came before the Reichstag, and this fervent anti-militarist vowed at the same time not to 'forsake our own fatherland in its hour of danger'.

By 1915, opposition within the SPD to the government's war policy began to emerge into the open, and Haase was prominent in this development. A co-signatory of the 'Demand of the Hour' statement denouncing the party's war policy, which was published in the socialist *Leipziger Volkszeitung* in summer 1915, he resigned from the party chairmanship a few months later and embarked on a course of opposition that led to his leadership (with Wilhelm Dittmann) of the Social Democratic *Arbeitsgemeinschaft* in spring 1916 and of the USPD in April 1917. The end of the war and the November Revolution generally saw this sober, cautious man act as a moderating force, committed ultimately to parliamentarism. He was co-chairman (with Friedrich Ebert) of the new revolutionary government, the Council of People's Representatives, until compelled to resign in December 1918 by the left wing of the USPD. The events of the following months revealed Haase's limitations as a revolutionary leader: above all, he lacked decisiveness in situations of crisis, preferring to act as a mediator between the warring factions of his party. Although he was to speak in spring 1919 in favour of proletarian dictatorship, he, unlike the Spartacists and the USPD radicals, regarded this as only a short-term measure designed to secure the revolution from right-wing assault, and to act as a stepping-stone to a longer-term socialist parliamentary state. Widely respected for his integrity, this somewhat idealistic, humanist and pacifist politician died on 7 November 1919 in Berlin, four weeks after being shot by a deranged gunman as he entered the Reichstag. The USPD soon discovered that Haase was irreplaceable.

## *Further Reading*

H. Haase, *Deutschlands Friedensschlüsse. Eine Reichstagsrede*, Berlin, 1919. See also E. Haase (ed.), *Hugo Haase. Sein Leben und Wirken. Mit einer Auswahl von Briefen, Reden und Aufsätzen*, Berlin, 1929; D.W. Morgan, *The Socialist Left and the German Revolution. A History of the German Independent Social Democratic Party 1917–1922*, London, 1975; K.R. Calkins, *Hugo Haase. Democrat und Revolutionary*, Durham, North Carolina, 1979; H. Krause, *USPD. Zur Geschichte der Unabhängigen Sozialdemokratischen Partei Deutschlands*, Frankfurt am Main, 1975.

# HAMM, Eduard (1879–1944)

This prominent DDP leader in Bavaria and Reich Minister was born into a middle-class family in Passau on 16 October 1879, and after obtaining a law degree from the University of Munich joined the civil service of his home state, first in its Ministry of Interior, and then during the war in a series of co-ordinating roles to do with food production between the Bavarian and Reich governments. In 1918 he was appointed *Legationsrat* in the Bavarian Ministry of External Affairs. In the following year he joined the DDP, was elected to represent it in the Landtag, and became Minister for Trade and Transport in the second administration of SPD Minister-President, Johannes Hoffmann. In the subsequent cabinet of Gustav von Kahr that was set up after the 1920 Landtag elections, Hamm was the only DDP representative and retained the same portfolio as before. He became embroiled in the bitter constitutional wrangle that erupted in summer 1921 between the von Kahr and Reich governments, when he found it difficult to reconcile his particularist sympathies with his support for the sovereign authority of the Reich. In a further episode in this dispute a year later, when Bavaria declared invalid the Law for the Defence of the Republic and issued its own Decree for the Defence of the Constitution of the Republic, Hamm tried to mediate between the two sides, ultimately without success, and he resigned his government post in July 1922. Only later did his continuing efforts to find a solution bear fruit, with Bavaria agreeing to accept the Law in return for a number of other constitutional concessions.

While a Reichstag deputy from 1920 until 1924, Hamm served in a number of Reich governments: from November 1922 until August 1923 he was State Secretary in the Wilhelm Cuno administration, and from November 1923 until January 1925 he was Reich Minister of Economics in the two cabinets led by Chancellor Wilhelm Marx. In the latter capacity he had to deal with a series of matters which were of crucial importance for the economic development of the Republic, including, above all, the reform of the currency, and the agreement on reparations enshrined in the Dawes Plan. Hamm proved to be a competent, reliable and hard-working minister, well regarded by colleagues. In spring 1924 he was among those right-wing leaders of the DDP who supported the idea of their party entering a coalition government that included the DNVP, and in the heated internal debate about this Hamm and Otto Gessler, among others, came close to seceding and forming a new liberal party with a Bavarian base. Unable to secure a Reichstag seat after the December 1924 elections, Hamm withdrew from direct participation in high politics to become, in January 1925, a top executive with the German Industry and Trade Assembly (Industrie- und Handelstag), where he remained until 1933. During this period he was also editor of the influential *Deutsche Wirtschaftszeitung*.

After 1933 Hamm returned to the practise of law in the insurance business, but later was also drawn into the conservative resistance circle around Carl Goerdeler. Arrested in connection with the July Plot in 1944, he suffered brutal treatment from the Gestapo, and took his own life while still in custody in Berlin on 23 September 1944.

## Further Reading

E. Hamm, *Die wirtschaftspolitische Interessenvertretung*, Berlin, 1929. See also W. Stephen, *Aufstieg und Verfall des Linksliberalismus 1918–1933. Geschichte der Deutschen Demokratischen Partei*, Göttingen, 1973; R. Pois, *The Bourgeois Democrats of Weimar Germany*, Philadelphia, 1976; B.B. Frye, *Liberal Democrats in the Weimar Republic*, Carbondale, 1985; L.E. Jones, *German Liberalism and the Dissolution of the Weimar Party System, 1918–1933*, Chapel Hill, 1988.

## HAUSSMANN, Conrad (1857–1922)

A major figure in the German liberal movement at a national and provincial level before and after the First World War, Haussmann was descended from a well-known Württemberg political family. A lawyer by profession, he entered the Reichstag in 1890 for the South German People's Party and subsequently for the Progressive People's Party, and then after 1918, for the DDP. At the time of his death in 1922 he was clearly, with 32 years' uninterrupted service, one of the Reichstag's elder statesmen, widely respected for his wisdom and good sense. He was at the centre of national affairs from at least 1916 onwards, criticizing the Treaty of Brest-Litovsk with Russia, and proposing Prince Max of Baden for the Chancellorship in autumn 1918. He himself served as State Secretary in his cabinet. In the November Revolution, he and Gustav Noske were asked by the Governor of Kiel to try to quell the sailors' revolt, a tribute to the status enjoyed by these two Reichstag members. Later, in 1919-20, Haussmann's powers of persuasion and discretion were fully in demand as he chaired the National Assembly's Constitutional Committee which speedily produced the draft of the Republic's new constitution.

After 1918, Haussmann clearly identified with the DDP's progressive wing and carried with him into the new party the ideals and lofty ambitions of the 1848 liberals. He was no starry-eyed dreamer of the impossible, however, but a deeply pragmatic politician who believed in striving for the attainable, provided no conflict with basic principle was involved. In 1919 he was strongly critical of those members of his party whom he considered were pandering to the Social Democrats in regard to the question of economic change. He was convinced that socialization would not provide satisfactory answers to Germany's pressing problems. Instead, he wanted the DDP to capture the high political ground and direct government from the centre in an independent manner that was faithful to middle-class interests and values. He led his party's condemnation of the Treaty of Versailles, and wanted it to emerge as the focal point of national resistance. Again, in 1921, he was to the fore in denouncing the London Ultimatum on Germany's reparations payments. But on both occasions he discovered that he could not even unite his own party. Haussmann's decidedly nationalist stance, which was in evidence later the same year over Upper Silesia, sat rather uncomfortably among the DDP's leaders, and the end of his career coincided with a marked and irrevocable decline in its fortunes.

## Further Reading

C. Haussmann, *Schlaglichter. Reichstagsbriefe und Aufzeichnungen* (edited by U. Zeller), Frankfurt am Main, 1924. See also F. Henning, *Die Haussmanns. Die Rolle einer schwäbischen Familie in der deutschen Politik des 19. und 20. Jahrhunderts*, Gerlingen, 1988; L.E. Jones, *German Liberalism and the Dissolution of the Weimar Party System, 1918-1933*, Chapel Hill, 1988.

## HEILMANN, Ernst (1881-1940)

Leader of the SPD delegation in the Prussian Landtag for most of the Weimar years and an influential voice also in the Reichstag, Heilmann was born into a middle-class Jewish family in Berlin's Charlottenburg on 13 April 1881, and qualified as a lawyer. Joining the SPD in 1898, he took to party journalism rather than law, and from 1909 until the outbreak of war was chief editor of the *Chemnitzer Volksstimme*. At the same time he belonged to the inner circle of the socialist journal *Die Glocke*, in which he published a series of patriotic articles. Decidedly on the right wing of the SPD, therefore, he volunteered for army service in 1914, returning badly wounded three years later.

A member of the Prussian State Assembly (Landesversammlung) in 1919, Heilmann made career advances thanks to his skills as a parliamentary tactician and public speaker, and also to his lack of interest in ministerial office, which commended him to other party leaders. A firm and intelligent advocate of parliamentary democracy, which for him incorporated the best elements of socialism, nationalism and constitutionalism, he wanted to preserve the integrity of Prussia through a political alliance with the moderate bourgeois parties. After he had been formally confirmed as leader of the SPD's delegation in the Prussian Landtag in November 1921, he went on to forge a close personal and working relationship with his counterpart in the Centre Party, Joseph Hess, which was a major factor in the remarkable stability of coalition politics in Germany's largest state until July 1932. As the 'uncrowned king of Prussia', an epithet supplied by a party colleague, Heilmann was the *éminence grise* of Prussian politics, working closely with Minister President Otto Braun, and generally exercising authority at the heart of the state's affairs. A member of the Constitutional Convention in Prussia in 1919-20, of the Landtag until 1933 and of the Reichstag from 1928 to 1933, he continued his journalistic work inside and outside the SPD, contributing to *Internationale Korrespondenz* and *Das Freie Wort*, among other journals.

The only serious problem he faced in politics arose in 1924 when it was revealed that he had connections with the corrupt financier, Julius Barmat. Though he had not apparently profited from the association, Heilmann had been friendly with him, advised him on business contacts and introduced him to clients. Despite being a particular target of the DNVP on the committee set up by the Prussian Landtag to investigate the Barmat scandal, Heilmann was able to ride the storm without too much damage to his reputation.

In June 1933, he was arrested and consigned to a series of concentration camps for the next seven years. On 3 April 1940 he was finally murdered in brutal fashion in Buchenwald.

## Further Reading

E. Heilmann, *Geschichte der Arbeiterbewegung in Chemnitz und dem Erzgebirge*, Chemnitz, 1911. See also P. Lösche, *Ernst Heilmann. Ein Widerstandskämpfer aus Charlottenburg*, Berlin, 1981; D. Orlow, *Weimar Prussia 1918-1925. The Unlikely Rock of Democracy*, Pittsburgh, 1986.

## HEINE, Wolfgang (1861-1944)

Heine's social and political background contrasted sharply with that of the large majority of his colleagues in the SPD. He was born into an upper middle-class family in Posen, West Prussia (later Poznań), on 3 May 1861, and cut his early political teeth as a member of an anti-Semitic fraternity at university, when he studied law, and of the Christian Social movement which espoused, among other ideas, racism and nationalism. Even after joining the SPD, a number of party associates detected a lingering element of anti-Semitism in his outlook. A leading pre-war revisionist in the SPD, he contributed to prominent socialist journals, including the *Sozialistische Monatshefte* and *Neue Gesellschaft*, and as a Reichstag deputy from 1898 until 1918 associated with his party's right-wing. A staunch German and Prussian nationalist throughout his career, this self-confident, abrasive and somewhat domineering politician firmly supported the German government's war policy from beginning to end.

The November Revolution pitched Heine into the political limelight. As Minister of Justice in Prussia for four months and then from early spring 1919 the first republican Prussian Minister of the Interior, he occupied a pivotal position in the organization and administration of Germany's largest and most important state. A determined opponent of left-wing radicalism, he encouraged the formation of civil militia units to defend the Republic, but it is more in the realm of administrative reform that he is best remembered. He established the new posts of parliamentary undersecretaries to act as co-ordinators of policy between cabinet and legislature, an innovation that had much to commend it. However, in his efforts to democratize the Prussian civil service and to institute an equal employment policy, Heine was markedly less successful. He set too much store by the professionalism of civil servants, erroneously believing that despite the conservative authoritarian attitudes of a large number of them, they would loyally serve the new republican state. Thus, he acted only with extreme caution when it came to making personnel changes, which the Kapp Putsch revealed as an unrealistic approach. His 'ideology of experts', whereby specialists of no particular political affiliation would run the Prussian administration, was similarly a failure. Consequently, a programme of fundamental administrative reform beneficial to the long-term interests of the Republic never actually materialized. Otherwise, Heine deserves credit for promoting coalition strategies with the middle-class parties in Prussia, and for supervising the passage of the draft constitution for the state through the Constitutional Convention and cabinet in 1919–20. In March 1920, when the Kapp Putsch revealed the ineffectiveness and indeed the naivety of some of his policies, he was forced to resign as Minister of the Interior, to be succeeded by Carl Severing. Thereafter, Heine disappeared from the front rank of the SPD, but continued to voice opinions about constitutional and administrative reform. He was also involved in his professional capacity as a lawyer in representing leading SPD personalities in court cases, such as his friend, Severing, and the Reich President, Friedrich Ebert. Emigrating in 1933 to Switzerland, Heine died in Ascona on 4 May 1944.

## Further Reading

Heine's memoirs, *Politische Aufzeichnungen*, are to be found in his *Nachlass* at the International Institute for Social History, Amsterdam. He also wrote *Wer ist schuld am Bürgerkrieg?*, Berlin, 1919. See also D. Orlow, *Weimar Prussia, 1918–1925. The Unlikely Rock of Democracy*, Pittsburgh, 1986; H. Schulze, *Otto Braun oder Preussens demokratische Sendung. Eine Biographie*, Berlin, 1977.

# HELD, Heinrich (1868–1938)

Held, who exerted a dominating influence on Bavarian politics from his position as Prime Minister from 1924 until 1933, was not a Bavarian by birth. He was born the son of a salesman in the village of Erbach in Hesse-Nassau on 6 June 1868 and completed his university studies in law, history and political science with a doctorate.

Taking up journalism, he subsequently moved to Bavaria and married into a publishing family, whose *Regensburger Morgenblatt* he edited from 1899 to 1914 (renamed *Der Regensburger Anzeiger* in 1910). Eventually, he became co-owner of the publishing firm and was able to use the newspaper to help his rise in the Centre Party, which he began to represent in the Bavarian Landtag in 1907, continuing until 1933. A protégé of Georg Heim, Held was elected leader of the Centre's parliamentary faction in 1914, and shortly thereafter also party chairman in Bavaria. During the First World War he emerged as a stout supporter of the Reich's annexationist policy.

A co-founder of the BVP, the Centre Party's sister party in Bavaria, Held became its leader in the Bavarian Landtag in 1919, and prior to his appointment as Prime Minister had emerged as the most influential and decisive figure in the BVP. His brand of moderate conservatism, coupled with strong sympathy for the monarchist cause, was well suited to the mood of most Bavarians following the turbulence of the early post-war years. A one-time president of the German Catholic Assembly, he brought a devout Catholicism to bear on his conduct of public office, allied to a steadfast respect for constitutional procedures. Although committed to the cause of federalist privileges and interests, he generally avoided the kind of confrontation that had disfigured relations between the Bavarian and Reich governments from 1918 to 1923. The vexed issue of constitutional reform in the Reich was one of his enduring interests. Held sought to give Bavaria a period of political stability and economic development, a prerequisite of which he saw as the containment of political extremism. He was sharply anti-Leftist, but also took a tough stance towards the NSDAP, whose progress in Bavaria after 1925 was rather patchy. He was opposed to the ideology as well as the political irresponsibility of Hitler, the more so when the party began its breakthrough into national prominence after 1929–30. The BVP candidate in the Reich presidential elections in 1925, when he attracted just under 1 million votes, Held was forced to preside over a minority administration in Bavaria after 1930 but still managed to take a robust line in defence of his party's interests, which continued to enjoy the support of the Catholic Church. The von Papen coup against the Prussian government in July 1932 caused deep consternation in particularist Bavaria, though Held's position was weakening all the time despite his best efforts. He gave some thought in early 1933 to a restoration of the Wittelsbach dynasty as a way of forestalling a Nazi takeover of Bavaria, but finally renounced the idea on political and practical grounds. In March 1933 his government was replaced by Reich Commissioner Ritter von Epp, and Held withdrew to private life, something of a broken man. He died in Regensburg on 4 August 1938.

## Further Reading

H. Held, *Abgrenzung der Zuständigkeiten zwischen Reich und Ländern*, Munich, 1929. See also the brief biographical sketch by his son, J. Held, *Heinrich Held. Ein Leben für Bayern*, Regensburg, 1958. Also of interest are K. Schwend, *Ein Mann des Rechts. In memoriam Heinrich Held*, Regensburg, 1958; R. Kessler, *Heinrich Held als Parlamentarier. Eine Teilbiographie 1868–1924*, Berlin, 1971; F. Wiesemann, *Die Vorgeschichte der nationalsozialistischen Machtübernahme in Bayern 1932–33*, Berlin, 1975.

## HELFFERICH, Karl (1872–1924)

Born the son of a weaving mill owner in Neustadt an der Haardt, Pfalz, on 22 July 1872, Helfferich completed his doctorate and *Habilitationsschrift* before emerging as one of Wilhelmine Germany's leading academic economists. Brilliant, energetic and ambitious, he joined the Reich Colonial Office in 1901 as an expert on currency reform and economic development, and five years later moved to the Deutsche Bank, where he became a leading adviser and an influential voice in German high finance. He was involved in the Bank's multifarious overseas activities, including the Baghdad Railway project, and in 1910 was appointed to the central committee of the Reichsbank. The second phase of his career involved his wartime service in the bureaucracy, beginning with his appointment as Secretary of the Reich Treasury Office, where he exercised significant but not entirely successful influence on the financing of the war. In May 1916 he became head of the Reich Interior Office and Vice-Chancellor of the Reich. However, he began to encounter increasingly serious political difficulties in the Reichstag, which finally caused his resignation in autumn 1917. He was not particularly suited to political office, lacking sympathetic insight and tolerance of opposing views, especially if they appeared to him to lack intellectual substance. He had shown only sporadic interest in politics before 1914 and rejected any ideas of reform during the conflict.

Helfferich's lack of political sensitivity and ultimately sound judgement was fully revealed during his brief career as a DNVP politician and Reichstag deputy. A passionate opponent of the Republic, he actively propagated a series of right-wing myths about the war and its outcome, excoriated the governments of the day for accepting the Treaty of Versailles and the reparations demands, and ensured that his own party, on whose governing body he sat, would have no compromise with the 'system'. Although he continued to expound convincingly on financial and economic matters, he often did so in a strident, demagogic fashion which was essentially counter-productive. His polemical attacks on political opponents, notably Matthias Erzberger and Walther Rathenau, were legendary, and did much to poison the atmosphere of post-war German politics. That he himself was frequently the object of violent attacks may help explain but does not excuse his intemperance. The cause of national reconciliation which he deemed essential to Germany's recovery from defeat was significantly undermined by his behaviour. On the other hand, as creator of the basic plan to stabilize the currency in 1923, he played a major role in ending the catastrophic inflation. Subsequently canvassed as a candidate for the presidency of the Reichsbank, Helfferich lost out to Hjalmar Schacht. In 1924 he was an outspoken critic of the Dawes Plan, describing it as a 'second Versailles'. His career was brought to a premature end when he was killed in a railway accident in Bellinzona, Switzerland, on 23 April 1924. Contemporaries viewed his loss as a tragedy for the DNVP, 'the only man in the party who could have been permitted to appear at an international forum of statesmen', according to the *Frankfurter Zeitung*.

*Further Reading*

K. Helfferich, *Das Geld*, Leipzig, 1903; *Fort mit Erzberger!*, Berlin, 1919; *Die Politik der Erfüllung*, Munich, 1922. See also J.G. Williamson, *Karl Helfferich 1872–1924. Economist, Financier, Politician*, Princeton, 1971, which also provides a full list of Helfferich's publications (pp. 417–24); J.W. Reichert (ed.), *Karl Helfferich. Reichstagsreden 1922–1924*, Berlin, 1925; L. Hertzman, *DNVP. Right-Wing Opposition in the Weimar Republic, 1918–1924*, Lincoln, Nebraska, 1963; A. Stupperich, *Volksgemeinschaft oder Arbeitersolidarität. Studien zur Arbeitnehmerpolitik in der Deutschnationalen Volkspartei (1918–1933)*, Göttingen, 1982.

## HELLPACH, Willy (1877–1955)

A distinguished academic and prominent DDP leader for most of the 1920s, Hellpach was born into a middle-class family in Oels, Silesia, on 26 February 1877, and graduated in medicine from Greifswald University and then in psychology from the University of Leipzig. In 1906 he completed his *Habilitationsschrift* at Karlsruhe's College of Technology, and before the First World War authored a number of important works in the field of social psychology. Only during the war did he begin to be attracted to politics in so far as it could improve the social and material condition of mankind.

Returning from medical service at the Front in 1918, he joined the DDP, using his gifts as 'an extraordinarily brilliant orator' (Erich Eyck) to make his way into the party hierarchy at both a regional and national level. As Minister of Education in Baden from 1922 until 1925, he created a widely-admired new structure for vocational education. As Minister-President of that state from 1924 to 1925, he promoted a good working relationship among most of the parties. However, when the DDP turned to him in 1925 to be its candidate in the Reich presidential election, it was not really on account of his commendable record in Baden, but rather because the more prominent Democrats were unwilling to enter a contest in which there was no chance of success and some likelihood of humiliation. Hellpach was not a particularly good candidate, mainly because he failed to arouse much enthusiasm for his campaign beyond the relatively small party circles. In the first ballot a modest 1.5 million votes were cast for him, and there was a widespread belief that he lacked the qualities for high public office. In 1925 also, with the DDP no longer part of the coalition government in Baden, Hellpach accepted an academic post at the University of Heidelberg.

Although elected to serve the DDP in the Reichstag in May 1928, he was becoming increasingly frustrated by the failure of political liberalism to establish itself as a major force in Weimar politics. He began publicly to criticize his party for not doing more to promote the idea of a united bourgeois party of the Centre, and in a desperate but unsuccessful attempt to shake it out of its lethargy, resigned his parliamentary seat and other party offices in March 1930. He continued to agitate for a complete realignment of the party system as a prerequisite not only for the creation of a united bourgeois political movement, but also for the very survival of the parliamentary Republic. Hellpach's perceptive observations made little impact on the DDP, however, and it was no surprise when he withdrew from it to join the newly-established German State Party. That proved to be another disillusioning experience for him, and he resigned from it in November 1930, abandoning active participation in politics altogether.

Hellpach is also best remembered for his well-publicized efforts to encourage Jews to assimilate completely into German society, to the point, in fact, where they would cease to exist as a distinctive racial or religious grouping. Throughout his political life, he remained a staunch non-Jewish adversary of anti-Semitism, and attracted considerable support from Jews, for instance, during his presidential campaign. He was one of the few in the DDP in 1930 who had a realistic appreciation of the rising threat of National Socialism.

After 1930 and throughout the Third Reich era, Hellpach's activity concentrated exclusively on his academic interests and his research at the University of Heidelberg. He died in that town on 6 July 1955.

## Further Reading

W.H. Hellpach, *Wesensgestalt der deutschen Schule*, Leipzig, 1925; *Politische Prognose für Deutschland*, Berlin, 1928; *Wirken im Wirren. Lebenserinnerungen. Eine Rechenschaft über Wert und Glück, Schuld und Sturz meiner Generation*, 2 vols, Hamburg, 1948–49 (volume 2 covers 1914–25); *Der deutsche Charakter*, Bonn, 1954. See also C. Führ and H.G. Zier (eds), *Willy Hellpach – Memoiren 1925–1945*, Cologne, 1987.

# HERGT, Oskar (1869–1967)

Born the son of a salesman in Naumburg an der Saale on 22 October 1869 and a university graduate in law, Hergt was a career civil servant in the Prussian administration from 1904 until 1918. Without formal party affiliation but sympathetic to the Free Conservatives, his successful career in the Ministry of Finance in Prussia led to appointments as *Regierungspräsident* in Silesia in 1915 and 1916, and then as Prussian Finance Minister in 1917–18. On joining the DNVP in late 1918, he was immediately elected party chairman in recognition of his capacity for balanced judgement, astuteness and unifying leadership style. A member of the Prussian State Assembly in 1919–21 and leader of his party's delegation to the Prussian Constitutional Convention at the same time, he intimated a desire to lead the DNVP into co-operation with moderate bourgeois parties, including the Centre Party. But this initiative, in September 1919, like similar ones in the following years at a national level, was undermined by the radical wing of his own party. A member of the Reichstag from 1920 until 1933, and chairman of the DNVP parliamentary faction until the mid-1920s, Hergt was widely regarded as a moderate conservative nationalist who sought a constructive role for his party in a parliamentary system to which it was formally opposed. But fairly often he was compelled by his extremist colleagues, against his better judgement, to play the role of hot-blooded rabble-rouser. In March 1920 he refused to be drawn into the Kapp putsch, despite appeals from General von

Lüttwitz, though he undoubtedly shared to an extent the positive attitude adopted towards it by many party members.

A sharp critic of the 'fulfilment policy' in German foreign affairs in the early 1920s, Hergt reacted to the calling off of the campaign of passive resistance to the French in the Ruhr by the Stresemann cabinet by proposing a vote of no confidence in the government in the Reichstag. His anti-French sentiments were as robust as his dislike for Poland, as he clearly showed in a speech in 1927, just as Foreign Minister Stresemann was trying to arrange a commercial agreement with Warsaw. His efforts to bring the DNVP into government were stepped up in 1923-24 and the good showing of the party in Reichstag elections in May 1924 strengthened his hand. Later that same year, however, Hergt's personal standing was dealt a considerable blow when his resignation of the DNVP's parliamentary faction leadership and of the party itself was forced by the débâcle over the Dawes Plan. Although ideologically opposed to the Plan, he was blamed by the party's right wing for the 48 DNVP votes that secured the safe passage of the Plan Bill through the Reichstag.

In the fractured DNVP, Hergt was still a force to be reckoned with, however, and he returned to the centre of national politics when appointed chairman of the Reichstag's Foreign Affairs Committee from 1925 until 1927 and, more significantly, Reich Minister of Justice and Vice-Chancellor in the fourth Wilhelm Marx cabinet, from January 1927 until June 1928. He proved a reliable and constructive member of government. A somewhat tentative attempt to regain the party chairmanship followed in October 1928, but Alfred Hugenberg was the rising star in the DNVP. Hergt remained in the party hierarchy until 1933 without ever retrieving the position of power he had enjoyed earlier. Following the *Machtergreifung*, he withdrew entirely from politics. He died in Göttingen on 9 May 1967.

## Further Reading

See L. Hertzman, *DNVP. Right-Wing Opposition in the Weimar Republic, 1918-1924*, Lincoln, Nebraska, 1963; W. Liebe, *Die Deutschnationale Volkpartei 1918-1924*, Düsseldorf 1956; A. Thimme, *Flucht in den Mythos. Die Deutschnationale Volkspartei und die Niederlage von 1918*, Göttingen, 1969; J.A. Leopold, *Alfred Hugenberg. The Radical Nationalist Campaign against the Weimar Republic*, New Haven, 1977; H. Weiss and P. Hoser (eds), *Die Deutschnationalen und die Zerstörung der Weimarer Republik. Aus dem Tagebuch von Reinhold Quaatz, 1928-1933*, Munich, 1989.

## HERMES, Andreas (1878-1964)

An agrarian expert of wide international experience before the First World War, Hermes, who was born in Cologne on 16 July 1878, quickly made his mark in the national political arena after 1918 as a member of the Centre Party. His professional expertise was fully deployed as Reich Minister of Food Supply in the cabinets led by Hermann Müller, Konstantin Fehrenbach and Joseph Wirth between March 1920 and March 1922, when he had responsibility for not only feeding the German population in the difficult aftermath of the war but also laying the foundation for the recovery of agriculture on a long-term basis. Both tasks were discharged with considerable efficiency. Appointed Reich Minister of Finance in November 1921, however, he was less successful in tackling the country's fiscal and budgetary problems, and simple-mindedly blamed French policy for the collapse of the currency and the hyperinflation crisis in 1923. He demitted office in August 1923. Thereafter, his principal sphere of activity lay in the development of small farmers' and agrarian politics in general, occupying posts as leader of the Catholic Peasant Leagues from 1928 to 1933 and president of the United Association of German Co-operatives from 1930 to 1933. But his reputation was besmirched by allegations of inconsistency, weak compromising and even of corruption. Above all, Dr Hermes was heavily criticized by farmers in his role as chief German negotiator after 1927 for the Polish trade treaties, which appeared to open the door to an influx of cheap foodstuffs. Although a co-founder of the Green Front, an umbrella organization of agrarian interest groups, in February 1929, he failed to provide decisive leadership or realistic schemes for dealing with the ever-increasing economic and political problems of agriculture, which the industrial depression of the early 1930s only exacerbated.

Arrested by the National Socialist regime in March 1933 and sentenced to a brief term of imprisonment for petty larceny the following year, Hermes later became involved with Carl Goerdeler's resistance circle. He was arrested and sentenced to death by the People's Court, but managed to survive the war. He reconstructed his political career after 1945 in the Federal Republic, emerging as a key factor in the rehabilitation of agriculture. He led the German Peasants' Association in 1948–54 and the German Raiffeisenverband in 1948–61. He died in Krälingen in the Eifel on 4 January 1964.

## Further Reading

A. Hermes, *Unser Kampf gegen Gewalt und Willkür*, Berlin 1923. See also H. Barmeyer, *Andreas Hermes und die Organisation der deutschen Landwirtschaft. Christliche Bauernvereine, Reichslandbund, Grüne Front, Reichsnährstand 1928 bis 1933*, Stuttgart, 1971; D. Gessner, *Agrarverbände in der Weimarer Republik*, Düsseldorf, 1976; H. Becker, *Handlungsspielräume der Agrarpolitik in der Weimarer Republik zwischen 1923 und 1929*, Stuttgart, 1990.

## HERTZ, Paul (1888–1961)

A major figure in the USPD and after 1922 in the left-wing of the SPD, Hertz was born into a comfortably-off Jewish business family in Worms on 23 June 1888, and after completing a commercial training course went on to earn a doctorate in political science in 1914. Joining the SPD in 1905, he spent some time as a trade union official before being called up for army service in the First World War. His pacifism led him into the USPD in 1917, and later that year he was discharged from the army. From November 1918 until March 1922 he was an editor on the USPD's main organ, *Die Freiheit*, and from this position became heavily involved in the often bitter internecine struggles that characterized the party's development. Finally, in 1922, he supported the USPD's fusion with the SPD. A Berlin town councillor from 1919 until 1925 and a Reichstag deputy from 1920 until 1933, Hertz emerged as one of the up-and-coming younger generation of SPD leaders who consistently identified with a decidedly left-wing point of view. In August 1923, for example, he led a group of left-wingers in the party's Reichstag faction in calling for a tougher SPD line towards the Cuno government. The so-called 'Hertz Resolution', issued after a meeting of this group, criticized the government's inactivity on important economic and political matters of the day, and demanded heavier taxation on property. The consequent hardening of the SPD's attitude helped precipitate the collapse of the government.

During the remainder of the 1920s, Hertz developed alongside Rudolf Hilferding as a leading economic expert in the SPD, adding significantly to the debate over funding for the unemployment insurance scheme which so much exercised the Hermann Müller-led Grand Coalition government in 1928–30. He rejected an invitation to take over the Reich Ministry of Finance when Hilferding resigned in December 1929. Grudgingly accepting the SPD's policy of toleration towards the Brüning administration, Hertz nevertheless was no more successful than any of his colleagues in finding a solution to Germany's mass unemployment problem. The ADGB's plan in spring 1932 he rejected as likely to cause inflation, for he appears at least to have agreed with Brüning that nothing could be undertaken which might have invited a recurrence of the 1923 crisis.

Appointed to the SPD's executive committee at its national congress in April 1933, Hertz shortly afterwards emigrated to Prague, where he was deeply involved in reconstituting the party apparatus in exile. This well-educated, articulate and urbane socialist soon ran into difficulties, however, with fellow executive committee members over his secret membership of the 'New Left' Neu Beginnen group, as well as his advocacy of a positive response to overtures from the KPD in 1935 for a common anti-fascist front. He resigned from the executive committee of the SPD in 1938 and the following year settled in the United States. Returning to West Berlin in 1949, he became a leading member of the city's Senate, specializing in economic and financial affairs, until his death on 23 October 1961.

## Further Reading

Bürgermeister-Reuter-Stiftung (ed), *Dr Paul Hertz hat das Wort. Ausgewählte Reichstagsreden*, Berlin, 1962; S. Miller and H. Potthoff, *A History of German Social Democracy. From 1848 to the Present*, Leamington Spa, 1986; R. Breitman, *German Socialism and Weimar Democracy*, Chapel Hill, 1981; W.H. Maehl, *The German Socialist Party. Champion of the First Republic, 1918–1933*, Philadelphia, 1986.

## HEUSS, Theodor (1884–1963)

The first President of the Federal Republic of Germany from August 1949 until September 1959 and a notable liberal politician of the later Weimar era was born near

Heilbronn, Swabia, on 31 January 1884. Even before embarking on his study of political economy and history at the universities of Munich and Berlin, he had developed a considerable political consciousness. A disciple and protégé of Friedrich Naumann, whose secretary he became before the First World War, Heuss contributed articles to *Die Hilfe*, the chief organ of the national liberal movement, and from 1912 until 1918 acted as chief editor of the democratic *Neckar-Zeitung*. Having completed his studies with a doctorate from the University of Munich, he pursued his post-war career with vigour and increasing success in both the political and academic spheres. Throughout the 1920s he produced a number of thoughtful works on the nature of politics, democracy and constitutionalism, while at the same time making his way in the DDP, which he had joined in 1918. Shortly before that, he had been a signatory to the founding manifesto of the Democratic People's League (Volksbund), the brain child of Walther Rathenau in Berlin in early November 1918. It was designed to unite the German bourgeoisie against the totalitarian imperatives of the radical German Left, but collapsed after only a few weeks.

Employed on the editorial staff of the liberal weekly journal *Deutsche Politik* from 1918 to 1922, and a lecturer in modern history and constitutional theory at the Deutsche Hochschule für Politik in Berlin from 1920 until 1933, Heuss also found time to have editorial responsibility for another liberal publication, *Die Deutsche Nation*. He was an admirer but not a member of the literary circle around Stefan George. As a DDP Reichstag deputy from May 1924 until May 1928, he had a prominent role in a number of controversies, for instance in defending the reputation of Reich President Friedrich Ebert when he was denounced as a traitor by political opponents and a Magdeburg court in late 1924, and in his support of the Law for the Protection of German Youth from Trashy and Erotic Literature in 1926 against a majority of the DDP. Joining the German State Party in 1930 and representing it in the Reichstag until 1933, Heuss emerged as an uncompromising and perceptive critic of the NSDAP, particularly with the publication of his book, *Hitlers Weg*, in 1932, which emphasized the opprobrious racist and anti-Semitic content of the *Führer*'s *Weltanschauung*, as well as its crusading anti-modernism. He was scathing about Hitler's crude exploitation of the fear and despair engendered by Germany's long-standing economic and political crises, culminating in the Depression. Gregor Strasser's famous exposition of the NSDAP's economic programme in the Reichstag in May 1932 was similarly dismissed as demagogic and impracticable. Nevertheless, Heuss vehemently argued against the German State Party allowing itself to be absorbed into a larger movement of the political middle in 1932, and because of this attitude, it has to be said that he shared the myopia and lack of realism that characterized leading liberals in Germany at that time.

In March 1933, Heuss wanted the small State Party delegation in the Reichstag to vote against the Enabling Bill, but was outvoted and supported it out of a sense of party discipline. During the Third Reich he withdrew from all political activity, wrote excellent biographies, including one on his mentor, Friedrich Naumann, and re-engaged in journalism. Minister of Culture in Baden-Württemberg immediately after the war for a brief period, he was elected chairman of the Free Democratic Party in 1948 and made a significant contribution to the framing of the Basic Law before assuming the Federal Presidency. Together with Konrad Adenauer, he was a chief architect of a Germany based on sound democratic principles and the rule of law, allowing her to rejoin the civilized comity of nations after all the barbarism of the Nazi era. He died in Stuttgart on 12 December 1963.

*Further Reading*
Among the most noteworthy of works by Heuss are *Zwischen Gestern und Morgen*, Stuggart, 1919; *Die Neue Demokratie*, Berlin, 1920; *Kapp-Lüttwitz. Das Verbrechen gegen die Nation*, Berlin, 1920; *Demokratie und Selbstverwaltung*, Berlin, 1921; *Staat und Volk. Betrachtungen über Wirtschaft, Politik und Kultur*, Berlin, 1926; *Politik. Ein Nachschlagebuch für Theorie und Geschichte*, Halberstadt, 1927; *Hitlers Weg. Eine historischpolitische Studie über den Nationalsozialismus*, Stuttgart, 1932 (new edn, Tübingen, 1968); *Friedrich Naumann. Der Mann, das Werk, die Zeit*, Stuttgart, 1937; *Vorspiele des Lebens. Jugenderinnerungen*, Tübingen, 1953; *Erinnerungen 1905–1933*, Tübingen, 1963; *An und über Juden*, Düsseldorf, 1964; *Die Machtergreifung und das Ermächtigungsgesetz* (edited by Eberhard Pikart), Tübingen, 1967. See also M. Ekstein, *Theodor Heuss und die Weimarer Republik. Ein Beitrag zur Geschichte des deutschen Liberalismus*, Stuttgart, 1969; J.C. Hess, *Theodor Heuss vor 1933. Ein Beitrag zur Geschichte des demokratischen Denkens in Deutschland*, Stuttgart, 1973; W. Wiedner, *Theodor Heuss. Das Demokratie- und Staatsverständnis im Zeitablauf. Betrachtungen der Jahre 1902–1963*, Ratingen, 1973; H.P. Mensing (ed.), *Unserem Vaterlande zugute. Der Briefwechsel 1948–1963. Theodor Heuss, Konrad Adenauer*, Berlin, 1989; H. Möller, *Theodor Heuss. Staatsmann und Schriftsteller*, Bonn, 1990.

# HILFERDING, Rudolf (1877–1941)

The principal economic and political theoretician of the SPD during the Weimar era and Reich Finance Minister on two occasions, Hilferding was born into an upper middle-class Jewish business family in Vienna on 10 August 1877, and initially trained and worked in that city as a paediatrician. Already a member of a socialist student group while at medical school, his interests turned more to questions of political economy and politics in the early 1900s, and as co-editor of *Marx-Studien* from 1904 (until 1923) he soon emerged as a prominent figure of the Austro-Marxist school. He also contributed articles on socialism to the journal *Die Neue Zeit*, which was edited by Karl Kautsky. In 1904 Hilferding published an impressive analysis of Böhm-Bawerk's critique of Marx. Moving to Berlin in 1906, he taught at the SPD's party school and was soon promoted to the editorial board of *Vorwärts*. His reputation as a major thinker in the party was made with the publication of his *magnum opus*, *Das Finanzkapital*, in 1910. In some respects an adaption of Marx's *Das Kapital* to changed economic conditions, the book also contained some original ideas on the relationship between investment banks and industry, the role of cartels and competition, and the importance of investment opportunities for imperialism. Above all, the work painted a more realistic picture of the state's active involvement in the modern industrial economy and the implications for the political power of the proletariat. In

1914 he protested against the SPD's decision to approve the war credits Bill in the Reichstag. From 1916 until 1918 he served as a military doctor in the Austrian army.

Returning to Berlin at the end of the war, Hilferding took Prussian citizenship, joined the USPD and became the chief editor of its main publication, *Die Freiheit*. An advocate of selective nationalization in industry, which he saw as a key factor in bringing the working class to the centre of political power, he rejected the notion of radical revolutionary government and was a consistent opponent of the KPD, particularly in 1920 when his party debated the issue of affiliation to the Communist International. He rejoined the SPD in 1922, represented it in the Reichstag from 1924 until 1933, served for a number of years on the party's executive committee, and generally enjoyed wide recognition for his intellectual capacity and political judgement. He was a major contributor to the SPD's Heidelberg Programme of 1925, developed the thesis of 'organized capitalism', and expounded a series of stimulating ideas as editor of the journal, *Die Gesellschaft*. He delivered the keynote address at the party's national congress in 1924, 1925 and 1927, discussing the links between economic developments and party strategy, and playing a vital role in the formulation of the SPD's coalition policy. His interpretation of the concept of democratic socialism became the standard party line. Hilferding also achieved prominence on the national political stage, beginning with his membership of the Socialization Commission of the Council of People's Representatives in 1918–19, and then as one of the German delegates who negotiated the Rapallo Treaty with the Soviet Union.

It was for his role as Reich Minister of Finance from August to October 1923 and from June 1928 until December 1929 that he was brought to the attention of a wider audience. During his first period of office he was unable to translate his expert knowledge of finance into decisive action on currency reform, thus allowing his great rival, Karl Helfferich, to come up with the idea of the Rentenmark. His resignation became unavoidable. As a member some years later of the Grand Coalition government, Hilferding was confronted by even more demanding problems concerning reparations, the budget and the rising costs of the unemployment insurance scheme. Lacking the full support of his own party and under fire from Reichsbank president Hjalmar Schacht, his proposals on government financing proved inadequate to the mounting crisis and once again he was compelled to resign. Despite this setback, he continued as a dominant figure in the SPD until forced by the *Machtergreifung* to emigrate in March 1933 to Denmark, then Switzerland and finally, in 1938, to France, where he continued his writing for the party and socialism. Arrested by the Vichy authorities in early 1941, he was handed over to the Gestapo, who murdered him in La Santé prison, Paris, on 2 February of that year.

## Further Reading

R. Hilferding, *Das Finanzkapital*, 2 vols, Frankfurt am Main, 1968 (original edn 1910). See also A. Stein, *Rudolf Hilferding und die deutsche Arbeiterbewegung*, Hamburg, 1946; W. Blumenberg, *Rudolf Hilferding. Kämpfer für die Freiheit*, Hanover, 1959; A. Möller, *Im Gedanken an Reichsfinanzminister Rudolf Hilferding*, Bonn. 1971; R. Breitman, *German Socialism and Weimar Democracy*, Chapel Hill, 1981; W. Smaldone, 'Rudolf Hilferding and the Theoretical

Foundations of German Social Democracy, 1902–1933', *Central European History*, 21, 1988, pp. 267–99; G. Könke, *Organisierter Kapitalismus. Sozialdemokratie und Staat. Eine Studie zur Ideologie der sozialdemokratischen Arbeiterbewegung in der Weimarer Republik, 1924–1932*, Stuttgart, 1987; I. Kershaw (ed.), *Weimar: Why Did German Democracy Fail?*, London, 1990.

## HINDENBURG, Paul von (1847–1934)

Hindenburg's historical significance lies in the content of the second phase of a career which began for him at the age of 67 years when, in 1914, he was recalled from retirement to assume command of the German army in East Prussia. Until then, Paul von Hindenburg und Beneckendorff, who was born in Posen, West Prussia (later Poznań), on 2 October 1847, had enjoyed a successful but by no means outstanding career in the army. After serving in the Prusso-Austrian War in 1866 and the Franco-Prussian War in 1870–71, he was appointed to the General Staff in 1879 and finished up with the rank of commanding general of the Fourth Army. His status as war hero *par excellence* dates from his triumphant command at the Battle of Tannenberg against Russia in 1914, which led to his appointment later that year to commander-in-chief of the German armies in the East and subsequently to his promotion to general field marshal. In August 1916 he succeeded General Erich von Falkenhayn as Supreme Commander of the entire German army, which allowed him to emerge, together with General Erich Ludendorff, at the head of a virtual military dictatorship in Germany until 1918. With defeat and the Royal abdication in November 1918, he once again went into retirement, though retained the status of a national hero, which the fallacious 'stab-in-the-back' legend helped to consolidate.

The most crucial part of this second phase of von Hindenburg's career began in May 1925 when as the candidate mainly of the traditional conservative-nationalist Right he was elected to the most important office in the Weimar Republic, the Reich Presidency, which had been made vacant by the death of its first incumbent, the socialist Friedrich Ebert. During the first four or five years of his tenure, he took pains to act strictly according to the constitution of a state which, as a diehard monarchist, Junker and anti-socialist, he really deeply despised. The economic and political turbulence created by the onset of the Great Depression in 1929–30 finally allowed him to reveal his true colours as an authoritarian who was determined, with increasingly overt encouragement from reactionary circles in the army, industry and agriculture, to destroy the parliamentary democratic system of government. Using the emergency powers granted the President under Article 48 of the Weimar Constitution, he installed Heinrich Brüning, the Centre Party politician, as Reich Chancellor in charge of a presidential cabinet which effectively shut out the Reichstag from the governing process. Indeed, the Weimar Republic, as an authentic parliamentary democracy, arguably ended in early 1930. Over the next few years rule by emergency degree became the norm, thus allowing authoritarian trends in government to be progressively strengthened through not only the Brüning administration but also its successors in 1932, the von Papen and von Schleicher cabinets. Nevertheless, the advent to power of the NSDAP in 1933 was not inevitable. Von Hindenburg formed a poor impression of the 'Bohemian corporal', Hitler, and only following pressure from various quarters, including his immediate entourage, did he finally relent, somewhat against his better judgement and instinct, and agree to Hitler's appointment as Reich Chancellor. It was not the outcome the by now senile President had originally envisaged – he would have much preferred a restoration of the *Kaisserreich* with all its institutions of power – but his attitudes and actions since 1930 undoubtedly contributed in substantial measure to it, given the wider context in Germany. His re-election as President in April 1932 represented for him confirmation that his course of action had the approval of most Germans.

After 1933 von Hindenburg's status as the representative of the old, conservative Prusso-Germany was fully exploited by Hitler in his drive to consolidate the Third Reich. The carefully stage-managed ceremony at Potsdam's Garrison Church in March 1933, when Hitler and the President came together to symbolize the unity of the nationalist cause, was perhaps the most striking example of how von Hindenburg was used to sanctify the new regime. Some time before his death on his Neudeck estate in East Prussia on 2 August 1934, he had served his political purpose, to no good end.

## Further Reading

Generalfeldmarshall von Hindenburg, *Aus meinem Leben*, Leipzig, 1920; F. Endres (ed.), *Hindenburg. Briefe, Reden, Berichte*, Munich, 1934. Among the many biographies, the most noteworthy are J.W. Wheeler-Bennett, *Hindenburg. The Wooden Titan*, London, 1936; W. Görlitz, *Hindenburg. Ein Lebensbild*, Bonn, 1953; A. Dorpalen, *Hindenburg and the Weimar Republic*, Princeton, 1964; W. Ruge, *Hindenburg. Portrait eines Militaristen*, Cologne, 1980; W. Maser, *Hindenburg. Eine politische Biographie*, Rastatt, 1989. Note also W. Hubatsch, *Hindenburg und der Staat. Aus den Papieren des Generalfeldmarshalls und Reichspräsidenten von 1878 bis 1934*, Göttingen, 1966; M. Kitchen, *The Silent Dictatorship*, London, 1976; H.-O. Meissner, *Junge Jahre im Reichspräsidentenpalais. Erinnerungen an Ebert und Hindenburg 1919–1934*, Esslingen, 1988.

# HIRSCH, Paul (1868–1940)

Once described by Count Harry Kessler as 'in the best sense of the word, a Prussian Jew – conscientious, reliable', Hirsch achieved prominence in the early post-war period as a leading member of the SPD and as Prime Minister of Prussia from 1918 until 1920. Born into a respectable, middle-class Jewish family in Berlin in 1868, he developed a professional and political expertise in local government while a rising star in the Berlin SPD, and served as one of the few representatives of the party in the Prussian House of Deputies from 1910 until 1913. He supported the party's stance on war credits in 1914, and during the war displayed a keen sense of patriotism. A member of the executive committee of the Berlin Workers' and Soldiers' Council in November 1918, he was then appointed one of the SPD representatives of the

Political Cabinet for Prussia, acting as its co-chairman (with Heinrich Stroebel of the USPD). He was also one of the seven Prussian delegates to the Reichskonferenz, an assembly of officials from the various German states, which met in Berlin in November 1918 to discuss measures for the preservation of the Reich's territorial integrity. Hirsch was adamant that Prussia should remain unaltered in this respect, and the following year he was a fierce critic of Matthias Erzberger's plans for Reich reform which he found incompatible with Prussian interests. Hirsch's loyalty to his home state was also much in evidence with regard to the Polish–German conflict over the eastern territories, in which his vehement support for the national cause left no doubt about his patriotic credentials.

Assuming the offices of Prime Minister and Minister of the Interior in Prussia (1918–19), he was at the centre of political activity which often threatened to get out of hand. His dismissal of the radical socialist chief of police in Berlin, Emil Eichhorn, in early January 1919, helped precipitate the Spartacist revolt later that month. He saw his principal task, however, as establishing the Prussian administrative machine on a solid, democratic basis. He was convinced that the key to creating democracy in Prussia lay in the selection of local executives by democratically-elected town and district legislative bodies, thus to inaugurate a system of municipal self-rule. But while he may have had the correct ideas, Hirsch lacked the essential quality of decisive leadership. He disliked the rough and tumble of politics, preferring to avoid confrontation as much as possible by entertaining compromise. Consequently, his democratic reform programme was only partially fulfilled. In any case, while he believed that a democratic Prussia was the best guarantee of a democratic Germany, the SPD in the Reich took the different view that a unitary state complemented by local self-administration was the desirable ideal. He was unable to fight his corner for too long, for in the governmental reconstruction in Prussia in the immediate aftermath of the Kapp Putsch, he was dismissed. Nevertheless, he continued to serve in the Landtag until 1933 and played a significant role in maintaining good relations with other parties of the Centre and moderate Right. From 1925 until 1933 he was also *Bürgermeister* of Dortmund. Forced into exile in 1933, he died in the United States in 1940.

## Further Reading

P. Hirsch (ed.), *Der preussische Landtag 1921–1924*, Berlin, 1924; *Der Weg der Sozialdemokratie zur Macht in Preussen*, Berlin, 1929; *Flucht vor Hitler. Erinnerungen an die Kapitulation der ersten deutschen Republik 1933*, Frankfurt am Main, 1979. See also D. Orlow, *Weimar Prussia 1918–1925. The Unlikely Rock of Democracy*, Pittsburgh, 1986.

## HIRTSIEFER, Heinrich (1876–1941)

This Centre Party politician's major contribution to the development of the Weimar Republic was made through his position of Prussian Minister of Welfare from 1921 until 1932, and as Deputy Prime Minister of Prussia from October 1931 until July 1932. His background and early political experience shaped a sympathetic and generally effective attitude towards the creation and extension of public welfare provision in economic circumstances which were hardly favourable. He was born into a working-class Catholic family in Essen on 26 April 1876, and after completing an apprenticeship as a locksmith, made his way as an official in the Christian-Social Metalworkers' Union, whose secretary he eventually became in 1920. From 1907 until 1914 he also represented the Centre Party on the Essen town council. After army service in the First World War, he was a member of the Prussian State Assembly from 1919, and from 1921 until 1933 of the Landtag.

As Prussian Minister of Welfare, Hirtsiefer emerged as a key figure in the development of the Republic's *Sozialpolitik*, and he took particular interest in youth welfare provision, not only because of a basic humanitarian concern that was inspired by Catholic social teaching, but also because he sought to anchor the democratic state in the younger generation. He faced an uphill struggle during the early 1920s when the Prussian government had other priorities, but in the relatively stable middle years of that decade he succeeded in making advances in the housing, medical and youth sectors of welfare. Finding appropriate levels of funding was a perennial challenge, but he acquitted himself quite well until the Depression threw up daunting obstacles. He could then do little to prevent the swift dissolution of important parts of the welfare system as his attention concentrated more and more on coping with the consequences of mass unemployment. Throughout his tenure of office, he sought to improve and modernize welfare provision, as his writings on the subject make clear.

In the early 1930s, this unassertive politician found the challenges emanating in particular from the Right to the democratic order rather too much to handle. He tried manfully to keep the coalition parties in Prussia in reasonable harmony, but he had no answer to von Papen's coup in July 1932 which he had to face as acting head of the government in the absence of the indisposed Otto Braun. Hirtsiefer opposed any use of violence to defend Prussia, supporting referral of a complaint to the Supreme Court. The new mood of German politics, however, had no place for people of his ilk – decent, sensible and conscientious democrats.

Arrested on corruption charges in September 1933 and sent to a concentration camp for almost a year, he was released without being convicted and retired to private life. He died in Berlin on 15 May 1941.

## Further Reading
H. Hirtsiefer, *Wohlfahrtspflege in Preussen 1919–1923*, Berlin, 1924; *Die Wohnungswirtschaft in Preussen*, Eberswalde-Berlin, 1929; H. Hirtsiefer (ed.), *Jugendpflege in Preussen*, Eberswalde-Berlin, 1930. See also H. Hömig, *Das preussische Zentrum in der Weimarer Republik*, Mainz, 1979.

# HITLER, Adolf (1889–1945)

The *Führer* of the NSDAP and Chancellor of the German Reich from 1933 to 1945 was born in the small Lower Austrian town of Braunau am Inn on 20 April 1889, the son of a minor customs official. After an unsuccessful period at secondary school in Linz, he left home in 1907 for Vienna, where he hoped to train as an artist. Refused entry to the Academy of Fine Arts, he spent the next six years living on the margins of society, eking out a miserable existence in the city's male hostels, and developing a pathological hatred of Jews, Marxists, liberals and other groups he saw as representative of a modernist urban-industrial culture. The Pan-Germanism of Georg von Schönerer and the demagogic racism of Karl Lueger supplemented his steady diet of resentment-filled influences, which by the time he left for Munich in 1913 had already provided Hitler with a political philosophy that was the basis for his subsequent career.

Volunteering for service when war was declared in August 1914, he enlisted in the 16th Bavarian Infantry Regiment, glad of the opportunity of giving some meaning to his aimless, disorganized life. His bravery at the Front was rewarded with the Iron Cross (First Class); he finished with the rank of lance-corporal. While recovering from a gas attack in a Pomeranian hospital he heard with disbelief the news of Germany's surrender and the November Revolution and, according to his own account, then decided to enter politics. Joining the German Workers' Party in Munich in late 1919 in the course of his work as an educational training officer of the Bavarian Reichswehr, he soon established his credentials as an orator and propagandist, co-authored the official programme in February 1920 of what then became known as the National Socialist German Workers' Party, and in July of the following year asserted his dictatorial leadership over the party. In these early years, he gave the NSDAP an edge over a score of similar-minded organizations in Munich by the extraordinary fanaticism and propagandistic flair with which he expounded his views. He saw himself as a 'drummer' for the nationalist cause, which demanded the overthrow of the Republic by violent revolutionary means and its replacement by some kind of authoritarian system. His efforts culminated in the abortive putsch in Munich in November 1923. Henceforth, the modest 'drummer' aimed to become the messianic, uncompromising leader of national Germany.

Having turned his trial for high treason in Munich in early 1924 into a propagandistic *tour de force* for the *völkisch*-nationalist ethos of the NSDAP, Hitler served a brief sentence in Landsberg prison, during which he wrote *Mein Kampf*, and re-emerged politically wiser but more determined than before to attain his objective of total power. The refounded NSDAP was organizationally rationalized around his undisputed authority, and attracted during a quiet period in its fortunes a hard core of true believers, the so-called *Alte Kämpfer*. Renouncing putschist tactics in favour of the legal parliamentary road to power, Hitler laid the foundations of a mass movement, designed to stretch into every part of Germany and every social class. With an appeal fashioned after the 1928 Reichstag elections to attract above all the broad range of the middle classes, however, the NSDAP was poised to exploit quite ruthlessly the despair and disorientation that accompanied the onset of mass unemployment during the Depression. Already the second largest party in the Reichstag as a result of the September 1930 elections, the NSDAP's meteoric rise culminated in Hitler succumbing without loss of face to von Hindenburg in the Reich presidential elections in April

1932, and in the party becoming the largest in German history at the Reichstag elections in July 1932. The NSDAP's mixture of chauvinism, anti-Marxism and anti-Semitism drew support from all sections of the community, but in particular from the Protestant lower middle and upper middle classes in northern, central and eastern Germany. The charismatic, quasi-mystical status of the *Führer* himself was an indispensable element of this success. Despite this advance by mid-1932, he was still dependent on the support of sections of the conservative élites in industry, agriculture and the army to bring him into the Reich Chancellery in January 1933. The elimination of all internal political opposition rapidly followed, and the totalitarian Third Reich, with Hitler as its focal point and supreme authority, was on course to stamp its uniquely nefarious *Weltanschauung* on a wider world.

## Further Reading

A. Hitler, *Mein Kampf*, 2 vols, Munich, 1925–26; *Hitler's Secret Book* (introduction by Telford Taylor), New York, 1961. See also E. Jäckel and A. Kuhn (eds), *Hitler. Sämtliche Aufzeichnungen 1905–1924*, Stuttgart, 1980; M. Domarus (ed.), *Hitler. Reden und Proklamationen 1932–1945*, 4 vols, Munich, 1965; H.R. Trevor-Roper (ed.), *Hitler's Table Talk 1941–44. His Private Conversations*, London, 1953.

Among the biographies that can be recommended are A. Bullock, *Hitler. A Study in Tyranny*, revised edn, London, 1964; A. Bullock, *Hitler and Stalin. Parallel Lives*, London, 1991; J.C. Fest, *Hitler*, London, 1974; B. F. Smith, *Adolf Hitler. His Family, Childhood and Youth*, Stanford, 1967; A. Tyrell, *Vom 'Trommler' zum 'Führer'. Der Wandel von Hitlers Selbstverständnis zwischen 1919 und 1924 und die Entwicklung der NSDAP*, Munich, 1975; R. Zitelmann, *Hitler. Selbstverständnis eines Revolutionärs*, Hamburg, 1987; R. Zitelmann, *Adolf Hitler. Eine politische Biographie*, Göttingen, 1989; I. Kershaw, *Hitler*, London, 1991. See also G. Schreiber, *Hitler-Interpretationen 1923–1983. Ergebnisse, Methoden und Probleme der Forschung*, 2nd revised edn, Darmstadt, 1988.

## HOERNLE, Edwin (1883–1952)

The energetic and able agrarian expert of the KPD in the later Weimar period was born the son of a Protestant clergyman in Cannstatt, Württemberg, on 11 December 1883, and trained himself for the church. This career was abandoned when he discovered politics, and specifically the SDP, for whom he became active as both a journalist and local organizer in Berlin. He became one of the large number of left-wing radicals in the party from a Württemberg background who went on to become prominent in the foundation and leadership of the Spartacist League and then the KPD. He helped build up the youth and children's sections of the party in 1919–20, while in 1921–22 he was one of the two permanent KPD representatives in Moscow (the other being Jakob Walcher), with responsibility for promoting contact between the Comintern and the German party. During this time he got to know Stalin. Returning to Berlin in 1922, he was nominated to serve on the party's central committee for two years, and from 1924 until 1933 sat for the party in the Reichstag. Apart from developing a specialist interest in agriculture and ways of bringing the party closer to the small farming community, he also concerned himself with education. In several works, he criticized the class bias of progressive educationalists as serving simply the interests of monopoly capitalism, and proffered instead a theory of proletarian and international education which was widely respected in party circles.

In 1933 Hoernle fled to Moscow, where he was employed for several years by the International Institute of Agriculture. He prepared an agrarian programme for the underground KPD in September 1934 which carried a commitment to wholesale land reform to the benefit of small farmers in a post-Nazi Germany. In 1943 he was a cofounder of the Soviet-sponsored National Committee for a Free Germany, and he returned to Berlin in May 1945 with the Red Army. He played an important part in establishing Communist power in the Soviet zone, with particular responsibility for implementing a programme of land reform which was heavily influenced by his own previously-stated ideas. From 1949 until his death in Bad Liebenstein, Thuringia, on 21 July 1952, he was head of the Political-Agrarian Faculty and vice-president of the German Academy of Administration in the DDR.

## *Further Reading*

E. Hoernle, *Grundfragen der proletarischen Erziehung*, Berlin, 1929; *La Situation des paysans en Allemagne hitlérienne*, Paris, 1939. See also H. Weber, *Kommunismus in Deutschland 1918–1945*, Darmstadt, 1983; B. Fowkes, *Communism in Germany under the Weimar Republic*, London, 1983; J. Wächtler, *Zwischen Revolutionserwartung und Untergang. Die Vorbereitung der KPD auf die Illegalität in den Jahren 1929–1933*, Frankfurt am Main, 1983.

## HOETZSCH, Otto (1876–1946)

As foreign affairs spokesman for the DNVP during most of the 1920s, Hoetzsch earned wide respect for his constructive attitude to the complex and divisive issue of *Erfüllungspolitik*, particularly in the Stresemann era. Born into an artisanal family in Leipzig on 14 February 1876, he read history and political science at university, and as a professional academic historian took his *Habilitation* in 1906 at the University of Berlin. His principal sphere of research was eastern European and Russian history, which influenced his political view of the need for Russo–German understanding and co-operation. From 1906 until 1913 he taught at the Royal Academy in Posen (later Poznań), and from 1913 at the University of Berlin, by which time he was being recognized as one of Germany's leading specialists on eastern European affairs. Professor Hoetzsch's political interests had also been clearly defined by the outbreak of the First World War. Active in *völkisch* student circles while still an undergraduate, he subsequently joined the Pan-German League and in 1904 was appointed to its national committee. He was also heavily involved in the Ostmarkenverein and its campaign to preserve the values of the German *Volkstum* in the East. As such, he developed a strong antipathy towards Poland, an attitude which continued to exert a limiting influence on his vision of eastern European problems at a later date in his career. During the war he fully supported the German government's imperialist-expansionist aims, which he could not easily reconcile, however, with its treatment of Russia at Brest-Litovsk.

In November 1918, Hoetzsch published in the conservative newspaper, the *Kreuzzeitung*, for which he had been writing articles on foreign affairs since 1914, the ideas he believed had to be implemented if conservatism as a coherent ideology, and a conservative party, were to survive the abdication of the Kaiser and the revolutionary events of 1918–19. Above all, he laid out guidelines for the development of a mass conservative party, and the following month he put his services at the disposal of the newly-founded DNVP, having been a member since before the war of the German Conservative Party. He quickly established his credentials as one of the best minds in the DNVP while a member of the Prussian Constitutional Convention from 1919 until 1921, and as a Reichstag deputy from 1921 until 1930. For some years he served on the Reichstag's powerful Foreign Affairs Committee, including a spell as its secretary. A moderate nationalist, he emerged as a perceptive and well-informed critic of German foreign policy, able to put to good advantage his excellent contacts with the government and with important members of the Berlin diplomatic corps. A supporter of the Dawes Plan and appreciative of the changes in the international scene brought about by the Locarno Accords, he was instrumental in guiding his party by 1927–28 to a generally more positive attitude towards Stresemann's conduct of foreign affairs, at the price, however, of making himself anathema to his former colleagues in the Pan German League. As something of a Russophile, he welcomed both the Rapallo Pact and, in 1926, the Treaty of Berlin with the Soviet Union, seeing these initiatives as a desirable counterweight to Germany's improving relations with the West. His commentaries on these developments were conveyed in the conservative journals *Der Tag* and *Osteuropa*, the latter of which he was editor from 1925.

Hoetzsch could not accommodate himself to the strident course the DNVP took under the leadership after 1928 of Alfred Hugenberg. Following a number of disagreements over matters of foreign affairs, he resigned from the party in November 1929 in protest at Hugenberg's campaign against the Young Plan, and joined the Conservative People's Party the following year. But his political prominence was not sustained. Dismissed by the Nazi regime from his Berlin professorship in 1935, he died in the ruined capital on 27 August 1946.

## Further Reading

O. Hoetzsch, *Deutschlands Weltlage*, Berlin, 1921; 'Die Aussenpolitik der Deutschnationalen Volkspartei', *Europäische Gespräche*, 6, 1926, pp. 339–51; *Germany's Domestic and Foreign Policies*, New Haven, 1929; *Osteuropa and der deutsche Osten*, Königsberg, 1934. See also P.-C. Witt, 'Eine Denkschrift Otto Hoetzschs vom 5. November 1919', *Vierteljahrshefte für Zeitgesschichte*, 21, 1973, pp. 337–53; R.P. Grathwol, *Stresemann and the DNVP. Reconciliation or Revenge in German Foreign Policy 1924–1928*, Lawrence, Kansas, 1980; G. Voigt, *Otto Hoetzsch 1876–1946. Wissenschaft und Politik im Leben eines deutschen Historikers*, East Berlin, 1978; U. Liszkowski, *Osteuropaforschung und Politik. Ein Beitrag zum historisch-politischen Denken und Wirken von Otto Hoetzsch*, Berlin, 1988.

# HÖPKER-ASCHOFF, Hermann (1883–1954)

One of the most perceptive liberal politicians of the Weimar era, and 'an impressive character' (Arnold Brecht), Höpker-Aschoff was born into a middle-class family in Herford, Westphalia, on 31 January 1883, took a degree and a doctorate in law and worked his way through the Prussian legal system to become in 1921 a judge in a court of appeal in Hamm. A member of the DDP from 1919, he represented it, and from 1930 the German State Party, in the Prussian Landtag, also representing the latter party in the Reichstag until 1932. In March 1925, he was elected Prussian Prime Minister in somewhat farcical circumstances for three days only, when neither the SPD nor the Centre Party could find a candidate for that office of their own. Höpker-Aschoff enjoyed sufficient goodwill from most parties in the Landtag to be elected, but found it impossible to form a cabinet. Otto Braun was once again elected Prime Minister a few days later and at once appointed his predecessor Minister of Finance, a post he occupied until October 1931. During that period, he fully mastered the problems confronting his ministry and established a reputation as something of a financial expert in conditions that were far from propitious. An ardent patriot and firm upholder of democratic ideals, he fully appreciated the importance of financial stability and prudent housekeeping in Germany's largest state, not least in terms of helping to secure the parliamentary Republic. An influential member of the cabinet, he enjoyed the full support and trust of Otto Braun.

Despite Höpker-Aschoff's sound management, however, the difficulties arising from the Depression increased to the point in 1931 where he and Braun feared they might occasion a premature dissolution of the Landtag, which they believed would result in the Weimar coalition parties losing their majority. To avoid this, a scheme was drafted to carry out a Reich reform by emergency decree and fuse the Reich and Prussian governments. Höpker-Aschoff had long been an advocate of a centralized Reich financial administration, and the scheme was partly designed to bring this about. In any case, he had become convinced by September 1931 that Prussia would collapse unless rescued financially by the Reich. But when the Reichsbank blocked the scheme, Höpker-Aschoff's position was made untenable and at the further insistence of the Centre Party he was compelled to resign in October 1931. Nevertheless, he continued to campaign in parliament for a comprehensive *Reichsreform*.

Within his own party, Höpker-Aschoff was to the fore in promoting the idea of a united liberal party of the moderate Centre, which in the eyes of some colleagues in 1929 made him a possible candidate to challenge Koch-Weser for the leadership. That came to nothing, and his growing frustration with the blurred profile of the DDP caused him to cross over to the German State Party in 1930, whereupon he tried unsuccessfully to find a basis for union with the DVP. His ideal of a single liberal party drawing support from white-collar employees, independent businessmen, intellectuals and professionals was no longer a realistic option by the early 1930s in Germany, particularly in view of the NSDAP's catch-all appeal across the broad spectrum of the bourgeoisie. His last political initiative also met with failure when, in August 1932, he attempted to mediate in the legal dispute between the von Papen government and the Prussian government that had been usurped, with a view to a settlement out of court. But this well-intentioned move floundered for want of co-operation on both sides.

Höpker-Aschoff withdrew to private life throughout the era of the Third Reich, but reappeared in 1945 to act as a financial adviser to the provisional government set up in Westphalia by the British occupation authorities. An early member of the Free Democratic Party, he served in the Parliamentary Council which prepared the way for the establishment of the Federal Republic, and in September 1951 was appointed the first president of the Federal Constitutional Court in Karlsruhe, a post he held until his death on 15 January 1954.

*Further Reading*

H. Höpker-Aschoff, *Deutscher Einheitsstaat. Ein Beitrag zur Rationalisierung der Verwaltung*, Berlin, 1928. See also W. Stephan, *Aufstieg und Verfall des Linksliberalismus 1918–1933. Geschichte der Deutschen Demokratischen Partei*, Göttingen, 1973; R. Pois, *The Bourgeois Democrats of Weimar Germany*, Philadelphia, 1976.

## HÖRSING, Friedrich Otto (1874–1937)

The high-profile SPD leader and founder of the Reichsbanner Schwarz-Rot-Gold paramilitary organization was born the son of an innkeeper in Gross-schillingken, East Prussia, on 18 July 1874. After completing an apprenticeship as a blacksmith, he spent a number of years working in various parts of the country, including three years (1901–1904) in Kiel. In 1905 he was appointed secretary of the German Metal-workers' Union in Kattowitz (now Katowice), and, having joined the SPD in 1894, served as its district secretary in Oppeln, Lower Silesia, from 1908 until 1914. Called up in 1914, he saw active service on the Eastern Front, reaching the rank of staff sergeant, and in recognition of his organizational talent was put in charge of a large prisoner-of-war camp in Romania.

After 1918, Hörsing's political career developed rapidly. Chairman of the Workers' and Soldiers' Council in Upper Silesia in 1918–19, he was then appointed State Commissioner for Upper Silesia, and later in 1919 State Commissioner for Silesia and Posen (later Poznań). In February 1920 he became Governor (*Oberpräsident*) of the province of Prussian Saxony, based in Magdeburg. His was a particularly controversial posting because, lacking a higher education and any sort of formal administrative training, he was seen as an 'outsider', a blatantly political appointment to what was the highest office in the Prussian administration. His personality also added to the difficulty: Hörsing was abrasive, overbearing and vain. But he was also decisive in action, patriotic, and fiercely loyal to the Republic, as shown by his firm attitude towards disturbances from both left- and right-wing political radicals. His swift and successful response to the so-called 'March Action' by the KPD in 1921 made him a figure of loathing on the radical Left in particular. His determination to offer muscular support to the Republic lay behind his creation of the Reichsbanner in Magdeburg in February 1924. It was to be a counterweight to the various paramilitary groups which had already displayed a strong anti-republican animus, such as the Stahlhelm, the SA, and the KPD's Rotfrontkämpferbund. He was chairman of the Reichsbanner until July 1931.

His confrontational style made Hörsing the 'terror of the Prussian administration', according to Carl Severing, and he became something of a liability in the reasonably harmonious political circles of Prussia. Conflicts with his own party leadership increased in frequency, and not surprisingly, he was dismissed as *Oberpräsident* by his party colleague, the Minister of the Interior in Prussia, Albert Grzesinski, in July 1927. He concentrated thereafter on developing the Reichsbanner as the largest organization of its type in Germany – with 3 million members by the early 1930s – though his relations with the SPD progressively deteriorated, particularly when it was made clear to him that neither the party nor the trade unions thought much of his plans to combat mass unemployment. To propagate his ideas he bought for a brief period in 1931 his own newspaper, the *Deutscher Volkskurier, Blatt für Arbeitsbeschaffung, Wirtschaft und Politik*, which further alienated him from his party. In July 1931, he was expelled from both the SPD and the Reichsbanner (to be replaced by Karl Höltermann). With characteristic vigour, he responded by establishing his own party, the Sozialrepublikanische Partei Deutschlands, and a newspaper, *Neue Kampffront*. This initiative failed to make any headway, despite strong canvassing among his former Reichsbanner comrades. In 1933 he retired to private life, dying in Berlin on 16 August 1937.

## Further Reading

F.O. Hörsing, 'Das Reichsbanner Schwarz-Rot-Gold', in Bernhard Harms (ed.), *Volk und Reich der Deutschen*, Volume 2, Berlin, 1929; Dr M. Curius (ed.), *Otto Hörsings Kriegsplan zur Niederringung der Arbeitslosigkeit*, Berlin-Schmargendorf, 1931. See also K. Rohe, *Das Reichsbanner Schwarz Rot Gold. Ein Beitrag zur Geschichte und Struktur der politischen Kampfverbände zur Zeit der Weimarer Republik*, Düsseldorf, 1966; H. Gotschlich, *Zwischen Kampf und Kapitulation. Zur Geschichte des Reichsbanners Schwarz-Rot-Gold*, East Berlin, 1987.

## HUGENBERG, Alfred (1865–1951)

Hugenberg emerged as a principal gravedigger of the Weimar Republic in at least two vital respects: he used his extensive press, publishing and film empire to influence and mobilize the broad range of the German middle classes against parliamentary democracy, and from the time he took over as chairman of the DNVP in October 1928, he directed his party along a radically nationalist and anti-Marxist course which at certain junctures, notably in 1929 in the campaign of the extreme Right against the Young Plan, and in 1931 with the formation of the Harzburg Front of right-wing organizations, aided and abetted the rise to power of the NSDAP. It was Hugenberg's press that created an aura of bourgeois respectability around Hitler, allowing him access to sections of society which provided the bedrock of Nazi support before and after 1933.

Hugenberg, born into a nationalist middle-class home in Hanover on 19 June 1865, the son of a National Liberal finance adviser in the civil service, and with degrees in law and political economy following study at several leading German universities, became actively involved in radical right-wing politics at an early age. In 1890 he was a co-founder of the Pan German League, served on its executive committee until 1905, and retained intimate links with the organization throughout his political career. Alternating business interests – as director of the Berg-Metallbank (1907–1909) – with service in the Prussian government (Finance Ministry) over a number of years, he made his major breakthrough in 1909 when appointed chairman of the Krupp concern, a position he held until 1919. A strong supporter of German imperialist ambitions during the First World War, he took the decisive step towards becoming an industrial tycoon in his own right during the inflationary early 1920s when he revealed a high order of business acumen, judgement and ruthlessness to construct his media-based empire, making him one of the most influential and successful industrialists of the period. The Scherl publishing house and UFA (Universal Film) were but two of his acquisitions. From this position he was uniquely placed to influence public opinion with his vehement anti-republicanism. Hugenberg is perhaps best understood politically as a reactionary conservative nationalist of the old school, albeit of a particularly radical type. Once he had asserted virtual dictatorial control over a party he had represented in the Reichstag since 1920, he was determined to replace the democratic Republic with an authoritarian system of government in which he aimed to play a central role, even when his inflexibility and extremism alienated and finally drove from the DNVP influential groups who proceeded to form alternative conservative-nationalist splinter parties. He felt he could control and manipulate Hitler and the NSDAP for his own ends, and it was too late before he realized a fundamental error of judgement.

Appointed Reich Minister of Economics and Agriculture in Hitler's first cabinet, he was forced out six months later when the DNVP was dissolved. For Hitler, he had simply fulfilled his purpose and was now supernumerary. He remained a Reichstag deputy until 1945 but was of no further political significance, and instead concentrated on managing those parts of his business which he had not been pressurized into selling to the Third Reich. Hugenberg survived the war and a de-nazification trial in 1949, when he was labelled no more than a 'fellow traveller' of the Nazis, with a considerable part of his fortune and business intact. He died on 12 March 1951 in Kükenbruch, near Rinteln.

## Further Reading

A. Hugenberg, *Streiflichter aus Vergangenheit und Gegenwart*, Berlin, 1927; *Die Soziale Frage in Deutschland*, Berlin, 1932; and his apologetic memoirs, *Hugenberg und die Hitler-Diktatur*, 2 vols, Detmold, 1949. See also D. Guratzsch, *Macht durch Organisation. Die Grundlagen des Hugenbergschen Presseimperiums*, Düsseldorf, 1974; J.A. Leopold, *Alfred Hugenberg. The Radical Nationalist Campaign against the Weimar Republic*, New Haven, 1977; H. Holzbach, *Das 'System Hugenberg'. Die Organisation bürgerlicher Sammlungspolitik vor dem Aufstieg der*

NSDAP, Stuttgart, 1981; H. Weiss and P. Hoser (eds), *Die Deutschnationalen und die Zerstörung der Weimarer Republik. Aus dem Tagebuch von Reinhold Quaatz, 1928–1933*, Munich, 1989.

## JARRES, Karl (1874–1951)

The long-serving and highly respected Lord Mayor of the industrial city of Duisburg (1914–1933) was also prominent as one of the most influential spokesmen of the DVP, particularly of its right wing, during the 1920s. Jarres, born in Remscheid on 21 September 1874, took a doctorate in law, and served as a *Beigeordneter* in Düren and Cologne as well as for four years as Lord Mayor of Remscheid before moving to his post in Duisburg. In October 1923 he chaired a top-level meeting in Hagen, Westphalia, of national political leaders, industrialists and bankers which gave support to the policy of abandoning the campaign of passive resistance against the French occupiers of the Ruhr because Germany faced, it was feared, an economic and political disaster if the crisis could not be quickly resolved. Jarres, who had earlier that year been jailed by the occupation authorities for a lack of co-operation, and who had been acting as a co-ordinator between the Reich government and centres of resistance, personally advised his party leader, Gustav Stresemann, then Chancellor, of the hopelessness of the situation. A few weeks later, on the withdrawal of SPD ministers from the cabinet, Jarres was appointed Reich Minister of the Interior, a post he continued to hold in the succeeding cabinets of Wilhelm Marx from November 1923 until January 1925. As such, his responsibilities were concerned partly at least with mopping up after the failed National Socialist, Communist and separatist insurrections.

A nationalist of impeccable conservative credentials, he was nominated by the Loebell Committee, a bipartisan organization of middle-class parties and interest groups, as its candidate in the Reich presidential election of March 1925, a move supported by both the DVP and DNVP, and personally endorsed by Stresemann. Dr Jarres emerged from the first round as the most popular candidate, with 10.7 million votes. But this amounted to less than 40 per cent of the total popular vote and thus was insufficient to give him the absolute majority required by the Weimar Constitution for the election of the Reich President. He did not contest the second ballot, von Hindenburg being the preferred candidate of the Right. In July 1926, the DVP leader and Baron Wilhelm von Gayl of the DNVP initiated a campaign to bring their parties into a formal parliamentary alliance in the Reichstag and Prussian Landtag. They had already since 1921 shared the leadership of a special working association (*Arbeitsgemeinschaft*) of their respective parties in the Prussian State Council, and now wanted to extend the influence in politics of the conservative, national and Christian ethos. But although the DNVP and the DVP's right wing responded enthusiastically to the proposal, Stresemann and more liberal elements did not and reaffirmed their unequivocal support for an independent and liberal DVP. Thereafter, Jarres remained a substantial voice and opinion-maker in the DVP without achieving further prominence at a national level. Like his *confrère*, Konrad Adenauer, in Cologne, he was deeply engaged in developing the economic and social life of Duisburg, with generally qualified success.

Dismissed at Lord Mayor in 1933, Jarres withdrew from public life. He died in Duisburg on 22 October 1951.

## Further Reading

G. Abramowski (ed.), *Akten der Reichskanzlei. Weimarer Republik. Die Kabinette Marx I und II: 30. November 1923 bis 3. Juni 1924; 3. Juni 1924 bis 15. Januar 1925*, 2 vols, Boppard,1973. See also L.E. Jones, *German Liberalism and the Dissolution of the Weimar Party System, 1918–1933*, Chapel Hill, 1988.

# JOOS, Joseph (1878–1965)

Catholic labour leader and distinguished theoretician of the Centre Party, Joos was born into a working-class family in Wintzenheim, near Colmar, on 13 November 1878, and completed an apprenticeship as a pattern-maker. His early political activity as a party member was concentrated in the press of the Catholic labour movement, culminating in 1905 in his appointment as editor of the *Westdeutsche Arbeiter-Zeitung*, where he remained despite many other commitments until 1933. He served his party in the National Assembly and subsequently in the Reichstag throughout the Weimar era, always as a representative of its democratic-social left wing. He produced a number of perceptive books and articles concerning the Centre's philosophy and place in modern society which identified him as one of the most serious thinkers in its ranks. He believed very firmly in the contribution his party had to make to the successful development of the parliamentary Republic, and towards this end was prepared to countenance coalition policies with the Left and Right. In early 1927, for example, he co-authored a Centre Party manifesto regarding the creation of a broad middle-class political alliance for government, a theme to which he returned in 1932.

The mid- and late 1920s saw Joos emerging as a national politician of considerable stature. Elected leader in 1927 of the Reichsverband der katholischen Arbeiter- und Arbeiterinnenvereine (National Association of Catholic Labour Unions), he also became chairman of the Catholic Labour International the following year, thus adding to his existing duties as chairman of the Catholic youth movement, the Windthorstbünde, and as a member of the national executive of the Reichsbanner Schwarz-Rot-Gold, the paramilitary organization. On Wilhelm Marx's resignation as chairman of the Centre Party in 1928, Joos was a candidate for the position along with Adam Stegerwald and Monsignor Ludwig Kaas, attracting 92 votes against the latter's winning 184 at the party's congress in December of that year. Joos was duly made deputy chairman. His commitment to the Republic in the Depression years never faltered, as revealed by his active involvement in the Deutschlandbund, set up with government funding to combat the demagogic propaganda of the anti-democratic extremists, and also by his leading role in negotiations between his party and the NSDAP in August 1932 regarding the possibilities of forming a coalition government. Joos had no time for the ideology of National Socialism, but he genuinely, if naively, thought that if the parliamentary process could be reactivated in a meaningful fashion on the basis of co-operation with the NSDAP, the cause of the Republic would be served. In other words, it was to be an association of political expediency, designed in the first instance to bring down the Papen cabinet, which Joos despised.

In 1933 Joos voted for the Enabling Bill out of a sense of party discipline, and during the last few months of the Centre Party's existence he shared its leadership with Heinrich Brüning and Carl Ulitzka. He remained active thereafter in the Catholic social movement. As he was of French nationality, he was stripped of his German citizenship in 1938 and interned as an alien in Dachau concentration camp from 1941 until the end of the war. In the early post-war period he was chairman of a German Catholic men's association. Joos died in St Gallen, Switzerland, on 11 March 1965.

## Further Reading

J. Joos, *Die katholische Arbeiterschaft und die nationale Bewegung*, Munich, 1925; *Die politische Ideenwelt des Zentrums*, Karlsruhe, 1928; *Leben auf Widerruf. Begegnungen und Beobachtungen im Konzentrationslager Dachau 1941–1945*, Olten, 1946; *Am Räderwerk der Zeit. Erinnerungen aus der katholischen und sozialen Bewegung und Politik*, Augsburg, 1950; *So sah ich sie. Menschen und Geschehnisse*, Augsburg, 1958. See also O. Wachtling, *Joseph Joos. Journalist, Arbeiterführer, Zentrumspolitiker. Politische Biographie 1878–1933*, Mainz, 1974.

## JUCHACZ, Marie (1879–1956)

Having been elected on a Social Democratic slate to the National Assembly in January 1919, Juchacz was the first woman to address a German parliamentary body when the following month she spoke of the importance of feminist issues. From then until 1933 she was a permanent and notable member of the Reichstag, devoting most of her time to social welfare and women's affairs. Juchacz was born a carpenter's daughter in Landsberg/Wartheland on 15 March 1879, completing only a primary school education before working in a succession of manual occupations. Following the failure of her marriage in 1903, she moved to Berlin where she became involved in the Social Democratic educational association for women. A talent for public speaking was developed and she steadily made her way in the party's apparatus. From 1913 to 1917 she was women's secretary of the SPD in Cologne before being appointed leader of the party's Women's Office with a place on the main executive (*Parteivorstand*). During this period, in the absence of Clara Zetkin, she occasionally edited the radical women's journal *Die Gleichheit*.

Juchacz's work in social affairs was rewarded in December 1919 when she took the chair of the national committee of the newly-founded voluntary socialist welfare organization, the Arbeiterwohlfahrt (AWO), which thereafter remained her principal sphere of activity. Under her guidance the AWO developed a membership of over 100,000, providing a comprehensive range of welfare facilities for the working class, but the organization had great difficulty in carving out an entirely coherent place for itself in a welfare system which was dominated by 'bourgeois' values in a capitalist society. Nevertheless, the AWO did allow a socialist influence in the politics and administration of welfare and drew into it for the first time large numbers of working-class women, many of whom were consequently attracted to the political orbit of the SPD. As such, the AWO under Juchacz's leadership attained a position of considerable social and political significance until its work was abruptly terminated by the National Socialist regime.

In 1933 she emigrated with her second husband (Emil Kirschmann) to the Saarland and then, following that district's incorporation into the Reich in 1935, to France. In 1940 she moved to the USA, returning to the Federal Republic in 1949. Honorary chairperson of the resurrected AWO for a few years, Juchacz died in Bonn on 28 January 1956.

## Further Reading

M. Juchacz, *Die Arbeiterwohlfahrt. Voraussetzungen und Entwicklungen*, Berlin, 1924. See also F.M. Roehl, *Marie Juchacz und die Arbeiterwohlfahrt*, Hanover, 1956; J. Geier, *'Praktischer Sozialismus oder Mildtätigkeit?' Die Geschichte der Arbeiterwohlfahrt Essen 1919–1933*, Essen, 1989; R. Pore, *A Conflict of Interest. Women in German Social Democracy 1919–1933*, Westport, 1981; C. Wickert, *Unsere Erwählten: Sozialdemokratische Frauen im Deutschen Reichstag und im Preussischen Landtag 1919 bis 1933*, Göttingen, 1986; R. Bridenthal, A. Grossmann and M. Kaplan (eds), *When Biology became Destiny. Women in Weimar and Nazi Germany*, New York, 1985; U. Frevert *Women in German History*, Oxford, 1989.

## KAAS, Ludwig (1881–1952)

A distinguished theological scholar who led the Centre Party from December 1928 until mid-1933, Kaas was born to lower middle-class parents in Trier on 23 May 1881, and was ordained a Catholic priest in 1906. Appointed an adviser to the papal nuncio in Germany (Pacelli) in 1917, he taught Church Law at the University of Trier in 1918 and then at the University of Bonn until 1924; political pressures then compelled him to relinquish his professorship. A representative of the Centre Party in the National Assembly and, further, in the Reichstag until 1933, he was a man of considerable intelligence and strength of character on the conservative right wing of his party, constantly alert to the implications of political developments for the interests of the Catholic Church. A papal domestic prelate from 1921 – an honorary ecclesiastical title bestowed by the Pope for life – Monsignor Kaas was a powerful if infrequent speaker in the Reichstag and the Prussian State Council, which he had joined the same year, particularly on matters of foreign policy. In November 1928, for instance, and speaking as a member of the German delegation to the League of Nations, he issued a ringing condemnation of Stresemann's foreign policy, suggesting it had brought few rewards to Germany. A year later, he was demanding a more aggressive foreign policy, to include German renunciation of the demilitarized status of the Rhineland.

A dramatic new phase in his career began when Kaas assumed the leadership of his party, steering it decidedly to the right in defence of traditional, conservative Catholic and political values. Having given his personal endorsement in 1929 to Heinrich Brüning as chairman of the party's Reichstag delegation, he had no reservations about supporting his chancellorship, especially as he favoured the policies at home and abroad which Brüning adopted. Kaas was infuriated, therefore, by the manner in which the Chancellor was dismissed in May 1932, and refused his successor, von Papen, a fellow party member until that moment, any support. This dissonance was one factor that persuaded the Centre Party to explore a parliamentary coalition with the NSDAP in August 1932. A few months later, with the party maintaining its electoral support at a remarkably constant level despite the pressures created by the Depression, Kaas was asked by Reich President von Hindenburg to determine whether a cabinet could be formed on the basis of a parliamentary coalition. The initiative proved abortive when he was unable to engage in serious discussion either the NSDAP or DNVP.

Kaas persisted in his search for a coalition government involving the Centre Party even after Hitler's appointment as Chancellor, and yet again following the Reichstag elections in March 1933. He then led the party in support of the Enabling Bill, and from Rome played a not unimportant role in the negotiations that paved the way for the Nazi–Vatican Concordat of July 1933, which he believed would secure the future of the Church in the Third Reich. He pursued his research interests at the Holy See until his death there on 15 April 1952.

## Further Reading

L. Kaas, *Die geistliche Gerichtsbarkeit der katholischen Kirche in Preussen in Vergangenheit und Gegenwart mit besonderer Berücksichtigung des Wesens der Monarchie*, 2 vols, Stuttgart, 1915–16; *Kriegsverschollenheit und Wiederverheiratung nach staatlichem und kirchlichem Recht*, Paderborn, 1919. See also R. Morsey, *Die deutsche Zentrumspartei 1917–1923*, Düsseldorf, 1966; R. Morsey (ed.), *Die Protokolle der Reichstagsfraktion und des Fraktionsvorstands der deutschen Zentrumspartei*, Mainz, 1969; D. Junker, *Die deutsche Zentrumspartei und Hitler, 1932/33. Ein Beitrag zur Problematik des politischen Katholizismus in Deutschland*, Stuttgart, 1969; G. May, *Ludwig Kaas. Der Priester, der Politiker und der Gelehrte aus der Schule von Ulrich Stutz*, 3 vols, Amsterdam, 1981–82.

# KAHL, Wilhelm (1849–1932)

'The Nestor of German jurisprudence' (Erich Eyck) and elder statesman of the DVP in the Weimar era, Kahl had a distinguished career as a university law professor and as a substantial personality in the German liberal movement both before and after the First World War. Born in Kleinheubach on 17 June 1849 into a comfortable middle-class home with good connections to the legal profession, he took his doctorate and *Habilitation* in law, and proceeded to hold several academic posts before being appointed to a professorship in 1895 at the University of Berlin. A specialist in criminal law, he served, eventually as chairman, on a governmental commission from 1911 whose remit was to draft a new criminal code. The advent of the First World War interrupted this undertaking, however, and it was not revived until the 1920s when, once again, he was able to bring his erudition to bear as chairman of the Reichstag's Legal Affairs Committee. Through no fault of his a new criminal code never actually materialized before 1933.

A member of the National Liberal Party from 1874, serving eventually on its national executive, Kahl joined the DVP in 1918 and played an important part in formulating its programme. As a member of the National Assembly, he also made a perceptive contribution to discussions on the new Weimar Constitution. He went on to make his mark as a widely respected and influential leader of the DVP in the Reichstag until 1932, associated with the party's left wing, but also serving as chairman for many years of the parliamentary delegation. His initial attitude towards the Republic had been more than circumspect, for in March 1920 he joined with other party colleagues in publicly welcoming the Kapp Putsch and the provisional government that briefly followed. After this episode, Kahl went to some lengths to underline his own and the DVP's support for governmental legislation aimed at protecting the political authority of the state from insurrectionists and radicals. Like his good friend and subsequent party leader, Gustav Stresemann, Professor Kahl made his peace with the democratic Republic. When Reich President Ebert was accused in 1924 of unpatriotic behaviour during the war, he conspicuously rallied to his defence.

A member of the DVP's national executive, chairman of its annual congresses, and honorary co-chairman of the Liberal Association, which sought to promote the cause of a united liberal party, Kahl was at the heart of his party's increasingly troubled development in the later 1920s, and viewed with alarm and disapproval its domination by industrial interests. Though he did not display the marked disillusionment of Stresemann with the party, he sought to keep it on a recognizably liberal track by tentatively exploring unity possibilities with the DDP in 1930, and the following year with the moderate Right. At one time it was even suggested in some quarters that he become chairman of a united liberal party, but all these ideas came to nothing. However, his unease at the direction of the DVP under Dingeldey was forcefully expressed in October 1931 when he defied his leader and continued supporting the Brüning government. It was one of his last notable political acts, for Kahl died in Berlin on 14 May 1932.

## Further Reading
W. Kahl, *Das neue Strafgesetzbuch*, Berlin, 1907; *Die Deutsche Volkspartei und das Reich*, Berlin, 1919. See also W. Hartenstein, *Die Anfänge der Deutschen Volkspartei 1918–1920*, Düsseldorf, 1962; L.E. Jones, *German Liberalism and the Dissolution of the Weimar Party System, 1918–1933*, Chapel Hill, 1988.

# KAHR, Gustav Ritter von (1862–1934)

A successful career civil servant who was thrust, somewhat reluctantly at first, into the centre of the political turbulence in Bavaria during the early 1920s, von Kahr was born in Weissenburg on 29 November 1862 into a prominent upper middle-class Protestant family which had given faithful service to crown and state since the beginning of the nineteenth century. His father had been president of the Bavarian Administrative Court and he himself was a law graduate of the University of Munich. After holding various posts in outlying areas, he was appointed to a position in the Bavarian Ministry of the Interior which, for his work in looking after historic monuments, led in 1911 to his elevation to the nobility. In 1917 he became *Regierungspräsident* of Upper Bavaria.

Despite a lack of previous political experience or involvement, von Kahr was chosen by the BVP to be Prime Minister of Bavaria in March 1920. His devotion to the monarchist-conservative cause and to the position of the Catholic Church was the basis for his political career, supplemented by a fanatical hatred of Marxism which, in his view, included the SPD. His government received powerful backing from the most important bastions of power in Bavaria, including the right-wing Home Guard (*Einwohnerwehr*), which he shielded from demands for its disbandment from the Allies and the Reich authorities. His sense of personal infallibility and grand manner made him a hero of the traditional Right, but these characteristics also led to a lack of decisive action: too often his schemes came to nothing, to the growing exasperation of his supporters. His frequently expressed determination to restore the Wittelsbach dynasty was but one unfulfilled plan. After a series of crises with the Reich, the last one in August 1921 concerning a presidential proclamation, von Kahr lost the backing of the BVP in the Landtag and had to resign, having achieved little of substance during his term of office. He returned to his former position as *Regierungspräsident* until once more, in September 1923, recalled to political office as General State Commissioner, armed with virtually dictatorial powers, a reflection of the progressive instability in Bavarian politics created above all by the action of the far Right. By the time of his new appointment, his close contacts with the latter had become notorious.

Von Kahr's aims were not entirely clear, apart from a resolve to crush the Left and restore the monarchy, thus to recreate a strong Bavaria within, eventually, a strong, non-republican Germany of an authoritarian-conservative type. His ideas for Bavaria's economic regeneration lacked coherence, and his attitude to the NSDAP and other radicals in the nationalist camp was essentially ambivalent. He continued his defiance of Berlin, notably when he cancelled the Law for the Protection of the Republic, and when he forced the Reichswehr to take an oath of allegiance to the Bavarian government, but on many other occasions he simply dithered, thereby adding further to an already very confused political situation. In November 1923, when Hitler thought von Kahr was his ally in the fight against Berlin and when the latter probably felt he had brought the NSDAP into his orbit of control, the crisis culminated in farce at the Bürgerbräukeller. Hitler coerced von Kahr and leading associates into supporting the proclamation of the 'national revolution', only for the General State Commissioner, once free of intimidation, to order the dispersal of the revolutionaries by the forces of the state. The rapid collapse of the putsch marked the end of the political upheaval in Bavaria, but the events that led to it inevitably rebounded on the government, and von Kahr resigned in February 1924. A prosecution witness at Hitler's trial for high treason in Munich in the spring of that year, he then resumed his career in the civil service, securing appointment, like his father before him, to the presidency of the Bavarian Administrative Court. Retired in 1930, he fell victim to Hitler's revenge four years later during the Röhm putsch: von Kahr was murdered in Dachau concentration camp on 30 June 1934.

## Further Reading

G. von Kahr, 'Reden zur bayerischen Politik. Ausgewählte Reden des bayerischen Ministerpräsidenten', *Politische Zeitfragen*, 2, 1920, nos 22–24, pp. 345–91. See also H.J. Gordon, *Hitler and the Beer Hall Putsch*, Princeton, 1972; H. Fenske, *Konservatismus und Rechtsradikalismus in Bayern nach 1918*, Bad Homburg, 1969; F. Wiesemann, *Die Vorgeschichte der nationalsozialistischen Machtübernahme in Bayern 1932/33*, Berlin, 1975; D.R. Dorondo, *Bavaria and German Federalism. Reich to Republic, 1918–33, 1945–49*, London, 1991.

## KAPP, Wolfgang (1858–1922)

The leader of the notorious putsch against the Republic in March 1920, when he seized the authority and title of Reich Chancellor for a few days, Kapp was born on 24 July 1858 in New York, where his father, a liberal revolutionary in 1848 and later Reichstag deputy, had fled to escape the reactionary crackdown that ensued. On the family's return to Germany in 1870, he pursued his studies at the universities of Tübingen, Göttingen and Berlin, completing a doctorate in law, and managed the family estate at Pilsen (later Pilzeň). Although he appeared to epitomise the archetypal upper-class Prussian, he was in fact an exemplar of the 'feudalized' bourgeoisie who identified wholly with the Junker aristocracy. A member of the German Conservative Party, he was a *Landrat* (district magistrate) in his home province of Guben from 1890 to 1899, served for seven years as a highly placed civil servant, and from 1906 to 1920 was General Director of Estates in East Prussia – an honorary position based on co-operative land credit institutes. As a founder of the Society for Internal Colonization, he was particularly concerned after 1908 with plans for rural settlement in East Prussia, working closely with the Agrarian League (Bund der Landwirte). Politically, Dr Kapp was a staunch conservative-agrarian and militant nationalist, with a profound antipathy towards Poles. His longer-term aim in politics was to create a mass movement of the Right, embracing the lower classes with promises of social reform, which would rival and in time supplant the SPD.

One of the most extreme chauvinists during the First World War and a well-known critic of Chancellor Bethmann-Hollweg, Kapp was a co-founder (with Admiral von Tirpitz) and deputy chairman (1917–18) of the radical right-wing German Fatherland Party. A member of the last imperial Reichstag in 1918, he joined the DNVP after the November Revolution, serving on its national executive as the representative of East Prussia.

A propagandist in 1919 of a military dictatorship and of a war against Poland to recover the lost province of West Prussia, Kapp was already before his coup attempt a known agitator of a radical nationalist type who excoriated the democratic Republic in language which possibly only a Hitler could emulate. The enduring economic and political crisis in Germany in the early post-war period, the activity of the Communists, and also the dismay and resentment in military circles at the severe reductions in the army establishment, combined to provide the background to the putsch. The politically ambitious Kapp found a willing accomplice in General Walther von Lüttwitz, commander of the First Army District in Berlin, to whom the Ehrhardt Brigade was responsible. On the latter's occupation of the government sector in Berlin on 13 March 1920, the Reich cabinet fled to Dresden, and further to Stuttgart, uncertain of its future, particularly after General Hans von Seeckt, chief of the Truppenamt, had declared that 'Reichswehr does not fire on Reichswehr'. But the putsch was a clumsily executed affair, lacking clear direction and leadership, and was quickly defeated by two principal forms of resistance: a general strike by the socialist trade unions, who saw the episode as an assault on 'their' parliamentary Republic, and the refusal of the higher civil service to co-operate. Kapp was left with no option but to resign and effect an ignominious exit from the capital. He went into exile in Sweden. He did not return to Germany until spring 1922, by which time he was in poor health. He died in Leipzig while awaiting trial for his part in the attempted coup on 12 June 1922.

The political implications of the affair were considerable. Governments in several major states, including Prussia and Bavaria, were soon replaced, the date of the next Reichstag elections was brought forward, revolutionary activity was further encouraged, notably in the Ruhr, and subsequently in Hamburg, central Germany and Munich, and the status and role of the army became even more problematical. Above all, the Kapp Putsch gave an unequivocal warning to the Republic of the ever-present danger from the Right.

## Further Reading

J. Erger, *Der Kapp-Lüttwitz-Putsch. Ein Beitrag zur deutschen Innenpolitik 1919–1920*, Düsseldorf, 1967; E. Könnemann (ed.), *Arbeiterklasse siegt über Kapp und Lüttwitz. Quellen*, 2 vols, East Berlin, 1971; G. Krüger, *Die Brigade Ehrhardt*, Hamburg, 1971; G. Eliasberg, *Der Ruhrkrieg von 1920*, Bad Godesberg, 1974; D. Orlow, 'Preussen und der Kapp Putsch', *Vierteljahrshefte für Zeitgeschichte*, 26, 1978, pp. 191–236.

## KEIL, Wilhelm (1870–1968)

Born into a working-class family in Helsa, near Kassel, on 24 July 1870, and a turner by trade, Keil cut his political teeth in the increasingly bitter struggle between the radical and revisionist wings of the SPD in Württemberg before the First World War. As an editor from 1896 until 1903 and chief editor until 1911 of the principal party newspaper in that state, the *Schwäbische Tagwacht*, he had come round to the revisionist view on most aspects of party policy, but was compelled to resign by the radicals, complaining that personal quarrels were making his life in the party unbearable. Until the outbreak of war, therefore, he confined his activities to his duties as a member of the regional party executive and of the Württemberg Landtag, where he sat from 1900 until 1933. As a right-wing socialist and patriot, he supported the SPD's approval of war credits in August 1914, and three months later he was reinstated as chief editor of the *Tagwacht* in order to bring its policy into harmony with the national and regional party line. He remained its chief editor until 1930, and a freelance contributor from then until its prohibition in 1933.

A Reichstag member from 1910 until October 1932 – he was not put on the SPD list of candidates for the November Reichstag election that year – Keil emerged as a well-informed party spokesman on financial and tax matters. Having made a noted contribution to discussion of the draft Weimar Constitution in 1918–19, he proceeded to express clear and helpful thoughts about the ongoing debate on tax and financial reform. Following the collapse of the Kapp Putsch, for instance, he called for nationalization of both the coal and potash industries, which he believed would serve the dual purpose of raising production and also strengthening the miners' confidence in socialism and the Republic. In October 1921 he warned the government that the SPD would not agree to new consumer taxes unless it presented a comprehensive plan to halt inflation. At the same time, in the early 1920s, he was heavily involved in the politics of Württemberg. A proponent of coalition policies with the moderate bourgeois parties after the war, he was president of the Württemberg State Assembly in 1919, and Minister of Labour and Agriculture from November 1921 until June 1923. Chairman of the party regional executive committee for many years, Keil was proposed by it for the post of Prime Minister (*Staatspräsident*) in 1928: his candidature was defeated by a change in coalition government, when the Centre Party decided to join the DNVP and Peasants' League rather than the SPD.

Proclaiming at the 1925 SPD national congress that his party was 'the true upholder of the democratic Republic' and 'the champion of the poor, the workers and the disinherited', Keil was always eager to have the SPD in national government rather than being a mere onlooker, as it was from 1923 until 1928. He was critical of its failure to find an acceptable way of maintaining the Grand Coalition in March 1930, and the following September, at a meeting in Dresden of German municipal bodies, he created something of a sensation by advocating SPD support for, rather than mere toleration of, Brüning's government if it wished to prevent the NSDAP from coming to power. Unlike many of his colleagues, he had a realistic understanding, even in 1930, of the danger posed by Hitler. By the same token, he criticized the SPD's failure to show more flexibility in its dealings with the von Papen cabinet, arguing that however distasteful it was, it at least acted as a barrier to the National Socialists.

After 1933 Keil regarded any illegal resistance by the party as senseless, and consequently withdrew from politics until the end of the Third Reich. He was never arrested, imprisoned or seriously harassed by the regime. He resumed his long political career in 1945 at the age of seventy-five years, and from 1946 until 1952 served as President of the Baden-Württemberg Landtag. Keil died in Ludwigsburg on 5 April 1968.

## Further Reading

W. Keil, *Erlebnisse eines Sozialdemokraten*, 2 vols, Stuttgart, 1948. See also W. Pyta, *Gegen Hitler und für die Republik. Die Auseinandersetzung der deutschen Sozialdemokratie mit der NSDAP in der Weimarer Republik*, Düsseldorf, 1989; R. Schaefer, *SPD in der Ära Brüning. Tolerierung oder Mobilisierung? Handlungsspielräume und Strategien sozialdemokratischer Politik 1930–1932*, Frankfurt am Main, 1990.

## KOCH-WESER, Erich (1875–1944)

The leader of the DDP from 1924 until 1930 came into Weimar politics after enjoying a meteoric rise in Prussian municipal administration during the imperial era. Born in Bremerhaven on 26 February 1875, and of partly Jewish origin, he took a degree in law and political science, and secured his first major appointment as Mayor of Delmenhorst in 1901. Until 1909 he also sat in the Oldenburg state assembly, before moving as *Stadtdirektor* to his town of birth and in 1913 to Kassel as Lord Mayor, where he remained until 1919. As such he was a member of the Prussian Upper House (Herrenhaus) and of the German Municipal Assembly (Städtetag) until 1918. His political sympathies already lay with the liberal cause, and he emerged as a disciple of Friedrich Naumann's national-social philosophy on the left wing of the National Liberal Party.

A co-founder of the DDP in 1918, Koch-Weser made an outstanding contribution to the framing of the Weimar Constitution and was already on course as one of the most humane, moderate and perceptive politicians of his generation. Although not a particularly forceful personality, his intelligence and extraordinary ability to grasp problems quickly drew admiration from colleagues and opponents alike. A member of the National Assembly and of the Reichstag in the period 1919–30, he was elected to the DDP's national executive committee in July 1919, and three months later was appointed Reich Minister of the Interior, a post he retained through a number of cabinets until May 1921. He also served as Vice-Chancellor in the short-lived Hermann Müller cabinet in 1920. As Interior Minister he acquitted himself very well indeed, despite having to address a host of complex issues, including the enforcement of the Disarmament Law in recalcitrant Bavaria. A vigorous proponent of constitutional centralism that allowed, nevertheless, considerable scope for devolution of power to the states, he was given an opportunity here to put into practice what he preached in order to reach a settlement acceptable to both sides. As he was to appreciate more fully later, however, the real challenge in the debate over *Reichsreform* was to find a formula which reconciled Prussian interests to those of the Reich.

Elected party chairman and leader of its parliamentary delegation in January 1924, Koch-Weser's main task was to revive political liberalism as an important political force, for there were already a number of indications that not only the DDP but also the DVP had passed the peak of their popularity with the middle-class electorate. Until 1929 he dismissed the idea of a united liberal party as unrealistic, preferring instead to promote closer working ties with the DVP, and to make the DDP a more willing coalition partner in government. When Chancellor Hans Luther resigned in December 1925, Koch-Weser was asked to form a cabinet (after Fehrenbach had declined to do so) on the basis of a grand coalition. However, his efforts came unstuck, thanks mainly to the opposition of the SPD. When Luther was again charged with forming a government he designated the DDP leader as his Interior Minister, but when the BVP objected, Koch-Weser gracefully and unselfishly withdrew, while ensuring that his party stayed in the coalition. But he received another chance to demonstrate his sound ministerial qualities when he served as Reich Minister of Justice in the Müller-led 'Grand Coalition' government from June 1928 until April 1929.

By the late 1920s, when German middle-class politics was in considerable flux, Koch-Weser had to recognize that his pursuit of policies based on principle as well as interest had only confused the DDP's ideological identity even further than had been the case when he became party leader, and aggravated the legitimacy crisis which had afflicted the party since 1923–24. Despite his excellent personal qualities and many fine speeches in favour of democratic-liberal reform at home and a realistic foreign policy, his leadership had obvious limitations. Above all, he had been unable to salvage the DDP's electoral fortunes. In 1929–30, Koch-Weser campaigned for a realignment of the party system in a way beneficial to the liberal Centre, envisaging an entirely new party capable of attracting support from the left-wing of his own party to moderate sections of the DNVP. This initiative soon proved abortive, as did another attempt to reach agreement with the DVP alone. All that came of his manoeuvring was a merger of the DDP with the Young German Order and the People's National Reich Association (Volksnationale Reichsvereinigung) to form the German State Party. But when the Young Germans seceded just after the Reichstag elections in September 1930, Koch-Weser felt obliged to resign as party leader and quit politics altogether. From October 1930 until his emigration to Brazil in autumn 1933, he worked at his flourishing Berlin law practice. He died in Rolandia, Brazil, on 19 October 1944.

*Further Reading*

E. Koch-Weser (with Hermann Luppe), *Der grossdeutsche Einheitsstaat. Das Ziel und der Weg*, Berlin, 1927; E. Koch-Weser, *Einheitsstaat und Selbstverwaltung*, Berlin, 1928; *Deutschlands Aussenpolitik in der Nachkriegszeit 1919–1929*, Berlin, 1929; *Und dennoch aufwärts! Eine deutsche Nachkriegsbilanz*, Berlin, 1933; *Hitler and Beyond. A German Testament*, New York, 1945. See also E. Pörtner, 'Koch-Wesers Verfassungsentwurf. Ein Beitrag zur Ideengeschichte der deutschen Emigration', *Vierteljahrshefte für Zeitgeschichte*, 14, 1966, pp. 280–98; G. Arns, 'Erich Koch-Wesers Aufzeichnungen vom 13. Februar 1919', *Vierteljahrshefte für Zeitgeschichte*, 17, 1969, pp. 96–115; W. Stephan, *Aufstieg und Verfall des Linksliberalismus 1918–1933. Geschichte der Deutschen Demokratischen Partei*, Göttingen, 1973; L.E. Jones, *German Liberalism and the Dissolution of the Weimar Party System, 1918–1933*, Chapel Hill, 1988; D. Langewiesche, *Liberalismus in Deutschland*, Frankfurt am Main, 1988.

## KOENEN, Wilhelm (1886-1963)

Later eulogized as personifying the revolutionary proletarian struggle in Germany in the twentieth century, Koenen was born on 7 April 1886 into a politically active working-class family in Hamburg, though he made his own mark principally in central parts of the country. Joining the SPD in the early 1900s, he edited the party newspaper in Halle from 1911 until 1914, but during the war became associated with the radicals in the party who seceded in 1917 to found the USPD. During 1918–19, he emerged as one of the most energetic and decisive leaders of the council movement. While a USPD deputy in the National Assembly, he was instrumental (with Bernhard Düwell) in organizing the movement in Halle-Merseburg in a particularly radical manner. For a brief period in early 1919 it assumed control of the Prussian Mining Office in Halle, which supervised all mines in central Germany, and demanded a wholesale programme of socialization and democratization. A general strike was launched to press these demands and for a time proved effective. Koenen opposed any measure of socialization from above which would deprive the workers of their right to participate in decision-making: it had to come from below, which in his view meant an extension of the council system. Although the overall operation petered out, Koenen had demonstrated an advanced understanding of key issues in the labour sphere, especially where workers' control and participation were concerned. Always alert to the revolutionary potential in any given political situation, his impatience for a thoroughgoing proletarian assault on the state was again revealed in the immediate aftermath of the Kapp Putsch when he supported left-wing and trade union demands for a workers' government and the elimination from positions of power of 'bourgeois reactionaries'.

Appointed a secretary at USPD headquarters in 1920, he was an advocate of amalgamation with the KPD, and when the party split over the issue towards the end of that year he led its left wing over to the Communist side. A member of the KPD's central committee from that time until 1924, and again in 1929–33, he emerged as a leader of the so-called Centre Group amidst the faction fighting that characterized the party's development. A keen observer of the wider political scene, he continued to urge the cause of revolutionary action by the proletariat – for example, in June 1922, in the wake of Walther Rathenau's murder, where he believed there was a chance of the state being taken over. An outspoken critic of the Dawes Plan in the Reichstag, where he sat from 1920 until 1932, Koenen was consistently able to define a coherent party perspective on the most important matters of national politics, while within the party he developed specialist knowledge of organizational and trade union affairs. He addressed these issues very often in the journal *Internationale Presse-Korrespondenz*, and was also noted for his admiration of the Soviet Union. From 1926 until 1932 he served on the Berlin city council, and from April 1932 until its dissolution in March 1933 he was a deputy in the Prussian Landtag. Here, on 4 February 1933, he delivered a passionate denunciation of the NSDAP.

Fleeing Germany in spring 1933, he spent the next twelve years as an exile, latterly in London, working on behalf of the underground Communist movement. He returned to the Soviet zone of Germany at the end of 1945 and played a major role in constructing the power base of the SED in Saxony. From 1949 until his death in East Berlin on 19 October 1963, Koenen was a hardline member of the party's central committee.

## Further Reading

W. Koenen, *Meine Begegnungen mit Lenin*, East Berlin, 1957; 'Zur Frage der Möglichkeit einer Arbeiterregierung nach dem Kapp-Putsch', *Beiträge zur Geschichte der deutschen Arbeiterbewegung*, 4, 1962, pp. 342–52. See also H. Naumann: 'Verkörperung des Kampfes dreier Generationen der revolutionären Arbeiterbewegung', *Beiträge zur Geschichte der deutschen Arbeiterbewegung*, 13, 1971, pp.287–95; H. Naumann, *Wilhelm Koenen*, Leipzig, 1977; H. Weber, *Kommunismus in Deutschland 1918–1945*, Darmstadt, 1983.

## KÖHLER, Heinrich (1878–1949)

This Centre Party politician's appearance on the national stage was brief but highly controversial. Appointed Reich Minister of Finance in Wilhelm Marx's fourth cabinet that came into office in January 1927, Köhler, who had been a very successful finance minister in his home state of Baden from 1920 until 1927, believed that the interests of big business had dictated national policy for too long and that the public sector interest required more recognition. As a career civil servant, he had, in particular, considerable sympathy for the plight of the country's officials, whose standard of living had declined drastically since the end of the war: the hyperinflation crisis resulted in their salary levels falling further behind. He resolved to increase their salaries by up to 33 per cent, and in the Reichstag in autumn 1927 he was given all-party support for his proposal. But his policy came under fierce attack from the Reichsbank, trade unions and even the reparations overseer, the American banker, Parker Gilbert. Köhler justified the increases as representing the ending of a major social injustice, and also on the basis that the Republic's servants were entitled to think that the state was concerned for their material welfare and morale. The broader political implications were still being felt during Brüning's chancellorship when the issue of civil service pay reappeared within the framework of his retrenchment policy.

Köhler became involved in a second major controversy when, in early 1928, he publicly stated that he did not think, as Reich Finance Minister enjoying an intimate overview of the country's budgetary condition, that Germany would be able in the future to carry out her obligations under the Dawes Plan. His government colleagues were acutely embarrassed by this gaffe. In more general terms, a number of influential personalities were critical of what they regarded as the inflationary tendencies of his financial strategy, which they alleged contributed in no small measure to Germany's severe budget crisis even before the Depression struck.

Köhler was born into a Catholic household in Karlsruhe on 29 September 1878 and represented the Centre Party in the town council from 1911 to 1913 before taking a seat in the Baden Lower House. During the First World War he served the German civil administration in occupied Belgium as a customs commissioner. After 1918 he joined the Baden state government as press officer of the Minister of the Interior and then in 1920 became Minister of Finance. In 1923–24 and again in 1926 he headed the government as *Staatspräsident*. Following his period as Reich Finance Minister, he sat for the Centre Party in the Reichstag from 1928 until 1932, contributing to some effect to discussion of financial and budgetary matters. From 1933 to 1939 he was a financial consultant in industry. Köhler came out of retirement after 1945 to assist in the reconstruction of government in Baden and was subsequently appointed Deputy Prime Minister of Baden-Württemberg (northern sector). From 1946 until his death in Karlsruhe on 6 February 1949 he held a series of further governmental posts, including the chairmanship of the North Baden state presidium.

## Further Reading

J. Becker (ed.), *Heinrich Köhler. Lebenserinnerungen des Politikers und Staatsmannes 1878–1949*, Stuttgart, 1964; R. Morsey, *Die deutsche Zentrumspartei 1917–1923*, Düsseldorf, 1966; H. Rehberger, *Die Gleichschaltung des Landes Baden 1932–33*, Heidelberg, 1966; W. Benz, *Süddeutschland in der Weimarer Republik. Ein Beitrag zur deutschen Innenpolitik 1918–1923*, Berlin, 1970; T. Schnabel (ed.), *Die Machtergreifung in Südwestdeutschland. Das Ende der Weimarer Republik in Baden und Württemberg, 1928–1933*, Stuttgart, 1982.

# KÖSTER, Adolf (1883–1930)

In a career tragically cut short while in his prime, Köster brought his patriotism, learning and humanist socialism with enthusiasm and intelligence to the cause of the democratic Republic in his capacity as politician and senior diplomat. His conviction that a state based on sound parliamentary principles was the only feasible option for an advanced industrial country like Germany was carried into every activity.

He was born on 8 March 1883 in Verden/Aller, the son of an army sergeant and customs official. After studying theology at several universities, he took his doctorate at Erlangen in 1907 with a dissertation entitled 'Pascal's Ethics', and went on to take his *Habilitation* five years later. From 1912–13 he was lecturer in pedagogy and philosophy at Munich's Technische Hochschule, putting his name to a number of literary-theological works. A member of the SPD from 1906, he was not called up for military service in 1914 because of a heart complaint, and instead spent the war years as a reporter at the Front for *Vorwärts* and the *Berliner Tageblatt*.

Köster's political career began in earnest with his appointment as an assistant in the Reich Chancellery in November 1918, where he was given the specific task of collecting and editing documents for an official White Book by the German government on the events preceding its peace offer to the Allies in October 1918. He had to break off from this task (Arnold Brecht completed the work, which was published in 1919) when in April 1919 he was appointed Prussian State Commissioner in Schleswig-

Holstein and German State Commissioner for the impending plebiscite in Schleswig. His work in overseeing the plebiscite in March 1920 drew wide admiration, and he was rewarded with the post of Reich Foreign Minister in Hermann Müller's first cabinet (March–June 1920). When the Reichstag elections that were held in June 1920 belatedly took place in Schleswig-Holstein (February 1921), Köster was elected to serve the SPD. As Reich Minister of the Interior in the second Wirth cabinet from October 1921 until November 1922, he was confronted with the problem of continuing political unrest, which culminated in Walther Rathenau's assassination in June 1922. Köster was instrumental in the introduction of the consequent Law for the Protection of the Republic. From 1923 until 1928 he served with distinction as German ambassador to Latvia, and from 1928 until his death in Belgrade on 18 February 1930 as ambassador to Yugoslavia.

*Further Reading*

A. Köster, *Secrets of German Progress*, London, 1917; *Der Kampf um Schleswig*, Berlin, 1921. See also K. Doss, *Reichsminister Adolf Köster, 1883–1930. Ein Leben für die Weimarer Republik*, Düsseldorf, 1978.

## KUBE, Wilhelm (1887–1943)

Before joining the NSDAP in February 1928 and then developing as one of its leading personalities during the last, critical phase of the Weimar Republic, Kube had already pursued a variegated career on the right wing of German politics, both before and after the First World War. He was born the son of an army sergeant and later minor civil servant on 13 November 1887 in Glogau, attended the Gymnasium zum Grauen Kloster in Berlin and took a degree in history and political economy at the University of Berlin in 1912. While a student he had co-founded the Deutsch-Völkischer Studentenbund, and in his graduation year was appointed chairman of the Völkische Akademikerverband in Berlin. Employed as a journalist and publicist on conservative newspapers in Breslau and Wismar, his political engagement continued with his membership of the Deutschsoziale Partei in 1911–13, in his capacity from 1913 until 1920 as general secretary of the German Conservative Party in Silesia, and for a brief period in 1917–18 as general secretary of the German Conservative Association. He briefly saw military service in 1918 as a member of the Home Guard, having been excused frontline duty because of a heart complaint.

From 1920 until 1923, Kube was general secretary of the Silesian section of the DNVP and leader of its affiliated youth group, the Reichsverband der Bismarck-Jugend; in 1922 he served the party as a branch secretary and a city councillor in Berlin. On joining the *völkisch* movement in 1923, he founded and led the Deutscher Bismarck-Orden, a youth group, and the following year entered the Reichstag as a deputy for the Deutschvölkische Freiheitspartei (German Racist-Nationalist Freedom Party), remaining there under various *völkisch* guises until joining the NSDAP. Ironically, his own extremist organization, the Völkisch-Soziale Arbeitsgemeinschaft

Gross-Berlins, which he founded in 1926, had been frequently harassed by the National Socialists.

Elected to the Prussian Landtag for the NSDAP in May 1928, Kube's experience and skill as a public speaker – he had 'a voice like a rhinoceros', according to Hitler – proved invaluable to a party somewhat lacking in political talent. Under his chairmanship from 1929, the National Socialist delegation came increasingly to the fore in the assembly, latterly becoming the major scourge of the socialist-led Prussian government. From September 1928 until 1933 he was also *Gauleiter* of Ostmark, and assumed a number of other important responsibilities, such as acting as one of the party's national electoral supervisors for the Reichstag elections in July 1932. Kube was never far from controversy, as in January 1932, when he attacked the Protestant churches for their lack of support for the anti-republican opposition and proposed that a single *Reichskirche* should replace them. Thanks to his pressure, the NSDAP organized its own church party to contest parish elections in the Old Prussian Union in November 1932 under the name of 'Glaubensbewegung Deutsche Christen'.

As *Oberpräsident* of Brandenburg (March 1933) and *Gauleiter* of Kurmark (May 1933), Kube played a vigorous part in the consolidation of the National Socialist takeover of power, with particular responsibility for dealing with political appointments, subject to higher authority. In November 1933 he was elected to the Reichstag for Frankfurt an der Oder. But his career was shattered in 1936 when his involvement in an unseemly divorce led to a confrontation with the chairman of the Party Court, Walter Buch, whose wife was alleged by Kube to be of Jewish ancestry. He was forced to resign all his offices, though was permitted to retain the title of *Gauleiter*. Rehabilitated in 1941 and appointed Commissioner-General for Belorussia, where he established a benevolent despotism because he considered the indigenous population to be Aryan, Kube was assassinated by a Soviet partisan at his headquarters in Minsk on 22 September 1943.

## Further Reading

W. Kube (ed.), *Deutsch-völkische Hochschulblätter*, Berlin 1911–18; W. Kube, *Nach der Aufrichtung des Dritten Reiches. Nationalsozialistische Aufsätze und Reden*, Langensalza, 1933; W. Kube (ed.), *Almanach der nationalsozialistischen Revolution*, Berlin, 1934. See also G. Altensteig, *Wilhelm Kube*, Leipzig, 1933; H. Heiber, 'Aus den Akten des Gauleiters Kube. Dokumentation', *Vierteljahrshefte für Zeitgeschichte*, 4, 1956, pp. 67–92.

Of further interest are L. Hertzman, *DNVP. Right-Wing Opposition in the Weimar Republic 1918–1924*, Lincoln, Nebraska, 1963; P. Hüttenberger, *Die Gauleiter*, Stuttgart, 1969; J. Striesow, *Die Deutschnationale Volkspartei und die Völkisch-Radikalen 1918–1922*, 2 vols, Frankfurt am Main, 1981.

# KÜLZ, Wilhelm (1875–1948)

An outstanding career in local government, liberal party politics on the national stage, and in the Reich cabinet gave Külz a respected and influential position at various levels in the life of the Weimar Republic. Born the son of a Protestant pastor in Borna, near Leipzig, on 18 February 1875, he completed a doctorate in legal studies and pursued a career in government administration, becoming mayor of Bückeburg in 1904 and Lord Mayor of Zittau in 1912; for a brief period between these posts, in 1907–08, he was Reich Commissioner in the German colony of South West Africa.

Külz joined the DDP in 1919, representing it in the National Assembly and then in the Reichstag until 1930; from 1930 until 1932 he sat for the German State Party. As a spokesman for local government affairs he was always well informed, the more so as he was a Deputy Mayor of Dresden from 1923 and Lord Mayor of that city from 1931 until dismissed by the National Socialist regime in March 1933. When Hans Luther was assembling his second cabinet in early 1926 his first choice for the post of Reich Interior Minister was Erich Koch-Weser, but when the BVP objected to his appointment, Luther turned to Külz, who continued to serve in the following Marx administration until January 1927. He had an eventful period of office, having to deal with the settlement issue of the former German princes, the conflict over the national flag and, even more controversially, the Law for the Protection of Youth from Trashy and Erotic Literature. He was responsible for the preparation and presentation of the draft Bill in the Reichstag, and thus addressed head-on questions of definition of the literature to be banned, and of freedom of artistic and literary expression. His own party divided sharply on the matter, and when it came to a vote in December 1926 only 12 of the 30-strong delegation supported him. However, several liberal notables, including Theodor Heuss and Gertrud Bäumer, welcomed the measure. The DDP consequently forfeited some middle-class electoral backing, and Külz's personal standing in the party became somewhat ambivalent. A final area of conflict arose when he proposed in 1926 changes which would have altered the powers of implementation relating to Article 48 of the Constitution, but the matter had to be dropped in the face of strong opposition, not least from the Reich President. Külz did not lose sight of the wider issue of *Reichsreform* later, in the early 1930s, when he had it accepted as a major priority in the programme of the German State Party.

During the Third Reich, Külz was employed as a financial consultant, but returned to active politics after 1945 as a co-founder of the Liberal Democratic Party in the Soviet zone of Germany. But until his death in East Berlin on 10 April 1948 he co-operated in a number of ways with the Communist Party (SED), even when it became obvious that bourgeois liberalism had no place in that part of the divided country.

## Further Reading

W. Külz, *Deutsche Wiedergeburt*, East Berlin, 1947. See also A. Behrendt, *Wilhelm Külz. Aus dem Leben eines Suchenden*, East Berlin, 1968; K.-H. Minuth (ed.), *Akten der Reichskanzlei. Weimarer Republik. Die Kabinette Luther I und II: 15. Januar 1925 bis 5. Dezember 1925; 20. Januar 1926 bis 12. Mai 1926*, 2 vols, Boppard, 1977; H. Robel (ed.), *Wilhelm Külz. Ein Liberaler zwischen Ost und West. Aufzeichnungen 1947–1948*, Munich, 1989.

# LANDSBERG, Otto (1869-1957)

Landsberg, whose political importance centres very largely on his high-profile role in the November Revolution and its immediate aftermath, was born into a comfortable middle-class Jewish home in Rybnik, Upper Silesia, on 4 December 1869. A law graduate of the University of Berlin, he joined the SPD in 1890, representing it in the Reichstag from 1912 until 1918, in the National Assembly and again in the Reichstag from December 1924 until 1933. Decidedly on the reformist wing of the party, he supported the war credits motion in parliament in 1914, and adhered to a firm patriotic line throughout the First World War. At the SPD party congress in Würzburg in October 1917 he spoke out in favour of achieving socialism within the framework of a parliamentary democracy, and also of bringing about a reunification of the German socialist movement. By 1918 he was a respected party spokesman on legal matters.

As one of the three Majority Socialist members in the Council of People's Representatives in late 1918 – the term 'People's Representatives' was suggested by him as preferable to the Bolshevik 'Commissar' – Landsberg fully backed Ebert's alliance with the army high command and tough stance towards the radical Left. For this reason he was a figure of hate among left-wing USPD and Communist followers. He also adopted a hard line towards the German–Polish conflict in the eastern provinces, and in December 1918 came out in favour of a German declaration of war against the Poles, for whom he harboured a particular loathing. As an overall advocate of the use of force in that disturbed period, Landsberg backed a military response to the sailors' revolt in Kiel and Wilhelmshaven. It was also he who advised the government to transfer to the relative tranquillity of Weimar during the worst of the upheavals in late 1918 and early 1919.

An SPD deputy in the National Assembly, Landsberg was appointed Reich Minister of Justice in the cabinet head by Philipp Scheidemann (February–June 1919), and was a member of the German delegation which received the Allied peace terms at Versailles. He refused to sign the treaty and resigned with the rest of the cabinet. When a vote on it was taken in the National Assembly, he was absent. During those first six months of 1919, a proposal to appoint him a Prussian minister without portfolio was rejected by Prussian ministers suspicious of possible central government encroachment on Prussia's authority. In spring 1920 he forcefully but unsuccessfully objected in the National Assembly to the appointment of the German nationalist, Walther von Keudall, as Reich Minister of the Interior, because of his notable involvement in the Kapp Putsch. From mid-1920 until early 1923, Landsberg spent a difficult and frustrating time as German ambassador to Belgium. He was recalled to Berlin when Belgium joined with France in occupying the Ruhr. He built up a flourishing law practice in Berlin from 1923, acting for Reich President Ebert in the infamous slander case in Magdeburg the following year. A founder member in 1891 of the Association to Combat Anti-Semitism (Verein zur Abwehr des Antisemitismus), he became conspicuously involved in this activity as the political Right emerged as an increasingly powerful force. Landsberg's role in the Reichstag after

1924 was much quieter, though he contributed effectively to the debate when the draft of the new criminal code was brought before the house in May 1927, as well as to discussion of emergency powers under Article 48 when this became an issue in the early days of the Brüning administration.

In 1933 Landsberg went into exile in the Netherlands, where he died on 9 December 1957.

## Further Reading

O. Landsberg, *Student und Politik*, Berlin, 1925; *Die politische Krise der Gegenwart*, Berlin, 1931. See also W.E Mosse and A. Paucker (eds), *Deutsches Judentum in Krieg und Revolution 1916–1923*, Tübingen, 1971; E. Matthias and S. Miller (eds), *Die Regierung der Volksbeauftragten 1918/19*, 2 vols, Düsseldorf, 1969; A.J. Ryder, *The German Revolution of 1918. A Study of German Socialism in War and Revolt*, London, 1967; E. Hamburger, *Juden im öffentlichen Leben in Deutschland*, Tübingen, 1968; S. Miller, *Die Bürde der Macht. Die deutsche Sozialdemokratie 1918–1920*, Düsseldorf, 1978.

# LEDEBOUR, Georg (1850–1947)

Ledebour, a radical socialist revolutionary of the early years of the Weimar Republic, was born to middle-class parents in Hanover on 7 March 1850. After participating in the Franco-Prussian war, he worked as a journalist and teacher before joining the SPD in 1890. Described as 'a pugnacious character' (Arnold Brecht), he diversified his political activities increasingly within the centre-leftist stream of the party, especially following his election to the Reichstag in 1900 and his acquaintanceship with the likes of Karl Kautsky and August Bebel. A noted polemicist in parliament and in the party executive, he developed a radical posture on many important issues which made it inevitable that in August 1914 he should oppose the SPD's stance on war credits. During the war Ledebour moved more and more into the ranks of the party's internal opposition and in February 1915 resigned from the national executive. He represented German socialists at the Zimmerwald Conference in Berne in September 1915, grew close to Hugo Haase, and in 1916 emerged as one of the leaders of a new parliamentary faction within the SPD, the Social Democratic Working Association (Arbeitsgemeinschaft), which was an important stage in the process that finally led to the foundation of the USPD the following year.

The revolutionary upheaval which began in November 1918 created a perfect sphere of political activity for Ledebour's radical zeal. Rejecting an invitation from Friedrich Ebert to join the Council of People's Representatives, he channelled his considerable energy into the supervisory council of the Workers' and Soldiers' Councils in Berlin. When the Congress of Councils elected a *Zentralrat* in December 1918, he and the rest of the USPD refused to participate because of a conflict over the extent of its power. In January 1919 he played a significant role in opposing the Council of People's Representatives, ultimately through the use of violence and involvement in the Spartacus revolt. He was fortunate to escape with his life and shortly thereafter turned his trial in Berlin into something of a personal triumph on behalf of the cause of revolution.

Ledebour was one of the few prominent USPD leaders who resisted all efforts to persuade him to join the KPD. He vigorously opposed his party's proposed affiliation to the Communist International in 1920, and at its conference in Gera in 1922 was equally resistant to the idea of it linking up with the SPD. He and a small group of loyal supporters continued to believe in a middle way between the SPD and KPD, hoping that the worsening economic and financial crisis would give the USPD a boost. When it came to a vote on the unity issue, all but the Ledebour group responded in the affirmative. He vowed to continue with an independent USPD, comprising approximately 10,000 members, based mainly in Berlin and the Ruhr. At the Reichstag elections in May 1924, it attracted 235,000 votes, or 0.8 per cent of the total popular vote. His Reichstag career, which had been resumed in June 1920, came to an end at this juncture. In 1925 his group suffered a further split after a policy clash between himself and Theodor Liebknecht. Ledebour's supporters, numbering some 3000, now united in the Socialist League (Sozialistischer Bund), which existed on the periphery of political life until 1932, when it followed many other leftist splinter groups into the Socialist Workers' Party.

In 1933, at the age of 83, he went into exile in Switzerland, dying in Berne on 31 March 1947.

## Further Reading

G. Ledebour (ed.), *Der Ledebour-Prozess. Gesamtdarstellung des Prozessses gegen Ledebour wegen Aufruhr*, Berlin, 1919. See also M. Ledebour (ed.), *Georg Ledebour. Mensch und Kämpfer*, Frankfurt am Main, 1954; U. Ratz, *Georg Ledebour, 1850–1947. Weg und Wirken eines sozialistischen Politikers*, Berlin, 1969; H. Krause, *USPD. Zur Geschichte der Unabhängigen Sozialdemokratischen Partei Deutschlands*, Frankfurt am Main, 1975; E. Matthias, *Zwischen Räten und Geheimräten. Die deutsche Revolutionsregierung 1918–1919*, Düsseldorf, 1970; C.B. Burdick and R.H. Lutz (eds), *The Political Institutions of the German Revolution 1918–1919*, New York, 1966; E. Kolb and R. Rürup (eds), *Der Zentralrat der deutschen sozialistischen Republik 1918–1919. Quellen zur Geschichte der Rätebewegung in Deutschland 1918/19*, Leiden, 1968.

# LEVI, Paul (1883–1930)

An intellectual tower of strength in various sections of the socialist and Communist movements during the 1920s, Levi was born into a Jewish manufacturing family in Hechingen on 11 March 1883, and took a doctorate in legal studies from the University of Heidelberg before joining the SPD in 1909. He first attracted public attention as Rosa Luxemburg's defence lawyer in her sedition case in early 1914 – a relationship which had a profound impact on his political and emotional development. During the First World War, the latter part of which he spent in Switzerland, he joined Luxemburg in membership of the Spartacus League.

During the post-war revolutionary period, Levi became one of the League's most influential figures, responsible above all for its acceptance of Bolshevism as its ideological and organizational guide. A founder member of the KPD, his advocacy of contesting the National Assembly elections was overruled by a vast majority of party members, though by 1920, by which time the far-leftist element had departed, the party did accept the notion of participating in parliamentary institutions. In June 1920, in consequence, he, a member of the KPD Central Committee, was returned to the Reichstag as one of two Communist deputies (the other being Clara Zetkin). They were the first Communists to sit in parliament in German history. At the unity congress of the KPD and USPD later that year, he was elected to the party chairmanship. However, his occupancy of this office proved short-lived: following a series of differences with the Communist International he resigned. After the failure of the so-called March Action in 1921, which Levi criticized as irresponsible putschism, he was expelled from the KPD altogether. A splinter group which he created with some leaders of the *Obleute* (shop stewards') wing of the party, the Kommunistische Arbeitsgemeinschaft, was ineffective in pursuing a non-violent revolutionary strategy, and he rejoined the SPD via the USPD in 1922.

For the remainder of the 1920s, Levi operated as the constructive leader of the SPD's left wing, which aimed above all for a reunification of the German working-class movement, without subservience to Moscow or the introduction of Leninist organizational techniques. Party life was to be organized along more democratic and political and less bureaucratic lines. Levi expressed these and other views of this grouping in his periodical, *Sozialistische Politik und Wirtschaft*, and, from 1927, in *Der Klassenkampf*. But he also exercised influence throughout the party. In the wake of Walther Rathenau's murder in 1922, for example, it was he who suggested that socialists and trade unionists, together with left-wingers in the Centre Party, form a government to combat the threat from the reactionary Right. Later, in 1928, in the controversy over the pocket battleship A, he criticized the SPD-led government's stance as a betrayal of socialist tradition and argued for an immediate end to the party's coalition policy. When Rudolf Hilferding subsequently moved that a party congress in early 1929 establish an official position on the general matter of national defence, and that a special commission be set up to examine the possibility of presenting a programme to the congress, Levi was appointed a member. He was not a fundamental opponent of the concept of national defence, but resented the anti-republican spirit of the officer corps which made the army an unreliable defender of the Republic.

During the last year of his life, Levi came into public view wearing his defence lawyer's hat in the Jörns–Bornstein case, particularly as he was able to reveal in court further information regarding the circumstances and manner of Rosa Luxemburg's death in 1919. He died in Berlin on 9 February 1930.

## Further Reading

P. Levi, *Unser Weg. Wider den Putschismus* (Berlin 1921); *Der Jörns-Prozess. Rede des Verteidigers Dr Paul Levi*, Berlin, 1929. See also C. Beradt, *Paul Levi. Ein demokratischer Sozialist in der*

*Weimarer Republik*, Frankfurt am Main, 1969; C. Beradt (ed.), *Zwischen Spartakus und Sozialdemokratie. Schriften, Reden und Briefe Paul Levis*, Frankfurt am Main, 1969; R. Lowenthal, 'The Bolshevisation of the Spartakus League', St Anthony's Papers, no. 9, *International Communism*, London, 1960, pp. 23–71; S. Quack, *Geistig frei und niemandes Knecht. Paul Levi und Rosa Luxemburg*, Cologne, 1983; T. Bergmann, *'Gegen den Strom'. Die Geschichte der Kommunistischen-Partei-Opposition*, Hamburg, 1988.

# LIEBKNECHT, Karl (1871–1919)

The revolutionary Communist martyr was born the son of the founder of the SPD, Wilhelm Liebknecht, in Leipzig on 13 August 1871, and quickly became deeply involved himself in the socialist movement, especially its radical stream. As a qualified lawyer, he represented workers and socialist sympathizers in political court cases and soon made his mark as one of the most outspoken and militant members of the SPD in the Prussian House of Deputies, where he sat from 1910 until expelled in 1916 when convicted of treason; he also sat in the Reichstag for much of the same period. Founder of the Socialist Youth International and a Berlin city councillor, he used his political base in the capital to write prolifically on a range of important issues of concern to socialism, and to strengthen the leftist element in the party. Dedicated to the concept and practice of class warfare, Liebknecht was a confirmed revolutionary before the First World War, with imperialism, capitalism and militarism the principal objects of his scorn and denunciation. For his rabid anti-militarist speeches and advocacy of a policy of propaganda and agitation inside army barracks and among the younger generation as part of his scheme for universal disarmament and international reconciliation, he received a prison sentence in 1907. In 1914 he did not at first reject the principle of national defence and as a member of the SPD parliamentary delegation he voted for the war credits in the Reichstag. But he was the first to break ranks when a few months later, on 2 December, he voted against the second War Loans Bill when it came before the house. Thereafter, he was on a collision course with his own party and the imperial authorities.

In May 1915 appeared his notorious pamphlet, *Der Hauptfeind steht im eigenen Land* (*The Main Enemy is at Home*), and on 1 January 1916 emerged the 'Group International' around Liebknecht and Rosa Luxemburg, to be known as the Spartacus Group, which began publication of its own radical periodical. When convicted in 1916 by the Reich Military Court for anti-war agitation in the streets and sentenced to four years' imprisonment, he was expelled from the SPD's parliamentary delegation and from the party altogether at the end of that year. He had consequently become something of a martyr for the Berlin radicals, even before his release from prison following a political amnesty in October 1918. He immediately resumed his anti-militarist and anti-Hohenzollern street agitation, calling for proletarian revolution before the events in November 1918 had taken place.

It is highly questionable whether his intellectual but particularly his political talents were equal to the tasks he set himself in 1918 and early 1919. He was at the centre of radical ferment in Berlin, impatient for action. On 9 November he proclaimed the Free Socialist Republic of Germany from the Royal Palace, just a few hours after Philipp Scheidemann of the Majority Socialists had declared a German Republic. Liebknecht's Spartacist League, which had its founding conference two days later, was quickly pushed out from its position as a propaganda group within the USPD to become a vehicle for a revolution on the Soviet Bolshevik model. Declining an invitation to join the Council of People's Representatives, and showing contempt for other allegedly 'moderate' revolutionary bodies, Liebknecht concentrated on whipping up mass emotions on the streets. At the founding conference of the German Communist Party (KPD) in Berlin at the end of December 1918, he strongly influenced the decision not to participate in National Assembly elections but to seize power through the masses. That he did not have a mandate for such a plan had been shown by his failure to be selected for attendance at the National Congress of Workers' and Soldiers' Councils in Berlin some days previously. Instead, he established a revolutionary committee in early January 1919 to direct the imminent Spartacist Rising and act as a provisional government. Liebknecht was arrested and murdered by *Freikorps* soldiers a few days later, on 15 January, in Berlin's Tiergarten.

## Further Reading

K. Liebknecht, *Gesammelte Reden und Schriften*, 8 vols, East Berlin, 1958–68; *Politische Aufzeichnungen aus seinem Nachlass*, Berlin, 1921. For further reference, see E. Hannover and H. Hannover, *Der Mord an Rosa Luxemburg und Karl Liebknecht. Dokumentation eines politischen Verbrechens*, Frankfurt am Main, 1967; G. Schmidt, *Spartakus. Rosa Luxemburg und Karl Liebknecht*, Frankfurt am Main, 1971; G.A. Ritter and S. Miller (eds), *Die deutsche Revolution 1918–1919. Dokumente*, new edn, Hamburg, 1975; H. Weber (ed.), *Der Gründungsparteitag der KPD. Protokoll und Materialien*, Frankfurt am Main, 1969. Two noteworthy biographies are H. Wohlgemuth, *Karl Liebknecht. Eine Biographie*, East Berlin, 1975; and H. Trotnow, *Karl Liebknecht (1871–1919). A Political Biography*, New York, 1985. See also E. Waldman, *The Spartacist Rising of 1919 and the Crisis of the German Socialist Movement*, Milwaukee, 1958.

# LÖBE, Paul (1875–1967)

The leading Social Democratic parliamentarian and president of the Reichstag was born into a working-class home in Liegnitz on 14 December 1875, and completed his apprenticeship as a compositor. In 1895 he joined the SPD and the trade union movement, and from 1900 until 1920 was chief editor of the party's *Volkswacht* newspaper in Breslau, where he was also a town councillor from 1904 until 1919. A member of the reformist wing of the party, he was in the intellectual circle around the *Sozialistische Monatshefte* and *Neue Gesellschaft* journals, and fully supported the SPD's co-operative stance towards the government during the First World War. A member of the Silesian provincial assembly from 1915 until 1920, he helped establish a people's council (Volksrat) in Breslau, and in 1921 was appointed to the Prussian State Council (Staatsrat). When the three USPD politicians resigned from the Council of People's Representatives in late December 1918, he was one of those selected by his party to replace them, but declined the invitation because of his commitments in Breslau and also because he felt he was not adequately conversant with conditions in Berlin.

A member of the National Assembly, he then sat in the Reichstag from 1920 until 1933 for the SPD, for whose parliamentary delegation he acted as co-chairman. As president of the Reichstag from 1924 until replaced by Hermann Goering following the NSDAP triumph at the July 1932 national elections, Löbe earned cross-party respect for his sensible, even-handed and polite conduct of affairs. His task was especially challenging in the early 1930s when he frequently had to resort to expulsions and police intervention to restore a semblance of order. Goebbels, for example, was ordered to leave the house after grossly insulting the Reich President. As a party politician, Löbe was less successful, on the whole. He could be rather indecisive and inconsistent in argument, and stirred controversy at injudicious moments. When Walther Rathenau was murdered, Löbe claimed that those politicians who vilified government leaders were partially responsible. A year later, he caused widespread dismay in his own party when he stated that the working masses no longer saw the Republic as worth defending because the capitalists and militarists were as powerful as they had been in the Kaiser's time. His solution was the traditional socialist prescription of a reversal to the class struggle. In a further awkward move in December 1926, he embarrassed the army by demanding in an open letter to army minister Otto Gessler a new method of recruitment. He advocated a parliamentary committee to supervise recruitment procedures to ensure that the army was not giving preference to those from a conservative, right-wing background. What he had in mind, of course, was an increase in pro-republican personnel from the working class, thus to strengthen the army's commitment to the Republic if possible. Löbe was not devoid of a touch of realism in the early 1930s, unlike a good number of his colleagues, and in spring 1932 stated quite openly that the SPD had no choice but to support von Hindenburg's re-election as Reich President in order simply to thwart Hitler. His other major function in the Weimar era was his vice-presidency of the Pan-Europa Union.

At the last SPD party conference in early 1933, Löbe was elected to the national executive committee (*Parteivorstand*), but in contrast to the many leaders who quickly fled into exile abroad, he stayed in Germany, clinging to the belief that a legal oppositional stance could serve to moderate terrorism. Detained by the regime for six months in 1933, he subsequently made contact with Goerdeler's resistance circle, and in the aftermath of the July Plot in 1944 was arrested and sent to a concentration camp. He survived that experience to become a member of the Parliamentary Council in the early post-war years in Western Germany, and a SPD deputy in the Federal Parliament (Bundestag) from 1949 to 1953. He died in Bonn at the age of 92 on 3 August 1967.

## Further Reading

P. Löbe, *Sozialismus, ja oder nein*, Berlin, 1932; *Erinnerungen eines Reichstagspräsidenten*, Berlin, 1949; *Der Weg war lang. Lebenserinnerungen*, Berlin, 1954. See also A. Scholz and W.G. Oschilewski (eds), *Lebendige Tradition. Paul Löbe zum achtzigsten Geburtstag am 14. Dezember 1955*, Berlin, 1955; W.S. Schütz, *Der gerade Weg. Paul Löbe und die deutsche Einheit*, Berlin, 1966.

## LUTHER, Hans (1879-1962)

The holder of a string of top-level ministerial and administrative posts in the Weimar and early Third Reich periods, Luther was born into a middle-class business family in Berlin on 10 March 1879 and had a brilliant career as an undergraduate and postgraduate law student in Berlin, Kiel and Geneva. He climbed the civil service promotion ladder very rapidly, being appointed *Stadtrat* in Magdeburg in 1907, secretary of the Prussian (and then German) Municipal Assembly (Städtetag) in 1913, and Lord Mayor of Essen in 1918, where he remained until 1922. Not affiliated to any political party but close to the DVP, he served as a highly capable Reich Minister of Agriculture in Chancellor Wilhelm Cuno's cabinet from December 1922 until August 1923, and again in the following Stresemann administration from August until October 1923. Dr Luther made his first significant political impact as Reich Minister of Finance under several chancellors from October 1923 until January 1925. Although not the intellectual equal of his predecessor (Hilferding), he was undoubtedly his superior in terms of ability to take decisive action. He was responsible for establishing the new currency, the Rentenmark, following the trauma of hyperinflation, thus laying the first essential foundation for national economic recovery. In aiming for a balanced budget, he introduced a range of tax increases and reductions in public expenditure, while debts written off in 1923 were made subject to tax. Public finances were stabilized and the spectre of hyperinflation was banished. For these accomplishments, Luther deserves to be regarded as the key minister of that period.

As Reich Chancellor from January 1925 until May 1926, Luther faced many complex challenges at home and abroad, but he brought to his task considerable intelligence, patience and statesmanship. In his first cabinet, besides problems over tariff policy and the economy, he had to deal with the crucial area of Germany's foreign relations. Despite certain differences with Stresemann, he supported the Locarno programme, though paid the price of losing the DNVP's support. His second cabinet collapsed over the flag decree of May 1926, which allowed German missions abroad to use the old imperial colours. Out of office, he founded the Bund zur Erneuerung des Reiches (League for the Regeneration of the Reich), which in 1928 presented far-reaching proposals for changing the constitutional status of Prussia and its relationship to the Reich. As President of the Reichsbank from 1930 until 1933, he could hardly have had a more difficult time, and despite using a series of emergency decrees to try to control and stabilize crucial sectors of the banking and financial system, he was unable to prevent catastrophes such as the collapse in July

1931 of the Darmstadt Bank, or to help alleviate the overall economic situation. Hjalmar Schacht was a constant and acerbic critic throughout Luther's tenure.

Forced to resign from the Reichsbank by Hitler in 1933, Luther was given the opportunity to serve his country as ambassador to Washington from 1933 until 1937. He attended to his duties with diligence and dignity, and above all in a manner which satisfied his political masters. He never became a National Socialist; rather his dislike of parliamentary democracy and his generally conservative disposition allowed him to engage in the Third Reich without too much soul-searching. Luther died in Düsseldorf on 11 May 1962.

## Further Reading

H. Luther (ed.), *Stresemann-Buch. Aussprüche, Aufsätze*, Berlin, 1923; *Weimar und Bonn. Zwei Vorträge*, Munich, 1951; *Politiker ohne Partei. Erinnerungen*, Stuttgart, 1960; *Vor dem Abgrund 1930–1933. Reichsbankpräsident in Krisenzeiten*, Berlin, 1964. See also K.-H. Minuth (ed.), *Akten der Reichskanzlei. Weimarer Republik. Die Kabinette Luther I und II: 15. Januar 1925 bis 5. Dezember 1925; 20. Januar 1926 bis 12. Dezember 1926*, 2 vols, Boppard, 1977; H. James, *The Reichsbank and Public Finance in Germany, 1924–1933*, Frankfurt am Main, 1985.

## LUXEMBURG, Rosa (1870–1919)

A major theoretician and committed revolutionary of the radical socialist movement before and after the First World War, Luxemburg was of Polish Jewish parentage, born in Zamość on 5 March 1870, but educated in Zürich, where she had fled to escape persecution. In 1898 she arrived in Berlin and shortly thereafter joined the SPD, emerging as a champion of its revolutionary Marxist wing. A prolific and intellectually profound writer, she expounded with clarity and passion her ideas on the major political topics of the day. A militant anti-imperialist, she brilliantly enunciated her theory of imperialism in a 1913 publication, *The Accumulation of Capital*, but she was equally devastating in her critiques of nationalism, militarism and revisionism within the SPD. In the mid-1900s she developed the theory of the mass strike weapon as a means to achieve revolution: mobilization of the masses for action was a consistent element in her appeals, and formed the basis of her later ideas on spontaneous revolution. Rejecting the Bolshevik model, she favoured freedom of expression and individual rights within a 'true democracy'. However, while she can be identified as a political leader of challenging ideas, her lack of practical understanding of the dynamics of revolutionary agitation is equally apparent.

Co-founder in December 1913 of the left-radical *Sozialdemokratische Korrespondenz*, Luxemburg was sentenced in February 1914 to one year's imprisonment for inciting soldiers to disobey orders, to a further term of two months in February 1915, and to a third term from 1916 until 1918. Her theses on *The Tasks of International Social Democracy* (1916) were accepted by disparate elements of the radical Left as a point of crystallization, and served as the founding text of the Spartacus Group. In 1917 the latter joined up with the USPD.

Released from prison in November 1918, Luxemburg played a crucial but ephemeral role in the revolutionary events of that period. She was prominent in establishing the Spartacus League and was at the heart of the radical flux in Berlin. Failing to secure election to the National Congress of Workers' and Soldiers' Councils in Berlin in December 1918, she turned her attention to assisting Liebknecht in the creation of the German Communist Party and its organ, *Die Rote Fahne*. The revolutionary propaganda of this small group attracted little support from the workers, but it was none the less determined by early January 1919 to take to the streets. Previously opposed to the idea of an uprising as counter-productive, Luxemburg could not resist the direction of her supporters and reluctantly joined in. Her murder on 15 January by right-wing troops shocked the nation but gave her the status of political martyrdom on the far Left. For conservative and nationalist Germany, however, she personified the restless, cosmopolitan Jewish revolutionary intellectual who inspired in them fear and loathing.

## Further Reading

R. Luxemburg, *Briefe aus dem Gefängnis*, Berlin, 1932. See also C. Zetkin and A. Warski (eds), *Gesammelte Werke von Rosa Luxemburg*, 3 vols, Berlin, 1928; R. Looker (ed.), *Rosa Luxemburg. Selected Political Writings*, London, 1972; S.E. Bonner (ed.), *The Letters of Rosa Luxemburg*, Boulder, Colorado, 1978; A. Laschitza and G. Adler (eds), *Herzlichst Ihre Rosa. Ausgewählte Briefe*, Berlin, 1989. Among the most noteworthy biographies are P. Frölich, *Rosa Luxemburg*, new edn, London, 1972; J.P Nettl, *Rosa Luxemburg*, 2 vols, London, 1966; H. Schulze-Wilde, *Rosa Luxemburg. Eine Biographie*, Munich, 1970; E. Ettinger, *Rosa Luxemburg. A Life*, London, 1987; R. Abraham, *Rosa Luxemburg*, Oxford, 1989. See also A. Laschitza and G. Radczun, *Rosa Luxemburg. Ihr Wirken in der deutschen Arbeiterbewegung*, Frankfurt am Main, 1971.

# MARX, Wilhelm (1863–1946)

Leader of the Centre Party and Reich Chancellor on no fewer than four occasions in the 1920s, there can be little doubt about Marx's importance to Weimar politics, despite his lack of colour and flair. He was a man of solid qualities: diligence, reliability, perseverance and an unshakeable commitment to duty. Pervading all of these was a devout Catholicism. Born in Cologne on 15 January 1863, he took a doctorate in law and built a successful professional career as a judge: in 1921 he attained the rank of Provincial Court president (*Landgerichtspräsident*) in Limburg, and from 1921 until 1923 was, on account of his chairmanship of the Centre Party's Reichstag delegation, *Senatspräsident* in the Supreme Court. Elected to the Prussian House of Deputies in 1899 and to the Reichstag in 1910 (remaining in both until 1918), his political career progressed along steady but unspectacular lines. His prewar involvement in the social-charitable organization, Volksverein für das katholische Deutschland, brought him into its deputy chairmanship from 1919 until 1921, and to the chairmanship itself from 1922 until 1933. A member of the National Assembly and Reichstag from 1919 until 1932, he was also chairman of the

Centre Party from 1922 until 1928, and continued to sit in the Prussian Lower House until 1921.

Appointed Reich Chancellor for the first time in November 1923 after the fall of Stresemann's government, Marx conducted affairs under an emergency law of limited duration. He achieved drastic changes in the composition of the German courts and in both criminal and civic procedure, including the abolition of the all-lay jury system. His government also managed to see through the measures for currency reform and stabilization, with the assistance of the recently appointed president of the Reichsbank, Hjalmar Schacht. When the Reichstag refused the government's request for a prolongation of the enabling law in March 1924, it collapsed a few months later. Marx immediately formed his second cabinet, which came to grief in December 1924 over the issue of the Dawes Plan. He was Prime Minister designate of Prussia for a short spell in early 1925, but lost a vote of confidence in the Landtag, allowing Otto Braun to resume in that office. An active member of the pro-republican paramilitary group, Reichsbanner Schwarz-Rot-Gold, since its foundation in 1924, Marx remained firmly in the political limelight through his candidature for the Reich Presidency in spring 1925. Sponsored by his party in the first round, he received 3.9 million votes, and went into the second ballot with the support of the three Weimar coalition parties against the candidate of the Right, von Hindenburg. Largely because of the Catholic BVP's support for the Prussian Protestant field marshal, Marx lost narrowly, by 13.7 million votes to 14.6 million. As Reich Minister of Justice in Hans Luther's second cabinet (January–May 1926), he had little time to make an enduring impression, though he carefully monitored the legal reforms which he had ushered in while Chancellor in 1923–25. His third and fourth administrations from May 1926 until June 1928 were involved especially in applying the Locarno spirit to the conduct of foreign affairs and in tackling problems of social welfare, including the organization of unemployment insurance. The new scheme of unemployment benefit that was introduced in 1927 was widely regarded as the centrepiece of the entire welfare system in the Weimar Republic. Throughout this period of office, Marx displayed admirable patience in juggling with a variegated alliance of coalition partners. It finally broke in February 1928 over an issue to which he attached great importance: the schools question. A Centre Party Bill to permit Catholic schools in states where the system was non-denominational ran into DVP opposition. The period of relative political and economic stability in Germany over much of which Marx presided as Reich Chancellor was drawing to a close. He resigned as leader of his party in the country and in the Reichstag, but continued to be politically active until 1933.

After many years in retirement, which spanned the National Socialist era, Marx died in Bonn on 5 August 1946, his memoirs unwritten.

## Further Reading

H. Stehkämper (ed.), *Der Nachlass des Reichskanzlers Wilhelm Marx*, 4 vols, Cologne, 1968; U. von Hehl, *Wilhelm Marx, 1863–1946. Eine politische Biographie*, Mainz, 1987. See also G. Gruenthal, *Reichsschulgesetz und Zentrumspartei in der Weimarer Republik*, Düsseldorf, 1968; R. Morsey, *Die Deutsche Zentrumspartei 1917–1923*, Düsseldorf, 1966; R. Morsey, *Der Untergang des politischen Katholizismus. Die Zentrumspartei zwischen christlichem Selbstverständnis und 'Nationaler Erhebung' 1923–1933*, Stuttgart, 1977; M. Stürmer, *Koalition und Opposition in der Weimarer Republik 1924–1928*, Düsseldorf, 1967; G. Abramowski (ed.), *Akten der Reichskanzlei. Weimarer Republik. Die Kabinette Marx I und II*, 2 vols, Boppard, 1973; and in the same series, G. Abramowski (ed.), *Die Kabinette Marx III und IV*, 2 vols, Boppard, 1988.

## MOLDENHAUER, Paul (1876–1946)

This prominent DVP politician and Reich minister was born into a middle-class home in Cologne on 2 December 1876 and completed both his doctorate and *Habilitationsschrift* in economics and law. In 1903 he took up a teaching post at Cologne's Handelshochschule, and from 1907 until 1920 had a professorship. From 1920 until 1929 he held a similar position, specializing in insurance matters, at the University of Cologne. After the First World War he joined the DVP and, with a firm commitment to the free enterprise system, became associated with the party's right wing. In 1923 he became a member of the so-called 'Kalle Committee', a special body established by leaders of the chemical industry to represent their political interests within the DVP and other non-socialist parties. Wilhelm Kalle, a DVP representative in the Prussian Landtag, was its unofficial chairman. A member of the Prussian Lower House himself from 1919 until 1921, Moldenhauer served in the Reichstag from 1920 until 1932, where he was a forthright party spokesman on social welfare. During the 1920s he also made clear his opposition to the idea of a united liberal party. In November 1929 he was appointed Reich Minister of Economics, but one month later succeeded Rudolf Hilferding as Reich Finance Minister in the 'Grand Coalition' government led by Hermann Müller.

In January 1930, Moldenhauer was in the German delegation at the second Hague Conference, where he was significantly involved in final negotiations concerning the Young Plan on reparations. He was responsible for the government agreeing that the Reichsbank be required by German law to participate in the International Bank, something which had been hitherto resisted by the President of the Reichsbank, Hjalmar Schacht. At home, Moldenhauer was immediately confronted by a crisis in the national finances, and had to explain to the Reichstag that the 700 million marks saved by the Reich as a result of the changes made to reparations payments by the Young Plan could not be used to reduce taxes, as hoped, but merely covered the deficit of that fiscal year. To further ensure the Treasury's cash position, he took the extraordinary step of granting a Swedish firm a matches monopoly in Germany in return for a loan of 500 million marks. However, the continued decline in tax revenues and the rapid growth of demand for unemployment benefit brought about a more serious financial crisis for government which effectively ruined his reform programme. While he succeeded in raising some taxes, he signally failed to raise others: thus a proposed special head tax on all adult citizens (*Bürgersteuer*) and a planned levy on salaries of government employees were abandoned mainly due to opposition from his own party's industrial wing. But the fundamental bone of contention was the unemployment insurance scheme which was being bailed out financially by the Reich in a way that could not be sustained for much longer. Moldenhauer had succeeded in having contributions to the scheme from employers and workers increased from 3 per cent to 3.5 per cent of the earnings level, but by February 1930 this had proved inadequate. A further proposal by him to raise the level to 4 per cent was defeated by the DVP, and a compromise formula which had the support of all parties except the SPD likewise floundered. The Müller government consequently collapsed.

Moldenhauer continued to serve the Brüning administration, but when his budget programme was rejected by the DVP Reichstag delegation he was compelled to resign his portfolio in June 1930. Continuing until 1932 as a Reichstag deputy, he held a number of academic posts in Berlin from 1931 until 1943. His attitude towards the National Socialist regime was not entirely unsympathetic. He died in Cologne on 2 February 1946.

## Further Reading

P. Moldenhauer, *Die rheinische Republik*, Berlin, 1920; *Internationale Sozialpolitik*, Leipzig, 1927. See also I. Maurer, *Reichsfinanzen und Grosse Koalition. Zur Geschichte des Reichskabinetts Müller (1928–1930)*, Frankfurt am Main, 1973; H. Timm, *Die Deutsche Sozialpolitik und der Bruch der Grossen Koalition im März 1930*, 2nd edn, Düsseldorf, 1982; K. Borchardt, *Wachstum, Krisen, Handlungsspielräume der Wirtschaftspolitik*, Göttingen, 1982; H. James, *The Reichsbank and Public Finance in Germany 1924–1933*, Frankfurt am Main, 1985.

## MÜLLER, Hermann (1876–1931)

From a middle-class background in Mannheim, where he was born on 18 May 1876, Müller was employed as a commercial traveller when he joined the SPD in 1893. Editor of the socialist newspaper *Görlitzer Volkszeitung* from 1899 until appointed a full-time official on the party national executive seven years later, he was a cautious, reliable and hard-working activist in his particular areas of responsibility, the press and foreign contacts. He also played a useful role in organizing the youth movement which was brought under the party's control in the late 1900s. As a 'centrist', he was generally sympathetic to the reformist wing of the SPD and had no ideological or political difficulty in supporting the official policy of co-operation with the government during the war. In 1916 he entered the Reichstag, where he remained, with an interlude in the National Assembly in 1919–20, until 1931. He was a highly influential figure, acting for periods in the 1920s as chairman of the party's parliamentary delegation, as chairman of the party itself from 1919 to 1927, and as a member of its national executive. His reputation as a clever, thoughtful and pragmatic politician, able to conciliate in difficult situations, extended well beyond the SPD. He expressed the view that flexible tactics had to be adopted if the party were to develop as an effective force in the parliamentary system, even if it meant forming coalitions with non-socialist parties: socialism was attainable by way of the democratic process, but it involved compromise.

During the November Revolution, Müller played a leading role in the Berlin Workers' and Soldiers' Council movement. From June 1919 until March 1920 he was Reich Foreign Minister in the Bauer cabinet, and as such was one of the two German signatories (the other was Johannes Bell of the Centre Party) to the Treaty of Versailles. When Bauer resigned, Müller was appointed Reich Chancellor in a coalition government, though was not really successful. Faced with left-wing revolts in central Germany and particularly in the Ruhr, and with continuing tensions in international affairs, he too often appeared hesitant, and failed to inspire a sense of collegial loyalty among ministers. Moreover, his initiative in establishing a new Socialization Commission did not yield substantial results.

As Reich Chancellor in the 'Grand Coalition' government from June 1928 until March 1930, Müller experienced one frustration after another, not only with partners such as the DVP but also with his own party, so that he was at times left isolated. Controversial issues, including the proposed pocket battleship A, reparations, the budget and the funding of the unemployment insurance scheme, drew heavily on his political and personal resources. Somewhat ironically, he enjoyed good relations with President von Hindenburg, who averred that while it was unfortunate that he was a socialist, Müller was the best Chancellor he ever had. The dominance of interest-group politics in the coalition government had become apparent by 1929, so that it was not surprising that a clash of interest between the DVP and SPD over funding of the unemployment insurance system should have led to the collapse of Müller's administration. Its demise marked the effective end of parliamentary democracy as the basis of government in the Weimar Republic. Müller died in Berlin almost exactly a year later, on 20 March 1931.

## Further Reading

H. Müller, *Die November-Revolution. Erinnerungen*, Berlin, 1931. Worth consulting are J. Holzer, *Parteien und Massen. Die politische Krise in Deutschland 1928–1930*, Wiesbaden, 1975; I. Maurer, *Reichsfinanzen und Grosse Koalition. Zur Geschichte des Reichskabinetts Müller (1928–1930)*, Frankfurt am Main, 1973; H. Timm, *Die deutsche Sozialpolitik und der Bruch der Grossen Koalition im März 1930*, new edn, Düsseldorf, 1982; M. Vogt (ed.), *Akten der Reichskanzlei. Weimarer Republik. Das Kabinett Müller I: 27. März bis 21. Juni 1920*, Boppard, 1971; M Vogt (ed.), *Akten der Reichskanzlei. Weimarer Republik: Das Kabinett Müller II. 28. Juni 1928 bis 27. März 1930*, Boppard, 1970.

# NEUMANN, Heinz (1902–1937)

One of the youngest, most dynamic and ambitious leaders of the KPD before 1933, Neumann was born into a Berlin middle-class family on 6 July 1902, and joined the party at the age of 18 as he was about to embark on an undergraduate career in economics and philosophy. Party activity was soon his principal and then exclusive interest, however, and in 1922 he became a full-time official at headquarters, and editor of the main party newspaper, *Die Rote Fahne*. Associated with the left opposition element at first, he then became heavily involved in the abortive putschist events of 1923. In 1925, by which time he had developed strong Russian contacts, he was commissioned by the Moscow Politburo to write a refutation of Arkady Maslow's critique of Lenin, *The Two Revolutions of 1917*. Neumann's stinging reply, *Maslows Offensive gegen den Leninismus*, satisfied his masters. From 1925 until 1928 he was the KPD representative to the Comintern in Moscow, where he was able further to extend his circle of friends through his excellent command of Russian. He was a confirmed and highly motivated Stalin loyalist, and when he returned to Berlin in 1928 he was one of a triumvirate (Ernst Thälmann and Hermann Remmele were the others) who instituted a rigid programme of Stalinization which rendered the KPD almost totally subservient to Moscow.

In October 1928 Neumann replaced Heinrich Süsskind as chief editor of *Die Rote Fahne*, and the following year became a member of the party's central committee and also of its secretariat. Over the next few years he was at the centre of much of the acrimonious internecine feuding that characterized the KPD, and was dismissively described by colleague Clara Zetkin as 'an agent provocateur of expulsions and splits'. He also was the target of criticism from Dimitri Manuilsky for his alleged 'revolutionary impatience'. Neumann, who had put forward the theory that fascism was preparing the way for revolution, was more alert than most other KPD leaders to the emerging threat of National Socialism. This view did not sit comfortably with the official party line, based on the ultra-leftist strategy that the 'social fascist' SPD was the main enemy. Thus, despite the astonishing performance of the NSDAP in the September 1930 Reichstag elections, the KPD intensified its assault on the SPD, particularly in view of its policy of toleration towards the 'fascist' Brüning government. Coining the blood-thirsty slogan, 'Hit the fascists wherever you meet them!', Neumann reacted to the NSDAP success in the Reichstag elections of July 1932 by suggesting once again that his party should give priority to attacking the National Socialists. For this he was dismissed from the leadership in August 1932 and compelled to give up the seat in the Reichstag which he had held since September 1930. At the third party congress in October 1932, he was blamed for a whole series of misdemeanours, including 'softening the principled struggle against social democracy', 'underestimating fascism' and 'unprincipled opposition'. What this meant was that nothing was to be allowed to interfere with the Moscow-dictated anti-SPD stance of the party. A month later, as if to emphasize this point, the Communists joined with the NSDAP in support of the Berlin transport workers' strike.

Following his expulsion, Neumann was employed by the Comintern in Spain for a brief time, and then moved to Switzerland where he was arrested in 1934 and nearly sent back to Germany. He succeeded in reaching Moscow, where he earned a living as a translator. In spring 1937 he was arrested by the secret police on Stalin's orders and murdered in unknown circumstances.

## Further Reading

H. Neumann, *Was ist Bolschewisierung?*, Berlin, 1924; *Der ultralinke Menschewismus*, Berlin, 1925. See also the autobiography of his wife, M. Buber-Neumann, *Von Potsdam nach Moskau*.

*Stationen eines Irrweges*, Stuttgart, 1957, and her study, *Kriegsschauplätze der Weltrevolution. Ein Bericht aus der Praxis der Komintern 1919–1943*, Stuttgart, 1967. Further useful reading: O.K. Flechtheim, *Die Kommunistische Partei Deutschlands in der Weimarer Republik*, new edn, Frankfurt am Main, 1969; H. Weber, *Die Wandlung des deutschen Kommunismus. Die Stalinisierung der KPD in der Weimarer Republik*, 2 vols, Frankfurt am Main, 1969; J.J. Ward, 'Smash the Fascists': German Communist Efforts to Counter the Nazis, 1930–31', *Central European History*, 14, no. 1, 1981, pp. 30–62; H. Weber, *Hauptfeind Sozialdemokratie. Strategie und Taktik der KPD, 1929–1933*, Düsseldorf, 1982; H. Weber (ed.), *Die Generallinie. Rundschreiben des Zentralkomitees der KPD an die Bezirke 1929–1933*, Düsseldorf, 1981; R. Fischer, *Stalin and German Communism. A Study in the Origins of the State Party*, Cambridge, Massachusetts, 1948; R. Leviné-Meyer, *Inside German Communism. Memoirs of Party Life in the Weimar Republic*, London, 1977; B. Fowkes, *Communism in Germany under the Weimar Republic*, London, 1984; T. Bergmann, *'Gegen den Strom'. Die Geschichte der Kommunistischen-Partei-Opposition*, Hamburg, 1988.

## NOSKE, Gustav (1868–1946)

The prominent SPD leader who played a decisive role as a self-styled 'bloodhound' in the November Revolution was born into a working-class home in Brandenburg/ Havel on 9 July 1868, and subsequently earned his living as a basket-weaver. A trade unionist and SPD member from 1886, Noske moved into party journalism and from 1902 until his election to the Reichstag in 1906 was editor of the right-wing socialist newspaper, *Chemnitzer Volksstimme*. In his first major parliamentary address in 1907 he controversially affirmed the validity of the defensive war concept, and in the years before the First World War emerged as the party's expert on military and colonial affairs, asserting Germany's right to colonies. This practical, sober, shrewd and patriotic reformist socialist had little time for the party's intellectuals and he once referred disparagingly to Marxism as 'an occult science'. He was the personification of the reliable party apparatchik. In 1913 he was the first socialist member of the Reichstag to be invited on an inspection tour of the naval dockyards. In August 1914 he had no hesitation in supporting the war effort.

Noske spent a brief period at the beginning of the conflict as a war correspondent, but for most of those years his involvement in politics was uneventful. This lull was in stark contrast to his fundamentally important contribution to the revolutionary post-war era from 1918 to 1920.

Despite being a staunch patriot, Noske publicly supported the idea of the Kaiser's abdication, believing it would secure for Germany a decent peace. On 4 November 1918 he was sent by the SPD at the government's request as Reich Commissioner to Kiel to help control the sailors' revolt. With great courage and skill, he negotiated a compromise settlement. He was promptly elected co-chairman of the Sailors' Council and Governor of Kiel. When the USPD delegates withdrew from the Council of People's Representatives in December 1918, he was appointed to fill one of the vacancies, and in the Scheidemann government formed in early 1919 he was made Minister of Defence, the role for which he is best remembered. His anti-Bolshevism, patriotism and dedication to law and order dictated that he adopt a tough attitude to the radicals of the Left. For this purpose he enlisted the services of the conservative-monarchist army officer corps and the ultra-rightist *Freikorps*. As he famously remarked: 'somebody has to be the bloodhound. I will not shirk this responsibility'. The consequent brutal use of force won him admiration on the Right and even from foreign observers such as Winston Churchill, who described him as 'a man of the people . . . acting without fear in a public cause'. But Noske was anathema not only to Communists and other radicals on the Left: he was hated by many ordinary working-class socialists and many sections of his own party. In a broader historical perspective, he has to be criticized for not even anticipating the long-term implications for the democratic Republic of allowing the reactionary Reichswehr to remain as a coherent force of opposition to the state. And although Noske had earned the trust and respect of many generals for his actions, including Walter Reinhardt, chief of the army high command, this did not prevent the Reichswehr from adopting an unhelpfully ambivalent stance towards the Kapp Putsch in March 1920, which brought about the Defence Minister's resignation. His blind trust in the officer corps was blamed for his failure to spare the government this unhappy and potentially disastrous experience. He found himself also dropped as a political liability from the SPD's list of candidates for the Reichstag elections in June 1920. The Prussian government, and particularly Carl Severing, saved him from total oblivion by appointing him Governor (*Oberpräsident*) of Hanover later that year. He had a notably successful career in that position until dismissed by the National Socialists in 1933. He kept a watchful eye on national politics, but his advice, as when he urged the SPD and trade unions to respond positively to Chancellor von Schleicher's overtures in December 1932, was invariably disregarded. A political career that had once promised so much had thus come to a disappointingly premature end. For the SPD, the deep divisions which Noske helped create in the German working-class movement were never healed.

In retirement during the Third Reich, Noske was nevertheless arrested on suspicion of being implicated in the July 1944 Plot, and would have been executed had not the Allies arrived in time to liberate him. He died in Hanover on 30 November 1946.

## Further Reading

G. Noske, *Kolonialpolitik und Sozialdemokratie*, Stuttgart, 1914; *Wie ich wurde*, Berlin, 1919; *Von Kiel bis Kapp. Zur Geschichte der deutschen Revolution*, Berlin, 1920; *Aufstieg und Niedergang der deutschen Sozialdemokratie. Erlebtes aus Aufstieg und Niedergang einer Demokratie*, Offenbach, 1947. Further useful studies include U. Czisnik, *Gustav Noske. Ein Sozialdemokratischer Staatsmann*, Göttingen, 1969; H.-C. Schröder, *Gustav Noske und die Kolonialpolitik des deutschen Kaiserreichs*, Bonn, 1979; W. Wette, *Gustav Noske. Eine politische Biographie*, Düsseldorf, 1987.

## PAPEN, Franz von (1879–1969)

Reich Chancellor in succession to Heinrich Brüning from June until November 1932 and a confidant of President von Hindenburg, von Papen's significance during the critical final phase of the Weimar Republic was considerable, particularly when, out of office, he played the classic role of intermediary between the forces of traditional conservative nationalism and the NSDAP. Ultimately, Hitler's appointment to the Chancellorship owed not a little to the ability of von Papen to convince von Hindenburg and representatives of the industrial, agrarian and military élites that the *Führer* could be politically contained and made to serve and perpetuate their privileged interests and status: the NSDAP would provide the mass base of popular support in the country, while the élitist groups would exercise the real power. It was a disastrously erroneous understanding of the dynamics of National Socialism, but then von Papen had not been an especially perceptive politician in a career that had been rather unremarkable until his elevation to the Chancellor's office.

Von Papen was born into a long-established Catholic noble family on 29 October 1879 in Werl, Westphalia. He opted for a military career, and after serving as a lieutenant in a cavalry regiment was assigned in 1911 to General Staff duties in Berlin. Accepted as a permanent member of the General Staff in March 1913, he took up the post of military attaché in Washington later that year and became so entangled in the American–Mexican war in 1914–15 that he was asked to leave by the US government. No sooner back in Germany, he was despatched as a battalion commander to the Western Front, and subsequently saw further service in Turkey and Palestine as a General Staff officer with the rank of major.

After 1918 von Papen abandoned his military career to enter politics as a member of the Centre Party. He was not in any way prominent in the revolutionary upheavals and was first elected to the Prussian Landtag in 1921, remaining there until 1932. As a member of the ultra-conservative, aristocratic Herrenklub in Berlin, he found a natural haven on the far-right monarchist wing of his party. His marriage in 1905 into the wealthy Boch-Galhaus family brought him into contact with influential industrialists in the Saar, and in 1923 he became chairman of the management board of the conservative Catholic newspaper, the organ of the Centre Party, *Germania*. It was from this base that von Papen, lacking political experience at the top level and previously not even considered for ministerial appointment, was asked by von Hindenburg to form a government in June 1932. His group of predominantly non-party-affiliated ministers from the conservative upper reaches of German society was dubbed 'the cabinet of barons', and its authority, in the absence of any worthwhile popular support, rested on the powers and authority of the Reich President. Nevertheless, the new Chancellor set about his task with vigour: the ban on the SA and the wearing in public of party uniform by NSDAP members was rescinded; the administration was purged of liberals, republicans and socialists to some extent; and in July 1932 he used the bloody Altona riot involving National Socialists and Communists to depose the properly elected SPD-led government in Prussia, appointing himself Reich Commissioner of Germany's largest province. This blatantly unconstitutional act was a foretaste of what was to come six months later, albeit on a grander scale.

The political crisis that had existed since early 1930 could only be exacerbated by von Papen's reactionary policies and by his failure to attract adequate support in the Reichstag or in the country at large. Even his success at the Lausanne Conference on reparations and his inauguration of a work creation scheme to alleviate unemployment failed to prevent his dismissal on 17 November. By that time, in any case, the destiny of the Weimar Republic had become a matter of political intrigue of the basest kind from which only Hitler emerged as a winner.

Von Papen was Vice-Chancellor from January 1933 until July 1934, resigning after narrowly escaping murder during the Röhm putsch. But he continued to serve the Third Reich in diplomatic posts in Vienna from 1934 to 1939, and in Ankara from 1939 until 1944. He was arraigned before the Nuremberg Military Tribunal on various counts, but was fully acquitted in October 1946. In February 1947, however, a German denazification court sentenced him to eight years in a labour camp and loss of property for having been a 'major offender' of the Nazi regime. On appeal, he was released in January 1949. Von Papen died in Oberasbach, Baden, on 2 May 1969.

## Further Reading

Franz von Papen, *Memoirs*, London, 1952; *Vom Scheitern einer Demokratie 1930-1933*, Mainz, 1968. See also T. Trumpp, *Franz von Papen, der preussisch-deutsche Dualismus und die NSDAP in Preussen*, Marburg, 1963; H. Marcon, *Arbeitsbeschaffungspolitik der Regierungen von Papen und Schleicher*, Frankfurt am Main, 1974; H. Grund, *'Preussenschlag' und Staatsgerichtshof im Jahre 1932*, Baden-Baden, 1976; J.A. Bach, *Franz von Papen in der Weimarer Republik. Aktivitäten in Politik und Presse 1918–1932*, Düsseldorf, 1977; U. Hörster-Philipps, *Konservative Politik in der Endphase der Weimarer Republik. Die Regierung Franz von Papen*, Cologne, 1982; H.M. Adams and R.K. Adams, *Rebel Patriot*, Santa Barbara, 1987 – a highly apologetic account; K.-H. Minuth (ed.), *Akten der Reichskanzlei. Weimarer Republik. Das Kabinett von Papen. 1. Juni bis 3. Dezember 1932*, 2 vols, Boppard, 1989.

# PIECK, Wilhelm (1876–1960)

A leading Communist of the Weimar era who rose to the highest offices in the German Democratic Republic after its creation in 1949, Pieck came from a working-class background in Guben, where he was born on 3 January 1876. After completing an apprenticeship as a joiner, he joined the SPD and from 1908 until 1910 represented it on the city council of Bremen. His radical views took him into the SPD's internal opposition, and in 1914 he was dismissed from his position as secretary of the party's education committee in Berlin for forcefully expressing his rejection of the party's stance on war credits. He served in the army for a few years but deserted in the Netherlands at the beginning of 1918 and went into hiding until the end of the war.

Pieck returned to Germany in good time to play a prominent role in radical revolutionary politics in Berlin. At the founding conference of the Spartacus League on 11 November 1918 he was elected to the central committee, while retaining, like his colleagues, membership of the USPD. He became directly involved in the preparations for an uprising, helping Karl Liebknecht to set up the Spartacists' Revolutionary Committee to act as a provisional government. In the course of the subsequent street fighting in January 1919 he was arrested by *Freikorps* units along with Liebknecht and Rosa Luxemburg, but was spared for divulging information about his associates and allowed to escape.

As a co-founder and member of the central committee of the KPD on 1 January 1919, Pieck emerged as one of the most dedicated and energetic party leaders of the 1920s and early 1930s. He owed unswerving loyalty to Moscow and the Comintern. While a deputy in the Prussian Landtag from 1921 until 1928, he held an administrative post in Comintern and acted as the political leader of the KPD's Berlin-Brandenburg district. Elected to the Reichstag in 1928, where he sat until 1933, he also occupied a position in the Comintern's presidium from 1931, and from 1929 until 1933 he was leader of the German section of the Internationale Rote Hilfe, the Communist aid organization. In 1930 he became a member of the Prussian State Council, and served for a second time in the Prussian Landtag in 1932–33. In his first notable speech in the Reichstag in the aftermath of the suppression of a Communist riot in Berlin in May 1929 (*Blutmai*), Pieck vehemently denounced the Berlin police chief, Karl Zörgiebel, for 'slaughtering workers', and called for a general strike of Berlin workers to force his resignation. The language used by the Communist deputy was widely condemned as inflammatory and irresponsible.

In the early 1930s, Pieck gave voice in the party to his fears of National Socialism and on occasion urged a change in its tactics towards the 'social fascist' SPD that would allow more time and resources to be deployed against the grave threat from that quarter. But he was always careful not to be seen to challenge the leadership of Ernst Thälmann or the Moscow-directed strategy against the Social Democrats. Indeed, as late as February 1933 he rejected the idea that had been mooted in sections of the party of forging a non-aggression policy *vis-à-vis* the socialists and the trade unions, emphasizing instead the KPD's self-proclaimed status as the only genuine party of the working class.

Pieck fled Germany in spring 1933 and spent the pre-war years shuttling between Moscow and Paris on Communist Party business. The outbreak of the German–Soviet war in 1941 saw him back in Moscow beaming propaganda to German troops. In 1943 he helped establish the Communist-sponsored National Committee for a Free Germany, and in June 1945 returned to Berlin, courtesy of the Red Army. He was prominently engaged in the re-establishment of the Communist Party and the creation in 1946 of what was termed the Socialist Unity Party of Germany. He and Otto Grotewohl were elected chairmen of the party. In 1949, Pieck reached the pinnacle of party and state office in Soviet-dominated eastern Germany when he was appointed the first President of the German Democratic Republic. He proved a stout and at times quite ruthless defender of that barren and wholly corrupt regime, as in 1953 when he called on Russian tanks to quell the rising in East Berlin. He held the Presidency until his death in East Berlin on 7 September 1960.

## Further Reading

Wilhelm Pieck, *Wir kämpfen für ein Rätedeutschland*, Moscow, 1934; *Der neue Weg zum gemeinsamen Kampf für den Sturz der Hitlerdiktatur*, 4th edn, East Berlin, 1954 (first published in Moscow, 1935); *Zur Geschichte der Kommunistischen Partei Deutschlands. 30 Jahre Kampf*, East Berlin, 1949; *Reden und Aufsätze*, Vols I–IV (*Parlamentsreden. Auswahl aus den Jahren 1906–1933*), East Berlin, 1951–55; *Gesammelte Reden und Schriften*, Vols I–III (1904–1927), East Berlin, 1959–61. See also F. Erpenbeck, *Wilhelm Pieck. Ein Lebensbild*, East Berlin, 1951; H. Vosske, *Wilhelm Pieck. Bilder und Dokumente*, East Berlin, 1977; O.K. Flechtheim, *Die KPD in der Weimarer Republik*, Frankfurt am Main, 1969; S. Bahne, *Die KPD und das Ende von Weimar*, Frankfurt am Main, 1976; J. Wächtler, *Zwischen Revolutionserwartung und Untergang. Die Vorbereitung der KPD auf die Illegalität in den Jahren 1929–1933*, Frankfurt am Main, 1983; H. Weber, *Kommunismus in Deutschland 1918–1945*, Darmstadt, 1983; R. Luz, *KPD. Weimarer Staat und politische Einheit der Arbeiterbewegung in der Nachkriegskrise, 1919–1922/23*, Konstanz, 1987.

## POPITZ, Johannes (1884–1945)

A high-profile civil servant whose direct influence on the fiscal and financial policies of the Reich government during the mid-1920s can hardly be underestimated, Popitz was born in Leipzig on 2 December 1884. After a brilliant career at university, where he read law, economics and political science, he received his first significant appointment as a Privy Councillor (*Geheimrat*) in 1919. A professorship at the University of Berlin followed in 1923, and when called in as State Secretary in the Reich Ministry of Finance two years later he was already widely acknowledged as Germany's leading expert on financial law. He immediately made his mark through the creation of an important new tax law in August 1925 which regulated the disorder caused in that sphere by the hyperinflation crisis. He then proceeded to formulate over the next four years a broad range of innovative policies for the national administration of finance in co-operation with, among others, Rudolf Hilferding, the Finance Minister in the 'Grand Coalition' cabinet of Heinrich Müller. Popitz was particularly concerned with the problem of 'fiscal equilibrium' (*Finanzausgleich*) between central government and the federal states. But he discovered that fiscal equilibrium was determined less by expert opinion than by a complicated process of political negotiation involving government at various levels, and the parties. He referred disdainfully to this as government by 'polycracy'.

Professor Popitz was politically conservative, but his fiercest critics came from the Right, none more vehement than Hjalmar Schacht, president of the Reichsbank, who repeatedly demanded that a tighter fiscal policy be adopted. Popitz had already come into conflict with Parker Gilbert, the American reparations expert, over budget imbalance, and when Schacht accused him of irresponsibility in financial management in December 1929, he was forced to resign. After a period in academia, he returned to the centre of national affairs in October 1932 when chosen by Chancellor von Papen to take charge of the Prussian Ministry of Finance in the wake of his unconstitutional deposition of the Prussian administration.

In January 1933 the non-Nazi Popitz was named Minister without Portfolio and Reich Commissioner of the Prussian Ministry of Finance, and from April 1933 until July 1944 he was Prussian State Minister and Minister of Finance – a key role, in fact, in the administrative structure of the Third Reich. He dismissed evidence of National Socialist violence and lawlessness as a temporary aberration, and expressed ideas about the need to create a new master class (*Herrenschlicht*) in Germany, thus in conformity with Hitler's racialist theories. In 1937 he was awarded the prestigious Golden Badge of Honour of the NSDAP in recognition of his services to the regime. However, Popitz began to mix in conservative resistance circles shortly thereafter, and more resolutely during the Second World War, on account of the persecution of the Jews and what he came to believe was inevitable catastrophe under the *Führer*'s leadership. By 1943 he had completed a detailed preliminary constitution which stressed the rule of law, good morals, individual liberty, protection of property and Christianity. It was a curious amalgam of liberal and ultra-conservative notions, for he accorded a primary role to the Wehrmacht as a model for the spiritual rebirth of the nation, and envisaged a unitary state run by a state council and not a parliament. In 1943 he held secret discussions with *Reichsführer SS* Heinrich Himmler with the aim of persuading him to reach a settlement with the Western Allies. He was arrested for his involvement in the July Plot of 1944 and hanged in Berlin's Plötzensee prison on 2 February 1945.

## Further Reading

J. Popitz, *Der Finanzausgleich und seine Bedeutung für die Finanzlage des Reichs, der Länder und Gemeinden*, Berlin, 1930. See H. Herzfeld, 'Johannes Popitz. Ein Beitrag zum Schicksal des deutschen Beamtentums', in *Forschungen zu Staat und Verfassung. Festschrift für Fritz Hartung*, Berlin, 1958, pp. 345–65; H. Dieckmann, *Johannes Popitz. Entwicklung und Wirksamkeit in der Zeit der Weimarer Republik*, Berlin, 1960; L.-A. Bentin, *Johannes Popitz und Carl Schmitt. Zur wirtschaftlichen Theorie des totalen Staates in Deutschland*, Munich, 1972; H. Mommsen, *Beamtentum im Dritten Reich*, Stuttgart, 1966; J. Caplan, *Government without Administration. State and Civil Service in Weimar and Nazi Germany*, Oxford, 1988; P. Hoffmann, *Widerstand, Staatsstreich, Attentat. Der Kampf der Opposition gegen Hitler*, Munich, 1970.

## PREUSS, Hugo (1860–1925)

The future constitutional expert of the early Weimar period was born into a comfortable Jewish commercial family in Berlin on 28 October 1860, and at the early age of 29 had already completed his *Habititationsschrift* (postdoctoral dissertation) in constitutional law at the University of Berlin. Intellectually a disciple of Otto Gierke, he went on to develop while lecturing at the University a distinctive democratic slant to the latter's theory of syndicalism. Above all, perhaps, Preuss was deeply influenced by Gierke's theory of the organic nature of state institutions, as revealed in his many excellent contributions to Theodor Barth's journal *Nation*, and in several outstanding books, including *History of the Development of German Municipal Law* (1906) and *The*

*German People and Politics* (1915). Having been denied a chair at the University of Berlin on account of his Jewishness and left-liberal political views – Preuss was for many years until 1918 an active member of the Progressive People's Party – he at last secured a professorship in constitutional law at the newly created Handelshochschule in the capital in 1906. He subsequently was appointed rector of that institution, the post he held when the November Revolution opened the way to a new career in national politics for him.

Preuss, who in July 1917 had presented to Chancellor Bethmann-Hollweg a paper delineating how Germany could affect democratic reform within the framework of the monarchy, and thus rejoin the western European community of nations was, in late 1918, clearly the man to tackle the vexed question of a new constitutional order for the country. In an article in the *Berliner Tageblatt* on 14 November he denounced the whole nature of authoritarian government and rejected the earlier notion of changing the nature of the state in partnership with the Hohenzollerns. With the Kaiser gone, an entirely different set of constitutional possibilities presented themselves, and Preuss intimated his eagerness for leading the way. Now a member of the DDP, he was appointed State Secretary in the Reich Ministry of the Interior by the Council of People's Representatives, with the specific tasks of preparing the ground for elections to the National Assembly and of drawing up a draft constitution for the new Republic. His first draft was completed by Christmas 1918, but underwent some modification before being presented to the Assembly in February 1919. Further changes were made in the specially convened Constitutional Convention, particularly as regards the relationship between central government and individual states: Preuss was a firm advocate of a strong, centralized authority and had been keen to abolish the powers and privileges of Prussia. A compromise of sorts was eventually agreed on this matter, as indeed on other features, including the nature and extent of presidential power. The final version that was approved by the Assembly in July 1919, however, fully incorporated his major ideas on a liberal-democratic parliamentary basis for the republican state. For this outstanding achievement, Preuss became widely known as the 'father' of the Weimar Constitution.

Appointed the Republic's first Minister of the Interior in Philipp Scheidemann's cabinet in February 1919, Preuss resigned with his colleagues four months later in protest at the terms of the Treaty of Versailles. He was never again nominated for cabinet office by his party, and had to be content, therefore, with a seat in the Prussian Landtag, where he made distinguished contributions to affairs concerning constitutional development and local government, in which he had had a considered interest since his service as a city councillor and magistrate in Berlin before 1914. Although he was among a number of Jews who played a conspicuous part in the early days of the DDP, Preuss had a somewhat ambivalent position in the party. His sarcasm, high intellectualism and slight air of *hauteur* won him few friends in the party hierarchy, and this possibly goes some way towards explaining a political career which did not fulfil the rich promise of 1919. He died in Berlin a few days before his sixty-fifth birthday on 9 October 1925.

## Further Reading

Among the most notable of works by Hugo Preuss are: *Entwicklungsgeschichte der deutschen Städteverfassung*, Berlin, 1906; *Zur preussischen Verwaltungsreform*, Berlin, 1910; *Das Deutsche Volk und die Politik*, Berlin, 1915; *Deutschlands Staatsumwälzung. Die verfassungsmässigen Grundlagen der deutschen Republik*, Berlin, 1920; *Deutschlands Republikanische Reichsverfassung*, Berlin, 1921; *Um die Reichsverfassung von Weimar*, Berlin, 1924; *Reich und Länder*, Berlin, 1926.

Also of interest are C. Schmitt, 'Hugo Preuss in der deutschen Staatlehre', *Die Neue Rundschau*, May 1930, pp. 289–303; G. Schmoller, *Walther Rathenau und Hugo Preuss. Die Staatsmänner des neuen Deutschlands*, Munich, 1922; E. Maste, 'Hugo Preuss. Vater der Weimarer Verfassung. Zur 100. Wiederkehr des Geburtstages von Hugo Preuss am 28. Oktober', in *Das Parlament. Aus Politik und Zeitgeschichte*, B43/60, 26 October 1960, pp. 695–702; K.-D. Bracher, *Die Entstehung der Weimarer Verfassung*, Hanover, 1963; S. Grassmann, *Hugo Preuss und die deutsche Selbstverwaltung*, Lübeck, 1965; E.R Huber, *Deutsche Verfassungsgeschichte seit 1789*, Volume 5, *Weltkrieg, Revolution und Reichserneuerung, 1914–1919*, Stuttgart, 1978; E. Portner, *Die Verfassungspolitik der Liberalen 1919. Ein Beitrag zur Deutung der Weimarer Reichsverfassung*, Bonn, 1973; G. Schulz, *Zwischen Demokratie und Diktatur. Verfassungspolitik und Reichsreform in der Weimarer Republik*, Vol. I (1919–1930), Vol. II (1930–1933), Berlin, 1987.

## PÜNDER, Hermann (1888–1976)

Hermann Pünder is one of a small and exclusive group of top civil servants who could reasonably claim to have not merely co-ordinated government policy in the Weimar era but also helped to influence it to an important degree. He was born in Trier on 1 April 1888 into a conservative upper middle-class Catholic family. On completion of a doctorate in law in 1910, he made his career in the Prussian civil service. He had barely joined the staff of the Prussian Ministry of Justice in 1914 when he was called up for military service as an officer from 1914 until 1918. He finished with the rank of major. After the end of the war he resumed his professional career, climbing rapidly up the promotion ladder to become one of the ablest administrators of his generation: he was an adviser to the State Secretary in the Reich Ministry of Finance from 1919 until 1921, leader of the minister's office in the same ministry from 1921 until 1925, ministerial director in the Reich Chancellery from 1925 until 1926 and, finally, State Secretary in the Chancellery from 1926 until 1932. From this latter strategic position, he advised and co-ordinated the work of several Reich chancellors, foreign secretaries and other leading members of government.

Dr Pünder displayed rare tact, judgement and loyalty throughout, and enjoyed a mutually respectful relationship with Gustav Stresemann. But, as his interesting and informative memoirs reveal, he had a particularly close and fruitful understanding with Heinrich Brüning. Pünder was himself a member of the Centre Party, and this factor undoubtedly helped in his dealings with the Chancellor. In addition, and more importantly, he harboured a genuine admiration for Brüning's political qualities and had no hesitation in regarding him as an international statesman of the first rank. Pünder's opinion has to be taken seriously because he developed an uncannily perceptive and well-informed appreciation of leading politicians and their policies. He also brought his expertise to bear on international affairs for he led German delegations to a number of major conferences and meetings, including those under the auspices of the League of Nations. His period as State Secretary ended with his resignation in summer 1932 over the increasingly high-handed and even unconstitutional approach to policy of the von Papen cabinet. Shortly afterwards, Pünder was appointed *Regierungspräsident* in Münster, but was dismissed by the National Socialists in July 1933.

Pünder's life in the Third Reich was undisturbed until July 1944, when his by no means significant links to the conservative resistance – Carl Goerdeler was simply a friend – led to his arrest, arraignment before the People's Court and detention in several concentration camps. Liberated by the Americans in May 1945, he immediately resumed an active political role in the western part of divided Germany. Co-founder of the Christian Democratic Party in the Rhineland, he succeeded Konrad Adenauer in October 1945 as Lord Mayor of shattered Cologne. From March 1948 until autumn 1949 he supervised economic regeneration programmes in the West, and from 1949 until 1957 sat in the Federal Parliament for the CDU, involving himself extensively in schemes of European co-operation. He died after a long retirement on 3 October 1976 in Fulda.

## Further Reading

H. Pünder (ed.), *Zur Geschichte des Reichskanzlerpalais und der Reichskanzlei*, Berlin, 1928; *Der Reichspräsident in der Weimarer Republik*, Frankfurt am Main, 1961; *Politik in der Reichskanzlei. Aufzeichnungen aus den Jahren 1929–1932*, (edited by T. Vogelsang), Stuttgart, 1961; *Von Preussen nach Europa. Lebenserinnerungen*, Stuttgart, 1968. See also H. Mommsen, 'Die Stellung der Beamtenschaft in Reich, Ländern, und Gemeinden in der Ära Brüning', *Vierteljahrshefte für Zeitgeschichte*, 21, 1973, pp. 151–65; W. Runge, *Politik und Beamtentum im Parteienstaat. Die Demokratisierung der politischen Beamten in Preussen zwischen 1918 und 1933*, Stuttgart, 1965; J. Caplan, *Government without Administration. State and Civil Service in Weimar and Nazi Germany*, Oxford, 1988.

# RADBRUCH, Gustav (1878–1949)

Before deciding to enter politics by way of the SPD in 1919, this highly intelligent, outstanding scholar was already well on his way to recognition as one of the most important legal and constitutional theorists in Germany this century. Born into a wealthy business family in Lübeck on 21 November 1878, he took his *Habilitation* in 1903 and taught at the University of Heidelberg for many years before the First World War. While there he produced two works, *Introduction to the Study of Law* in 1910 and *Introduction to Legal Philosophy* in 1914, which made his reputation as a profound and original thinker. His ideas bore the influence of Kantian philosophy, idealism and a mild patriotism, but above all, of Franz von Liszt, the controversial founder of the modern school of criminal law. Radbruch's experiences as a soldier at the Front converted him to an ethical, humanist socialism, which he felt compelled to translate into political action at the end of the war.

Appointed to the Chair of criminal law and legal philosophy at the University of Kiel in 1919, he made his first definitive statement in politics the following year when, showing great courage and strength of character, he prevented irresponsible acts of violence in that city during the Kapp Putsch, while making a vigorous defence of the Republic. The SPD rewarded him with a Reichstag seat in the June 1920 elections, and in October 1921 a place in Chancellor Wirth's second cabinet as Reich Minister of Justice. He held this post until November 1922, and was reappointed to it in Gustav Stresemann's administration of August–November 1923. These periods were eventful and challenging. As a progressive jurist, he set about revising the criminal law code *(Strafgesetzbuch)* in such a way as to encourage the rehabilitation of the offender in society and generally to make the exercise of justice more humane: for instance, he proposed the abolition of the death penalty. His revised version was masterful, but failed to be implemented because of opposition from the conservative political Right. He did succeed, however, in pushing on to the statute book one of the most significant pieces of youth legislation in the Weimar era, the *Jugendgerichtsgesetz* (Juvenile Courts Law) in 1923, which incorporated the liberal educational-rehabilitative ethos. Following the murder of Walther Rathenau in 1922, Radbruch was convinced the Republic had to be defended with all legal means, and consequently prepared the Law for the Protection of the Republic and a Special Court for the Protection of the Republic in Leipzig. For him, the Law was to be directed against the Right, but he was apparently unaware that in future it could just as easily be employed against the Left. His measures in any case underlined the fact that the Republic could not rely on the existing judicial system for support. A final area of acute conflict which he faced concerned the crisis over the Saxon government in autumn 1923 which he tried without success to resolve with tactful persuasion rather than military force.

Radbruch declined re-election on the party list to the Reichstag in 1924 and four years later rejected an offer from Hermann Müller to take up the post of Reich Minister of Justice in his government. He remained active in the SPD, contributing to the debate on legal and constitutional matters. Most notably, he developed the argument that the capital–labour divide could only be bridged by a coalition government in which both were represented. For him, democracy reflected the current state of the class struggle and made it possible to continue that struggle with non-revolutionary methods. At the same time, he became rather critical of his party leaders for allegedly failing to make a sufficient effort to convince the people of the intrinsic value of democracy. He himself attempted to make a modest contribution in this respect when the opportunity arose in public – for example, when he gave the official address in the Reichstag in celebration of Constitution Day in August 1928.

His retirement in 1924 from the national political stage also allowed Professor Radbruch to devote more time to his academic interests. In 1926, when he was already a renowned teacher and scholar used to large and appreciative student audiences for his first-class lectures, he took up a Chair at the University of

Heidelberg. Given his academic and political status, it was not altogether surprising that in 1933 he should be the first Social Democratic and pro-republican professor to be dismissed by the National Socialist regime. Twelve years later he was restored to his former position, and until his death on 23 November 1949 he helped rebuild the law faculty at Heidelberg.

## Further Reading

G. Radbruch, *Einführung in die Rechtswissenschaft*, Berlin, 1910; *Einführung in die Rechtsphilosophie*, Berlin, 1914; *Der Innere Weg. Aufriss meines Leben*, Göttingen, 1951; *Schriften. Gesamtausgabe* (edited by A. Kaufmann), Vol I. *Rechtsphilosophie*, Heidelberg, 1987; *Briefe* (edited by E. Wolf), Göttingen, 1968. See also H. de With, *Gustav Radbruch. Reichsmmister der Justiz*, Cologne, 1978; A. Kaufmann, *Gustav Radbruch. Rechtsdenker, Philosoph, Sozialdemokrat*, Munich, 1987.

## RATHENAU, Walther (1867–1922)

The multi-talented scion of one of Germany's most powerful industrial families, Rathenau was a towering intellectual and political influence in the earliest phase of the Republic's history. Born in Berlin on 29 September 1867, the elder son of the Jewish founder and principal owner of AEG, he took a doctorate in physics and qualified as an engineer, and quickly developed a perceptive and highly progressive view of the role of the economy in an industrializing society. After some years spent gaining experience in a variety of companies affiliated to AEG, he became its president on the death of his father in 1915. By that time he had distinguished himself not only as an extremely successful entrepreneur in his own right, but also as an imaginative and challenging thinker, whose philosophy combined elements of Hegel, Marx, Spengler, Nietzsche, Max Weber and Friedrich Naumann. He wrote extensively on a wide range of social, economic, philosophical and cultural themes, but it was mainly during the First World War that he developed his blueprint for Germany's post-war recovery: the economy would have to be completely reorganized, and its productive and distributive processes rationalized. This demanded considerable state intervention, on the one hand, and the concentration of economic power in the hands of a capitalist élite chosen on the basis of education and merit, not inherited wealth or privilege. He had gained valuable insights into the overall working of the economy in 1914–15 when he had helped organize the War Raw Materials Department of the Prussian Ministry of War. It has been suggested that his efforts allowed Germany to engage in a prolonged conflict. Throughout the war he continued to support the German war effort with numerous memoranda concerning the mobilization of the country's resources. At the same time, however, he was firmly against annexationism and unconditional submarine warfare. By 1918 he had abandoned his erstwhile support for the Hohenzollerns and welcomed the Kaiser's abdication.

In November 1918, Rathenau founded his own political organization, the Democratic People's League, in order to propagate his economic and political ideas for a new Germany. But it collapsed for lack of support after less than a fortnight. For many observers, this failure underlined the utopian, unrealistic dimension of his personality and his lack of genuine leadership qualities in national politics. Undaunted, he helped arrange the Stinnes–Legien pact between employers and trade unions, and shifted his political home to the DDP. However, Rathenau remained essentially alienated from party politics and was never comfortable even in his own party, which refused to place him on its list of candidates for the National Assembly. His concept of an 'organic' economy was distrusted by most party leaders, especially, of course, those associated with its business wing. Thus, he remained something of an outsider in the DDP. His prominent role in the second Socialization Commission in 1920 and his proposal for the reorganization of the coal industry embarrassed many colleagues. Further discomfort was occasioned in May 1921 when he was appointed Minister for Reconstruction in Chancellor Wirth's first cabinet not simply on account of his economic views, but also because his membership of the government appeared to tie the party more closely to it without being given any more influence over policy.

Rathenau is perhaps best remembered in a strictly political sense for his term as Reich Foreign Minister from January until June 1922, and, in particular, for his espousal of the so-called policy of fulfilment (*Erfüllungspolitik*). As Wirth's confidant and trusted adviser, his influence was fundamentally important, if not decisive, in respect of reparations, the crisis over Upper Silesia and the Rapallo Treaty. As such, the left-wing Jewish intellectual was anathema to nationalist and far Right circles in Germany while at the same time a highly respected and admired figure abroad. His murder in Berlin on 24 June 1922 by members of the extreme rightist terrorist group Organisation Consul sent shock waves through the country, eliciting from Chancellor Wirth in the Reichstag the famous declaration, 'The enemy stands on the Right'. The Law for the Protection of the Republic was the government's immediate legislative response, though the vacuum created by the departure of Rathenau's unique personality was never filled.

## Further Reading

Of Rathenau's many writings, the following may be noted: *Zur Kritik der Zeit*, Berlin, 1912; *Zur Mechanik des Geistes*, Berlin, 1913; *Von kommenden Dingen*, Berlin, 1917; *Der neue Staat*, Berlin, 1919; *Was wird werden?*, Berlin, 1920; *Gesammelte Schriften in fünf Bänden*, Berlin, 1918; *Nachgelassene Schriften*, Berlin, 1928; *Politische Briefe*, Dresden, 1929. See also A. Brecht, *Walther Rathenau und das deutsche Volk*, Munich, 1950; J. Joll, *Intellectuals in Politics. Three Biographical Essays*, London, 1960, pp. 59–129; H. Graf Kessler, *Walther Rathenau, Sein Leben und Sein Werk*, Wiesbaden, 1962; H.W. Richter (ed.), *Walther Rathenau. Schriften und Reden*, Frankfurt am Main, 1964; H. Pogge von Strandmann (ed.), *Walther Rathenau. Tagebuch 1907–1922*, Düsseldorf, 1967; P. Berglar, *Walther Rathenau. Seine Zeit, sein Werk, seine Persönlichkeit*, Bremen, 1970; D. Felix: *Walther Rathenau and the Weimar Republic. The Politics of Reparation*, Baltimore, 1971; E. Schulin, *Walther Rathenau. Repräsentant, Kritiker und Opfer seiner Zeit*, Göttingen, 1977; E. Schulin (ed.), *Walther Rathenau. Hauptwerke und Gespräche*, Munich, 1977; H. Pogge von Strandmann (ed.), *Walther Rathenau. Notes and Diaries, 1907–1922*, Oxford, 1986; P. Berglar, *Walther Rathenau. Ein Leben zwischen Philosophie und Politik*, Graz, 1987.

# RAUMER, Hans von (1870–1965)

This highly successful industrialist, DVP politician and Reich minister was born into a privileged upper middle-class/aristocratic family in Dessau on 10 January 1870, and after completing a degree and doctorate in law was from 1905 until 1911 a district magistrate (*Landrat*). Moving into private industry, his ascent was swift: appointed managing director in 1915 of the central organization of the electro-technical industry (Bund der Elektrizitäts-Versorgungs-Unternehmungen Deutschlands), he also served from 1916 until 1918 as an adviser in the Reich Treasury Office.

In autumn 1918 von Raumer took the initiative which resulted in both sides of industry coming together in the Zentralarbeitsgemeinschaft der industriellen und gewerblichen Arbeitgeber und Arbeitnehmer Deutschlands, a body designed to reconcile the interests of employers and workers for the common good of the country as it strove to overcome the economic consequences of a lost war. He remained on its executive committee until it became redundant in the wake of the hyperinflation crisis in 1923–24. At the same time he had many other business interests: from 1919 until 1933 he headed the Zentralverband der Deutschen Elektrotechnischen Industrie, held directorships in numerous private companies, and throughout the Weimar period was a major influence in the committee of the powerful industrialists' body, the Reichsverband der deutschen Industrie. In summer 1922 he was one of several members asked by the Reichsverband to draft a comprehensive programme for Germany's economic regeneration, and the ensuing statement served as the basis of the programme adopted by it in 1925, as well as the outline of an official ideology for leading industrialists.

Von Raumer's political activity was no less considerable, particularly during the early 1920s. Elected to the Reichstag for the DVP in June 1920 and remaining a deputy and leader of its left wing until 1930, he saw ministerial office for the first time as Reich Treasurer in Konstantin Fehrenbach's cabinet from June 1920 until May 1921. He accepted Germany's reparation obligations as detailed by the Spa Conference in July 1920, and gained a reputation as a moderate in both domestic and foreign affairs, despite a hardening of many attitudes in his own party. However, his generally socially progressive outlook and conciliatory attitude towards the SPD did not extend to support for proposals on nationalization of the coal industry from the second Socialization Commission. In summer 1923 he took the lead in urging Gustav Stresemann to reach agreement with the Social Democrats on the formation of a coalition government, and produced a programme for tax reform, restoration of the eight-hour day and a role for labour in economic decision-making, towards that end. In the subsequent but short-lived Stresemann government, von Raumer was appointed Reich Minister of Economics. His resignation after only two months in office, which had been demanded by a majority of the DVP's Reichstag delegation, constituted a severe setback for the administration.

During the remainder of the 1920s von Raumer continued to preach the virtues of DVP co-operation with the SPD, and labour as a whole, and in spring 1930 he was one of several liberal-minded industrialists who came close to resurrecting the Zentralarbeitsgemeinschaft as a basis for a joint effort by employers and workers to defeat the Depression. The initiative floundered when the trade unions withdrew at a late stage in the negotiations. He was also an active promoter of German–Soviet economic relations which he believed could only be of immense potential benefit to Germany in terms of markets for her buoyant export industries. As the political crisis deepened with the rise of radicalism, von Raumer was unable to form a clear understanding of the NSDAP. While acknowledging that it stood on the far Right politically, he believed but was not certain that economically it was left-wing in orientation. The vague and contradictory statements by the party on its economic policy only confused the issue. In any event, he was among a group of industrialists from the more liberal, export-oriented branch of the economy who gave support to Chancellor Kurt von Schleicher's *Querfront* policy in December 1932. Earlier that year von Raumer had resigned his membership of the DVP. He went into permanent retirement in 1933 and died aged 95 in West Berlin on 3 November 1965.

## Further Reading

H. von Raumer: 'Unternehmer und Gewerkschaften in der Weimarer Zeit', *Deutsche Rundschau*, 80, 1954, pp. 425–34. See also G.D. Feldman and I. Steinisch, *Industrie und Gewerkschaften 1918–1924. Die überforderte Zentralarbeitsgemeinschaft*, Stuttgart, 1985; B. Weisbrod, *Die Schwerindustrie in der Weimarer Republik*, Wuppertal, 1978; A. Schildt, *Militärdiktatur mit Massenbasis? Die Querfrontkonzeption der Reichswehrführung um General von Schleicher am Ende der Weimarer Republik*, Frankfurt am Main, 1981; P. Wulf (ed.), *Akten der Reichskanzlei, Weimarer Republik. Das Kabinett Fehrenbach*, Boppard, 1972; K.D. Erdmann and M. Vogt (eds), *Akten der Reichskanzlei, Weirmarer Republik. Die Kabinette Stresemann I & II*, 2 vols, Boppard, 1978.

## REMMELE, Hermann (1880–1939)

Before his emergence as a leading Communist in the Weimar era, Remmele had considerable experience in the socialist and trade union movements. Born of peasant stock on 15 November 1880 in Ziegelhausen/Neckar, he completed an apprenticeship as a turner, and in 1897 joined both the SPD and the German Metalworkers' Union. Membership of the embryonic socialist youth movement followed in 1906, and from then until the First World War he worked as an official of the SPD in Mannheim, associating with its left wing. He served at the Front throughout the war years, but while on leave took part in the founding congress of the USPD in 1917. During the revolutionary period of 1918–19, Remmele was actively involved as the USPD's leader in Mannheim in the Workers' and Soldiers' Council, attempting to establish a Soviet-style councillor republic. On being appointed to the USPD's national executive, he vigorously prosecuted a policy of unity with the KPD. When the parties united in 1920, he was elected to the KPD's central committee and took a seat in the Reichstag, where he served until 1933.

In the perennial faction fighting and shifting alliances in the KPD, Remmele was usually identified as belonging to the leftist stream, but he was adept at accommodating himself to rapidly changing circumstances, which allowed him to remain at the forefront of the leadership cadre. As a member of the politburo in the years 1924-33, of the executive committee of the Comintern in 1926-32 and, for a period, chief editor of *Die Rote Fahne*, the main party newspaper, he was a substantial and influential figure. His ideas were invariably presented in the journal, *Die Internationale*, of which he was also chief editor for a time. Later, he was leader (*Bundesführer*) of the Kampfbund gegen den Faschismus, which in 1931 boasted some 80,000 members. In October 1923 he was an active agent in the KPD-led insurrection in Hamburg. In the mid-1920s he grew close to Ernst Thälmann and Heinz Neumann, and in 1928-29 joined them in a triumvirate in the leadership which exercised a dominating influence over the party during the period of the so-called ultra-leftist strategy, by which the supposedly 'social fascist' SPD was depicted as its major enemy. Remmele was an obedient servant of Comintern and an unconditional Stalin loyalist.

With the spectacular advance of National Socialism in the early 1930s, however, Remmele and Neumann began openly to question the party strategy, advocating more concentration on the danger from the NSDAP. When Neumann began to lose his struggle for control with Thälmann in early 1932, Remmele's own position consequently suffered. The advent of Hitler to power increased his criticism of the party leaders, arguing that the *Machtergreifung* was 'the greatest defeat of the proletariat since 1914.' His calls for a muscular response from the KPD went unheeded, as Thälmann faithfully toed the Moscow line, and his efforts to organize an oppositional group within the party from a base in Berlin-Wedding proved abortive. Previously stripped of all party offices, Remmele was expelled from the KPD in November 1933 amidst allegations that he was an undercover agent of the Gestapo. Emigrating to the Soviet Union, he fell victim like so many of his German *confrères* to Stalin's purges in 1937 and was subsequently murdered in an unknown place, probably sometime in 1939.

## Further Reading

H. Remmele, *Die Lehren des Berliner Blutmai und das drohende Verbot der KPD*, Berlin, 1929; *Der Kampf gegen den imperialistischen Krieg, die Verteidigung der Sowjetunion, das Wehrprogramm der SPD und die Aufgaben der KPD*, Berlin, 1929. See also S. Bahne, *Die KPD und das Ende von Weimar*, Frankfurt am Main, 1976; O.K. Flechtheim, *Die KPD in der Weimarer Republik*, Frankfurt am Main, 1969; H. Weber, *Die Wandlungen des deutschen Kommunismus. Die Stalinisierung der KPD in der Weimarer Republik*, 2 vols, Frankfurt am Main, 1969; H. Weber, *Hauptfeind Sozialdemokratie. Strategie und Taktik der KPD 1929-1933*, Düsseldorf, 1982; T. Kurz, *'Blutmai'. Sozialdemokraten und Kommunisten im Brennpunkt der Berliner Ereignisse von 1929*, Bonn and Berlin, 1990.

# RÖHM, Ernst (1887-1934)

The SA's Chief of Staff in the early 1930s, Röhm was born into an old Bavarian civil service family of monarchist sympathies in Munich on 28 November 1887, and after taking his leaving certificate (*Abitur*) at the humanist Maximilian grammar school in 1906 became a professional soldier in the King Ludwig regiment of the Royal Bavarian army. Wounded on three occasions during the First World War, he attained the rank of captain in 1917 and the following year was posted to the General Staff. He emerged from the conflict as a typical representative of a so-called 'lost generation', restless, dynamic, adventurist, brutal, and unable or unwilling to adjust to civilian society. His was an outlook permanently shaped by the excitement of battle, the comradeship of the trenches and an unshakeable belief in the superiority of the military ethos. Resentment at losing the war, and at the Treaty of Versailles, mixed in him with an aimless revolutionary dynamic and the heroic myth to produce, in political terms, hatred for the democratic Republic, Socialists, Marxists and Jews.

In spring 1919, Röhm joined the *Freikorps* Epp to suppress the Soviet Republic that had been set up in Munich. A few months later he was taken on as a staff officer at the Munich headquarters of the Reichswehr, with responsibility for looking after a considerable cache of illegal arms, many of which subsequently were channelled into the scores of right-wing paramilitary and nationalist organizations in Bavaria. An outstanding organizer, he also established a special intelligence unit of the army which made contact with groups of the political Right. In this connection, he came across Hitler, then employed by the army as a political training instructor, and became an early member himself of the German Workers' Party and, from February 1920, of the NSDAP. Röhm provided the party with both funds and introductions to important military and political leaders in Bavaria. Prominent also in extending the spectrum of paramilitary activity, including the creation of his own group in 1923 – the Reichskriegsflagge – he organized an umbrella association, the Deutscher Kampfbund, for an assault on the Republic in autumn 1923, with the NSDAP providing the political spearhead. The outcome was the abortive Beer Hall putsch, which caused Röhm's dismissal from the army a few days later, and a 15-month jail sentence. Released on 1 April 1924, he was commissioned by the still incarcerated *Führer* to reorganize the SA. Instead, he founded a cover organization, the Frontbann, for a number of *völkisch* paramilitary groups and gave every indication of wanting to be its leader independent of Hitler. In any case, the NSDAP leader had made a fundamental reappraisal of the National Socialist movement's future, and had concluded that any paramilitary group would have to be subordinated to the primacy of the political party. In short, Röhm's concept of militarism was no longer acceptable to Hitler. In April 1925 he withdrew from the movement and active politics altogether. After leading an unsatisfying, feckless existence for a few years he accepted the offer of a post as military adviser in Bolivia, remaining there from 1928 until 1930.

The electoral success of the NSDAP at the Reichstag elections in September 1930 and the rapid expansion of its paramilitary organization prompted Hitler to recall Röhm as SA Chief of Staff from 1 January 1931. Under his command the SA attracted some 800,000 members within two years, and as a force of intimidation, street terror and noisy propaganda, it became an indispensable asset in Hitler's quest for power. Composed largely of unemployed and *déclassé* proletarian elements but with a substantial lower middle-class contingent, the SA's domination of the streets against left-wing rivals, and its quasi-revolutionary *élan*, perfectly complemented the more directly political contribution of the party. Röhm was even more ambitious, for after the *Machtergreifung* he wanted a second 'socialist' revolution through which his SA would form the nucleus of a 'people's army', to the exclusion of the Reichswehr. From Hitler's standpoint, the assumption and consolidation of power in the state, which had been accomplished within six months of his appointment as Chancellor, rendered the SA redundant. Still dependent on the support and goodwill of the traditional conservative élites in industry, agriculture and, above all, the army, he could not afford to tolerate his close friend's schemes. The SA Chief of Staff, Reich Minister without Portfolio, Minister of the Bavarian State government and Reichstag member was politically expendable. The debauchery of his homosexual circle of friends provided a moral pretext for action. In the consequent 'Night of the Long Knives' in June 1934, Röhm was arrested and, after refusing an invitation to commit suicide, shot dead in Munich's Stadelheim prison on 1 July by the SS. The episode claimed the lives of hundreds of others, SA leaders as well as designated enemies of the regime, including General Kurt von Schleicher, Gregor Strasser and Gustav von Kahr. The SA itself was permanently emasculated as a political force.

## Further Reading

E. Röhm, *Die Geschichte eines Hochverräters*, Munich, 1928. See also Heinrich Bennecke, *Die Reichswehr und der 'Röhm-Putsch'*, Munich, 1964; H. Bennecke, *Hitler und die SA*, Munich, 1962; A. Werner, 'SA und NSDAP. SA: "Wehrverband", "Parteitruppe" oder "Revolutionsarmee"? Studien zur Geschichte der SA und der NSDAP 1920–1933', doctoral dissertation, University of Erlangen, 1964; C. Bloch, *Die SA und die Krise des NS-Regimes 1934*, Frankfurt am Main, 1970; P.H. Merkl, *The Making of a Stormtrooper*, Princeton, 1980; C.J Fischer, *Stormtroopers. A Social, Economic and Ideological Analysis 1929–1935*, London, 1983; R. Bessel, *Political Violence and the Rise of Nazism. The Storm Troopers in Eastern Germany 1925–1934*, New Haven and London, 1984; M. Jamin, *Zwischen den Klassen. Zur Sozialstruktur der SA-Führerschaft*, Wuppertal, 1984; K. Gossweiler, *Die Röhm-Affäre. Hintergründe, Zusammenhänge, Auswirkungen*, Cologne, 1983; H. Höhne, *Mordsache Röhm*, Hamburg, 1984; E.G. Reiche, *The Development of the SA in Nürnberg 1922–1934*, London, 1986; P. Longerich, *Die braunen Bataillone. Geschichte der SA*, Munich, 1989.

## ROSENBERG, Alfred (1893–1946)

The major ideologue of the NSDAP whose influence on Hitler during the early 1920s, in particular, was substantial, was born in Reval, Estonia, on 12 January 1893 to comfortably-off parents of a Baltic German background. After studying engineering and architecture in Riga and Moscow until March 1918, he fled revolutionary Russia, reaching Munich in December of that year. Associating immediately with fiercely anti-Bolshevik White Russian *émigrés*, he became a member of the sinister *völkisch* anti-Semitic Thule Society, and helped the radical poet and writer, Dietrich Eckart, to produce the journal, *Auf gut Deutsch*. Through Eckart he was introduced to the German Workers' Party and Hitler, who was impressed by Rosenberg's pseudo-intellectual theories on Bolshevism, international Jewry, freemasonry and Christianity, which supported his own virulent prejudices. Rosenberg wrote prolifically and his influence extended not only to Hitler's speeches and writings on anti-Semitism and Bolshevism, but also to the official party programme of February 1920 and the principal party newspaper, the *Völkischer Beobachter*, whose editor he became in February 1923 and again from 1925 until 1945.

After the failure of the Beer Hall putsch, in which he participated, Rosenberg was chosen by the imprisoned Hitler to lead the fragmented NSDAP, but proved so inept at dealing with the warring factions that he was relieved of this responsibility later in 1924. He was disliked by many of his colleagues for his rather pedantic, humourless and intellectually arrogant manner, while his qualities of political leadership had been shown to be poor. Nevertheless, he remained a figure of importance in the party, advising the *Führer* on foreign policy, explaining and propagating the National Socialist *Weltanschauung* and consolidating his status as the chief theoretician of the NSDAP against rivals such as Gottfried Feder and Artur Dinter. Founder and leader of the Kampfbund für deutsche Kultur in 1929, he began to edit and publish the following year the periodical *Nationalsozialistische Monatshefte*, and also in 1930 produced his magnus opus, *Der Mythos des 20. Jahrhunderts. Eine Wertung der seelischgeistigen Gestaltenkämpfe unserer Zeit*, a turgid pseudo-philosophical, mystical-racist denunciation of the perceived enemies of noble Aryan Germanic culture. But, for reasons of political expediency, Hitler was embarrassed by the book's strident anti-Christian and neo-pagan flavour and refused to allow it to be officially endorsed by the party. This did not prevent it becoming a largely unread bestseller. In 1930, Rosenberg was elected to the Reichstag for the electoral district of Hesse-Darmstadt, retaining the seat until 1945.

After 1933 his influence declined as the exigencies of power politics determined ranking in the Third Reich, though he was by no means a peripheral figure. From 1933 until 1945 he was head of the NSDAP's Foreign Affairs Department, and from 1934 was 'The *Führer*'s Delegate for the Supervision of the Entire Intellectual and Philosophical Education and Instruction of the NSDAP'. The importance of these offices was secondary, however, to other centres of power. In 1939 Rosenberg established in Frankfurt his Institute for the Investigation of the Jewish Question, and during the war organized a special task force which systematically looted Jewish treasures from homes, libraries and art galleries throughout German-occupied Europe. From 1941 until 1945 he was *Reichsminister* for the Occupied Eastern Territories, where his authority, brutally exercised as it was, was soon superseded by the even more savage extermination policy of the SS. Convicted by the Nuremberg Tribunal as a major war criminal, Rosenberg was hanged on 16 October 1946.

*Further Reading*

Among the most noteworthy of Rosenberg's writings are: *Unmoral im Talmud*, Munich, 1920; *Die Spur des Juden im Wandel der Zeiten*, Munich, 1920; *Das Verbrechen der Freimaurerei. Judentum, Jesuitismus, deutsches Christentum*, Munich, 1921; *Der staatsfeindliche Zionismus*, Hamburg, 1922; *Pest in Russland. Der Bolschewismus, seine Häupter, Handlanger und Opfer*,

Munich, 1922; *Wesen, Grundsätze und Ziele der Nationalsozialistischen Deutschen Arbeiterpartei*, Munich, 1923; *Die Protokolle der Weisen von Zion und die jüdische Weltpolitik*, Munich, 1923; *Der völkische Staatsgedanke*, Munich, 1924; *Die internationale Hochfinanz als Herrn der Arbeiterbewegung in allen Ländern*, Munich, 1924; *Novemberköpfe*, Berlin, 1927; *Der Weltverschwörerkongress zu Basel*, Munich, 1927; *Freimaurerische Weltpolitik im Lichte der Kritischen Forschung*, Munich, 1929; *Der Mythos des 20. Jahrhunderts*, Munich, 1930; *Die Entwicklung der deutschen Freiheitsbewegung*, Munich, 1933; *Kampf um die Macht. Aufsätze von 1921–1932* (edited by Thilo von Trotha), Munich, 1937; *Blut und Ehre. Ein Kampf für die deutsche Wiedergeburt. Reden und Aufsätze von 1919–1933*, Munich, 1939; *Schriften und Reden. Band I: 1917–1921, Band II: 1921–1923*, Munich, 1943; *Letzte Aufzeichnungen. Ideale und Idole der nationalsozialistischen Revolution.* (edited by H. Härtle), Göttingen, 1955; *Grossdeutschland. Traum und Tragödie. Rosenbergs Kritik am Hitlerismus* (edited by H. Härtle), Munich, 1970.

See also S. Lang and E. von Schenk (eds), *Porträt eines Menschheitsverbrechers nach den hinterlassenen Memoiren des ehemaligen Reichsministers Alfred Rosenberg*, St Gallen, 1947; H.G. Seraphim (ed.), *Das politische Tagebuch Alfred Rosenbergs 1934/35 und 1939/40*, Munich, 1964; R. Pois (ed.), *Alfred Rosenberg. Selected Writings*, London, 1970; R. Bollmus, *Das Amt Rosenberg und seine Gegner. Studien zum Machtkampf im nationalsozialistischen Herrschaftssystem*, Stuttgart, 1970; H.-D. Loock: *Quisling, Rosenberg und Terboven. Zur Vorgeschichte und Geschichte der nationalsozialistischen Revolution in Norwegen*, Stuttgart, 1970; R. Cecil, *The Myth of the Master Race. Alfred Rosenberg and Nazi Ideology*, London, 1972; R. Baumgärtner, *Weltanschauungskampf im Dritten Reich. Die Auseinandersetzung der Kirchen mit Alfred Rosenberg*, Mainz, 1977; J.B. Whisker, *The Social, Political and Religious Thought of Alfred Rosenberg. An Interpretative Essay*, London, 1982; F. Nova, *Alfred Rosenberg. Nazi Theorist of the Holocaust*, New York, 1986.

# SCHÄFFER, Fritz (1888–1967)

Born in Munich on 12 May 1888, the son of a minor civil servant, Schäffer completed his study of law with a doctorate from the University of Munich and, after serving in the army during the First World War, entered the Bavarian Ministry of the Interior. Of a strongly conservative, Catholic and monarchist disposition, he joined the BVP in 1919 and from 1920 until 1933 represented it in the Bavarian Landtag, developing specialist interests in problems of finance and federalism. A loyal Bavarian, he nevertheless was not a blind particularist and was perhaps more sympathetic to the status and role of central government than many of his party colleagues.

After serving for five years as chairman of the Munich district of the BVP, he was elected party chairman in 1929 and immediately forged a friendly and co-operative relationship with his counterpart in the Centre Party, Ludwig Kaas. Consequently, much of the tension which had plagued relations between the two parties earlier – highlighted by their different voting preferences in the 1925 Reich presidential election – largely disappeared. Schäffer led his party in firm support for the Brüning administration, whose economic and financial policies, in particular, he found wholly appropriate. Indeed, when appointed as State Councillor (*Staatsrat*) to lead the Bavarian Ministry of Finance in September 1931 in the Heinrich Held cabinet, he adopted similar measures. He was fully aware of the danger posed by the NSDAP, and for a period tried to bring it into government where it might be 'tamed'. But the NSDAP showed no interest, and his other thought, to have the party banned, simply was not feasible. In August 1932 Schäffer was part of the Centre/BVP delegation that negotiated with Hitler on a possible partnership in a Reich coalition government. The deteriorating political situation in the country as a whole had earlier, in 1931, persuaded him to assist in the establishment of a paramilitary organization under the wing of the BVP, the 30,000-strong Bayernwacht, which increasingly became involved in skirmishes with the SA. In the Reich presidential elections in spring 1932, Schäffer initially opposed not only Hitler but also von Hindenburg, thus attempting to reverse the BVP's stance of 1925. He wanted the Centre Party to link up with its sister party in support of a Brüning candidature, but when nothing came of the initiative, the BVP reluctantly fell in behind the Protestant field marshal for a second time.

In the final crisis of the Republic in late 1932 and early 1933, Schäffer's role was strangely ambivalent, or at least inconsistent in some respects. He apparently offered, if Franz von Papen is to be believed, to accept in January 1933 a ministerial post in a Hitler cabinet, not that such an invitation was ever forthcoming. When, at a meeting with the Reich President in February 1933, he failed to obtain assurances about Nazi intentions in Bavaria, he gave support to the notion of a Wittelsbach restoration. After an interview with Crown Prince Rupprecht, the head of the royal house, he put his scheme before the Bavarian cabinet. Prime Minister Held, however, was sceptical of the whole idea and it was abandoned. Shortly afterwards, the National Socialists appointed Ritter von Epp as Reich Commissioner in Bavaria, Schäffer was detained for a brief period and the BVP was dissolved. He retired to private civilian employment until arrested in connection with the July Plot in 1944 and sent to Dachau concentration camp.

Liberated by the Americans in May 1945, Schäffer was immediately appointed Prime Minister of Bavaria by the military authorities, only to be dismissed after a few months for alleged leniency towards former Nazis. A prosecution witness at former Chancellor Franz von Papen's denazification trial in 1947, he rebuilt his political career as a founder member of the Christian Social Union, the BVP's successor. From 1949 until 1957 he was a successful Federal Minister of Finance. Schäffer died on 29 March 1967 in Berchtesgaden.

## Further Reading

F. Schäffer, *Der Föderalismus in Deutschland*, Munich, 1928; *Die Aushöhlungs- und Aushungerungspolitik des Reiches gegenüber den Ländern*, Munich, 1928. See also P.C. Hartmann and O. Altendorfer (eds), *100 Jahre Fritz Schäffer. Politik in schwierigen Zeiten*, Passau, 1988; K. Schwend, *Bayern zwischen Monarchie und Diktatur. Beiträge zur bayerische Frage, 1918-1933*, Munich, 1954; K. Schwend, 'Die Bayerische Volkspartei', in E. Matthias and R. Morsey (eds), *Das Ende der Parteien. Darstellungen und Dokumente*, Düsseldorf, 1960, pp. 457-519; H. Fenske, *Konservatismus und Rechtsradikalismus in Bayern nach 1918*, Bad Homburg, 1969; W. Benz (ed.), *Politik in Bayern 1919-1933*.

*Berichte des württembergischen Gesandten Carl Moser von Filseck*, Stuttgart, 1971; K. Schönhoven, *Die Bayerische Volkspartei 1924–1932*, Düsseldorf, 1972; F. Wiesemann, *Die Vorgeschichte der nationalsozialistischen Machtübernahme in Bayern 1932/33*, Berlin, 1975; K. Schönhoven, 'Zwischen Anpassung und Ausschaltung. Die Bayerische Volkspartei in der Endphase der Weimarer Republik 1932–33', *Historische Zeitschrift*, 224, 1977, pp. 340–78.

## SCHEIDEMANN, Philipp (1865–1939)

One of the most important SPD leaders from 1913–14 onwards and Reich Chancellor of the first regular republican government in 1919, Scheidemann was born into a working-class home in Kassel on 26 July 1865, became a printer by trade, and joined the party in 1883. In Kassel three years later he began his journalistic career on an illegal socialist newspaper and went on to write for several others over a lengthy period, including the *Mitteldeutsche Sonntagszeitung*; in 1905 he was appointed chief editor of the *Kasseler Volksblatt*. Having failed to secure a Reichstag seat for Solingen in 1898, his second attempt in the same constituency five years later was successful, and during the pre-war era he emerged as the party's leading spokesman on agriculture. He remained a parliamentary deputy until 1933. An excellent orator, regarded by many colleagues as something of a careerist with a burning desire to make a name for himself and be accepted by the political and social establishment, he was untroubled by theoretical aspects of socialism or Marxism. He liked to think he could articulate the thoughts and feelings of the ordinary man in the street. Essentially a pragmatist, therefore, he took care not to be associated too closely with the various factions in the party before 1914, preferring to keep his options open in the nebulous centre. Only during the First World War did he move firmly to the moderate right-wing element. Elected to the SPD executive committee in 1911, and a co-chairman of the party's parliamentary delegation following the death of August Bebel in 1913, he fully supported the party policy on war credits, declaring: 'we are defending the Fatherland in order to conquer it'.

During the war the SPD's attitude was loyal towards the government – Scheidemann even travelling to the Netherlands as its emissary to dampen down anti-German sentiment – but based on a rejection of annexations and the right of all peoples to self-determination within the framework of a negotiated peace, an attitude personalized as the 'Scheidemann Peace'. But he warned in 1917 that a Russian-style revolution would occur in Germany unless the government undertook fundamental political reform. By October 1917, he was already anticipating the SPD playing a direct role in a post-war democratic parliamentary government. A year later, he became the first German socialist to hold senior government office when, as his party's representative, he joined Prince Max of Baden's coalition cabinet as Secretary of State. A few weeks later he demanded the Kaiser's abdication as a 'historical necessity'.

In the November Revolution, Scheidemann adopted a fierce anti-Bolshevik stance and without authorization proclaimed the establishment of a German Republic to a crowd assembled outside the Reichstag on 9 November 1918. He was a leading member of the Council of People's Representatives, and from February to June 1919 was Reich Chancellor in a 'Weimar Coalition' (SPD, DDP, Centre Party) administration. When presented with the peace terms, he declared at a session of the National Assembly in the University of Berlin on 12 May: 'what hand would not wither that ties itself and us to these chains'. On 20 June he and his cabinet resigned. Scheidemann, co-chairman of the SPD with Friedrich Ebert in 1918–19, and a member of the party executive committee until 1933, was elected Lord Mayor of Kassel at the end of 1919. He held this post until 1925, having survived a right-wing assassination attempt in 1922. He continued to exercise his oratorical talents in the Reichstag, notably in March 1920 when he launched a bitter attack on the Reichswehr for its role during the Kapp Putsch, and in December 1926 when he sought to weaken the Marx government by revealing the army's clandestine links with the Red Army and German paramilitary and nationalist groups. The speech caused a sensation, but was condemned as politically injudicious by all sides. Nevertheless, he continued to warn of the danger posed by the Right to the Republic.

Scheidemann fled Germany in 1933 and eventually settled into exile in Denmark, dying in Copenhagen on 29 November 1939.

## Further Reading

P. Scheidemann, *Der Zusammenbruch*, Berlin, 1921, *Die rechtsradikalen Verschwörer*, Berlin, 1923; *Memoiren eines Sozialdemokraten*, 2 vols, Dresden, 1928 (translated into English as *The Making of New Germany, Memoirs*, New York, 1929. See also J. Werthauer, *Das Blausäure. Attentat auf Scheidemann*, Berlin, 1923; U. Kluge, *Die deutsche Revolution 1918–1919*, Frankfurt am Main, 1985; S. Miller, *Burgfrieden und Klassenkampf. Die deutsche Sozialdemokratie im Ersten Weltkrieg*, Düsseldorf, 1974; S. Miller, *Die Bürde der Macht. Die deutsche Sozialdemokratie 1918–1920*, Düsseldorf, 1978; H.A. Winkler, *Die Sozialdemokratie und die Revolution 1918–1919*, Bonn, 1979; H. Schulze (ed.), *Akten der Reichskanzlei. Weimarer Republik. Das Kabinett Scheidemann: 13. Februar bis 20. Juni 1919*, Boppard, 1971.

# SCHIELE, Martin (1870–1939)

The influential agrarian leader and several times Reich minister was born in Gross-Schwarzlosen on 17 January 1870, completed a doctorate in estate management and developed business interests in both farming and commerce. A member of the German Conservative Party since the 1890s, he was elected to the Reichstag in 1914 and four years later helped found the DNVP, which he represented in parliament until March 1930. One of four DNVP members appointed to Hans Luther's cabinet in January 1925, Schiele, as Reich Minister of the Interior, spent much of his time criticizing Stresemann's foreign policy, and indeed resigned with his party colleagues in October of that year in protest at the Locarno Pact. In his subsequent diaries, the Foreign Minister was in turn scathing about Schiele's allegedly unscrupulous use of patronage while in office. Schiele rejoined government in January 1927 as Reich Minister of Agriculture in Wilhelm Marx's fourth administration, and made his mark by introducing early the following year an emergency programme for farmers already suffering a crisis. It was chiefly designed to help the livestock and dairy produce sectors in a way which followed on logically from the Tariffs Act of 1928. At the back of his mind was the belief that industry and agriculture were evenly balanced in the economy, a situation which had to be maintained because Germany was, to use his neologism, an *Agrarindustriestaat*. His efforts to improve his constituency could on occasion prove embarrassing to his government, however, as when in May 1927 he publicly demanded higher tariffs on agricultural products while Germany was eagerly proposing tariff reductions at the World Economic Conference in Geneva.

Schiele's profile as a leader of the agrarian interest was further enhanced when, a few months after leaving ministerial office, he was appointed executive president of the important pressure group, the National Agrarian League (Reichslandbund), which he continued to lead in a relatively moderate, responsible fashion until October 1930. In February 1929 he also co-founded and became the major driving force behind the Green Front, an umbrella organization of the four principal rural interest groups in Germany, whose objective was basically to create governmental sympathy for the worsening plight of farmers. Schiele's position in the DNVP was beginning to be somewhat shaky in the intransigently anti-republican Hugenberg era, and matters came to a head at the end of 1929 when, unable fully to accept the so-called 'Freedom Law' put forward by his party leader, he resigned and early the following year joined the splinter Christian National Peasants and Agrarian People's Party. When he joined Chancellor Brüning's government as Reich Minister of Agriculture in March 1930 he also resigned his DNVP seat in the Reichstag.

Schiele's latest appointment was warmly welcomed by farmers who saw him as a forthright champion of their interests and, supported by Reich President von Hindenburg, he demanded an extensive protectionist programme for them from the state. He put constant pressure on the Chancellor to meet his demands, much to the annoyance of industrialists and the Reich Minister of Labour, Adam Stegerwald, who felt the needs of industry were being neglected. The resultant programme of *Osthilfe* was designed to effect a refinancing and amortization of agricultural debts, a lowering of interest rates and other payments, and a reform of the credit structure in order to maintain existing agricultural enterprises. Higher tariffs and various other import controls completed the package. Before long, however, farmers complained that these measures were inadequate, but with the whole aid programme running into a financial scandal in which von Hindenburg was implicated, and Brüning having to consider other priorities, Schiele was unable to fulfil expectations. By early 1932 he was the target of bitter criticism from the National Agrarian League and other farming organizations, which became more politically radical. Out of office in May 1932, he was no longer prominently engaged in politics and went into retirement after 1933. He died in Suckow, Mecklenburg, on 16 February 1939.

## Further Reading

M. Schiele, *Der Schutz der deutschen Landwirtschaft*, Berlin, 1930. See also B. Buchta, *Die Junker und die Weimarer Republik. Charakter und Bedeutung der Osthilfe in den Jahren 1928–1933*, East Berlin, 1959; D. Hertz-Eichenrode, *Politik und Landwirtschaft in Ostpreussen 1919–1930*, Cologne, 1969; D. Gessner, *Agrarverbände in der Weimarer Republik*, Wiesbaden, 1976; D. Gessner, *Agrardepression und Präsidialregierungen in Deutschland 1930 bis 1933. Probleme des Agrarprotektionismus am Ende der Weimarer Republik*, Düsseldorf, 1977; D. Gessner, '"Grüne Front" oder "Harzburger Front". Der Reichs-Landbund in der letzten Phase der Weimarer Republik', *Vierteljahrshefte für Zeitgeschichte*, 29, 1981, no. 1, pp. 110–23; D. Abraham, *The Collapse of the Weimar Republic. Political Economy and Crisis*, 2nd edn, New York, 1986.

## SCHIFFER, Eugen (1860-1954)

A substantial personality in the upper echelons of the DDP leadership during the final phase of a long political career in German liberalism, Schiffer was born into a middle-class Jewish family in Breslau on 14 February 1860, and on completion of a law degree pursued a successful professional life in the Prussian judicial administration. From 1903 until 1918 he sat as a National Liberal Party deputy in the Prussian House of Deputies and also, from 1911 until 1917, in the Reichstag, where he was a prominent supporter of the Peace Resolution in July of that latter year. In 1916-17 he headed the Legal Department in the War Office of the Prussian Ministry of War, and from 1917 until his entry into government in early 1919 he was employed in the Reich Treasury Office, latterly as Secretary of State.

Joining the DDP in 1918, Schiffer had a powerful parliamentary base from which to exert influence for he enjoyed membership of the National Assembly in 1919-20, and then of both the Reichstag and the Prussian Landtag until spring 1924: in both the Assembly and Reichstag he was chairman of the DDP delegation. Appointed Vice-Chancellor and Reich Minister of Finance in Philipp Scheidemann's cabinet in February 1919, he immediately and categorically stated his opposition to any economic experiments, particularly socialization of industry, because of the extremely unstable condition of the economy and public finances, and committed himself to the restoration of the free enterprise system as soon as possible. However, in March 1919 the DDP delegation in the National Assembly voted in favour of the government's socialization Bill in order to maintain cabinet unity, which prompted Schiffer's resignation from office a month later in protest at the whole tenor of Scheidemann's social and economic programme. Thereafter, he consistently opposed his party's co-operation with the SPD in government, advocating instead a concentration of middle-class political interests within the 'Weimar coalition' framework. But despite his skills as a negotiator and political manager, he usually failed to unite the fragmented DDP on major issues. For example, in his capacity as chairman of the party's socialization committee in 1920 he could not construct a consensus on the question of socialisation measures, and similarly, his attempts to forge a more realistic party approach to foreign affairs, free of nationalist emotion and resentment over the

Treaty of Versailles, proved fruitless. Thus, while he accepted the London Ultimatum on reparations, most of his colleagues were against it.

Following the DDP's decision to enter the second cabinet of Gustav Bauer in October 1919, Schiffer served as Vice Chancellor and Reich Minister of Justice until compelled to resign when the trade unions criticized his somewhat ambiguous role during the Kapp Putsch. He was the only cabinet member to remain in Berlin as the insurgents took over the city, but his negotiating posture was not well received by other government ministers from their temporary haven in Stuttgart. Just over a year later, however, he returned to the centre of national politics when he joined Chancellor Wirth's first cabinet as Reich Minister of Justice in May–October 1921. In this brief period, he encouraged a programme of judicial and administrative reform and was primarily responsible for the establishment in Berlin of the Academy of Administration, whose president he subsequently became. As German Plenipotentiary for Upper Silesia in Wirth's second administration from October 1921 until May 1922, Schiffer carried out an arduous and complex task with considerable success. The regulation of the partition by a three-man commission resulted in the German–Polish Agreement, signed in Geneva in May 1922, which observers regarded as an important advance in international law. For his contribution, he spent 1922–23 as Germany's representative at the International Court in The Hague. On returning to Berlin, he supported the idea of the DDP joining the DNVP in a coalition government in spring 1924, but found that, once again, the party could not agree on a positive course of action. Increasingly frustrated by its failure to bring about liberal unity in the centre of German politics, Schiffer seceded from the party in October 1924 to found and lead the Liberal Association, whose aim was to create a united movement of political liberalism. The new grouping failed after several well-publicized attempts to mould a constructive relationship with the DDP and DVP, and in December 1925 he resigned at the age of 65 to make way for others not yet touched by disillusionment. Having previously given up his Reichstag seat in autumn 1924, he was now free to resume his legal career in Berlin and to accept several directorships in industry.

During the Third Reich, Schiffer became the central figure of an informal discussion group – the so-called 'Schiffer Circle' – which included prominent liberal and moderate conservative politicians from the Weimar era, as well as the later resistance hero, Helmuth James Graf von Moltke, but he managed to survive. Indeed, he was still fit enough to add a postscript to both his political and professional careers during the early post-war years in Soviet-occupied eastern Germany. In 1946 he was elected to the executive committee of the Liberal Democratic Party, and until 1948 he headed the central system of justice in the East. He also campaigned to preserve German unity. A remarkably varied, full life ended in East Berlin on 5 September 1954.

## Further Reading

E. Schiffer, *Deutschlands Finanzlage nach dem Kriege*, Berlin 1919; *Das erste Jahr nach der Revolution*, Berlin, 1919; *Von der Nationalversammlung zum Reichstag*, Berlin, 1920; *Die deutsche Justiz*, Berlin, 1928; *Sturm über Deutschland*, Berlin 1932; and his memoirs, *Ein Leben für den Liberalismus*, East Berlin 1951.

See also W. Stephan, *Aufstieg und Verfall des Linksliberalismus 1918–1933. Geschichte der Deutschen Demokratischen Partei*, Göttingen, 1973; J. Ramm, *Eugen Schiffer und die Reform der deutschen Justiz*, Neuwied, 1987; L.E. Jones, *German Liberalism and the Dissolution of the Weimar Party System 1918–1933*, Chapel Hill, 1988. On Schiffer during the Nazi period see Friedrich Meinecke, *Autobiographische Schriften*, Stuttgart, 1969.

# SCHLANGE-SCHÖNINGEN, Hans (1886-1960)

Born into a well-established family of estate owners in Schöningen, Pomerania, on 17 November 1886, Schlange-Schöningen followed in his early career a path that was traditional to his aristocratic caste: an army cadetship in an élite Prussian regiment followed by service as an officer in the First World War. After 1918 his natural political habitat had to be the DNVP, with its ultra-conservative, nationalist and monarchist outlook, and deep hostility to the parliamentary Republic. Indeed, in the early 1920s he was a prominent defender of the *völkisch* cause and complained bitterly to Carl Severing in the Prussian Landtag in early 1923 when he banned the Deutschvölkische Freiheitspartei. Schlange-Schöningen represented his party in that assembly from 1920 until 1928, and also in the Reichstag from 1924 to 1930. From 1924 to 1929 he was chairman of the DNVP's Pomeranian district branch, and served as deputy chairman of the party itself from 1926 until 1928.

During the course of the 1920s, however, he abandoned his total rejection of the Republic in favour of seeking a broader accommodation with it on a moderate conservative basis. Unable to see the rationale behind Alfred Hugenberg's stridently chauvinistic and intolerant stance, his alienation from reactionary conservatism culminated in his leaving the DNVP in early 1930 over the party chairman's tactics concerning the 'Freedom Law'. Schlange-Schöningen joined the Christian National Peasants' and Agrarian People's Party, representing it in the Reichstag until mid-1932. He became one of Chancellor Brüning's strongest supporters on the German Right, and tried before the autumn of 1930 to create a broad base of centre and moderate Right support for his government in the Reichstag. But the DVP rejected his overtures, as did a number of other prominent conservatives. He was increasingly aware of the threat posed by the National Socialists and strove to find a political grouping that would reflect his ideal of national unity, the antithesis of which was the sectarian and racial divisiveness preached by Hitler and Hugenberg.

By the early 1930s Schlange-Schöningen had developed a substantial reputation as an agrarian specialist. He had transformed his formerly backward estates into an efficient commercial enterprise, and he had written outstanding papers on various aspects of farming and estate management. These qualifications, in conjunction with his admiration for Heinrich Brüning, made him an obvious choice in 1931 for the post of Reich Commissioner for the Eastern Aid Programme (*Osthilfe*) in the Chancellor's cabinet; he was also Reich Minister without Portfolio. The Aid Programme was designed as a rescue operation by the national government for the depressed agrarian provinces of eastern Germany, particularly East Prussia, and incorporated measures to ease debts, mortgage payments and the credit mechanism. But the Reich Commissioner aroused the hostility of his fellow Junker estate owners by suggesting that the programme should also seek to resettle unemployed workers from industrial parts of Germany in the East. Some estates would be broken up and some arable land redistributed. But this domestic form of colonization was denounced by the estate owners as 'agrarian Bolshevism', and exerting political pressure through one of their own kind, Reich President von Hindenburg, they succeeded in making Schlange-Schöningen's position virtually untenable. The *Osthilfe* controversy played an important part in his Chancellor's downfall in May 1932.

During the final, critical phase of the Weimar Republic, he continued his endeavours to construct a meaningful political bloc of the moderate non-Catholic Right, encouraging the German National League, founded in 1932, to act as a spearhead of this initiative. But Schlange-Schöningen, by excluding from consideration the Centre Party and the SPD, entertained quite unrealistic expectations in this regard, particularly as the moderate Protestant bourgeois right-of-centre milieu had all but disappeared as a political factor by July 1932, as the Reichstag elections clearly showed.

During the Third Reich, Schlange-Schöningen was associated with the conservative-nationalist resistance circle around Carl Goerdeler, and was under consideration for the post of Reich Minister of Agriculture in a post-Hitler government, according to plans drawn up in 1943. He was not arrested in connection with the July Plot. After 1945 he assisted in the creation of the Christian Democratic Party in Western Germany, but scored his most noteworthy political success by organizing food supplies for the population. From 1950 until 1955 he was the Federal Republic's diplomatic representative in London. He died in Bad Godesberg on 20 July 1960.

## Further Reading

H. Schlange-Schöningen, *Acker und Arbeit*, Oldenburg i.O. 1932; *The Morning After. Memoirs*, London, 1948 (originally published as *Am Tage danach*, Hamburg, 1946). See also A. Chanady, 'The Disintegration of the German National People's Party, 1924–1930', *Journal of Modern History*, 39, 1967, pp. 65–91; H. Muth, 'Agrarpolitik und Parteipolitik im Frühjahr 1932', in F.A. Hermens and T. Schieder (eds), *Staat, Wirtschaft und Politik in der Weimarer Republik. Festschrift für Heinrich Brüning*, Berlin, 1967, pp. 317–360; G.J. Trittel, 'Hans Schlange-Schöningen. Ein vergessener Politiker der "Ersten Stunde"', *Vierteljahrshefte für Zeitgeschichte*, 25, 1987, pp. 25–63; J. Farquharson, 'The Consensus that Never Came. H. Schlange-Schöningen and the CDU, 1945–9', *European History Quarterly*, 19, 1989, pp. 353–83.

# SCHLEICHER, Kurt von (1882–1934)

Arguably the most decisive political influence in Germany during the early 1930s and the last Chancellor of the Weimar Republic, Schleicher personified the fateful way in which the Reichswehr developed as much of a political as of a purely military profile.

Inordinately ambitious for power, he had 'an overweening predilection for intrigue' (Wheeler-Bennett), often operating behind the scenes with a rare combination of guile, deviousness and lack of scruple. Born the son of an old family of the minor aristocracy in Brandenburg on 7 April 1882, he began his military career in 1900 as a subaltern in von Hindenburg's old regiment, the Third Foot Guards. Selected for service with the General Staff in 1913, Schleicher spent a brief period on the Eastern Front during the First World War, earning the Iron Cross, and after serving in various posts at Supreme Headquarters was appointed Adjutant in October 1918 to the Quartermaster-General, Wilhelm Groener, with whom he formed a firm personal friendship. Thereafter, he was never far from the centre of power in the army.

With the rank of major, von Schleicher was head of the Truppenamt in the Reichswehr Ministry from 1919 until 1926, during which time he acted as an essential coordinator between the army high command and the socialist-led government during the November Revolution, played an important role in the organization and equipping of the right-wing *Freikorps* units and, as an intimate of General Hans von Seeckt, Chief of the *Heeresleitung*, was heavily involved in promoting the German army's collaboration with the Red Army. It was also von Schleicher more than anyone else who was responsible for the success of the army's experiment in 'military government' from September 1923 until February 1924. By the end of his time in the Truppenamt, he exercised extensive control over the army's political affairs, supported by a network of friends and informants in government, the political parties and high society. Promoted in 1926 to the rank of colonel and to the leadership of the *Wehrmachtsabteilung* until 1929, he further consolidated his political base, which included excellent contacts with Reich President von Hindenburg and his circle. Indeed, in January 1928, he persuaded the President to appoint Groener, his friend and mentor from the war, Minister of Defence. A year later, Groener in a sense reciprocated by having von Schleicher made head of the newly created Ministry Bureau (*Ministeramt*) in the Reichswehr Ministry, with the rank of major-general. The Minister of Defence had complete trust in his protégé's political talents, which were now given unprecedented scope for expression. Over the next three years he was at the very heart of national politics, content to wield often crucial influence from his army office.

Von Schleicher played a key role in the appointment and dismissal of Chancellors Brüning and von Papen before assuming this office himself between 2 December 1932 and 28 January 1933. Lacking support in the country and in parliament, and distrusted by many of his fellow officers, he tried without success to create a broad crossparty nationalist and moderate alliance, to include the putative 'left wing' of the NSDAP around Gregor Strasser and sections of the trade union movement around Theodor Leipart and Adam Stegerwald. He even attempted subsequently to attract the backing of the SPD. All the time he was attracting only hostility from the traditional conservative élites in industry, agriculture and the army, who feared that the General's *Querfront* strategy amounted to a form of military-based socialism. His plans to break up and disperse the bankrupt Junker estates in the East, his ambivalence towards the capitalist free enterprise system, and his support for social welfare and job creation programmes in aid of the working classes were too much for the élites to tolerate. Using spokesmen such as von Papen and Hjalmar Schacht, they put pressure on von Hindenburg to withdraw his presidential base from the government and get rid of the irksome Chancellor. Unable to secure additional powers that would have allowed him to establish a form of military dictatorship early in 1933, Schleicher was left exposed and isolated, and a victim also of political intrigue. His dismissal removed the last important obstacle to Hitler's appointment as Chancellor, something which von Schleicher had spent a great deal of time and effort trying to avoid. His political and military career lay in ruins.

The general, in his enforced retirement, kept a close eye on political developments and retained some of his former contacts. But Hitler, never one to forget or forgive, had him and his wife murdered at their home in Berlin during the Röhm purge, on 30 June 1934.

## Further Reading

T. Vogelsang, *Reichswehr, Staat und NSDAP. Beiträge zur deutschen Geschichte 1930-1932*, Stuttgart, 1962; T. Vogelsang, *Kurt von Schleicher. Ein General als Politiker*, Göttingen, 1965; F.L. Carsten, *The Reichswehr and Politics 1918-1933*, Oxford, 1966; J. Wheeler-Bennett, *The Nemesis of Power. The German Army in Politics, 1918-1945*, London, 1953; A. Schildt, *Militärdiktatur mit Massenbasis? Die Querfrontkonzeption der Reichswehrführung um General von Schleicher am Ende der Weimarer Republik*, Frankfurt am Main, 1981; P. Hayes: '"A Question Mark with Epaulettes"? Kurt von Schleicher and Weimar Politics', *Journal of Modern History*, 52, 1980, pp. 35-65; H. Muth, 'Schleicher und die Gewerkschaften 1932. Ein Quellenproblem', *Vierteljahrshefte für Zeitgeschichte*, 29, 1981, pp. 189-215; F.-K. von Plehwe, *Reichskanzler Kurt von Schleicher. Weimars letzte Chance gegen Hitler*, Esslingen, 1983; A. Golecki (ed.), *Akten der Reichskanzlei. Weimarer Republik. Das Kabinett von Schleicher*, Boppard, 1986.

## SCHMIDT, Robert (1864-1943)

The respected economics spokesman from the revisionist right wing of the SPD and experienced Reich cabinet minister of the early and late 1920s made his considerable impact on Weimar politics after years of trade union, party and parliamentary activity in Imperial Germany. Schmidt was born into a working-class home in Berlin on 15 May 1864, completed an apprenticeship as a piano-maker, and from 1890 made his way as an official in the piano-makers' and woodworkers' trade unions. He also worked for a period as an editor on the SPD newspaper, *Vorwärts*. In 1902 he was elected to the General Commission of German Trade Unions, where until the end of the First World War he had responsibility for a variety of social, economic and insurance affairs. In 1907-08 he was an outspoken opponent of an independent socialist youth movement, believing it should be under party and trade union control. A Reichstag member in 1893-98 and 1903-18, he identified solidly with the revisionist stream in the SPD, particularly the likes of Wolfgang Heine, Eduard David, Otto Hué and Friedrich Stampfer, and, as he revealed to startled cabinet colleagues in

November 1923, he spent some years in prison for his socialist beliefs and activity. During the First World War he developed an informed interest in questions of food and agriculture which, in October 1918, earned him an appointment as Under-Secretary of State in the War Food Office in Prince Max of Baden's government.

Schmidt began his post-war ministerial career in Philipp Scheidemann's cabinet (February–June 1919), where he was responsible for food, an important ministry, given the suffering of the general population at that time from the effects of the Allied blockade and the disruption caused by the ending of the war. A calm and reserved man, he tackled the food problem with efficiency and some success, adopting a series of short-term pragmatic measures, though his longer-term aim was socialization of the most important parts of the economy. During the SPD's somewhat confused debate about the future of the economy in 1919, he emerged as a critic of colleague Rudolf Wissell's concept of a 'common economy' (*Gemeinwirtschaft*), claiming it was tantamount to an unacceptably diluted form of socialization that was incompatible with the SPD's Erfurt Programme of 1891. Schmidt resigned along with the rest of the cabinet in June 1919, though he had personally favoured German acceptance of the terms of the Versailles Treaty. He retained the Ministry of Food portfolio in the incoming Bauer administration, but was switched to the Ministry of Economics in July 1919 on Wissell's resignation. Later that year he grudgingly sanctioned a gradual dismantling of existing state controls, including those on prices of some non-essential goods, and reduced the number of enterprises regulated by government. He continued to supervise this process in the same ministerial capacity for the first Hermann Müller cabinet (March–June 1920).

Minister of Economics once again in the cabinets led by Joseph Wirth from May 1921 until November 1922, Schmidt presented a plan for the taxation of 'real values' (*Erfassung der Sachwerte*). He argued in cabinet that wage and salary earners, pensioners and those with savings accounts had suffered badly from inflation whereas owners of property in agriculture, industry and real estate had not been affected to nearly the same extent, because the value of their holdings had risen in proportion to the fall in the value of the mark. In view of the urgent need for tax revenue to meet the early reparations payments and to balance the budget, he continued, the government should consider this unearned increase in the value of property. He suggested that it seize about 20 per cent ownership of farms, commercial enterprises and housing. Farmers and householders would then pay off a compulsory mortgage, while firms would surrender roughly 20 per cent of their stock and pay dividends on it. He estimated that 20 billion marks could be raised annually, which was almost half of the projected reparations bill each year. Ingenious as Schmidt's proposal was, his Chancellor thought it too unwieldy to operate and it was effectively abandoned. When Schmidt returned to office as Vice-Chancellor and Reich Minister for Reconstruction in Gustav Stresemann's two cabinets (August–November 1923), his most noteworthy contribution was his stout defence of the principle of the eight-hour day in industry, which he described as the only material advantage of the November Revolution remaining to the working classes. Stresemann, trying to reconcile conflicting pressures within the cabinet, eventually decided on a compromise solution put forward by his Vice-Chancellor, whereby the eight-hour day was retained in principle but could be waived in specified exceptional conditions. Schmidt resigned from office along with fellow SPD ministers in protest at the government's interventionist policy in Saxony and Thuringia that autumn. He returned to cabinet for the last time when appointed in December 1929 to take over the Reich Ministry of Economics in Hermann Müller's Grand Coalition administration. He was a member of the German delegation to the Hague Conference on reparations in January 1930, and he tried hard but ultimately without success to maintain cabinet unity over the funding of the unemployment insurance scheme.

The collapse of the last parliamentary government of the Weimar Republic signalled the end of Schmidt's political activity in the SPD and the Reichstag, where he had sat since 1918. He died in Berlin on 16 September 1943.

## Further Reading
Scattered references to Schmidt's political career exist in a number of scholarly works on the SPD, most notably, H.A. Winkler, *Von der Revolution zur Stabilisierung. Arbeiter und Arbeiterbewegung in der Weimarer Republik 1918 bis 1924*, Hamburg, 1984; and H.A. Winkler, *Der Schein der Normalität. Arbeiter und Arbeiterbewegung in der Weimarer Republik 1924 bis 1930*, Hamburg, 1985.

# SCHOLZ, Ernst (1874–1932)

Before emerging as one of the DVP's most prominent leaders in Weimar politics, Scholz had enjoyed a successful career in local government administration in Imperial Germany. Born in Berlin of middle-class parents in 1874, he completed a doctorate in law, and after gaining experience in a number of posts was appointed Lord Mayor of Kassel in 1912. The following year he moved to a similar position at Charlottenburg, which was still independent of Berlin. Joining the Prussian Upper House (Herrenhaus) as a National Liberal in 1912, he saw service as an officer in the First World War, returning to his office in Charlottenburg from 1918 until 1920.

A member of the DVP from 1918, Scholz's recognized expertise in financial affairs led to his appointment as Reich Minister of Economics in the Konstantin Fehrenbach government from June 1920 until May 1921. Elected to the Reichstag in 1921, where he remained until 1932, his astute political talent and leadership qualities brought him the chairmanship of the party's parliamentary delegation from 1923 until 1932. His professional interests were simultaneously sustained through his chairmanship from 1922 until 1929 of the Reichsbund der Höheren Beamten Deutschlands.

As chairman of the DVP Reichstag delegation, Scholz faced the perennial task of achieving balance between the various factions, and for this purpose he invariably adopted a centrist position, at least in the early and mid-1920s. However, he was not afraid to take a vigorous line on certain issues that he knew would displease some colleagues. Thus, in autumn 1923 he pushed hard for the inclusion of the DNVP in Stresemann's cabinet, much to the latter's embarrassment, and shortly afterwards caused some dismay on the left wing of the party by his firm advocacy of the abolition of the eight-hour day. His public support of a pro-Russian orientation in German foreign policy, which included a widely noticed article in *Izvestia* in spring 1926, reminded Stresemann of the delicacy of his dealings with the Western Allies over the Locarno agreements. Later that year a blistering attack he made in a speech in Insterburg on the SPD's social and military policies contributed to the crisis which brought down the third cabinet of Wilhelm Marx. Because of his particularly good relations with Reich President von Hindenburg, Scholz himself was asked to form a government. He declined, and instead campaigned yet again for the DNVP's inclusion in cabinet – this time successfully. But the poor showing of the liberal parties in the 1928 Reichstag elections concentrated his mind on other matters, above all, the thorny issue of liberal unity. He completely ruled out a merger of the DVP and DDP, though he did favour some kind of parliamentary alliance which subsequently he wanted to extend across the moderate bourgeois spectrum as far as the left wing of the DNVP. At the same time, he kept his distance from the Liberal Association, whose objective was to bring about a united liberal political movement.

Scholz's relations with party chairman Stresemann deteriorated markedly following that Reichstag election. Having for a second time declined an offer from von Hindenburg to form a cabinet, Scholz ruled out the DVP's involvement in a coalition in which the SPD was included, only to be overruled by his chairman who, in a message to SPD leader Hermann Müller, offered alternative arrangements which resulted in him and Julius Curtius joining the Grand Coalition. The rift did not last long in view of Stresemann's premature death in October 1929. Scholz's election to the party chairmanship two months later represented a decisive triumph for the conservative business wing of the party, but new Reichstag elections in September 1930 revealed his inability to halt the DVP's electoral decline. He also suffered a personal defeat when, in a ballot for the presidency of the Reichstag in October that year, he lost to the incumbent Paul Löbe by 269 votes to 209. Moreover, his endeavours to construct a moderate bourgeois front in support of Brüning's government were cut short by the establishment of the German State Party, which took him completely by surprise. In a few short months, his hopes for the DVP had been rudely shattered. Suffering from ill health in any case, he drew the obvious conclusions and resigned as party chairman in November 1930, to be replaced by Eduard Dingeldey. Scholz was elevated to the honorary chairmanship of the party, and continued to act as chairman of the parliamentary delegation in the Reichstag.

Scholz was not exactly a spent force in politics. His relations with both Brüning and von Hindenburg remained very cordial, and when the Chancellor was refashioning his cabinet in October 1931 he offered Scholz the position of Reich Interior Minister. Not for the first time he declined the offer of high office, which may be seen as a revealing commentary on a fundamental weakness of Weimar liberal politicians in general – an unwillingness, emanating perhaps from a lack of confidence, to assert themselves at the top levels of governmental responsibility. Scholz died of ill health at the age of 58 years in Berlin.

## Further Reading

L. Döhn, *Politik und Interesse. Die Interessenstruktur der Deutschen Volkspartei*, Meisenheim, 1970; H. Romeyk, 'Die Deutsche Volkspartei in Rheinland und Westfalen 1918–1933', *Rheinische Vierteljahrsblätter*, 39, 1975, pp. 189–236; L.E. Jones, *German Liberalism and the Dissolution of the Weimar Party System, 1918–1933*, Chapel Hill, 1988; H. Booms, 'Die Deutsche Volkspartei', in E. Matthias and R. Morsey (eds), *Das Ende der Parteien. Darstellungen und Dokumente*, Düsseldorf, 1979, pp. 523–39.

## SCHWERIN VON KROSIGK, Lutz Graf (1887–1977)

A leading civil servant who became an important member of the last two Weimar cabinets, Schwerin von Krosigk, scion of an old aristocratic family, was born in Rathmannsdorf, Anhalt, on 22 August 1887. He travelled widely in Europe, getting to know Britain very well, took a law degree and in 1909 joined the Prussian judicial system as a career civil servant. During the First World War he served as an officer with a Pomeranian cavalry regiment and was awarded the Iron Cross (First Class) for bravery. Able and personable, he climbed the promotion ladder in the 1920s as a highly-placed official in the Reich Ministry of Finance, culminating in his appointment in 1929 as Ministerial Director and head of the Budget Department in that Ministry. From 1931 he had added responsibilities in the Reparations Department.

In political matters, Schwerin von Krosigk was very much a reflection of his privileged background: conservative, authoritarian, nationalist and monarchist, with an ill-concealed dislike for the democratic state which employed him. He was not a member of any political party, but naturally inclined towards the DNVP. He fully supported Chancellor Brüning's deflationary economic and financial strategy and played a crucial role in formulating his many emergency decrees in this sphere. After a personal appeal to his patriotic loyalty by Reich President von Hindenburg, he accepted somewhat reluctantly the post of Reich Minister of Finance in Franz von Papen's cabinet. Here he mixed with ministers of similar social and political disposition – the so-called 'cabinet of barons' – and he immediately took steps to reduce public expenditure. A loan to the Prussian government was stopped but, more importantly, deeper cuts than even under the previous government were made to the welfare programme. Schwerin von Krosigk shared his Chancellor's hostility to the *Sozialstaat* and to the notion that recovery from the Depression should be state-directed. The work creation plans which he drew up were designed merely as an aid to economic recovery and not a solution to the problem of mass unemployment. A member of the German delegation to the Lausanne Conference in June 1932, he lent substantial support to the successful campaign to have reparations cancelled. More generally, von Papen appreciated his crisp, constructive advice in cabinet discussions.

Schwerin von Krosigk retained his portfolio not only under Chancellor von Schleicher but also in Hitler's cabinet for the entire duration of the Third Reich, playing an indispensable part in the rearmament programme. For a few weeks in May 1945 he was a senior figure in the government of Admiral Dönitz. In April 1949 he was sentenced to ten years' imprisonment by the Nuremberg Tribunal for war crimes, but was released in January 1951. Before his death in Essen on 4 March 1977 he recorded his experiences in a number of historical works.

## Further Reading

L. Graf Schwerin von Krosigk, *Es geschah in Deutschland. Menschenbilder unseres Jahrhunderts*, Tübingen, 1951; *Staatsbankrott. Die Geschichte des deutschen Reiches von 1920 bis 1945*, Göttingen, 1974; *Memoiren*, Stuttgart, 1977. See also H. James, *The Reichsbank and Public Finance in Germany, 1924–1933*, Frankfurt am Main, 1985; H. Marcon, *Arbeitsbeschaffungspolitik der Regierungen Papen und Schleicher*, Berne, 1974; U. Hörster-Philipps, *Konservative Politik in der Endphase der Weimarer Republik. Die Regierung Franz von Papen*, Cologne, 1982.

# SEECKT, Hans von (1866–1936)

Though a professional soldier first and foremost, von Seeckt's position as chief of the *Heeresleitung* from March 1920 until 1926 permitted considerable latitude to impress his views on a whole range of important domestic and foreign policy matters, so that he emerged as one of the most powerful personalities in politics during the first half of the Weimar period. Born the son of an army general in Schleswig on 22 April 1866, he embarked on his military career in 1885 in the Kaiser Alexander Guards-Grenadier Regiment in Berlin and joined the General Staff of the Prussian army in 1899. In the First World War he fought with distinction on both the Western and Eastern Fronts, won promotion in May 1915 to the rank of major-general and a year later was appointed Chief of Staff of the Austro-Hungarian Twelfth Army. In January 1918 he was Chief of Staff of the Turkish Army. A member of the German delegation at the Paris Peace Conference, he earned further promotion in October 1919 to the rank of lieutenant-general and was made chief of the Truppenamt in the Reich Ministry of Defence.

General von Seeckt retained his monarchist convictions, yet before 1918 had understood the need for fundamental reforms in the *Kaiserreich*. Conservative, nationalist and aloof in his attitude towards the parliamentary Republic, he nevertheless rejected intolerant chauvinism, Pan-Germanism and racism. In 1893 he had married the daughter of a Jew and was always particularly contemptuous of the strident anti-Semitism of the radical Right. He also abhorred political adventurism, as his refusal of Reichswehr support for the Kapp putschists and Hitler in Munich in 1923, as well as his subjugation of Communist risings in central Germany and the Ruhr, clearly showed. Under his astute guidance the army was reorganized and re-equipped, making it an outstanding professional force. He also ensured that during his time in high office it developed as a 'state within a state', virtually independent of parliamentary interference. In any case, he had the Prussian officer's traditional sense of superiority towards politicians. Insisting on the army's non-political character, he created an ethos of loyalty to the nation-state and not to what he regarded as the transient Republic. But he did recognize limitations on his authority. Thus, when in early November 1923 Reich President Ebert transferred executive power and supreme command of the army to him, he pulled back from establishing a formal military dictatorship, and handed back these powers in February 1924.

Von Seeckt had strong interests in foreign affairs and in matters touching on Germany's territorial integrity. He had helped the *Freikorps* in Upper Silesia and consistently aimed at the destruction of independent Poland and the restoration of the 1914 borders. Towards this end, he was an enthusiastic advocate of military and diplomatic collaboration with the Soviet Union, despite his anti-Bolshevism, and welcomed the Treaty of Rapallo. He circumvented the military restrictions imposed at Versailles and fostered the army's links with the 'Black Reichswehr' and right-wing paramilitary groups, while adopting a cautious approach to Stresemann's diplomacy with the West. This vain, self-confident and somewhat enigmatic figure made a fatal political miscalculation in autumn 1926 when, without consulting Defence Minister Otto Gessler, he gave his permission for the former Crown Prince's son to take up a training post in the army. The symbolism of this action he either ignored or did not appreciate, and he was dismissed in October of that year. Now a general-colonel, von Seeckt was stunned to learn that his position had not been impregnable after all.

After joining the DVP, von Seeckt represented it in the Reichstag from 1930 until 1932, while developing a certain admiration for Hitler. He made a point of attending large nationalist demonstrations organized by the Stahlhelm in Koblenz in October 1930 and in Breslau in May 1931, and the meeting of the 'Harzburg Front' later that autumn. In 1934–35 he headed the German military mission to China. He died in Berlin on 27 December 1936.

## Further Reading

H. von Seeckt, *Gedanken eines Soldaten*, Berlin, 1929; and *Die Zukunft des Reiches. Urteile und Forderungen*, Berlin, 1929 (published in English as *The Future of the German Empire*, London, 1930; *Wege deutscher Aussenpolitik*, Leipzig, 1931; *Die Reichswehr*, Leipzig, 1933; *Deutschland zwischen Ost und West*, Hamburg, 1933. See also H. Meier-Welcker, *Seeckt*, Frankfurt am Main, 1967; K. Guske, *Das politische Denken des Generals von Seeckt*, Lübeck, 1971; O. Gessler, *Reichswehrpolitik in der Weimarer Zeit* (edited by K. Sendtner), Stuttgart, 1958; H. J. Gordon, *The Reichswehr and the German Republic, 1919–1926*, Princeton, 1957; O.E. Schüddekopf, *Heer und Republik. Quellen zur Politik der Reichswehrführung 1918–1933*, Frankfurt am Main, 1955; F.L. Carsten, *The Reichswehr and Politics, 1918–1933*, Oxford, 1966; H. Hürten (ed.), *Die Anfänge der Ära Seeckt. Militär und Innenpolitik 1920–1922*, Düsseldorf, 1979.

## SELDTE, Franz (1882–1947)

As co-founder and leader of the conservative-nationalist ex-servicemen's association, the Stahlhelm, in December 1918, Seldte exercised a considerable influence on right-wing politics throughout the Weimar period. Born in Magdeburg on 29 June 1882, he took a degree in chemistry from the Technical College in Brunswick, and subsequently managed the family's well-established chemical and soda water factory. He fought with enthusiasm at the Front as a captain in an infantry regiment in 1914–16, losing his left arm at the Somme and receiving the Iron Cross (First and Second Class). He spent the remainder of the war as a war correspondent.

The Stahlhelm was at first concerned with looking after the material needs of demobilised veterans, and its conservative outlook, though anti-republican, was relatively moderate. But after it had been banned in 1922–23 following the murder of Walther Rathenau, it increasingly developed along militantly anti-republican, anti-Marxist and ultra-nationalistic lines, though Seldte represented the less aggressive Magdeburg faction. He felt more comfortable with the DNVP than with the nascent NSDAP, and he succeeded for a long time in keeping the organization's distance from its direct counterpart, the SA, the paramilitary arm of Hitler's party. But in 1929, the 340,000-strong Stahlhelm lent its support, along with several other right-wing organizations, to the campaign against the Young Plan, and in October 1931 formed the so-called 'Harzburg Front' with the DNVP and NSDAP. Seldte thus emerged as one of the most determined opponents of the democratic system and was more than ready to join hands in 1933 with Hitler, who appointed him Reich Minister of Labour, which he remained until the end of the Third Reich. In this capacity Seldte proved to be a loyal and efficient administrator, though he revealed little other than a rather pedestrian intellectual approach to his responsibilities. He also held appointments as Labour Minister for Prussia, a State Councillor in Prussia, and Reichstag Deputy. With the dissolution of the Stahlhelm in 1935, Seldte, who had become a member of the NSDAP in April 1933, was elevated to the rank of *SA-Obergruppenführer*. He was charged with crimes by the post-war Nuremberg Tribunal but died in an American military hospital in Fürth, Bavaria, on 1 April 1947 before being tried.

## Further Reading

F. Seldte, *Fronterlebnis*, Leipzig, 1930; *Sozialpolitik im Dritten Reich 1933–1938*, Munich, 1939. See also A. Klotzbücher, *Der politische Weg des Stahlhelm, Bund der Frontsoldaten, in der Weimarer Republik. Ein Beitrag zur Geschichte der 'Nationalen Opposition' 1918–1933*, Erlangen, 1965; V.R. Berghahn, *Der Stahlhelm. Bund der Frontsoldaten 1918–1935*, Düsseldorf, 1966; J.M. Diehl, *Paramilitary Politics in Weimar Germany*, Bloomington, 1977; H.J. Mauch, *Nationalistische Wehrorganisationen in der Weimarer Republik. Zur Entwicklung und Ideologie des 'Paramilitarismus'*, Frankfurt am Main, 1982.

# SEVERING, Carl (1875–1952)

One of the most robust defenders of the democratic Republic in the ranks of the SPD, Severing was born into a working-class family in Herford on 1 June 1875, completed an apprenticeship as a locksmith, and at the age of 18 joined the SPD and the German Metalworkers' Union, rising to official posts in both organizations. Party secretary in the early 1900s in Bielefeld, which became his political base throughout his career, he was also business manager of the Union in Bielefeld from 1901 until 1912 and served as an SPD town councillor there from 1905 until 1924. A Reichstag deputy from 1907 until 1911, he edited the socialist newspaper in Bielefeld, *Volkswacht*, from 1912 to 1919. He earned a reputation as an effective public speaker and always sought to accord equal weight to party and trade union views on policy matters. As a committed member of the reformist wing of the SPD, he contributed articles regularly to the periodical *Neue Gesellschaft*, and from 1914 until the end of the war came out in unequivocal support of the party's *Burgfrieden* policy.

In November 1918 Severing played a conspicuous part in the Workers' and Soldiers' Council in Bielefeld, and in 1919 helped settle the coalminers' strike in the Ruhr. The following year his ability as a mediator was put to even more severe test when, as Reich and Prussian State Commissioner in the Ruhr, he succeeded in detaching from the workers' insurrection that erupted in the immediate aftermath of the Kapp Putsch those elements who were basically in favour of the Republic. The radicals who remained in the fight were ruthlessly put down by Reichswehr and *Freikorps* units, but his so-called 'Bielefeld Agreement', based on a compromise solution to the workers' economic and political demands, prevented a greater catastrophe. His firm, energetic action impressed the new Prussian Prime Minister, Otto Braun, so much that he appointed Severing to his cabinet as Minister of the Interior. He held this position in 1920–21, 1921–26 and again in 1930–32. A deputy to the National Assembly in 1919–20, he sat in the Reichstag from 1920 until 1933 and in the Prussian Landtag from 1921 until 1933, and was Reich Interior Minister in Müller's 'Grand Coalition' government from 1928 until 1930.

Essentially a pragmatist with little time for socialist theory or philosophy, Severing was motivated in all his political activity by a single-minded determination to secure the future of the democratic Republic on the basis of a democratic Prussia. As Prussian Interior Minister he at once set about democratizing the civil service, especially the police, by insisting that all political appointments should be of republican supporters. He made clear that the degree of political engagement by officials should vary in proportion to the level of appointment. Conservative anti-democratic officials were weeded out, in consultation with the SPD's coalition partners, with the result that the police force, especially, became widely recognized as an active defender of the democratic order. He had no hesitation in taking tough action to disarm and suppress paramilitary groups of the Left and Right, or in intervening purposely to deal with insurrectionists. He banned the NSDAP in Prussia in November 1922 and imposed a public speaking ban on Hitler; the Deutschvölkische Freiheitspartei was banned in March 1923; and he stood firm against the Communists in Saxony and Thuringia later that year. In the early 1930s he curtailed the policies of the National Socialist Interior Minister in Thuringia, Wilhelm Frick, and helped persuade the Reich government to ban the SA and SS in April 1932. On the other hand, Severing lent his weight to the pro-republican Reichsbanner Schwarz-Rot-Gold. He felt just as strongly that the SPD should seek to participate in government at every feasible opportunity and advocated co-operation with moderate bourgeois parties towards that end. The Republic would be established on a firm basis, he argued, if the largest democratic party displayed responsibility in office at all levels and took the lead in providing progressive social legislation. With his colleague Otto Braun, he created the model of 'Red Prussia', moderate but muscular in democratic spirit and action.

Severing's approach, however, was inevitably circumscribed by the depressing realities of Weimar society and politics in the early 1930s. Although as a member of cabinet he accepted the Brüning–Meyer compromise over the funding of the unemployment insurance scheme, his party as a whole did not, so that he was ultimately powerless to prevent the collapse of the Grand Coalition in March 1930 and the beginning of a crisis that was not resolved until January 1933. Worse still was the von Papen coup against the Prussian government led on a caretaker basis by Braun and him in July 1932. He took the controversial view that resistance in any form, whether from the trade unions, the SPD or the Reichsbanner, would have been hopeless, even irresponsible, in that it might have provoked a civil war which the socialist and labour movement would in any case have lost.

Severing withdrew into private life during the Third Reich, but after 1945 became active again on behalf of the SPD. He sat in the Landtag of North Rhine-Westphalia and from 1946 to 1948 edited the newspaper *Neue Presse* in Bielefeld. He died there on 23 July 1952.

## Further Reading

C. Severing, *1919/1920 im Wetter und Watterwinkel. Aufzeichnungen und Erinnerungen*, Bielefeld, 1927; *Mein Lebensweg*, 2 vols, Cologne, 1950. He also published under the pseudonym 'Wilhelm Gerviens', *Der 20. Juli 1932 in Wahrheit und Dichtung*, Bielefeld, 1946.

See also E. Eimers, *Das Verhältnis von Preussen und Reich in den ersten Jahren der Weimarer Republik*, West Berlin, 1969; H.P. Ehni, *Bollwerk Preussen? Preussen-Regierung, Reich-Länder-Problem und Sozialdemokratie 1928–1932*, Bonn, 1975; G. Eliasberg, *Der Ruhrkrieg von 1920*, Bad Godesberg, 1974; G. Jasper, 'Zur innerpolitischen Lage im Deutschland im Herbst 1929' (concerning a memorandum by Severing), *Vierteljahrshefte für Zeitgeschichte*, 8, 1960, pp. 280–89; H.H. Liang, *The Berlin Police Force in the Weimar Republic*, Berkeley, 1970; H. Schulze, *Otto Braun oder Preussens demokratische Sendung*, Frankfurt am Main, 1977; D. Orlow, *Weimar Prussia, 1918-1925. The Unlikely Rock of Democracy*, Pittsburgh, 1986; W. Benz and I. Geiss, *Staatsstreich gegen Preussen – 20. Juli 1932*, Düsseldorf, 1982.

# SOLLMANN, Wilhelm (1881–1951)

Described by Arnold Brecht as 'one of the most admirable characters I have come to know – manly, courageous, straightforward', Sollmann represented that type of Weimar politician for whom honest and critical discussion of issues across party boundaries was far more important than the pursuit of selfish personal or narrow party interests. He had a vital and informed understanding of Germany's post-war problems and felt rather fortunate to have the opportunity of contributing to her regeneration. Thus, despite his loyal membership of the SPD, he was an essentially pragmatic politician who advocated in the 1920s a policy of coalition with moderate middle-class parties.

Sollmann was born into a middle-class family near Coburg on 1 April 1881 and obtained qualifications in business studies at the Commercial College of Cologne. Involved while still a teenager in the temperance movement, he joined the SPD in 1906 and the following year founded a small youth group, Die Freie Jugend, in his home city. In 1911 he joined the editorial staff of the socialist newspaper, *Rheinische Zeitung*, worked on the *Fränkischer Volksfreund* in the following two years, then returned to the *Rheinische Zeitung*, becoming its chief editor from 1920 until 1933. A Reichstag member during the First World War, he sat in the National Assembly and once again in the Reichstag from 1920 to 1933. From 1915 he was chairman of the SPD in Cologne, and a city councillor until 1923.

A right-wing Social Democrat, he exerted a moderating influence on the Workers' and Soldiers' Council in Cologne, was a member of the German delegation to the Paris Peace Conference, and came out as a determined opponent of the Rhenish separatist movement in the early 1920s. Founder in 1920 and subsequently co-owner of the *Sozialdemokratischer Pressedienst*, a journal which encouraged intellectual debate in the party, Sollmann developed particular expertise in questions of international peace, education and relations between Church and state, making frequent statements on these in parliament. In 1923 he supported the idea of a grand coalition administration as the only solution to Germany's crushing economic and diplomatic problems, and served as Reich Minister of the Interior in Stresemann's two cabinets from August to November 1923. Complaining that the workers were making the most sacrifices in the inflation, he strongly advocated the retention of the eight-hour day in industry. Otherwise, he made an unsuccessful attempt to resolve peacefully the crisis in the Saxon government in October of that year.

Apart from his journalism, Sollmann spent the remainder of the Weimar period trying to broaden the appeal of the SPD in and out of parliament and to create some kind of consensus among democratic politicians on ways and means of strengthening the Republic. A member of the Inter-Parliamentary Union and of the Working Committee of German Associations (Arbeitsausschuss Deutscher Verbände), he spoke also at public meetings of the Deutschlandbund, a patriotic, democratic organization in the early 1930s, and urged resolution in the face of the growing National Socialist threat. In 1931 he criticized party colleagues Severing and Grzesinski, Prussian and Reich Interior Ministers, respectively, for not being tough enough against Hitler. In 1933 he lamented that the SPD had not managed to extend its influence to a broader section of the nation, particularly to the younger generation, for only in this way might the NSDAP advance have been halted.

Shortly after the *Machtergreifung*, Sollmann was brutally assaulted and hospitalized by SA men in Cologne, causing him to be absent from the vote in the Reichstag on the Enabling Bill. Elected to the SPD national executive committee in spring 1933, he fled to the Saar, where he published the newspaper *Deutsche Freiheit* until the area was reunited with the Reich two years later. He moved to Luxemburg and in 1937 to the United States, where the Quakers secured a teaching post for him at their Swarthmore College in Pennsylvania. He mixed also with exiled German socialists, propounding a *Volkssozialismus* (people's socialism) which would abandon the class struggle in favour of a patriotic, moderate socialism in the mould of Ferdinand Lassalle. He took American citizenship in 1943, but retained a keen interest in post-war West German politics, urging negotiations with the Russians on German reunification. He died at Mount Carmel, Connecticut, on 6 January 1951.

## Further Reading

W. Sollmann, *Die Revolution in Köln. Ein Bericht über Tatsachen*, Cologne, 1918; *Sozialismus der Tat*, Berlin, 1925. See also T.A. Knapp, 'Heinrich Brüning in Exile: Briefe an Wilhelm Sollmann', *Vierteljahrshefte für Zeitgeschichte*, 22, 1974, pp. 93–120; H. Kühn, *Wilhelm Sollmann, Rheinischer Sozialist, Kölner Patriot, demokratischer Weltbürger*, Cologne, 1981; U. Nyassi (ed.), *Der Nachlass Wilhelm Sollmanns*, Cologne, 1985; H. Weiler, *Die Reichsexekution gegen den Freistaat Sachsen unter Reichskanzler Dr. Stresemann im Oktober 1923*, Frankfurt am Main, 1987.

# STEGERWALD, Adam (1874–1945)

The foremost Catholic trade unionist and prominent political leader of the Weimar era was born into a background of rural poverty near Würzburg on 14 December 1874. An apprenticed joiner, in 1899 he founded the Christian trade union movement as an alternative to the socialist variety, becoming its general secretary three years later, and until 1919. From 1919–20 until 1929 he was chairman of the Christian German Trade Union League ( DGB), and of the Federation of Christian Trade Unions in Germany (Gesamtverband der Christlichen Gewerkschaften Deutschlands). He was party to the Stinnes–Legien Agreement in November 1918 and, at the same time, co-founded (with Gustav Hartmann of the Hirsch–Duncker trade unions) the Federation of German Democratic Trade Unions as a basis for consolidating the non-socialist elements of the working class. The initiative collapsed, however, after only a few weeks, though Stegerwald continued to seek ways of bolstering the nationally-minded, conservative forces of the working class. Thus in November 1920 he caused something of a political sensation at the tenth annual congress of the Christian trade unions in Essen when he made a fervent appeal for the establishment of a new middle-of-the road party that would be nationalist, Christian, democratic and social. In effect, he was calling for a socially heterogeneous, inter-confessional Christian people's party that would break the mould of the post-war party system in Germany. He envisaged his own union, the DGB, and the Centre Party, as the core of the proposed movement, but in the event his 'Essen Programme' evoked little positive response, despite considerable publicity surrounding the launch of *Der Deutsche*, a DGB daily newspaper.

Stegerwald's involvement in national politics had begun during the First World War when he was appointed head of the War Food Office in 1916, and elected to sit in the Prussian Herrenhaus in 1917–18. A member of the Centre Party's right wing in the National Assembly and then in the Reichstag until 1933, he made his early mark in the Prussian government as Minister of Welfare from 1919 until 1921 and Prime Minister from April until November 1921. He was far more successful in the former capacity, where he laid the foundations of the *Sozialstaat* in Germany's largest province, with particular emphasis on provision for the younger generation. On the other hand, his weak minority cabinet was no more than an interim administration and achieved nothing of significance. He thereafter left the Prussian scene to concentrate on politics at the Reich level. Deputy chairman of the Centre Party from 1920 until 1928, a challenger for the leadership of the party in December 1928 when he lost to Ludwig Kaas, and chairman in 1928–29 of its Reichstag delegation, he was asked by Reich President Ebert to form a cabinet in November 1923 on the collapse of the Stresemann government, but failed to secure the crucial participation of the DNVP. This was particularly disappointing for him as it signalled the effective end of his endeavours to implement his 'Essen Programme', latterly through the so-called Bürgerliche Arbeitsgemeinschaft comprising the DDP, DVP and Centre Party in the Reichstag.

Stegerwald's national ministerial career began with his appointment in 1929 as Reich Minister of Transport in the Grand Coalition, and continued, more importantly, with his acceptance of the Labour portfolio under Chancellor Brüning, his one-time personal assistant. He could hardly have landed a more daunting task, not only in view of the rising mass unemployment but also because he had to preside, as a former trade union leader, over the dismantling of the social welfare system. And because of that background he was viewed with deep suspicion by employers, who thwarted his efforts to revive dialogue between both sides of industry in November 1930, and by the conservative Right. His support for the resettlement of unemployed urban workers in the eastern provinces as part of the *Osthilfe* programme drew angry protests from estate owners, and led to President von Hindenburg referring to him as an 'agrarian Bolshevik'. His rejection of the WTB-Plan for relieving unemployment as reckless and inflationary also made him unpopular in socialist circles.

In early 1933, Stegerwald argued in Centre Party circles for its acceptance of the Enabling Bill, partly because as a conservative Catholic he was concerned that there should be no renewed conflict between Church and state, and partly also because he welcomed the prospect of the National Socialists destroying their mutual enemy, Marxism and the socialist Left. He lived privately until 1945. For a short time afterwards, he served as president of the government in part of Franconia and contributed to the foundation of the Christian Social Union, the BVP's successor in Bavarian politics. He died in Würzburg on 3 December 1945.

## Further Reading

A. Stegerwald, *Zur politischen Lage. Unsere Not und unsere Rettung*, Berlin, 1919; *Zusammenbruch und Wiederaufbau*, Berlin, 1922; *Aus meinem Leben*, Cologne, 1924; *Nicht Klassen, sondern Stände*, Stuttgart, 1925; *Zentrumspartei, Arbeiterschaft, Volk und Staat*, Berlin, 1928; *Die Notverordnung vom 5. Juni 1931. Ihr Hintergrund, Wesen und Ziel*, Berlin, 1931. See also R. Morsey: 'Zur Gründung der Tageszeitung "Der Deutsche" (1921)', *Publizistik*, 17, 1972, pp. 351–58; E.L. Evans, 'Adam Stegerwald and the Role of the Christian Trade

Unions in the Weimar Republic', *Catholic Historical Review*, 59, 1973-4, pp. 602-26; L.E. Jones, 'Adam Stegerwald und die Krise des deutschen Parteiensystems. Ein Beitrag zur Deutung des "Essener Programms" vom November 1920', *Vierteljahrshefte für Zeitgeschichte*, 27, 1979, pp. 1-29; H.J. Schorr, *Adam Stegerwald. Gewerkschaftler und Politiker in der ersten deutschen Republik*, Recklinghausen, 1966; M. Schneider, *Die Christlichen Gewerkschaften 1894-1933*, Bonn, 1982; W.L.L. Patch, *Christian Trade Unions in the Weimar Republic, 1918-1933. The Failure of 'Corporate Pluralism,'* New Haven, 1985.

# STRASSER, Gregor (1892-1934)

The most important NSDAP leader after Hitler in the *Kampfzeit* and a substantial figure in wider Weimar politics in his own right, Strasser was born the son of a royal court official in Geisenfeld, Upper Bavaria, on 31 May 1892. During the First World War he fought with the First Bavarian Foot Artillery Regiment, rising from corporal to lieutenant of the Reserve. He was seriously wounded several times and decorated for bravery with the Iron Cross (First and Second Class). The war was a crucially formative experience for him, particularly as regards his subsequent career in politics, when he was often seen as a quintessential representative of the 'Front generation', imbued with a militant nationalism, respect for military values and a belief in a non-Marxist 'German socialism' that stressed loyalty and racial comradeship within a people's community (*Volksgemeinschaft*). In the post-war era he articulated the disillusionment of young Germans with the Republic and their determination to create a better future in a state informed by a broadly neo-conservative ideology.

In 1919-20 Strasser completed the pharmacy course he had begun before the war and soon owned a chemist's business in Landshut. But his interest in politics was more important. A member of *Freikorps Epp* which terminated the Soviet Republic in Munich in spring 1919, he was involved in various paramilitary organizations in Bavaria, including the Verband Nationalgesinnter Soldaten and the Einwohnerwehr (Civil Guard), prior to joining the NSDAP and SA in autumn 1922. An active participant with his Landshut SA unit in the Beer Hall putsch, he received an 18-month prison sentence, but was able to begin his political career in the National Socialist movement during the period in 1924 when Hitler was in Landsberg jail. He was released from prison on being elected to the Bavarian Landtag in spring 1924 as a candidate of the Völkisch-Sozialer Block, and in July became the first Nazi to deliver a speech in a German parliament. He was one of the three-man directorate (*Reichsführerschaft*) of the National Socialist Freedom Party (NSFP), for which he secured a seat in the Reichstag in December 1924. Strasser developed as a formidable parliamentarian, noted for strongly-worded, passionate and at times rather coarse contributions, which earned him the sobriquet 'Terror of the Reichstag'.

Strasser rejoined the NSDAP in spring 1925 as a 'colleague' (*Mitarbeiter*) rather than a 'follower' (*Gefolgsmann*) of Hitler. Their relationship was never intimate; rather it was professional, sometimes warm, respectful but carrying an underlying strain and tension, which surfaced most notably in 1926 and late 1932. Strasser was appointed NSDAP

*Gauleiter* of Lower Bavaria in 1925 (until March 1929), but his efforts on behalf of the party were wholly concentrated in northern Germany, particularly the Ruhr, over the next few years. He was primarily responsible for fashioning an appeal based on 'German socialism' to the industrial working class, in contrast to the nationalist, anti-Semitic message being propagated by the party in southern Germany. His social-revolutionary brand of National Socialism provided the ideological base for a group of like-minded party leaders in the Arbeitsgemeinschaft Nord West, and inspired the formulation of an alternative draft programme for the party. Any suggestion that Hitler's position as leader might be challenged, especially by Strasser, was dispelled at a critical showdown party conference in Bamberg in February 1926. However, the cause of 'Strasserism', a vague, eclectic petty-bourgeois anti-capitalism within a nationalist, anti-Semitic framework, continued to be offered to the German people in the north for a few years more. Strasser bought the Kampfverlag to disseminate the views of the so-called 'Nazi Left', which, in reality, did not exist in any meaningful sense. The periodical, *Nationalsozialistiche Briefe*, was its leading forum for discussion of ideology and programmatic goals. This course of action continued with some vigour until the NSDAP's poor showing in the 1928 Reichstag elections led to a fundamental change of direction by both Strasser and the party.

Strasser, who had been Reich Propaganda Leader from September 1925 until December 1927, was appointed Reich Organization Leader in June 1928, and immediately initiated a complete overhaul that made the NSDAP the most efficiently run party in Germany, ready to take advantage of the political crisis of the Depression years. His significant contribution in this respect was complemented by his tireless activity as a propagandist, public speaker and political strategist. His earlier commitment to 'socialism' rapidly weakened, as shown by his refusal to support his brother Otto's clash with Hitler in 1930, and he developed a considerable status as a national politician with contacts across the broad right-wing spectrum. His widely publicized programmatic speech in the Reichstag in May 1932, 'Arbeit und Brot', consolidated that standing, but at the same time helped sharpen his growing differences with Hitler over party strategy. By mid-1932 he was advocating a policy of coalition with nationalist elements, while the *Führer* insisted on an uncompromising all-or-nothing approach to the objective of achieving power in the state. Chancellor Kurt von Schleicher's *Querfront* strategy envisaged the inclusion of Strasser in a new governmental alliance in which he would be Vice-Chancellor and Prime Minister of Prussia. But the enigmatic Nazi leader baulked at seceding from the NSDAP, particularly when he knew there was no 'Nazi Left' to call upon for support, and instead caused a major political sensation by resigning from his party offices (but not from the NSDAP itself) in December 1932. Paradoxically, perhaps, his exit facilitated the link-up between Hitler and the conservative élites in industry, agriculture and the army which quickly resulted in the *Führer*'s appointment as Chancellor.

Resigning his Reichstag seat in March 1933, Strasser withdrew from public life and took up employment in the pharmaceutical industry. Rumours circulated about his alleged clandestine contacts with enemies of the regime, including General von Schleicher, and Göring and Goebbels were keen to have him compromised in such a way as to justify, on their terms, decisive action. On 13 June 1934 Hitler secretly offered Strasser the post of Reich Minister of Economics, which was declined when it was made clear that Göring and Goebbels would not be dismissed. On 30 June 1934 Strasser was murdered by the SS at the Gestapo's Berlin headquarters – a victim of the 'Night of the Long Knives'.

## Further Reading

G. Strasser, *Freiheit und Brot. Ausgewählte Reden und Schriften eines Nationalsozialisten, Teil I; Hammer und Schwert. Ausgewählte Reden und Schriften eines Nationalsozialisten, Teil II*, Berlin 1928; *Das Hitlerbüchlein*, Berlin, 1928; *58 Jahre Young Plan*, Berlin, 1929; *Kampf um Deutschland. Reden und Aufsätze eines Nationalsozialisten*, Munich, 1932. See also G. Schildt, 'Die Arbeitsgemeinschaft Nord-West. Untersuchungen zur Geschichte der NSDAP 1925—6,' doctoral dissertation, University of Freiburg im Breisgau, 1964; U. Wörtz, 'Programmatik und Führerprinzip. Das Problem des Strasser-Kreises in der NSDAP', doctoral dissertation, University of Erlangen, 1966; R. Kühnl, *Die Nationalsozialistische Linke 1925–1930*, Meisenheim, 1966; J. Nyomarkay, *Charisma and Factionalism in the Nazi Party*, Minneapolis, 1967; U. Kissenkoetter, *Gregor Strasser und die NSDAP*, Stuttgart, 1978; P.D. Stachura, *Gregor Strasser and the Rise of Nazism*, London, 1983.

# STRESEMANN, Gustav (1878–1929)

The outstanding German statesman of the Weimar Republic, whose towering personality and scale of achievement, above all in foreign affairs, allows reference to a 'Stresemann era' in the mid- and late 1920s, was born the youngest of eight children to an innkeeper in Berlin on 10 May 1878. While still attending the city's Andreas-Realgymnasium he contributed articles on politics and culture to the progressive liberal newspaper *Dresdner Volks-Zeitung*, and as an undergraduate reading political economy and history at the universities of Berlin and Leipzig he was a member of the liberal fraternity Neo-Germania. In 1900, he took a doctorate with a thesis on 'The Growth of the Berlin Beer Bottle Industry'. From 1902 until 1918 he was secretary of the Association of Saxon Industrialists, and from 1911 until the end of the war a presidential member of the Hansa League for Trade, Commerce and Industry. Marriage in 1903 to Käthe Kleefeld, daughter of a baptized Jewish middle-class family, was followed four years later by Stresemann's election to the Reichstag for the National Liberal Party, making him at the age of 29 the youngest deputy. He served as a deputy until 1912, a second time from 1914 to 1918, and from then until his death in 1929 for the DVP. During the First World War, he succeeded his patron Ernst Bassermann as chairman and parliamentary leader of the National Liberals.

Before and during most of the war, Stresemann was a convinced monarchist, a supporter of Germany's naval and colonial expansion and a passionate annexationist with a commitment to a victorious peace. By 1917–18, however, his views were considerably modified and he began to advocate international reconciliation abroad and liberal constitutional reform at home. For some observers, Stresemann was thus being pragmatic and realistic, while for others he was simply opportunistic.

Founder and chairman of the right-wing liberal DVP from November 1918 until October 1929, and chairman of its Reichstag delegation from June 1920 to August 1923, when he was appointed Reich Chancellor, Stresemann emerged incontrovertibly as one of the decisive figures of early post-war politics in Germany, though for a few years he identified emotionally and ideologically with the *Kaiserreich*. By 1921–22, however, he had become a 'republican by rational choice' (*Vernunftsrepublikaner*), coming to terms with the Republic as the only realistic constitutional basis for government in Germany. His liberalism essentially conveyed his belief in the individual and his sense of responsibility. But he remained a nationalist while dismissing the radicalism of the Right, and his attitude to anti-Semitism was not without ambiguity. He faced many challenges and difficulties as leader of the DVP, a party divided into warring factions, which caused him on several occasions seriously to consider his resignation, and despite his many talents he presided over a slump in its electoral performance between 1920 and 1928. Stresemann was not in favour of a merger with the DDP, though in the later 1920s he pondered the advantages of creating a broad liberal party with the left wing of the DNVP and the right wing of the DDP. But his growing indecisiveness, which was partly attributable to his failing health, ruled out a concrete initiative in this regard.

In his brief period as Reich Chancellor (August–November 1923), Stresemann had to contend with a daunting series of important crises: hyperinflation, the campaign of passive resistance in the Ruhr, Rhineland separatism, the Beer Hall putsch in Munich and Communist uprisings in central Germany. But, remarkably, he took decisions which laid the foundations for the Republic's relative economic and political stabilization during the 'golden years' of the mid-1920s: the Rentenmark was introduced, reparations renegotiations produced the Dawes Plan the following year, the campaign of passive resistance was terminated, and the policy of obstruction in foreign affairs was renounced in favour of an attitude of co-operation that acknowledged international realities.

It is for his role as Germany's Foreign Secretary from August 1923 until October 1929 that Stresemann is best remembered and assessed as an historical personality. His overriding objective was the restoration of German sovereignty as a great power with equal rights, rejecting war as a means of attaining it. Instead, negotiation, understanding and reconciliation had to be employed, first, to reassure France about her security and, second, to use Germany's economic power to attract the Americans. In this endeavour he was not an idealist, let alone a 'good European', but rather a calculating realist, a nationalist and a power politician who looked to the longer-term realization of his goals. His view was that the policy of fulfilment (*Erfüllungspolitik*), despite the hostility it engendered on the political Right, was the only viable way to revise the Treaty of Versailles in Germany's favour. He hoped ultimately that Franco-German reconciliation would isolate Poland and clear the way for changes to the eastern frontier. Stresemann was as bitterly and irrevocably anti-Polish as a Hugenberg or Hitler. Within this broad framework, he engineered not only the Dawes Plan, but also the Locarno Agreements, Germany's entry to the League of Nations, the ending of military control in certain parts of the country, and the early evacuation of Allied forces from the Rhineland. At the same time, he was able to maintain the co-operation and friendship with the Soviet Union begun at Rapallo in the form of the Treaty of Berlin in 1926. The Kellogg–Briand Pact in 1928 and the Young Plan on reparations in 1929 completed an impressive list of achievements, for which Stresemann was awarded (with Aristide Briand, the French Foreign Minister) the Nobel Peace Prize in December 1926.

Vilified by the nationalistic Right, increasingly criticized by right-wing elements in the DVP, generally unappreciated by the German public, Stresemann finally succumbed to a long-standing illness on 3 October 1929 in Berlin.

## Further Reading

G. Stresemann, *Wirtschaftspolitische Zeitfragen*, Dresden, 1919; *Deutsche Gegenwart und Zukunft*, Stuttgart, 1917; *Weimar und die Politik*, Berlin, 1919; *Von der Revolution bis zum Frieden von Versailles. Reden und Aufsätze*, Berlin, 1919; *Die Märzereignisse und die Deutsche Volkspartei*, Berlin, 1920; *Reden und Schriften. Politik, Geschichte, Literatur 1897–1926*, 2 vols. Dresden, 1924; *Diaries, Letters and Papers* (edited by E. Sutton), 3 vols, London, 1935–40.

The best biographies are: A. Thimme, *Gustav Stresemann. Eine politische Biographie zur Geschichte der Weimarer Republik*, Frankfurt am Main, 1957; H. A. Turner, *Stresemann and the Politics of the Weimar Republic*, Princeton 1963; F. Hirsch, *Stresemann*, Göttingen, 1978; K.D. Erdmann, *Gustav Stresemann. The Revision of Versailles and the Weimar Parliamentary System*, London, 1980; K. Koszyk, *Gustav Stresemann. Der kaisertreu Demokrat. Eine Biographie*, Cologne, 1989. Also noteworthy is W. Michalka and M. Lee (eds), *Gustav Stresemann*, Darmstadt, 1982. On the broader issues of foreign policy, see W. Link, *Die amerikanische Stabilisierungspolitik in Deutschland 1921–1932*, Düsseldorf, 1970; M. Walsdorff, *West-orientierung und Ostpolitik. Stresemanns Russlandpolitik in der Locarno-Ära*, Bremen, 1971; J. Jacobsen, *Locarno Diplomacy. Germany and the West, 1925–1929*, Princeton, 1972; M.O. Maxelon, *Stresemann und Frankreich 1914–1929*, Düsseldorf, 1972; C.M. Kimmich, *Germany and the League of Nations*, Chicago, 1976; R.P. Grathwol, *Stresemann and the DNVP. Reconciliation or Revenge in German Foreign Policy, 1924–1928*, Lawrence, Kansas, 1980; P. Krüger, *Die Aussenpolitik der Republik von Weimar*, Darmstadt, 1985; M. Lee and W. Michalka, *German Foreign Policy, 1917–1933. Continuity or Break?*, Leamington Spa, 1987; B. Kent, *The Spoils of War. The Politics, Economics and Diplomacy of Reparations, 1918–1932*, Oxford, 1989; M. Berg, *Gustav Stresemann und die Vereinigten Staaten von Amerika. Weltwirtschaftliche Verflechtung und Revisionspolitik 1907–1929*, Baden-Baden, 1990.

# THALHEIMER, August (1884–1948)

As the dominant intellectual personality in the KPD during the early 1920s, Thalheimer exercised a substantial and frequently decisive influence on the party's political tactics and strategy. He was born to middle-class Jewish parents in the village of Affaltrach, Württemberg, on 18 March 1884, took a doctorate in linguistics and became a member of the SPD at the age of 20. From 1909 until 1914 he was chief editor of the radical social democratic newspaper *Freie Volkszeitung* in Göppingen, and was one of that small group of party members in Württemberg who subsequently went on to become Communists, first in the Spartacist movement, and then in the KPD. While editing the *Volksfreund* socialist newspaper in Brunswick from 1914 to 1916, he contributed to the first, and until 1919, the only, issue of *Die Internationale* (April 1915), the journal edited by Rosa Luxemburg and Franz Mehring. The group associated with the journal formed the nucleus of Spartacus during the First World War. Thalheimer was very much at the centre of this radical political activity until called up for military service in 1916–18.

A founder member of the KPD at the end of 1918, he was elected to the party's central committee and almost immediately formulated a theoretical context for its revolutionary politics. At the fifth congress of the KPD in November 1920, for instance, he vehemently rejected the 'bourgeois' Weimar Republic and coined the slogan, 'Initiative! Revolutionary Offensive', which paved the way for the policy that culminated in the disastrous 'March Action' by the party in 1921. Undaunted by this failure, he continued to assert the validity of the 'revolutionary offensive' policy, though his views were no longer unanimously accepted by his colleagues on the central committee or by the faction-ridden rank and file. Still, Thalheimer, a close associate of Heinrich Brandler, continued for a further period as the generally recognized 'brains' of the party. He presented himself as an orthodox Marxist, a disciple of Leninism and a stout champion of the Soviet Union as the self-styled socialist and workers' state. He convinced the KPD that the revolutionary example of the Bolsheviks had to be emulated in Germany at the earliest opportunity. The collapse of the Communist insurrection in central Germany in October 1923, however, effectively destroyed his standing in the party, and both he and Brandler were made the scapegoats. Expelled from the KPD in early 1924, Thalheimer made his way to Moscow, where he was admitted to the Russian party and employed as a lecturer at the Marx–Engels Institute.

On his return to Germany in 1928, Thalheimer declined an invitation to engage in KPD party journalism and instead assisted Brandler in establishing a small splinter group, the KPDO (Communist Party of Germany (Opposition)), in December of that year. His most notable contribution to political debate before 1933 was his thesis on National Socialism and fascism, the first and most successful attempt to apply a Marxist analysis to these phenomena, thus in stark contrast to the rather unsophisticated KPD official doctrine of social fascism. The major criticism of his challenging hypothesis was its naive comprehension of the nature of class relationships. Otherwise, it offered a realistic appraisal of the Nazi threat to the German socialist and working-class tradition.

Thalheimer fled to France in 1933 and then later to Cuba. He died in Havana on 19 September 1948.

## Further Reading

A. Thalheimer, *Einführung in den dialektischen Materialismus*, Vienna, and Berlin, 1928; *Wie schafft die Arbeiterklasse die Einheitsfront gegen den Faschismus?*, Berlin, 1932; see also his numerous articles in *Die Internationale*, 1919–23.

Of further interest are M. Kitchen, 'August Thalheimer's Theory of Fascism', *Journal of the*

*History of Ideas*, 33, 1973, pp. 67–78; T. Bergmann, *50 Jahre KPD (Opposition)*, Hanover, 1978; J. Kaestner, *Die politische Theorie August Thalheimers*, Frankfurt am Main, 1982; W.T. Angress, *Die Kampfzeit der KPD 1921–1923*, Düsseldorf, 1973; K.H. Tjaden, *Struktur und Funktion der 'KPD-Opposition' (KPO). Eine Organisationssoziologische Untersuchung zur 'Rechts-Opposition im deutschen Kommunismus zur Zeit der Weimarer Republik*, Meisenheim, 1964.

## THÄLMANN, Ernst (1886–1944)

Leader of the KPD during the second half of the Weimar period, Thälmann was born of lower middle-class parents in Hamburg on 16 April 1886. At the age of six he and his younger sister, Frieda, were put into care when their parents were sentenced to a term of imprisonment for petty larceny. Leaving primary school in 1900, he worked in the family business for two years, then left home, taking odd jobs in a small theatre and at Hamburg harbour. In May 1903 he joined the SPD and in February of the following year became a member of the German Transport Workers' Union. Called up in October 1906 for military service in a foot artillery regiment, he was declared medically unfit and returned in January 1907 to his parents' home. In the autumn of that year he went to sea for a while and on his return in 1908 became active in SPD and trade union affairs. Thälmann was called up for army service in January 1915 and fought as a private on the Western Front. Twice wounded, he deserted in November 1918.

Thälmann joined the USPD in Hamburg and became active once again in his union. An unsuccessful USPD candidate in the National Assembly elections in early 1919, he was elected in March of that year to serve in the Hamburg legislature (Bürgerschaft). In May 1919 he took over the chairmanship of the USPD branch in the city. He contested the Reichstag elections in June 1920 in Hamburg but failed to secure a seat. When the left wing of the USPD merged with the KPD in December 1920, he was elected to his new party's central committee, and in February 1921 he was re-elected to the Bürgerschaft, this time for the KPD. A few months later he made the first of many visits to Moscow, to attend the third congress of the Comintern, speaking on behalf of the 'Left' faction in the KPD. In the abortive Communist rising in Hamburg in October 1923, he played a prominent role as leader of the party in the city, despite the national leadership's opposition to it. Elected to the Reichstag in 1924, where he remained until 1933, Thälmann's advance the following year to the chairmanship of the KPD represented a considerable personal triumph as well as a victory for those in the party whose allegiance lay unswervingly with Moscow and the Comintern. He was an unequivocal Stalin loyalist who eventually succeeded in fashioning a highly disciplined and committed party in full accord with the Soviet dictator's wishes. His sudden high profile in the KPD was further consolidated in 1925 by his appointment as leader of the Rotfrontkämpferbund (Red Front Fighters' League), the paramilitary arm of the KPD, and by his nomination as the party's candidate in the Reich Presidential elections, in whose second ballot he attracted 1,931,151 votes, or 6.4 per cent of the total. By this time also, Thälmann was a member of the executive committee of the Comintern: in 1931 he joined its presidium. That sort of backing was important in autumn 1928 when he was nearly forced to resign at the insistence of the KPD Politburo over the so-called Wittorf case, which involved an unsuccessful cover-up by Thälmann of financial irregularities in the party's Hamburg branch. When Stalin and the Comintern went to considerable lengths to emphasize their trust in him, he was reinstated, stronger than ever.

In 1926 Thälmann eliminated the ultra-left faction led by Ruth Fischer from the party, and when two years later the reformist group around Heinrich Brandler was similarly expelled, his control over the KPD was and remained very solid. He accepted unconditionally the Comintern strategy in 1928–29 whereby the 'social fascist' SPD was identified as the principal enemy of the revolutionary proletarian movement in Germany, and adhered firmly to this line as directed by Stalin, despite the upsurge in popular support for the NSDAP in the wake of the Great Depression. Thälmann's leadership qualities, however, were limited. Although he was a fiery public speaker, he was essentially a stolid party functionary whose understanding of political issues was invariably deficient. His blind loyalty to Moscow was a grave disservice to a generation of thinking German Communists, and the substantial increase in popularity which the KPD enjoyed between 1930 and 1932 was due above all to the desperation and despair generated among the urban working class by the economic crisis and mass unemployment, and not to his leadership. Thus, the 5 million votes he received in the first ballot of the Reich Presidential election in March 1932 (13.2 per cent of the total), and the 3,700,000 votes in the second ballot (10.2 per cent of the total), are to be seen in that context. Temporary KPD alliances with the NSDAP, as when they acted to have the Prussian Landtag dissolved in spring 1931 and their joint support for the Berlin transport workers' strike in autumn 1932, only served to confuse the general public and reduce the KPD's credibility.

Thälmann's consistent and ill-judged underestimation of the NSDAP was not even seriously shaken when he was arrested by the Gestapo in March 1933 and sent to a concentration camp. Only long years of imprisonment and maltreatment brought home the sordid reality to him and many of his comrades. He was murdered in Buchenwald on 18 August 1944.

## Further Reading

E. Thälmann, *Was ist Sozialfaschismus?*, Berlin, 1930; *Volksrevolution über Deutschland*, Berlin, 1931; *Im Kampf gegen die faschistische Diktatur*, Berlin, 1932; *Der revolutionäre Ausweg und die KPD*, Berlin, 1932; *Reden und Aufsätze zur Geschichte der deutschen Arbeiterbewegung. Band I: Auswahl aus den Jahren Juni 1919 bis November 1928; Band II: Auswahl aus den Jahren November 1928 bis September 1930*, East Berlin, 1958; *Zwischen Erinnerungen und Erwartung. Autobiographische Aufzeichnungen* (edited by Kuratorium 'Gedenkstätte Ernst Thälmann'), Hamburg, 1977. See also W. Bredel, *Ernst Thälmann. Beitrag zu einem politischen Lebensbild*, East Berlin, 1950; H. Matern (introd.), *Ernst Thälmann. Bilder und Dokumente aus seinem Leben*, East Berlin, 1955; W. Wimmer, 'Ernst Thälmann – proletarischer Internationalist', *Beiträge zur Geschichte der deutschen Arbeiterbewegung*, 14, 1972, pp. 193–221; Institut für Marxismus-Leninismus, *Ernst Thälmann. Geschichte und Politik*, East Berlin, 1973; G. Hortzschansky, *Ernst Thälmann. Eine Biographie*, Frankfurt am Main, 1979.

Of further interest are S. Bahne, *Die KPD und das Ende von Weimar*, Frankfurt am Main, 1976; O.K. Flechtheim, *Die KPD in der Weimarer Republik*, Frankfurt am Main, 1969; E. Rosenhaft, *Beating the Fascists? The German Communists and Political Violence, 1929–1933*, Cambridge, 1983; H. Weber, *Die Wandlungen des deutschen Kommunismus. Die Stalinisierung der KPD in der Weimarer Republik*, 2 vols, Frankfurt am Main, 1969; H. Weber, *Hauptfeind Sozialdemokratie. Strategie und Taktik der KPD 1929–1933*, Düsseldorf, 1982; K.G.P. Schuster, *Der Rote Frontkämpferbund 1924–1929*, Düsseldorf, 1975.

# TREVIRANUS, Gottfried (1891-1971)

The popular and articulate leader of moderate conservative opinion in the late Weimar period and Reich Minister in Heinrich Brüning's cabinet, Treviranus was born into a middle-class home in Schieder, Lippe, on 20 March 1891, and was a professional naval officer from 1912 until his resignation with the rank of lieutenant-captain at the end of the First World War. A period of study at agricultural college led to his appointment from 1921 until 1930 as Director of the Chamber of Agriculture in Lippe. His political career was forged in the DNVP, which he represented in the Reichstag from 1924 until 1930. During this time he became a leading exponent of a moderate, progressive brand of conservatism which, although nationalistic and anti-Marxist, embraced an ideal of national unity based on mutual co-operation and responsibility within the parliamentary framework of the Republic. This viewpoint was incompatible with Alfred Hugenberg's strident anti-republicanism after his election to the party chairmanship in 1928, and a showdown occurred at the end of the following year over the DNVP leader's so-called 'Freedom Law'.

Treviranus was one of 12 members of the party's Reichstag delegation who seceded in December 1929 after a bitter argument concerning the infamous penal clause (paragraph 4) of Hugenberg's bill (the 'Freedom Law'), which in the event received little support in a referendum held later that month. As one of the most outspoken dissidents, he accused his leader of denying DNVP parliamentary representatives 'that freedom to act according to one's conscience required by our constitutional responsibility to the nation'. For his part, Hugenberg was determined to purge the party of those whom he regarded as having compromised with the Republic by supporting the policy of participation in government in 1925 and 1927, and that included Treviranus. Following their exit, the 12 former DNVP deputies linked up with a small number of deputies from the Christian National Peasants' and Agrarian People's Party to form a special parliamentary alliance, the Christian National Coalition, with Treviranus as its chairman. He aimed to use this grouping to construct a broader alliance of moderate conservatives drawn from a number of parties, including the DVP, that would ultimately result in the formation of a new political party to the left of the DNVP. Those hopes made little headway, however, against entrenched interests, and all that materialized was the Popular Conservative Union (Volkskonservative Vereinigung) in January 1930, of which he was the principal driving force. It explored links with disparate moderate nationalist and conservative elements, particularly the Christian trade unions and the white-collar employees' union, the Deutschnationaler Handlungsgehilfenverband (DHV). In late summer 1930, his supporters came together with Count Westarp's dissident DNVP group to establish the Conservative People's Party (Konservative Volkspartei) in time to fight the Reichstag elections in September. In the event, it attracted fewer than 300,000 votes and only four seats, but it enabled Treviranus to continue in the Reichstag until the party's virtual destruction in 1932, when its supporters flocked to the NSDAP. Through all this turmoil on the political Right, he retained his membership of the Stahlhelm.

The appointment in March 1930 of Treviranus to the post of Reich Minister for the Occupied Territories reflected in part the friendly relationship he had enjoyed with Heinrich Brüning since the war, and in part also the Chancellor's desire to extend his support as widely as possible across the moderate political spectrum. Both he and his new minister were seen as representatives of the 'Front generation' coming to power, and as such a certain amount of popular enthusiasm was engendered for a brief period. Treviranus did not have a particularly happy experience in his first ministerial post. After being charged by Rudolf Breitscheid (SPD) in the Reichstag in April 1930 of having a 'sea cadet's temperament', he caused a major diplomatic crisis when as principal speaker at a rally of the Patriotic Eastern Associations (Heimattreue Ostverbände) in August of that year, he vehemently attacked Poland and asserted Germany's determination to recover what he described as 'the lost regions of the East'. The Polish and French governments interpreted his statement as being something close to a declaration of war and lodged a furious official protest, while the British ambassador to Berlin chided the hapless minister as 'a young and apparently headstrong ex-naval officer'. Chancellor Brüning was forced to issue a public assurance to Poland that Germany had no intention of using force to settle differences but there was no denying the considerable damage inflicted by the incident on his government's status. In a cabinet reshuffle after the Reichstag elections in September, Treviranus was given a new responsibility, Reich Minister without Portfolio and Reich Commissioner for Eastern Aid (*Osthilfe*), which he retained until October 1931. Even here, of course, he was hardly free of controversy, given the political furore that accompanied this programme from beginning to end. He must have been grateful indeed when he was appointed to serve in the low-profile post of Reich Transport Minister from October 1931 to May 1932.

On leaving government, Treviranus returned to his former job as director of the Lippe Chamber of Agriculture, while continuing his political activity as chairman (from November 1932) of what had become the unimportant Popular Conservative Union. Always a steadfast opponent of the NSDAP, he could do little to halt Hitler's advance to the chancellorship. In 1933 Treviranus was dismissed from his post in Lippe and his Popular Conservative Union was banned. He spent the years from 1934 to 1945 in exile. After the war he was an adviser for a time to the American military administration but did not re-engage in politics. Treviranus later settled in Italy, and died in Florence on 7 June 1971.

## Further Reading

G.R. Treviranus, *Auf neuen Wegen*, Berlin 1930; *Das Ende von Weimar. Heinrich Brüning und seine Zeit*, Düsseldorf, 1968; *Für Deutschland im Exil*, Düsseldorf, 1973. See also A. Chanady,'The Disintegration of the German National People's Party, 1924–30', *Journal of Modern History*, 39, 1967, pp. 65–91; E. Jonas, *Die Volkskonservativen 1928–1933. Entwicklung, Struktur, Standort und staatspolitische Zielsetzung*, Düsseldorf, 1965; A. Thimme, *Flucht in den Mythos. Die Deutschnationale Volkspartei und die Niederlage von 1918*, Göttingen, 1969.

## ULBRICHT, Walter (1893-1973)

Best known as the authoritarian Communist leader of the former German Democratic Republic, Ulbricht was already a formidable figure in the KPD before and after 1933. He was born the son of a socialist master tailor in Leipzig on 13 June 1893, completed an apprenticeship as a joiner and before the First World War became actively involved in the working-class youth movement, which was under the tutelage of the SPD. He also joined the party in 1912. During the war he served in the army as a private but deserted on his way to the Western Front at the beginning of 1918.

Ulbricht was a founder member of the KPD in 1919, and as a talented and trustworthy organizer and manager made his way in the party hierarchy. He possessed little intellectual understanding of Marxism–Leninism and stayed clear of the vicious factionism of many of his colleagues. He believed in discipline and loyalty to the Soviet Union above all else. In 1921 he was appointed party secretary and political leader in Thuringia, where he was primarily responsible for planning and organizing the various Communist uprisings that took place there before 1923. Elected to the party's central committee in 1923, he was put in charge of a special department whose task was to create factory cells systematically as an essential component of a policy designed to bring the KPD into closer contact with workers and trade unions. The factory cell strategy itself formed an important part of the process of 'Bolshevization' implemented by the party in the mid-1920s. When he failed to be re-elected to the central committee in 1924 Ulbricht was sent to Moscow to be trained as a Comintern agent, and in this capacity he served briefly in Prague and Vienna. On his return to Berlin in 1925, he continued his career as a party functionary and represented the party in the Saxon Landtag. In 1927 he rejoined the central committee and the following year was elected to the Reichstag for the electoral district of South Westphalia, remaining a deputy until 1933. During the short interlude in autumn 1928 when party leader Ernst Thälmann was relieved of his post as a consequence of the Wittorf financial scandal, Ulbricht took his place as the KPD representative to the Comintern in Moscow.

As district secretary of Berlin-Brandenburg from 1929 until 1933, Ulbricht was at the heart of the KPD's political struggle. The experience of the bloody confrontation with the Berlin police in May 1929 as well as the growth in Nazi street terror convinced him of the need for an appropriate physical response from the Communist camp, which required renewed planning following the prohibition in 1929 of its paramilitary wing, the Red Front Fighters' League (RFB). He devised a programme of lightning demonstrations and aggressive street confrontation aimed at the police and NSDAP, emphasizing his belief in mass working-class action as an integral element of the KPD's revolutionary strategy. The result was the virtual civil war that raged in Berlin and other cities during the crisis of the Depression era in Germany.

Following some months in underground resistance to the Third Reich, Ulbricht fled in October 1933 to Prague, where he headed the exiled KPD office, and then in autumn 1936 to Paris. In 1936-38 he played an active role in the Spanish Civil War, eliminating party colleagues allegedly disloyal to Stalin. From 1938 to 1945 he lived in Moscow, serving in the Political Section of the Red Army and co-founding, in 1943, the anti-Nazi National Committee for a Free Germany. He returned to Berlin with the Red Army in spring 1945 with instructions from Stalin to establish the political hegemony of the Communist Party in the Soviet zone of occupation. In 1949 he was appointed Deputy Prime Minister of the German Democratic Republic and secretary-general the following year of the so-called Socialist Unity Party (SED), the successor to the KPD. Always the Soviet loyalist, he called on Russian tanks to suppress the workers' rising in East Berlin in 1953, and until his resignation from all party and state offices (First Secretary of the SED since 1953 and chairman of the Council of State from 1960) in May 1971, he developed the East German state as a subservient, corrupt and terroristic satellite of the Soviet Union under his dictatorial control. The construction of the Berlin Wall in 1961 and the East German army's participation in the invasion of Czechoslovakia in 1968 characterized his sectarian and ruthless political and ideological outlook. Ulbricht died in Döllnsee, just outside East Berlin, on 1 August 1973.

## Further Reading

W. Ulbricht, *Kriegsschauplatz Innerdeutschland*, Strasbourg, 1938; and *Zur Geschichte der deutschen Arbeiterbewegung. Aus Reden und Aufsätzen. Band I (1918-1933)*, East Berlin, 1953. See also J.R. Becher, *Walter Ulbricht. Ein deutscher Arbeitersohn*, East Berlin, 1958; H. Weber, *Von Rosa Luxemburg zu Walter Ulbricht. Wandlungen des deutschen Kommunismus*, Bonn, 1959; C. Stern, *Ulbricht. Eine politische Biographie*, Cologne, 1963; G. Zwerenz, *Walter Ulbricht*, Munich, 1966; L. Thoms, H. Vieillard and W. Berger, *Walter Ulbricht. Arbeiter, Revolutionär, Staatsmann. Eine biographische Skizze*, East Berlin, 1968; H. Weber, *Kommunismus in Deutschland 1918-1945*, Darmstadt, 1983.

## WELS, Otto (1873-1939)

Co-chairman of the SPD from 1919 to 1931 and chairman from 1931 until 1933, Reichstag deputy and leader of the party's parliamentary delegation, Wels exercised a unique and substantial influence in the Weimar period as the quintessential party boss, never seeking, and even declining on at least one occasion, ministerial office. He was born in Berlin on 15 September 1873 the son of a restauranteur who himself was active in the socialist movement, and after completing an apprenticeship as an upholsterer, joined the socialist youth organization at the age of 14 and the SPD four years later, in 1891. His youthful radicalism gradually abated as he climbed the trade union and party bureaucracies. In 1906 he became a paid official of the upholsterers' union and from 1907 until 1918 was leader of the SPD in Brandenburg, which under his guidance became a model of energetic and efficient management. It was these administrative and organizational qualities which brought Wels to the attention of August Bebel, who secured him a place on the party executive (*Vorstand*) in 1913. Elected already to the Reichstag the previous year, he served both bodies until 1918. In the many bitter controversies that erupted in the SPD before the First World War, he loyally delivered the block of votes under his control to whichever side was supported by the executive, though his personal preferences invariably lay with the centrist faction. Throughout the war, he fully supported the policy of *Burgfrieden*, emerged as a close ally of Friedrich Ebert and tightened the party organization in response to the establishment in 1917 of the USPD.

With the benefit of his long political experience in Berlin, Wels played an active and significant role in the November Revolution, particularly in the struggle with the radical Left for control of government and the streets. A member of the capital's Workers' and Soldiers' Council, he was also, more importantly, city commandant of Berlin from 10 November until the end of December 1918. He headed the Republikanische Soldatenwehr, a military formation designed to protect the government, but had to battle hard against units of similar type that were controlled by other bodies aspiring to power. When, in December 1918, he used troops to disperse a Spartacist demonstration in the northern proletarian district of Wedding, which resulted in fatalities, he was soundly condemned by the radical Left and Ebert was forced to order an official investigation into the incident. A few weeks later, Wels was held hostage for a brief period by men from the revolutionary People's Naval Division in Berlin's Royal Palace, and was freed only after further bloodshed. Badly shaken but with his reputation somewhat enhanced, he was relieved of his post of commandant. This troubled experience left him with an enduring antipathy for radicals and Communists which he brought to bear on many occasions in the years ahead.

A member of the National Assembly and then of the Reichstag to 1933, party executive committee stalwart, and from 1921 co-chairman of the SPD's annual congress, Wels was one of the solid rocks on which the party depended. Always loyal to friends and harsh towards enemies, he cut a tough, robust figure who kept the party machine in good working order and made successful efforts to ensure the continuity of leadership at the top. Party loyalty transcended all personal and policy differences, as far as he was concerned. Of average intellectual ability and somewhat limited vision, he was indispensable as an organizer and 'fixer'. In March 1920, he helped Carl Legien organize the general strike that was decisive in defeating the Kapp Putsch, and at his insistence Ebert dismissed Gustav Noske as Reich Minister of Defence in its immediate aftermath. He declined the offer to succeed Noske in that prestigious office, believing that a member of a party other than the SPD should be appointed: Otto Gessler (DDP) took over. Wels was a major influence on the party's coalition strategy, advising caution but prepared to work with the DVP, and ready to criticize his own party's performance in government when he felt it warranted: thus, by early 1930 he could not hide his dissatisfaction with the Grand Coalition, despite the friendship he enjoyed with Chancellor Hermann Müller. An architect of the SPD's policy of toleration towards the Brüning administration, Wels advised against the party or the paramilitary Reichsbanner, of which he has been a major sponsor since its creation in 1924, taking action against the Papen coup in Prussia in July 1932. He convinced his colleagues that circumstances were quite different from those at the time of the Kapp Putsch, and that a working-class uprising would not only be crushed, but would lead to a military dictatorship and the total destruction of the democratic Republic. He simply called for the forthcoming Reichstag elections to proceed as planned. While recognizing the relative weakness of the socialist Left as this juncture, Wels probably did not yet fully appreciate the gathering strength of the far Right.

Speaking as party leader in the Reichstag on 23 March 1933, Wels gained widespread admiration for an extraordinarily courageous speech opposing Hitler's Enabling Bill. Adumbrating the achievements and ideals of his party in a straightforward and patriotic manner, he concluded with the emotional words: 'At this historic moment, we German Social Democrats solemnly confess our adherence to the principles of humanity and justice, of liberty and socialism.' Fleeing Germany shortly afterwards, he reached Prague, where he became chairman of the exiled SPD (1933–39), using the contacts he had built up during many years as a member of the executive committee of the Socialist International (1920–39) in the struggle against the Third Reich. That fight he conducted from Paris after the fall of Czechoslovakia in 1938, until his death in the French capital on 16 September 1939.

## Further Reading

O. Wels, *Bolschewismus von rechts*, Berlin, 1920; *Die Sozialdemokratie gegen Poincaré und Helfferich*, Berlin, 1923; *Eiserne Front*, Berlin, 1932. See also H.J. Adolph, *Otto Wels und die Politik der deutschen Sozialdemokratie 1894–1939. Eine politische Biographie*, Berlin, 1971; R. Breitman, *German Socialism and Weimar Democracy*, Chapel Hill, 1981; W.L. Guttsman, *The German Social Democratic Party, 1875–1933*, London, 1981; H.A. Winkler, *Von der Revolution zur Stabilisierung. Arbeiter und Arbeiterbewegung in der Weimarer Republik 1918 bis 1924*, Berlin and Bonn, 1984; H.A. Winkler, *Der Schein der Normalität. Arbeiter und Arbeiterbewegung in der Weimarer Republik 1924 bis 1930*, Berlin and Bonn, 1985; H.A. Winkler, *Der Weg in die Katastrophe. Arbeiter und Arbeiterbewegung in der Weimarer Republik 1930 bis 1933*, Berlin, 1987.

# WESTARP, Kuno Graf von (1864-1945)

A scion of the Junker aristocracy, Westarp was born in Ludom on 12 August 1864, took a law degree and embarked on a career in the Prussian civil service. From 1893 to 1902 he served as a local magistrate (*Landrat*), as Police President of Berlin-Schöneberg from 1902 until 1908, and as a senior judicial official (*Oberverwaltungsgerichtsrat*) from 1908 to 1920. He was elected in 1908 to the Reichstag for the

German Conservative Party, and acted as chairman of its parliamentary delegation from 1912 until the end of the First World War.

A founder member of the DNVP in November 1918, Westarp represented it in the National Assembly, and from 1920 to 1930 in the Reichstag. From 1925 to 1929 he chaired the party's parliamentary group, while from March 1926 until July 1928 he was chairman of the party itself. He held traditional but moderate conservative, nationalist and monarchist views, proclaiming the DNVP to be 'the party of national idealism'. By the mid-1920s, he was prepared to make substantial concessions as part of a policy of political expediency designed to allow the party to participate in government. Thus, while he had been a vociferous critic of Stresemann's entire Locarno strategy in 1924–26, he exerted his authority as chairman to have the party as a whole accept in 1926–27 the Locarno agreements and Germany's entry into the League of Nations as the future basis of foreign policy. No less controversially, Westarp finally recognized the validity of the Law for the Protection of the Republic, which contained a clause forbidding the Kaiser to return to Germany. Some members of the ostensibly monarchist DNVP were understandably vexed by this astonishing *démarche*. He was constantly having to act as a bridge-builder between the various factions in the party and, perhaps inevitably, made powerful enemies, particularly Alfred Hugenberg.

Following the DNVP's poor showing in the 1928 Reichstag elections, Westarp's leadership was called seriously into question by the radicals, who ascribed the reversal to his willingness to compromise on matters of fundamental principle and to his guidance of the party in a direction increasingly well-disposed to the Republic. For his part, he had grown rather weary of the bitter internecine feuding and, more in relief than anger, stepped aside to allow Hugenberg to assume the party leadership in October 1928. The personal conflict between the two men, based on their quite different brands of conservatism, came to a head over the so-called 'Freedom Bill', when Hugenberg insisted that the DNVP Reichstag delegation fully support it. Westarp could not accept either its penal clause (paragraph 4) or his leader's dictatorial style, and resigned in November 1929 as chairman of the parliamentary delegation, while retaining in the meantime his party membership. He lent his full support to the campaign against the Young Plan, though tried to curb Hugenberg's wilder excesses from within the party. This tactic could no longer be credibly sustained after he publicly disagreed with the party leader in the Reichstag over support for some of Chancellor Brüning's financial and agrarian measures, and he finally resigned from the DNVP in July 1930. A few weeks later, he founded, together with some other dissident DNVP members, the Conservative People's Party (KVP). He was returned to the Reichstag as one of its four delegates as a result of the elections in September of that year, remaining there until the party had become defunct in 1932. During the early 1930s, Westarp made a series of unsuccessful efforts to construct a moderate bourgeois conservative party embracing a number of smaller conservative parties and groups. The nearest he came was in April 1932 when he chaired a loose right-wing pact, the 'National Front of German Estates', to contest the Prussian Landtag elections.

Throughout the 1920s and early 1930s, Westarp was a confidant of President von Hindenburg, who trusted him as someone of similar social and political background.

ber 1918 until February 1920 he was Finance Minister in Baden, and from March 1920 until May 1921 he served as Reich Finance Minister in the governments headed by Hermann Müller and Konstantin Fehrenbach. In this latter capacity he revealed his principal political assets: courage and decisiveness when it came to major policies. As a protégé of the murdered Matthias Erzberger, he continued the system of taxation that weighed heavily on the propertied classes because in his view it was socially just and politically necessary if Germany's reparations bill was to be met. He believed that unending protests about the Treaty of Versailles were counter-productive in respect of Germany's standing in world opinion, and that it was in her own best interests in the long-term to make a genuine effort to comply as far as possible. Only in this way, he argued, could the Allies be made to understand that there were limits to Germany's capacity to honour the Treaty. In short, Wirth had already before his time as Reich Chancellor developed an attitude in favour of a 'policy of fulfilment' (*Erfüllungspolitik*).

The acknowledged leader of the Centre Party's left wing when appointed Chancellor (and Foreign Minister in his first cabinet, May–October 1921), Wirth's first act was to accept the terms of the London Ultimatum on reparations, for an immediate invasion of the Ruhr had been threatened by the Allies. This marked the formal beginning of the 'policy of fulfilment' which was to make the Chancellor and the Foreign Minister in his second cabinet (from October 1921 until November 1922), Walther Rathenau, who was appointed in January 1922, figures of hate on the nationalist Right. Both men, who complemented each other rather effectively, were political realists who considered that only through compliance with reparations could an international environment be created in which revision of the Treaty of Versailles would become possible. Towards this end, they accepted that a fundamental change to the taxation system was necessary. The problem that was not easily solved, however, was how to secure political support in the Reichstag for a package of new taxes and other painful measures which would spread the burden equitably across the social spectrum. The urgency of this task was made clear at the beginning of 1922 when the Allies, spearheaded by the new French Prime Minister, Raymond Poincaré, refused Wirth's request for a moratorium on reparations payments for the duration of that year until an acceptable tax and financial stabilization programme was in place. The continuing decline in the exchange value of the German mark complicated matters for the Chancellor who understood fully, however, that the fate of his foreign policy rested ultimately on pushing through domestic and, principally, fiscal reforms. The Upper Silesian crisis, which caused his temporary resignation in October 1921, and opposition to his proposals at one time or another from the major political parties, meant that his fiscal reform programme was not approved by the Reichstag until April 1922. Although something of a compromise, it was Wirth's main domestic achievement. But it did not satisfy the Allies, so that the Genoa Conference in spring 1922 failed to reach agreement on reparations, and this issue continued to be a bone of contention to the end of Wirth's chancellorship.

As Chancellor, Wirth had many other difficult matters to confront: the Communist uprising in central Germany in March 1921, the disbandment of the *Freikorps* and

He frequently advised the President on matters concerning cabinet formation and even on suitability of certain candidates for the chancellorship. His opinions were not always accepted. For instance, he objected to General Wilhelm Groener's appointment as Reich Defence Minister in 1928 because he held him personally responsible for the Kaiser's decision to abdicate ten years previously. In spring 1932 Westarp exacted revenge of a sort when he conspicuously joined the campaign that led to Groener's resignation. Despite his qualified rapprochement with the Republic, Westarp remained at heart an admirer of authoritarian government. He advocated in influential circles increased powers for the President as a way of advancing this cause, and never abandoned entirely the notion of a partial monarchial restoration. He fully subscribed to the view of the President and his circle that Germany's political salvation depended to a considerable extent on the permanent exclusion of the SPD from power. In June 1932 von Hindenburg considered Westarp for the chancellorship before choosing, at General von Schleicher's behest, Franz von Papen. But he continued to advise the President and talked of returning to the DNVP if Hugenberg were removed as party leader.

Westarp spent the years of the Third Reich in retirement, and died in the rubble of Berlin on 30 July 1945.

## Further Reading

K. Graf von Westarp, *Am Grabe der Parteiherrschaft. Bilanz des deutschen Parlamentarismus von 1918–1932*, Berlin, 1932; *Konservative Politik im letzten Jahrzehnt des Kaiserreichs*, Berlin, 1935; *Das Ende der Monarchie am 9. November 1918. Abschliessender Bericht nach den Aussagen der Beteiligten*, Berlin, 1952 (published posthumously). See also E. Jonas, *Die Volkskonservativen 1928–1933. Entwicklung, Struktur, Standort und staatspolitische Zielsetzung*, Düsseldorf, 1965; A. Dorpalen, *Hindenburg and the Weimar Republic*, Princeton, 1964; J.A. Leopold, *Alfred Hugenberg. The Radical Nationalist Campaign against the Weimar Republic*, London, 1977; R.P. Grathwol, *Stresemann and the DNVP. Reconciliation or Revenge in German Foreign Policy 1924–1928*, Lawrence, Kansas, 1980; A. Stupperich, *Volksgemeinschaft oder Arbeitersolidarität. Studien zur Arbeitnehmerpolitik in der Deutschnationalen Volkspartei (1918–1933)*, Gottingen, 1982.

# WIRTH, Joseph (1879–1956)

The youngest-ever Reich Chancellor when appointed in 1920 at the age of 42, this mercurial and unconventional Centre Party politician pursued a south German Catholic form of democratic idealism, which he sought energetically to bring to bear for the good of the parliamentary Republic. Wirth was born into a lower middle-class home in Freiburg im Breisgau on 6 September 1879, took a doctorate in mathematics in 1905 and taught for a number of years at a Realgymnasium (vocationally-orientated grammar school). After joining the Centre Party in 1911, he was elected to represent it in the Baden Landtag from 1913 until 1920, the Imperial Reichstag from 1914 until 1918, the National Assembly and the Reichstag from 1920 until 1933. From Novem-

civil militia units, which provoked yet another constitutional crisis with Bavaria, and the assassination of his closest colleague in June 1922, Rathenau. His outrage at the latter episode provoked Wirth to an emotional attack on the intransigent nationalist camp in the Reichstag, ending with the declaration: 'There stands the enemy, where Mephisto drips his poison into a nation's wounds; there stands the enemy and there can be no doubt about it – the enemy stands on the Right!'. He brought in without delay the Law for the Protection of the Republic, which was designed to combat the activities of the extreme Right. Wirth himself took over the post of Reich Foreign Minister from June until November 1922. Perhaps the most significant result of his partnership with Rathenau had been the Treaty of Rapallo between Germany and Soviet Russia in April 1922, and for years before 1933 he was an active proponent of collaboration between both countries as a committee member of the German–Soviet Friendship Society, which brought him into contact with KPD sources.

Out of office, Wirth was no less indefatigable on behalf of the republican cause, despite his increasing isolation in a Centre Party moving inexorably to the Right. A co-founder of the Reichsbanner Schwarz-Rot-Gold in 1924, he called two years later for the foundation of a Republican Union to promote closer ties between the Centre Party, the DDP and SPD in a revitalized 'Weimar Coalition' alliance. As if to emphasize his disapproval of the Centre Party's course, he temporarily resigned from its Reichstag delegation in summer 1925, and in February 1927 he was the only deputy of his party to oppose a Reichstag vote of confidence in the Marx cabinet. Appointed Reich Minister for the Occupied Territories in the 'Grand Coalition' government in April 1929 – an unfortunate choice in view of his rabid anti-Polish stance – Wirth was a member of the German delegation to the first and second Hague Conferences on reparations (August 1929 and January 1930), where he was able to lend knowledgeable assistance to the framing of the Young Plan. From March 1930 until October 1931, he served in the trying post of Reich Interior Minister, which gave him a further opportunity to defend the republican cause against the rising National Socialist and Communist threat. However, some critics accused him of being insufficiently tough, pointing as an example to the defiant antics of the Nazi minister in Thuringia, Wilhelm Frick. His exclusion from the second Brüning cabinet, on the other hand, owed more to President von Hindenburg's insistence that the government should be cleared of those whom he perceived as 'left-wing'. Moreover, the President had never forgiven Wirth his denunciation of the Right in the Reichstag following Rathenau's murder.

In March 1933, Wirth voted for the Enabling Bill in deference to party unity, and shortly afterwards emigrated. He continued to be politically active before and after 1945, undertaking a series of unsuccessful initiatives designed to create a new democratic basis for an eastern-oriented post-Hitler Germany. In 1955 he received the Stalin Prize, and died the following year, on 3 January, in his town of birth.

## Further Reading

J. Wirth, *Reden während der Kanzlerschaft*, Berlin, 1925; and 'Die deutschen neutralitätspolitischen Jahre 1922–1932', *Blätter für Deutsch- und Internationale Politik*, 5, 1960, pp. 1013–20.

See also J. Becker, 'Joseph Wirth und die Krise des Zentrums während des IV. Kabinetts Marx (1927 bis 1928): Darstellung und Dokumente', *Zeitschrift für die Geschichte des Oberrheins*, 109, 1961, pp. 361–482; T.A. Knapp, 'Joseph Wirth and the Democratic Left in the German Center Party, 1918–1928', Ph.D. thesis, Catholic University of America, 1967; E. Laubach, *Die Politik der Kabinette Wirth 1921–1922*, Lübeck, 1968; I. Schulze-Bidlingmaier (ed.), *Akten der Reichskanzlei Weimarer Republik. Das Kabinett Wirth I und II: 10. Mai 1921 bis 26. Oktober 1921; 26. Oktober 1921 bis 22. November 1922*, 2 vols, Boppard, 1974.

## WISSELL, Rudolf (1869–1962)

Wissell's reputation rests largely on his dedicated efforts as a prominent trade union and SPD official to improve the material condition of the German working class within the framework of the Weimar *Sozialstaat*, and on his ideas for economic reform. He discovered at an early date, however, that his genuine idealism and commitment invariably were constrained by the painful political and financial realities of the period, so that little of substance had been achieved or left in place by 1933. Born the son of a middle-ranking civil servant in Göttingen on 8 March 1869, he completed an apprenticeship in machine construction, and was already a member of both the SPD and the German Metalworkers' Union before his compulsory military training in 1891–93. He served the socialist trade union movement in Lübeck as a secretary from 1901 to 1908, and the SPD as a deputy in that city's local council (*Bürgerschaft*) from 1905 to 1908. Wissell then moved to Berlin to head the national secretariat and Department of Social Affairs at the trade union's headquarters, holding these responsibilities until the end of the First World War. He was also a regular contributor as a right-of-centre party member to the journal *Sozialistische Monatshefte*, and from 1916 until 1929 was editor of a trade union publication. In March 1918 he was elected to the Reichstag.

Wissell's two-track career continued after 1918, but with the emphasis increasingly on the political. Appointed secretary and deputy chairman of the General Federation of German Trade Unions (ADGB) in November of that year, he joined the Council of People's Representatives the following month on the resignation from that body of the USPD contingent, and was given responsibility for social affairs (*Sozialpolitik*). In February 1919 he was appointed Reich Minister of Economics in the Scheidemann cabinet on the understanding that he would be allowed to socialize large sectors of the economy. He was no radical in this matter, as he demonstrated immediately on taking office when he refused to allow factory councils the right of control over mines and factories. He aimed for a moderate, orderly approach with government backing, but was convinced that a planned economy would not only promote greater economic efficiency but also lead the way towards socialism. His concept was given intellectual depth by Wickard von Möllendorff, undersecretary in his Ministry and a former aide to Walther Rathenau, who favoured a planned and controlled economy based on a corporatist structure, with production, pricing and distribution made subject to centralized direction.

Wissell's first proposals for the implementation of what was termed 'the common economy' (*Gemeinwirtschaft*) were approved by the National Assembly in March 1919, involving in particular the establishment of a National Coal Council to regulate the coal industry. A more comprehensive programme, however, which he argued for at the SPD congress in Weimar in June, was rejected by the Bauer cabinet in July 1919, causing him to resign.

In January 1920, Wissell was reappointed head of the ADGB's Social Affairs Department and elected to its national executive, remaining in both positions until 1923. Already a deputy in the National Assembly, he served in the Reichstag from June 1920 until March 1933, continuing to act as a principal SPD spokesman on economic and social affairs. From 1920 to 1925 he was a member of the National Economic Council (Reichswirtschaftsrat), a forum designed to encourage mutual understanding and decision-making in economic matters between workers and employers, and from 1924 to 1928 he chaired the state arbitration system in Berlin-Brandenburg. He was one of those officials bitterly criticized by employers for using his powers to impose wage settlements that were biased in favour of labour, and when his ministerial career was resumed with his appointment as Reich Minister of Labour in June 1928 he was confronted by a hostile business community. That situation was exacerbated when he became involved that autumn in the acrimonious Ruhr iron industry dispute, which employers regarded as part of their campaign against the state arbitration system and the authority of the minister to declare awards binding. After he had arranged, with the help of a specially appointed arbitrator, Carl Severing, a compromise solution which pleased neither side, Wissell's interventions in the labour market became more cautious. He was under pressure from cabinet colleagues to slow down the rate of wage increases because of the mounting budget deficit, but found that more of his energy was being used to defend the unemployment insurance scheme which, because of the rapid rise in the numbers of unemployed and the government's financial difficulties, became the subject of intense debate in cabinet. Finally, in March 1930, he rejected the Brüning–Meyer proposals for a settlement of the funding issue, and the Müller government resigned. Wissell's fellow SPD cabinet colleagues had been in favour of a compromise, but he swung the party behind his principled if politically injudicious stand with the support of the ADGB. From then until his dismissal following the von Papen coup in Prussia in July 1932, he resumed his role as an arbitrator in Berlin-Brandenburg.

Briefly arrested in spring 1933, Wissell remained in Germany, unlike many of his colleagues, during the Third Reich. He had some contact with the oppositional Leuschner circle. After 1945, at the age of 76, he re-engaged in trade union and SPD affairs in Berlin, without achieving national prominence. In 1949 he was made an honorary citizen of Berlin, and in 1954 was awarded the Federal Service Cross. He died in West Berlin on 13 December 1962. At his funeral oration, Willy Brandt referred to him as 'the personification of the social conscience of the Weimar Republic'.

## Further Reading

R. Wissell, *Praktische Wirtschaftspolitik. Unterlagen zur Beurteilung einer fünfmonatigen Wirtschaftsführung*, Berlin, 1919; *Kritik und Aufbau. Ein Beitrag zur Wirtschaftspolitik der letzten zwei Jahre*, Berlin, 1921; with R. Hilferding and R. Dissmann (eds), *Protokoll der Verhandlungen des ersten Reichskongress der Betriebsräte Deutschlands*, Berlin, 1921; and with K. Heinig and C. Mierendorff (eds), *Das Dawes Gutachten*, Berlin, 1924.

Wissell also authored a standard work on a quite different subject, *Des alten Handwerks Recht und Gewohnheit*, 2 vols, Berlin, 1929; a new edition has been published in six volumes under the editorship of E. Schraepler (Berlin, 1971, 1974, 1981, 1985, 1986, 1988): further details are given in R. Reith, 'The Social History of Crafts in Germany. A New Edition of the Work of Rudolf Wissell', *International Review of Social History*, XXXVI, 1991, pp. 92–102.

Of further interest are O. Bach (ed.), *Rudolf Wissell. Ein Leben für soziale Gerechtigkeit*, Berlin, 1959; E. Schraepler (ed.), *Rudolf Wissell. Aus meinen Lebensjahren*, Berlin, 1983; and D.E. Barclay, *Rudolf Wissell als Sozialpolitiker, 1890–1933*, Berlin, 1984. See also H. Mommsen, D. Petzina and B. Weisbrod (eds), *Industrielles System und politische Entwicklung in der Weimarer Republik*, 2 vols, Düsseldorf, 1973; L. Preller, *Sozialpolitik in der Weimarer Republik*, 2nd edn, Düsseldorf, 1978; H. Timm, *Die deutsche Sozialpolitik und Bruch der grossen Koalition im März 1930*, 2nd edn, Düsseldorf, 1982; H.G. Ehlert, *Die wirtschaftliche Zentralbehörde des Deutschen Reiches 1914 bis 1919. Das Problem der 'Gemeinwirtschaft' in Krieg und Frieden*, Wiesbaden, 1982.

## ZEIGNER, Erich (1886–1949)

Zeigner's significance in Weimar politics was largely confined to the dramatic events in Saxony in autumn 1923 when, as Prime Minister of a radical SPD–KPD coalition government, he was forcibly removed from office by a combination of the Stresemann cabinet, Reich President Friedrich Ebert and the Reichswehr. Born into a middle-class family in Erfurt on 17 February 1886, he had completed his study of law and political economy with a doctorate and had carved out a successful career in the Saxon government's legal system, resulting in his appointment in August 1921 as Minister of Justice. During his tenure of that office (until August 1923), his most noteworthy contribution was his placement of personnel loyal to the Republic in key areas of the judiciary, and his efforts to give the administration of justice a more sympathetic, human face.

Dr Zeigner joined the SPD in 1919 and quickly identified with its left wing, and as a perceived enemy of the nationalist cause was put on a death-list of socialist and Communist politicians and personalities by a *Freikorps* unit. Following elections in November 1922, he joined the Saxon Landtag, and in March of the following year he became Prime Minister of an exclusively Social Democratic cabinet with Communist support. The KPD, now pursuing a 'united front' strategy dictated by the Comintern in Moscow, agreed to support his government in return for promises of extensive social legislation and backing for the creation of so-called Proletarian Hundreds (*Hundertschaften*), paramilitary defence groups, to combat the threat of the extreme rightist and National Socialist forces. In a series of violent speeches in the Landtag,

Zeigner denounced the anti-republican attitudes of the Reichswehr and its links with organizations on the far Right. With a background of the passive resistance campaign against the French occupation of the Ruhr, hyperinflation and confrontation between the Bavarian and Reich authorities, the situation in Saxony reached crisis point, with Zeigner very much to the fore.

The KPD's adoption in early autumn 1923, on instructions from Moscow, of a revolutionary strategy that aimed at a working-class insurrection, and its readiness, as a tactical ploy, to join with the SPD in a new coalition government in Saxony, finally provoked the Reich government headed by Chancellor Gustav Stresemann into counteraction. The Saxon government, which from early October included two Communist ministers, and a third, the Saxon KPD leader Heinrich Brandler, as Assistant Secretary in the State Chancellery, openly called for an uprising while defying an order from the army commander in Saxony, General Alfred Müller, to disband the Proletarian Hundreds. With Zeigner adopting an increasingly radical posture and failing to respond to any overtures from the Reich authorities, Stresemann ordered in the army to depose what was, after all, a legally and constitutionally elected Saxon government. A Reich Commissioner, Dr Rudolf Heinze, a DVP member, was put in temporary charge of Saxony, though a few days later the Saxon Landtag elected a new Social Democratic cabinet led by Dr Karl Fellisch. 'Red Saxony' had not been destroyed, but its more radical proponents had. The entire episode proved fatal for the Stresemann cabinet because, when the SPD ministers resigned in protest at the way in which the Zeigner government had been removed, it collapsed after a matter of weeks.

Zeigner's provocative conduct of his office earned him not only the contempt of the SPD's national leadership, but also the extreme loathing of the Right. When, during the following year he was convicted for a number of crimes, including petty larceny and judicial corruption, which he had committed while in office under pressure from a blackmailer, his personal and political disgrace was complete. He received a three-year jail sentence, most of which he was obliged to serve. From the mid-1920s, on his release, until 1933, he returned to obscurity, lecturing at a sports and athletics college in Leipzig and writing the odd article for Social Democratic newspapers.

After 1933 Zeigner suffered considerable harassment from the Nazi regime and was once again imprisoned during the war. Hailed as something of a proletarian, anti-fascist hero by the regrouped Communists in the Soviet Zone of Occupation, he served as Lord Mayor of Leipzig from 1945 until his death in the city on 5 April 1949.

## Further Reading

Kommission zur Erforschung der örtlichen Arbeiterbewegung bei der SED-Stadtleitung, *Erich Zeigner. Eine biographische Skizze*, Leipzig, 1986. See also W. Hanisch, *Die Hundertschaften Arbeiterwehr. Die proletarischen Hundertschaften 1923 in Sachsen*, East Berlin, 1958; H.J. Gordon, 'Die Reichswehr und Sachsen, 1923', *Wehrwissenschaftliche Rundschau*, 11, 1961, pp. 677–92; K. Hohlfeld, *Die Reichsexekution gegen Sachsen im Jahre 1923: ihre Vorgeschichte und politische Bedeutung*, Erlangen, 1964; H.-J. Krusch, *Um die Einheitsfront und eine Arbeiterregierung*, East Berlin, 1966; W.T. Angress, *Die Kampfzeit der KPD 1921–1923*,

Düsseldorf, 1973; D.B. Pryce, 'The Reich Government versus Saxony, 1923: The Decision to Intervene', *Central European History*, 10, 1977, pp. 112–47; H.U. Ludewig, *Arbeiterbewegung und Aufstand. Eine Untersuchung zum Verhalten der Arbeiterparteien in den Aufstandsbewegungen der frühen Weimarer Republik 1920–1923*, Husum, 1973; H.A. Winkler, *Von der Revolution zur Stablisierung. Arbeiter und Arbeiterbewegung in der Weimarer Republik 1918 bis 1924*, Berlin and Bonn, 1984; H. Weiler, *Die Reichsexekution gegen den Freistaat Sachsen unter Reichskanzler Dr Stresemann im Oktober 1923*, Frankfurt am Main, 1987; G.D. Feldman, 'Saxony, the Reich, and the Problem of Unemployment in the German Inflation', *Archiv für Sozialgeschichte*, XXVII, 1987, pp. 103–44.

## ZETKIN, Clara (1857–1933)

One of the few women to make a substantial impact on Imperial German and Weimar politics, Clara Eisner was born the eldest daughter of the Jewish schoolmaster in the Saxon village of Niederau on 5 July 1857, and went on to qualify in the same profession. She joined the SPD when in her mid-twenties, but spent some years living in Paris married to an *émigré* Russian socialist, Ossip Zetkin. She gained experience as a publicist and member of the Socialist International, and it was at an International Workers' Congress in the French capital in 1889 that she made a famous speech entitled 'For the Liberation of Women', which was adopted subsequently as the manifesto of the working-class women's movement in Germany. On her return there in 1891 following the early death of her husband, Zetkin immediately set about constructing a firm niche for herself in the SPD. By the early 1900s, she was established as a leading Marxist revolutionary, in the company of Karl Liebknecht, Rosa Luxemburg and Franz Mehring, and editor of the ultra-radical theoretical journal for women, *Die Gleichheit*, which preached unrestricted access for women to the labour market and their full social and political emancipation. She was, in effect, the recognized first leader of the proletarian feminist movement.

Zetkin belonged to that group of pre-war Social Democrats in Stuttgart which was locked in virtually unending confrontation with the predominantly reformist leadership of the national party, and which furnished many notable leaders of the later Spartacist and Communist movements. One of the party's intellectuals who before 1914 sought to reconcile the ideas of Marx and Nietzsche within a meaningful theoretical framework, she was supportive not only of the socialist women's movement but also of the party-affiliated youth organization which took embryonic shape in 1903–04. She developed a theory of youth education based on a combination of revolutionary Marxism and concepts of liberal-progressive pedagogy. At a conference of the Social Democratic women's organization in Nuremberg in 1908, for example, she argued that through simultaneous encouragement of individual and group initiative, the youth movement could provide a much-needed radical dynamic to the party's development, as long as it was allowed to exist independently of adult control. As it transpired, however, the SPD, supported by the trade union leadership, successfully insisted on the younger people's subordination to the party executive.

After joining with some other radicals in September 1914 in public criticism of the SPD's *Burgfrieden* policy, Zetkin was harassed and briefly imprisoned by the authorities as the anti-war campaign intensified. Undaunted, she organized, in her capacity as secretary of the Women's Section of the Socialist International, an important conference in Berne in March 1915, attended by peace campaigners from various European countries. The following month, she contributed an article on this theme to the only issue of the radical periodical *Die Internationale* that appeared during the war. A founder member of the Spartacist group and of the USPD, she was forced to relinquish the editorship of *Die Gleichheit* to the SPD national executive, also in 1917. Until 1919 she used her seat for the USPD in the Württemberg Landtag as a convenient platform for her agitation.

In 1918–19 Zetkin vehemently rejected 'bourgeois' parliamentarianism in favour of a councillor system embracing the aim of the dictatorship of the proletariat and, continuing to advocate revolution by the masses, she crossed from the USPD to the KPD, to whose central committee she was immediately elected. In June 1920 she was one of the two Communists (the other being Paul Levi) elected for the first time to the Reichstag. During the early 1920s she propounded a fiercely anti-Western and pro-Soviet line of argument, affirming the crucial importance of the Bolshevik experience for the German working class. Maintaining a keen and influential interest in women's rights, anti-militarism and theoretical Marxism, Zetkin also made significant contributions to discussion of KPD tactics and strategy. A member of Comintern from 1921, she was caught up for a period in the party's internal feuding, then withdrew to Moscow, where she befriended Lenin. In the mid-1920s, she abandoned her long-standing commitment to international proletarian revolution to embrace the Stalinist hypothesis of 'socialism in one country'. This ideological shift in emphasis notwithstanding, she remained a fulsome apologist for the mass killings and brutalities that accompanied the Bolshevik seizure and consolidation of power.

When she returned once again to Germany in 1927, Zetkin played a prominent role in the expulsion of Heinz Neumann and his supporters from the KPD, denouncing him as an *agent provocateur*. Having retained her seat in the Reichstag despite her temporary exile in the Soviet Union, she emerged as more of a backstage influence in the KPD than a frontrunner. The only occasion she caught the public eye occurred at the end of August 1932 when the newly elected Reichstag convened for the first time. According to the rules of parliamentary procedure, the oldest deputy, regardless of party affiliation, presided over the organizational meeting during which the official President of the Reichstag was elected. The 75-year-old Communist seized the chance to insult the assembly and most of the nation by expressing her hopes for a Soviet Germany. What actually materialized was Hermann Goering's election to the presidency. Zetkin was in Moscow when the NSDAP came to power, and she died in this 'socialist paradise' (her words) on 20 June 1933.

## Further Reading

Clara Zetkin, *Erinnerungen an Lenin*, Berlin, 1929; *Clara Zetkin: Ausgewählte Reden und Schriften. Band II. Auswahl aus den Jahren 1918–23; Band III. Auswahl aus den Jahren 1924 bis*

*1933*, East Berlin, 1960. See also L. Dornemann, *Clara Zetkin. Leben und Wirken*, East Berlin, 1973; H. Weber, 'Zwischen kritischem und bürokratischem Kommunismus. Unbekannte Briefe von Clara Zetkin', *Archiv für Sozialgeschichte*, 11, 1971, pp. 417–48; K. Haferkorn and H. Karl (eds), *Clara Zetkin. Zur Theorie und Taktik der Kommunistischen Bewegung*, Leipzig, 1974; W. Thönnessen, *The Emancipation of Women. The Rise and Decline of the Women's Movement in German Social Democracy 1863–1933*, London, 1973; R.J. Evans, *The Feminist Movement in Germany, 1894–1933*, London, 1976; B. Greven-Aschoff, *Die bürgerliche Frauenbewegung in Deutschland 1894–1933*, Göttingen, 1981; R. Bridenthal, A. Grossmann and M. Kaplan (eds), *When Biology Became Destiny. Women in Weimar and Nazi Germany*, New York, 1985; R. Luz, *KPD, Weimarer Staat und politische Einheit der Arbeitbewegung in der Nachkriegskrise, 1919–1922/23*, Konstanz, 1987; U. Frevert, *Women in German History*, Oxford, 1990.

# Chronology of the Weimar Republic

## 1918

| | |
|---|---|
| 28–29 September | The German army high command advises the Kaiser to establish a parliamentary government and to negotiate an armistice. |
| 1 October | Prince Max of Baden appointed Chancellor. |
| 3–4 October | Germany proposes armistice to President Woodrow Wilson. |
| 23 October | President Wilson intimates that the Kaiser would have to abdicate before peace negotiations. |
| 28 October | Mutiny of the German naval fleet at Wilhelmshaven. |
| 3 November | Sailors' rebellion in Kiel. |
| 7 November | Wittelsbach monarchy overthrown in Bavaria and a Republic under the leadership of Kurt Eisner proclaimed in Munich. |
| 9 November | Abdication of the Kaiser; German Republic declared in Berlin. |
| 10 November | Friedrich Ebert replaces Prince Max of Baden as Chancellor in a coalition administration (SPD and USPD) called the Council of People's Representatives; Ebert–Groener Pact. |
| 11 November | Armistice concluded at Compiègne between Marshal Foch and Matthias Erzberger. |
| 15 November | Stinnes–Legien Agreement and establishment of Central Working Committee between industrialists and trade unions. Foundation of DVP. |
| 20 November | Foundation of DDP. |
| 24 November | Foundation of DNVP. |
| 16–20 December | Congress of Workers' and Soldiers' Councils in Berlin votes to hold elections for a National Assembly on 19 January 1919. |
| 25 December | Establishment of Stahlhelm. |
| 28–29 December | USPD ministers resign from Council of People's Representatives. |
| 30–31 December | Foundation of KPD. |

## 1919

| | |
|---|---|
| 5 January | Foundation of DAP, forerunner of NSDAP. |
| 5–12 January | Spartacist Rising in Berlin. |
| 15 January | Murder of Rosa Luxemburg and Karl Liebknecht. |
| 18 January | Inaugural session of Paris Peace Conference. |
| 19 January | Elections for the National Assembly. |
| 6 February | National Assembly convenes in Weimar. |
| 11 February | Friedrich Ebert elected Reich President. |
| 13 February | Formation of cabinet under Chancellor Philipp Scheidemann. |
| 21 February | Assassination of Kurt Eisner, Bavarian Prime Minister. |
| 7 April | Bavarian Soviet Republic proclaimed in Munich. |
| 2 May | Suppression of Bavarian Soviet Republic by *Freikorps* and Reichswehr troops. |
| 7 May | Peace terms announced to German delegation at Versailles. |
| 20 June | Resignation of Scheidemann cabinet over peace terms. |
| 21 June | Gustav Bauer becomes Chancellor. |
| 28 June | Treaty of Versailles signed. |
| 11 August | Weimar Constitution formally promulgated. |
| 14 August | Weimar Constitution takes effect. |
| 19 October | Adolf Hitler applies for membership of DAP. |

## 1920

| | |
|---|---|
| 10 January | Treaty of Versailles comes into effect. |
| 24 February | DAP renamed NSDAP. New Party Programme of Twenty-Five Points adopted. |
| 13 March | Beginning of Kapp Putsch (ends 17 March). |
| March–April | *Ruhrkrieg*: Communist uprisings in the Ruhr and central Germany. |
| 6 June | Reichstag elections. |
| 25 June | Konstantin Fehrenbach heads new cabinet. |
| 5–16 July | Spa Conference on reparations. |
| 16 October | USPD splits. |

| | |
|---|---|
| 4–7 December | Left wing of USPD joins the KPD. |

## 1921

| | |
|---|---|
| 24–29 January | Paris Conference on reparations. |
| 21 February – 14 March | London Conference on reparations. |
| 8 March | Occupation of several towns in the Ruhr by Allied troops. |
| 20 March | Plebiscite in Upper Silesia.<br>Communist uprising (March Action) in Saxony and Hamburg. |
| 27 April | Reparations Commission fixes German obligations at 132,000 million gold marks. |
| 5 May | London Ultimatum to Germany over reparations. |
| 10 May | Joseph Wirth appointed Chancellor; beginning of 'policy of fulfilment'. |
| 26–29 July | Hitler asserts his dictatorial leadership of the NSDAP. |
| 26 August | Murder of Matthias Erzberger. |
| 12 October | Partition of Upper Silesia by League of Nations. |
| 5 November | Otto Braun heads 'Grand Coalition' cabinet in Prussia. |

## 1922

| | |
|---|---|
| 10 April – 19 May | Genoa Conference. |
| 16 April | Germany and the Soviet Union conclude Treaty of Rapallo. |
| 24 June | Murder of Walther Rathenau, German Foreign Minister. |
| 18 July | Law for the Protection of the Republic passed by the Reichstag. |
| 24 September | The rump of the USPD joins SPD. |
| 22 November | New cabinet headed by Wilhelm Cuno takes office. |

## 1923

| | |
|---|---|
| 11 January | Ruhr occupied by French and Belgian troops in response to an alleged German default on reparations payments. |
| 13 January | Adoption of passive resistance by Germany to Ruhr invasion. |
| June–July | Hyperinflation destroys German currency. |

| | |
|---|---|
| 13 August – 23 November | Gustav Stresemann Chancellor. |
| 26 September | Passive resistance campaign in Ruhr is ended; State of Emergency proclaimed; Gustav von Kahr becomes General State Commissioner in Bavaria. |
| October–November | Separatist agitation in Rhineland. |
| 1 October | Black Reichswehr Putsch at Küstrin. |
| 21 October | Reichswehr ordered to depose SPD–KPD government in Saxony. |
| 29–30 October | Abortive Communist 'German October' Rising. |
| 3 November | SPD ministers withdraw from Stresemann cabinet in protest at government policy in Saxony and Bavaria. |
| 8–9 November | Hitler–Ludendorff Putsch in Munich. |
| 15 November | Introduction of Rentenmark. |
| 23 November | Collapse of Stresemann cabinet. |
| 30 November | Wilhelm Marx heads new government. |

## 1924

| | |
|---|---|
| 13 February | State of Emergency ended by President Ebert. |
| 22 February | Foundation of Reichsbanner Schwarz-Rot-Gold. |
| 1 April | Hitler sentenced to five years' imprisonment in Landsberg. |
| 9 April | Publication of Dawes Plan on reparations. |
| 16 April | Germany accepts Dawes Plan. |
| 4 May | Reichstag elections. |
| July | Foundation of Rotfrontkämpferbund (RFB). |
| 29 August | Reichstag accepts Dawes Plan. |
| 7 December | Reichstag elections. |
| 20 December | Hitler leaves prison. |

## 1925

| | |
|---|---|
| 15 January | Hans Luther is Chancellor in a new cabinet. |
| 27 February | Re-establishment of the NSDAP. |
| 28 February | Death of President Ebert. |

|  |  |
|---|---|
| 26 April | Field Marshal Paul von Hindenburg elected President. |
| 5–16 October | Locarno Conference. |
| 1 December | Locarno treaties signed in London. |

## 1926

|  |  |
|---|---|
| 24 April | Treaty of Berlin between Germany and Soviet Union. |
| 20 June | Plebiscite on compensation for estate losses by German royalty. |
| 8 September | Germany admitted to the League of Nations. |
| 17 September | Thoiry meeting between Briand and Stresemann, the French and German foreign ministers. |
| 6 October | Dismissal of General Hans von Seeckt as chief of army command. |
| 10 December | Stresemann awarded Nobel Peace Prize. |

## 1927

|  |  |
|---|---|
| 31 January | Inter-Allied Military Commission leaves Germany. |
| 4 May | Opening of World Economic Conference in Geneva. |
| 16 July | Law on Labour Exchanges and Unemployment Insurance (the most significant advance in the Republic's public welfare system). |

## 1928

|  |  |
|---|---|
| 14 January | Resignation of Reich Defence Minister Otto Gessler; succeeded by Wilhelm Groener. |
| 15 February | Cabinet collapses over the proposed Reich School Law. |
| 20 May | Reichstag elections. |
| 28 June | Hermann Müller appointed Chancellor of 'Grand Coalition' government. |
| 27 August | Kellogg–Briand Pact outlawing war. |
| October–December | Ruhr ironworkers' dispute and employers' lockout. |
| 20 October | Alfred Hugenberg elected leader of the DNVP. |
| 9 December | Monsignor Ludwig Kaas elected leader of the Centre Party. |

## 1929

| | |
|---|---|
| 1 May | Communist street violence in Berlin: RFB banned. |
| 7 June | Young Plan finalized. |
| 9 July | Beginning of right-wing campaign against the Young Plan. |
| 6–31 August | First Hague Conference on Young Plan; agreement on evacuation of Rhineland. |
| 3 October | Death of Stresemann. |
| 30 October | Wall Street Crash and beginning of the Great Depression. |
| 6 December | Dr Hjalmar Schacht, President of the Reichsbank, criticizes the Young Plan. |
| 22 December | Failure of nationalist plebiscite on the Young Plan. |

## 1930

| | |
|---|---|
| 3 January | Opening of Second Hague Conference on reparations. |
| 7 March | Dr Schacht resigns presidency of Reichsbank; Hans Luther succeeds him. |
| 12 March | Reichstag accepts Young Plan. |
| 27 March | Collapse of 'Grand Coalition' government. |
| 30 March | Heinrich Brüning heads a presidential cabinet. |
| 30 June | Evacuation of Rhineland by Allied troops completed. |
| 18 June | Dissolution of Reichstag. |
| 14 September | Reichstag elections: spectacular success of NSDAP (107 seats). |
| 30 December | Official unemployment of 4,380,000. |

## 1931

| | |
|---|---|
| 20 March | Proposed Austro-German Customs Union vetoed by France. |
| 11 May | Collapse of Creditanstalt in Vienna engenders fear of a banking crisis. |
| 20 June | Hoover moratorium on reparations and war debts. |
| 13 July | Banking crisis in Germany. |
| 11 October | Meeting of 'Harzburg Front' (right-wing forces). |
| 16 December | Formation of left-wing 'Iron Front' in response to the Right. |

## 1932

| | |
|---|---|
| 30 December | Official unemployment reaches 5,660,000. |
| 22 January | Hitler's address to the Industry Club in Düsseldorf. |
| 2 February | Opening of Geneva Disarmament Conference. |
| 10 April | Von Hindenburg re-elected President. |
| 13 April | SA and SS banned. |
| 24 April | Prussian state elections. |
| 12 May | Defence Minister Wilhelm Groener forced to resign. |
| 30 May | Chancellor Brüning dismissed. Franz von Papen named his successor (effective from 1 June). |
| 16 June | Von Papen government revokes ban on SA and SS. |
| 16 June – 9 July | Lausanne Conference; reparations cancelled. |
| 20 July | Prussian government deposed in von Papen coup. |
| 22 July | Germany walks out of the Geneva Disarmament Conference. |
| 31 July | Reichstag elections; NSDAP largest party (37.3 per cent of vote and 230 seats). |
| 13 August | Hindenburg rejects Hitler's demand for the chancellorship. |
| 12 September | Reichstag dissolved after no-confidence vote in the von Papen government. |
| 6 November | Reichstag elections: NSDAP loses 2 million votes. |
| 17 November | Resignation of von Papen cabinet. |
| 2 December | General Kurt von Schleicher appointed Chancellor. |

## 1933

| | |
|---|---|
| 4 January | Hitler–von Papen meeting in Cologne. |
| 28 January | Chancellor von Schleicher resigns. |
| 30 January | Hitler appointed Chancellor. |

# *Abbreviations and Glossary*

**ADGB**   Allgemeiner Deutscher Gewerkschaftsbund: General Federation of German Trade Unions.
**AEG**   Allgemeine Elektrizitäts-Gesellschaft: General Electric Company.
*Alte Kämpfer*   Old Fighters: those who joined the Nazi party during the mid-1920s.
**Arbeitsgemeinschaft Nord West**   Working Union of North and West German Gauleiters of the NSDAP, established in 1925.
*Auslandsdeutsche*   Ethnic Germans living in foreign countries.
**AWO**   Arbeiterwohlfahrt (Workers' Welfare): a voluntary socialist welfare organization created in 1919.
*Beigeordneter*   Chief Overseer attached to local government.
**BDF**   Bund Deutscher Frauenvereine: League of German Women's Associations.
**Black Reichswehr**   Clandestine army formations of the early 1920s.
*Blutorden*   Blood Order: Nazi party award to those members involved in the Beer Hall putsch.
*Blut und Boden*   Blood and Soil: Nazi party's agrarian ideology.
*Bürgermeister*   Town Mayor.
**Bürgerrat**   Locally elected citizens' council.
*Bürgerschaft*   Locally elected citizens' group (town council).
*Burgfrieden*   Civil truce, agreed to by all parties in Germany in August 1914.
**BVP**   Bayerische Volkspartei: Bavarian People's Party.
**CDU**   Christian Democratic Union (post-1945).
**Comintern**   Communist International.
**DAP**   Deutsche Arbeiterpartei: German Workers' Party.
**DDP**   Deutsche Demokratische Partei: German Democratic Party.
**DDR**   Deutsche Demokratische Republik: German Democratic Republic (defunct).
**Deutscher Kampfbund**   German Combat League: an umbrella organization of right-wing paramilitaries set up in September 1923.
**Deutschnationaler Handlungsgehilfenverband (DHV)**   German National Union of Commercial Employees, a right-wing, white-collar union.
**Deutschsoziale Partei**   German Social Party.
**Deutschvölkische Freiheitspartei**   German Racist-Nationalist Freedom Party (1922–28).
**DGB**   Deutscher Gewerkschaftsbund: German League of Trade Unions (Christian).
**DNVP**   Deutschnationale Volkspartei: German National People's Party.
**DVP**   Deutsche Volkspartei: German People's Party.
*Erfüllungspolitik*   Policy of fulfilment (that is, compliance with the Treaty of Versailles) in German foreign affairs in the 1920s.
**Feldherrnhalle**   Nationalist/Nazi shrine in Munich.

'Freedom Law'  Introduced by Alfred Hugenberg, the DNVP leader, as part of the nationalist campaign against the Young Plan in 1929–30.
*Freikorps*  Free Corps: irregular paramilitary units of the German Right during the early 1920s.
*Gauleiter*  Regional Leader of the Nazi Party.
*Gleichschaltung*  'Co-ordination': the programme of amalgamation and destruction of opposition groups forcibly imposed by the National Socialists in 1933–34.
*Habilitationsschrift*  Post-doctoral dissertation.
Handelshochschule  Commercial college.
Hauptarchiv der NSDAP  Central Archive of the NSDAP.
*Heeresleitung*  Army Command.
Heimatstadt  Home town; place of birth and residence.
Herrenhaus  Prussian Upper House (pre-1918).
Kampfbund gegen den Faschismus  Anti-Fascist Combat League (Communist).
*Kampfzeit*  Period of political struggle for the Nazi party before 1933.
KPD  Kommunistische Partei Deutschlands: German Communist Party.
KVP  Konservative Volkspartei: Conservative People's Party.
*Länder*  Federal German states.
Landbund  Rural League: important small farmers' organization.
*Landeshauptmann*  Provincial official appointed by the Reich Government, equivalent to Governor.
Landesversammlung  Provincial state assembly.
Landtag  Provincial state parliament.
Lebensborn  Programme of racial experimentation involving children under the direction of the SS.
*Legationsrat*  A civil service post (Bavarian state government).
Luftwaffe  German Air Force.
Machtergreifung  Seizure of Power by the NSDAP in 1933.
Nationale Frauendienst  National Women's Service (First World War).
NSDAP  Nationalsozialistische Deutsche Arbeiterpartei: National Socialist German Workers' Party (Nazi Party).
NSFP  Nationalsozialistischer Freiheitspartei: National Socialist Freedom Party (1924–25).
*Oberbürgermeister*  Lord Mayor (of a large town or city).
*Oberpräsident*  State Governor.
*Osthilfe*  Agrarian aid programme, introduced by Chancellor Heinrich Brüning for Germany's eastern provinces.
*Preussenschlag*  The illegal and unconstitutional deposition of the Prussian government by Chancellor Franz von Papen in July 1932.
*Pour le Mérite*  Germany's highest award for bravery in the First World War.
*Querfront*  The cross-party alliance attempted by Chancellor Kurt von Schleicher in December 1932.
*Regierungspräsident*  The senior administrative official in a government district.
Reichsbahn  German National Railways.
Reichsbank  German central bank, based in Berlin.
Reichsbanner Schwarz-Rot-Gold  Pro-republican paramilitary organization established in 1924 and dominated by the SPD.
Reichskirche  National Church.

*Reichsleiter der NSDAP*  Top-ranking Nazi party official.
**Reichsnährstand**  Reich Food Estate (post-1933).
**Reichsrat**  Upper Legislative Chamber.
*Reichsreform*  The term used to describe matters concerning constitutional and territorial reform.
*Reichsstatthalter*  The Reich Governor of a German state: a new position and title created by Hitler in April 1933.
**Reichsverband der deutschen Industrie**  National Association of German Industry: a powerful employers' pressure group.
**Reichswehr**  German army in the Weimar era.
**Rentenmark**  The new German currency introduced in 1923–24.
**RGO**  Revolutionäre Gewerkschafts-Opposition: Revolutionary Trade Union Opposition (Communist).
**Rotfrontkämpferbund (RFB)**  Red Front Fighter's League: the paramilitary organization of the German Communist Party (1924–29).
**RVDP**  Reichsverband der Deutschen Presse: National Association of the German Press.
**SA**  Sturmabteilung: Stormtroopers.
**SAPD**  Sozialistische Arbeiterpartei Deutschlands: Socialist Workers' Party of Germany.
**SED**  Sozialistische Einheitspartei: Socialist Unity Party (Communist), post-1945 in East Germany.
*Senatspräsident*  Top-ranking judicial official.
*Sozialpolitik*  Social welfare policy.
*Sozialstaat*  The term used to describe the provision of public welfare by the Weimar Republic.
**SPD**  Sozialdemokratische Partei Deutschlands: Social Democratic Party of Germany.
**SS**  Schutzstaffeln: literally 'protection squads', the élite Nazi organization.
*Staatsanwalt*  Public Prosecutor.
**Staatsgerichtshof**  Supreme Court of the Reich, situated in Leipzig.
**Staatsrat**  State Council (as in Prussia until 1933).
*Staatssekretär*  Civil service grade, roughly equivalent to Under-Secretary.
*Stadtdirektor*  Chief executive in local government.
*Stadtrat*  Town councillor.
**Stahlhelm, Bund der Frontsoldaten**  Steel Helmet, League of Frontline Soldiers: right-wing veterans' organization.
**Truppenamt**  General Staff Office in the German army after 1918.
**USPD**  Unabhängige Sozialdemokratische Partei Deutschlands: Independent Social Democratic Party of Germany.
*völkisch*  Racist-nationalist.
**Volksgemeinschaft**  People's Community.
*Volkstum*  Nationality, national characteristics.
**VVVD**  Vereinigte Vaterländische Verbände Deutschlands: United Patriotic Groups of Germany.
**Wehrmacht**  German armed forces: the term replaced 'Reichswehr' in May 1935.
*Weltanschauung*  'World outlook': ideology or philosophy
**WTB-Plan**  Woytinsky–Tarnow–Baade Plan to relieve unemployment, 1932, named after its authors.

**Zentralarbeitsgemeinschaft (ZAG)** Joint Central Committee of Employers' and Trade Unions' representatives, established in November 1918.

# Select Bibliography: The Weimar Republic

Texts already cited in the individual Further Reading lists attached to each subject entry are not reproduced here. Moreover, works published before 1975 are cited only occasionally in sections 3–8 below.

## 1. Biographical Reference Works

Benz, W. and Graml, H. (eds), *Biographisches Lexikon zur Weimarer Republik*, Munich, 1988.
Czech-Jochberg, E., *Die Politiker der Republik. Von Ebert bis Schleicher*, Leipzig, 1933.
Degener, H.A.L. (ed.), *Wer Ist's?*, Berlin, 1928.
*Das Deutsche Führerlexikon 1934–1935*, Berlin, 1934.
Grab, W. and Schoeps, J.H. (eds), *Juden in der Weimarer Republik*, Stuttgart, 1986.
Grossmann, R., *Fünfzig Köpfe der Zeit*, Berlin, 1926.
Höffkes, K., *Hitlers politische Generale. Die Gauleiter des Dritten Reiches. Ein biographisches Nachschlagewerk*, Tübingen, 1986.
Horkenbach, C. (ed), *Das Deutsche Reich von 1918 bis heute*, 4 vols, Berlin, 1930–33.
Lösche, P., Scholing, M. and Walter, F. (eds), *Vor dem Vergessen bewahren. Lebenswege Weimarer Sozialdemokraten*, Berlin, 1988.
Mann, B. (ed.), *Biographisches Handbuch für das preussische Abgeordnetenhaus 1867–1918*, Düsseldorf, 1988.
Morsey, R. (ed.), *Zeitgeschichte in Lebensbildern*, 2 vols, Mainz, 1973–75.
Osterroth, F., *Biographisches Lexikon des Sozialismus*, Hanover, 1960.
Pachnicke, H., *Führende Männer im alten und neuen Reich*, Berlin, 1930.
Rees, P., *Biographical Dictionary of the Extreme Right since 1890*, London, 1990.
Rössler, H., and Franz, G. (eds), *Biographisches Wörterbuch zur deutschen Geschichte*, 3 vols, Munich, 1973–75.
Schröder, W.H., *Sozialdemokratische Reichstagsabgeordnete und Reichstagskandidaten 1898–1918. Biographisch-statistisches Handbuch*, Düsseldorf, 1986.
Schumacher, M. (ed.), *MdR. Die Reichstagsabgeordneten der Weimarer Republik in der Zeit des Nationalsozialismus. Politische Verfolgung, Emigration und Ausbürgerung 1933–1945. Eine biographisches Dokumentation*, Düsseldorf, 1991.
Schwarz, M., *MdR. Biographisches Handbuch der Reichstage*, Hanover, 1965.
Smelser, R. and Zitelmann, R. (eds), *Die braune Elite. 22 biographische Skizzen*, 2nd edn, Darmstadt, 1990.
Stöcker, J., *Männer des deutschen Schicksals*, Berlin, 1949.

Stockhorst, E., *Fünftausend Köpfe*, Velbert-Kettwig, 1967.
Snyder, L.L., *Hitler's Elite. Biographical Sketches of Nazis who Shaped the Third Reich*, New York, 1989.
Treml, M. and Wiegand, W. (eds), *Geschichte und Kultur der Juden in Bayern. Band 2: Lebensläufe*, Munich, 1988.
Unger, E., *Politische Köpfe des sozialistischen Deutschlands*, Leipzig, 1920.
Walk, J., *Kurzbiographien zur Geschichte der Juden 1918–1945*, Munich, 1988.
Wistrich, R., *Who's Who in Nazi Germany*, London, 1982.
Zentner, C. and Bedürftig, F. (eds), *Das Grosse Lexikon des Dritten Reiches*, Munich, 1985.

## 2. Bibliographies

ABC-Clio, *The Weimar Republic. A Historical Bibliography*, Santa Barbara and Oxford, 1984.
*Bibliographie zur Zeitgeschichte*, Supplement of the *Vierteljahrshefte für Zeitgeschichte*, 1953ff.
Kehr, H. and Langmaid, J., *The Nazi Era 1919–1945. A Select Bibliography of Published Works from the Early Roots to 1980*, London, 1982.
Klotzbach, K., *Bibliographie zur Geschichte der deutschen Arbeiterbewegung 1914–1945*, 3rd edn, Bonn, 1981.
Meyer, G.P., *Bibliographie zur deutschen Revolution 1918/19*, Göttingen, 1977.
Stachura, P.D., *The Weimar Era and Hitler, 1918–1933. A Select Bibliography*, Oxford, 1977.
Ullmann, H.-P., *Bibliographie zur Geschichte der deutschen Parteien und Interessenverbände*, Göttingen, 1978.
Vogelsang, T. and Auerbach, H. (eds), *Bibliographie zur Zeitgeschichte 1953–1980*, Munich, 1982.
Wiener Library, *From Weimar to Hitler. Germany, 1918–1933*, London, 1964.

## 3. Edited Collections of Documents and Essays

Abelshauser, W. and Himmelmann, R. (eds), *Revolution in Rheinland und Westfalen. Quellen zur Wirtschaft, Gesellschaft und Politik, 1918–1923*, Essen, 1988.
Albertin, L. and Link, W. (eds), *Politische Parteien auf dem Wege zur parlamentarischen Demokratie in Deutschland*, Düsseldorf, 1981.
Benz, W. (ed.), *Pazifismus in Deutschland. Dokumente zur Friedensbewegung 1890–1939*, Frankfurt am Main, 1988.
Bessel, R. and Feuchtwanger, E.J. (eds), *Social Change and Political Development in Weimar Germany*, London, 1981.
Bracher, K.D., Funke, M. and Jacobsen, H.-A. (eds), *Die Weimarer Republik, 1918–1933. Politik, Wirtschaft, Gesellschaft*, Düsseldorf, 1987.
Broszat, M. and Dübber, U. (eds), *Deutschlands Weg in die Diktatur*, Berlin, 1983.
Feldman, G.D. and Holtfrerich, C.-L. (eds), *Konsequenzen der Inflation*, Berlin, 1989.
Childers, T. (ed.), *The Formation of the Nazi Constituency, 1918–1933*, London, 1986.
Dobkowski, M.N. and Wallimann, I. (eds), *Towards the Holocaust. The Social and Economic Collapse of the Weimar Republic*, New York, 1983.
Erdmann, K.D. and Schulze, H. (eds), *Weimar. Selbstpreisgabe einer Demokratie*, Düsseldorf, 1980.

Evans, R.J. and Geary, D. (eds), *The German Unemployed. Experiences and Consequences of Mass Unemployment from the Weimar Republic to the Third Reich*, London, 1987.
Flemming, J., Krohn, C.-D., Stegmann, D. and Witt, P.C. (eds), *Die Republik von Weimar*, 2 vols, Königstein, 1979.
Flemming, J. (ed.), *Familienleben im Schatten der Krise. Dokumente und Analysen zur Sozialgeschichte der Weimarer Republik*, Düsseldorf, 1988.
Gordon, H.J. (ed.), *The Hitler Trial before the People's Court in Munich*, 3 vols, Arlington, Virginia, 1976.
Holl, K. (ed.), *Wirtschaftskrise und liberale Demokratie*, Göttingen, 1978.
Jäckel, E. and Kuhn, A. (eds), *Hitler. Sämtliche Aufzeichnungen 1905–1924*, Stuttgart, 1980.
Jahn, P. and Brunner, D. (eds), *Die Gewerkschaften in der Endphase der Republik 1930–1933*, Cologne, 1988.
Kruedener, J. von (ed.), *Economic Crisis and Political Collapse. The Weimar Republic 1924–1933*, Oxford, 1990.
Kukuck, H.A., and Schiffmann, D. (eds), *Die Gewerkschaften von der Stabilisierung bis zur Weltwirtschaftskrise 1924–1930*, Cologne, 1986.
Laffan, M. (ed.), *The Burden of German History, 1918–1945*, London, 1988.
Langewiesche, D. and Tenorth, H.-E. (eds), *Die Weimarer Republik und die nationalsozialistische Diktatur*, Munich, 1989.
Lehnert, D. and Megerle, K. (eds), *Politische Identität und nationale Gedenktage. Zur politischen Kultur in der Weimarer Republik*, Opladen, 1989.
Lehnert, D. and Megerle, K. (eds), *Politische Teilkulturen zwischen Integration und Polarisierung. Zur politischen Kultur in der Weimarer Republik*, Berlin, 1990.
Maier, C.S. and Hoffmann, S. (eds), *The Rise of the Nazi Regime. Historical Reassessments*, Cambridge, Massachusetts, 1985.
Mann, R. (ed.), *Die Nationalsozialisten*, Stuttgart, 1980.
Michalka, W. (ed.), *Die nationalsozialistische Machtergreifung*, Paderborn, 1984.
Michalka, W. and Niedhart, G. (eds), *Die ungeliebte Republik. Dokumentation zur Innen- und Aussenpolitik Weimars, 1918–1933*, Munich, 1980.
Miller Lane, B. and Rupp, L.J. (eds), *Nazi Ideology before 1933*, Austin, 1978.
Noakes, J. and Pridham, G. (eds), *Nazism 1919–1945.*, Vol I, *The Rise to Power 1919–1934. A Documentary Reader*, Exeter, 1983.
Prinz, M. and Zitelmann, R. (eds), *Nationalsozialismus und Modernisierung*, Darmstadt, 1991.
Potthoff, H. and Weber, H. (eds), *Die SPD-Fraktion in der Nationalversammlung 1919–1920*, Düsseldorf, 1986.
Rittberger, V. (ed.), *1933. Wie die Republik der Diktatur erlag*, Stuttgart, 1983.
Ruck, M. (ed.), *Die Gewerkschaften in den Anfangsjahren der Republik 1919–1923*, Cologne, 1985.
Schönhoven, K. (ed.), *Die Gewerkschaften in Weltkrieg und Revolution 1914–1919*, Cologne, 1985.
Schulz, G. (ed.), *Weimarer Republik. Eine Nation im Umbruch*, Freiburg, 1987.
Stachura, P.D. (ed.), *The Nazi Machtergreifung*, London, 1983.
Stachura, P.D. (ed.), *Unemployment and The Great Depression in Weimar Germany*, London, 1986.
Stürmer, M. (ed.), *Die Weimarer Republik. Belagerte Civitas*, Königstein, 1980.
Treue, W. and Schmädeke, J. (eds), *Deutschland 1933. Machtzerfall der Demokratie und nationalsozialistische 'Machtergreifung'*, Berlin, 1984.

Turner, H.A. (ed.), *Hitler, Memoirs of a Confidant*, London, 1985.
Tyrell, A. (ed.), *Führer befiehl . . . Selbstzeugnisse aus der 'Kampfzeit' der NSDAP*, Düsseldorf, 1969.
Welch, D. (ed.), *Nazi Propaganda*, London, 1983.

## 4. General Accounts

Bracher, K.D., *Die Auflösung der Weimarer Republik. Eine Studie zum Problem des Machtverfalls in der Demokratie*, 6th edn, Königstein, 1978.
Dederke, K., *Reich und Republik. Deutschland 1917–1933*, 4th edn, Stuttgart, 1981.
Gessner, D., *Das Ende der Weimarer Republik. Fragen, Methoden und Ergebnisse interdisziplinärer Forschung*, Darmstadt, 1978.
Hentschel, V., *Weimars letzte Monate*, Düsseldorf, 1978.
Huber, E.R., *Deutsche Verfassungsgeschichte seit 1789*, Vol. 7, *Ausbau, Schutz und Untergang der Weimarer Republik*, Stuttgart, 1984.
Jasper, G., *Die gescheiterte Zähmung. Wege zur Machtergreifung Hitlers 1930–1934*, Frankfurt am Main, 1986.
Köhler, H., *Geschichte der Weimarer Republik*, Berlin, 1981.
Kolb, E., *The Weimar Republic*, London, 1988.
Kühnl, R., *Die Weimarer Republik*, Reinbek, 1985.
Möller, H., *Weimar. Die unvollendete Demokratie*, 2nd edn, Munich, 1987.
Mommsen, H., *Die verspielte Freiheit. Der Weg der Republik von Weimar in den Untergang 1918 bis 1933*, Berlin, 1989.
Nicholls, A.J., *Weimar and the Rise of Hitler*, 3rd edn, London, 1989.
Overesch, M. and Saal, F.W., *Die Weimarer Republik*, Düsseldorf, 1982.
Peukert, D., *The Weimar Republic*, London, 1991.
Ruge, W., *Weimar. Republik auf Zeit*, Cologne, 1980.
Schulz, G., *Aufstieg des Nationalsozialismus. Krise und Revolution in Deutschland*, Frankfurt am Main, 1975.
Schulze, H., *Weimar. Deutschland 1917–1933*, Berlin, 1982.

## 5. International Relations
(A) THE VERSAILLES SETTLEMENT 1918–19

Dockrill, M.L. and Gould, J.D., *Peace with Promise. Britain and the Peace Conferences 1919–1923*, London, 1981.
Floto, J., *Colonel House in Paris. A Study of American Policy at the Paris Peace Conference of 1919*, Princeton, 1980.
Jaffe, L.S., *The Decision to Disarm Germany. British Policy towards Postwar German Disarmament, 1914–1919*, London, 1985.
Köhler, H., *Novemberrevolution und Frankreich. Die französische Deutschlandpolitik 1918–19*, Düsseldorf, 1979.
Lentin, A., *Lloyd George, Woodrow Wilson and the Guilt of Germany*, London, 1985.
Lentin, A., *The Versailles Peace Settlement 1919*, London, 1991.
Nelson, K.L., *Victors Divided. America and the Allies in Germany, 1918-1923*, Berkeley, 1975.
Pommerin, R. (ed.), *Der Vertrag von Versailles*, Cologne, 1990.

Schwabe, K., *Woodrow Wilson, Revolutionary Germany, and Peacemaking 1918–1919*, Chapel Hill, 1985.
Sharp, A., *The Versailles Settlement. Peacemaking in Paris, 1919*, London, 1991.
Steinmeyer, G., *Die Grundlagen der französischen Deutschlandpolitik 1917–1919*, Stuttgart, 1979.
Stevenson, D., *French War Aims against Germany 1914–1919*, Oxford, 1982.
Walworth, A., *America's Moment: 1918. American Diplomacy at the End of World War I*, New York, 1977.
Walworth, A., *Wilson and His Peacemakers. American Diplomacy at the Paris Peace Conference, 1919*, New York, 1986.

(B) 1919-32

Becker, J. and Hildebrand, K. (eds), *Internationale Beziehungen in der Weltwirtschaftskrise 1929–1933*, Munich, 1980.
Beitel, W. and Nötzold, J., *Deutsch-sowjetische Wirtschaftsbeziehungen in der Zeit der Weimarer Republik*, Baden-Baden, 1979.
Bennett, E.W., *German Rearmament and the West, 1932–1933*, Princeton, 1979.
Campbell, F.G., *Confrontation in Central Europe. Weimar Germany and Czechoslovakia*, Chicago, 1975.
Dohrmann, B., *Die englische Europapolitik in der Wirtschaftskrise 1921–1923*, Munich, 1980.
Enssle, M., *Stresemann's Territorial Revisionism. Germany, Belgium and the Eupen–Malmédy Question, 1919–1929*, Wiesbaden, 1980.
Fink, C., *The Genoa Conference. European Diplomacy, 1921–22*, Chapel Hill, 1984.
Frommelt, R., *Paneuropa oder Mitteleuropa. Einigungsbestrebungen im Kalkül deutscher Wirtschaft und Politik 1925–1933*, Stuttgart, 1977.
Grupp, P., *Deutsche Aussenpolitik im Schatten von Versailles, 1918–1920*, Paderborn, 1988.
Haigh, R.H., Morris, D.S. and Peters, A.R., *German–Soviet Relations in the Weimar Era. Friendship from Necessity*, Totowa, New Jersey, 1985.
Hiden, J.W., *The Baltic States and Weimar 'Ostpolitik'*, London, 1987.
Hildebrand, K., *Das Deutsche Reich und die Sowjetunion im internationalen System 1918–1932*, Wiesbaden, 1977.
Knilling, F., *Deutschland, Frankreich und das Ende der Locarno–Ära 1928–1931. Studien zur internationalen Politik in der Anfangsphase der Weltwirtschaftskrise*, Munich, 1987.
Leffler, M.P., *The Elusive Quest. America's Pursuit of European Stability and French Security, 1919–1933*, Chapel Hill, 1979.
Luks, L., *Entstehung der kommunistischen Faschismustheorie. Die Auseinandersetzung der Komintern mit Faschismus und Nationalsozialismus 1921-1925*, Stuttgart, 1984.
Luza, R., *Austro-German Relations in the Anschluss Era*, Chicago, 1975.
Maier, C., *Recasting Bourgeois Europe. Stabilization in France, Germany and Italy in the Decade after World War I*, Princeton, 1975.
Mayer, K.J., *Die Weimarer Republik und das Problem der Sicherheit in den deutsch–französischen Beziehungen 1918–1925*, Frankfurt am Main, 1990.
McKale, D.M., *Curt Prüfer. German Diplomat from the Kaiser to Hitler*, Lawrence, Kansas, 1989.
Nadolny, S., *Abrüstungsdiplomatie 1932/33. Deutschland auf der Genfer Konferenz im Übergang von Weimar zu Hitler*, Munich, 1978.

Schuker, S.A., *The End of French Predominance in Europe. The Financial Crisis of 1924 and the Adoption of the Dawes Plan*, Chapel Hill, 1976.
Stehlin, S.A., *Weimar and the Vatican 1919–1933*, Princeton, 1983.
Suval, S., *The Anschluss Question in the Weimar Era. A Study of Nationalism in Germany and Austria, 1918–1932*, Baltimore, 1974.
Trachtenberg, M., *Reparations in World Politics. France and European Economic Diplomacy, 1916–1923*, New York, 1980.
Vincent, C.P., *The Politics of Hunger. The Allied Blockade of Germany, 1915–1919*, Athens, Ohio, 1985.
Williamson, D.G., *The British in Germany, 1918–1930*, Oxford, 1990.
Wurm, C.A., *Die französische Sicherheitspolitik in der Phase der Umorientierung 1924–1926*, Frankfurt am Main, 1979.

## 6. Political Developments

Aretz, J., *Katholische Arbeiterbewegung und Nationalsozialismus. Der Verband Katholischer Arbeiter- und Knappenvereine Westdeutschlands, 1923–1945*, Mainz, 1978.
Baker, L., *Days of Sorrow and Pain. Leo Baeck and the Berlin Jews*, London, 1982.
Bieber, H.-J., *Gewerkschaften in Krieg und Revolution*, 2 vols, Hamburg, 1981.
Bockel, R. von, *Kurt Hiller und die Gruppe Revolutionärer Pazifisten (1926–1933)*, Hamburg, 1990.
Bölling, R., *Volksschullehrer und Politik. Der Deutsche Lehrerverein 1918–1933*, Göttingen, 1978.
Borg, D.R., *The Old Prussian Church and the Weimar Republic. A Study in Political Adjustment, 1917–1927*, London, 1985.
Braunthal, G., *Socialist Labor and Politics in Weimar Germany. The General Federation of German Trade Unions*, New Haven, 1981.
Büsch, O., Wölk, M. and Wölk, W. (eds), *Wählerbewegungen in der deutschen Geschichte. Analysen und Berichte zu den Reichstagswahlen 1871–1933*, Berlin, 1978.
Donat, H. and Holl, K. (eds), *Die Friedensbewegung. Organisierter Pazifismus in Deutschland, Österreich und der Schweiz*, Düsseldorf, 1983.
Dupeau, L., *'Nationalbolschewismus' in Deutschland 1919–1933*, Munich, 1983.
Eksteins, M., *The Limits of Reason. The German Democratic Press and the Collapse of Weimar Democracy*, Oxford, 1975.
Falter, J., Lindenberg, T. and Schumann, S., *Wahlen und Abstimmungen in der Weimarer Republik. Materialien zum Wahlverhalten 1919–1932*, Munich, 1986.
Fritsche, P., *Rehearsals for Fascism. Populism and Political Mobilization in Weimar Germany*, Oxford, 1990.
Hänisch, D., *Sozialstrukturelle Bestimmungsgründe des Wahlverhaltens in der Weimarer Republik*, Duisburg, 1983.
Hasselhorn, F., *Wie wählte Göttingen? Wahlverhalten und soziale Basis der Parteien in Göttingen 1924–1933*, Göttingen, 1983.
Herf, J., *Reactionary Modernism. Technology, Culture and Politics in Weimar and the Third Reich*, Cambridge, 1984.
Hess, J.C., *'Das ganze Deutschland soll es sein'. Demokratischer Nationalismus in der Weimarer Republik am Beispiel der Deutschen Demokratischen Partei*, Stuttgart, 1978.
Holzer, J., *Parteien und Massen. Die politische Krise in Deutschland 1928-1930*, Wiesbaden, 1975.

Jacke, J., *Kirche zwischen Monarchie und Republik. Der preussische Protestantismus nach dem Zusammenbruch von 1918*, Hamburg, 1976.

Jung, O., *Direkte Demokratie in der Weimarer Republik*, Frankfurt am Main, 1989.

Large, D.C., *The Politics of Law and Order. A History of the Bavarian Einwohnerwehr, 1918–1921*, Philadelphia, 1980.

Luthardt, W. (ed.), *Sozialdemokratische Arbeiterbewegung und Weimarer Republik. Materialien zur gesellschaftlichen Entwicklung 1927–1933*, 2 vols, Frankfurt am Main, 1978.

Mohler, A., *Die Konservative Revolution in Deutschland 1918–1932*, 3rd edn, Darmstadt, 1989.

Moses, J.A., *Trade Unionism in Germany from Bismarck to Hitler. Vol 2: 1919–1933*, London, 1982.

Neugebauer-Wölk, M., *Wählergenerationen in Preussen zwischen Kaiserreich und Republik*, Berlin, 1987.

Nöcker, H., *Der preussische Reichstagswähler in Kaiserreich und Republik, 1912 und 1924*, Berlin, 1987.

Niewyk, D.K., *The Jews in Weimar Germany*, Baton Rouge, 1982.

Novak, K., *Evangelische Kirche und Weimarer Republik. Zum politischen Weg des deutschen Protestantismus zwischen 1918 und 1932*, 2nd edn, Göttingen, 1988.

Petzold, J., *Wegbereiter des deutschen Faschismus. Die Jungkonservativen in der Weimarer Republik*, Cologne, 1978.

Potthoff, H., *Gewerkschaften und Politik zwischen Revolution und Inflation*, Düsseldorf, 1979.

Potthoff, H., *Freie Gewerkschaften 1918–1933. Der Allgemeine Deutsche Gewerkschaftsbund in der Weimarer Republik*, Düsseldorf, 1987.

Priamus, H.-J., *Angestellte und Demokratie. Die nationalliberale Angestelltenbewegung in der Weimarer Republik*, Stuttgart, 1979.

Ruck, M., *Die freien Gewerkschaften in Ruhrkampf 1923*, Cologne, 1986.

Ruck, M., *Gewerkschaften-Staat-Unternehmer. Die Gewerkschaften im sozialen und politischen Kräftefeld 1914 bis 1933*, Cologne, 1990.

Schanbacher, E., *Parlamentarische Wahlen und Wahlsystem in der Weimarer Republik*, Düsseldorf, 1982.

Schmidt, E.-H., *Heimatheer und Revolution 1918*, Stuttgart, 1981.

Schönhoven, K., *Reformismus und Radikalismus. Gespaltene Arbeiterbewegung im Weimarer Sozialstaat*, Munich, 1989.

Schüren, U., *Der Volksentscheid zur Fürstenenteignung 1926*, Düsseldorf, 1978.

Stark, G., *Entrepreneurs of Ideology. Neoconservative Publishers in Germany 1890–1933*, Chapel Hill, 1981.

Sühl, K., *SPD und öffentlicher Dienst in der Weimarer Republik*, Opladen, 1988.

Tampke, J., *The Ruhr and Revolution. The Revolutionary Movement in the Rhenish-Westphalian Region, 1914–1919*, London, 1979.

Vogel, W., *Katholische Kirche und nationale Kampfverbände in der Weimarer Republik*, Mainz, 1989.

West, F.C., *A Crisis of the Weimar Republic. A Study of the German Referendum of 20 June 1926*, Philadelphia, 1986.

## 7. Economic and Social Developments

Bähr, J., *Staatliche Schlichtung in der Weimarer Republik. Tarifpolitik, Korporatismus und industrieller Konflikt zwischen Inflation und Deflation, 1919–1932*, Berlin, 1989.
Bischoff, S., *Arbeitszeitrecht in der Weimarer Republik*, Berlin, 1987.
Blaich, F., *Die Wirtschaftskrise 1925/26 und die Reichsregierung. Von der Erwerbslosenfürsorge zur Konjunkturpolitik*, Kallmünz, 1977.
Blaich, F., *Der Schwarze Freitag. Inflation und Wirtschaftskrise*, Munich, 1985.
Bogs, W., *Die Sozialversicherung in der Weimarer Republik*, Munich, 1981.
Borchardt, K., *Perspectives on Modern German Economic History and Policy*, Cambridge, 1991.
Büsch, O. and Feldman, G.D. (eds), *Historische Prozesse der deutschen Inflation 1914–1924*, Berlin, 1978.
Büsch, O. and Haus, W., *Berlin als Hauptstadt der Weimarer Republik 1919–1933*, Berlin, 1987.
Büttner, U., *Hamburg in der Staats- und Wirtschaftskrise 1928–1931*, Hamburg, 1982.
Dudek, P., *Erziehung durch Arbeit. Arbeitslagerbewegung und freiwilliger Arbeitsdienst 1920–1935*, Opladen, 1988.
Feldman, G.D., Holtfrerisch, C.-L. and Writt, P.-C. (eds), *The German Inflation Reconsidered. A Preliminary Balance*, New York, 1982.
Feldman, G.D., *Vom Weltkrieg zur Wirtschaftskrise. Studien zur deutschen Wirtschafts- und Sozialgeschichte 1914–1932*, Göttingen, 1984.
Feldman, G.D. (ed), *Die Nachwirkungen der Inflation auf die deutsche Geschichte 1924–1933*, Munich, 1985.
Feldman, G.D., Holtfrerich, C.-L., Ritter, G.A. and Writt, P.-C. (eds), *Die Anpassung an die Inflation*, Berlin, 1986.
Fiedler, G., *Jugend im Krieg. Bürgerliche Jugendbewegung, Erster Weltkrieg und sozialer Wandel, 1914–1923*, Cologne, 1989.
Flemming, J., *Landwirtschaftliche Interessen und Demokratie. Ländliche Gesellschaft, Agrarverbände und Staat 1890–1925*, Bonn, 1978.
Freyberg, T. von, *Industrielle Rationalisierung in der Weimarer Republik*, Frankfurt am Main, 1989.
Fromm, E., *The Working Class in Weimar Germany. A Psychological and Sociological Study*, Leamington Spa, 1984.
Führer, K.C., *Arbeitslosigkeit und die Entstehung der Arbeitslosenversicherung in Deutschland 1902–1927*, Berlin, 1990.
Götz von Olenhusen, I., *Jugendreich, Gottes Reich, Deutsches Reich. Junge Generation, Religion und Politik 1928–1933*, Cologne, 1987.
Grübler, M., *Die Spitzenverbände der Wirtschaft und das erste Kabinett Brüning*, Düsseldorf, 1982.
Grzywatz, B., *Arbeit und Bevölkerung im Berlin der Weimarer Republik*, Berlin, 1988.
Guttsman, W.L., *Workers' Culture in Weimar Germany*, Oxford, 1990.
Hagemann, K., *Frauenalltag und Männerpolitik. Alltagsleben und gesellschaftliches Handeln von Arbeiterfrauen in der Weimarer Republik*, Bonn, 1990.
Henze, J., *Sechsstundenschicht im Ruhrbergbau 1918–1920*, Freiburg im Breisgau, 1988.
Hertz-Eichenrode, D., *Wirtschaftskrise und Arbeitsbeschaffung. Konjunkturpolitik 1925/26 und die Grundlagen der Krisenpolitik Brünings*, Frankfurt am Main, 1982.
Holtfrerich, C.-L., *The German Inflation 1914–1923. Causes and Effect in International Perspective*, New York, 1986.

Hughes, M.L., *Paying for the German Inflation*, Chapel Hill, 1988.
James, H., *The German Slump. Politics and Economics, 1924–1936*, Oxford, 1986.
Kindt, W. (ed.), *Die deutsche Jugendbewegung 1920 bis 1933. Die Bündische Zeit*, Düsseldorf, 1974.
Kunz, A., *Civil Servants and the Politics of Inflation in Germany, 1914–1924*, Berlin, 1986.
Lyth, P.J., *Inflation and the Merchant Economy. The Hamburg Mittelstand 1914–1924*, Oxford, 1990.
McNeil, W.C., *American Money and the Weimar Republic*, New York, 1988.
Mitterauer, M., *Sozialgeschichte der Jugend*, Frankfurt am Main, 1986.
Moeller, R., *Peasants, Politics and Pressure Groups in War and Inflation. A Study of the Rhineland and Westphalia, 1914–1924*, Chapel Hill, 1986.
Mommsen, H., *Klassenkampf oder Mitbestimmung. Zum Problem der Kontrolle wirtschaftlicher Macht in der Weimarer Republik*, Cologne, 1978.
Neebe, R., *Grossindustrie, Staat und NSDAP 1930–1933. Paul Silverberg und der Reichsverband der deutschen Industrie in der Krise der Weimarer Republik*, Göttingen, 1981.
Niehuss, M., *Arbeiterschaft in Krieg und Inflation. Soziale Schichtung und Lage der Arbeiter in Augsburg und Linz 1910 bis 1925*, Berlin, 1985.
Nussbaum, M., *Wirtschaft und Staat in Deutschland während der Weimarer Republik*, East Berlin, 1978.
Peukert, D.J.K., *Grenzen der Sozialdisziplinierung. Aufstieg und Krise der deutschen Jugendfürsorge 1878 bis 1932*, Cologne, 1986.
Peukert, D.J.K., *Jugend zwischen Krieg und Krise. Lebenswelten von Arbeiterjungen in der Weimarer Republik*, Cologne, 1987.
Prinz, M., *Vom neuen Mittelstand zum Volksgenossen. Die Entwicklung des sozialen Status der Angestellten von der Weimarer Republik bis zum Ende der NS-Zeit*, Munich, 1986.
Richter, F., *Beiträge zur Industrie- und Handwerks-geschichtliche Ostpreussen 1919–1939*, Stuttgart, 1988.
Ritter, G.A., *Staat, Arbeiterschaft und Arbeiterbewegung in Deutschland*, Berlin, 1980.
Rüther, M., *Arbeiterschaft in Köln 1928–1945*, Cologne, 1990.
Schneider, M., *Das Arbeitsbeschaffungsprogramm des ADGB. Zur gewerkschaftlichen Politik in der Endphase der Weimarer Republik*, Bonn, 1975.
Schneider, M., *Unternehmer und Demokratie. Die freien Gewerkschaften in der unternehmerischen Ideologie der Jahre 1918 bis 1933*, Bonn, 1975.
Schötz, H.O., *Der Kampf um die Mark 1923/24. Die deutsche Währungsstabilisierung unter dem Einfluss der nationalen Interessen Frankreichs, Grossbritanniens und der USA*, Berlin, 1987.
Schuker, S.A., *American 'Reparations' to Germany, 1919–1933*, Princeton, 1988.
Stachura, P.D., *The German Youth Movement 1900–1945*, London, 1981.
Stachura, P.D., *The Weimar Republic and the Younger Proletariat. An Economic and Social Analysis*, London, 1989.
Unterstell, R., *Mittelstand in der Weimarer Republik. Die soziale Entwicklung und politische Orientierung von Handwerk, Kleinhandel und Hausbesitz 1919–1933*, Frankfurt am Main, 1989.
Usborne, C., *The Politics of the Body in Weimar Germany*, London, 1991.
Webb, S.B., *Hyperinflation and Stabilization in Weimar Germany*, Oxford, 1990.
Whalen, R.W., *Bitter Wounds. German Victims of the Great War, 1914–1939*, Ithaca, 1985.
Wolffsohn, M., *Industrie und Handwerk im Konflikt mit staatlicher Wirtschaftspolitik? Studien zur Politik der Arbeitsbeschaffung in Deutschland 1930–1934*, Berlin, 1977.

Zollitsch, W., *Arbeiter zwischen Weltwirtschaftskrise und Nationalsozialismus. Ein Beitrag zur Sozialgeschichte der Jahre 1928 bis 1936*, Göttingen, 1990.

## 8. The Rise of National Socialism

Allen, W.S. (ed.), *The Infancy of Nazism. The Memoirs of ex-Gauleiter Albert Krebs, 1923–1933*, New York, 1976.
Ayçoberry, P., *The Nazi Question. An Essay on the Interpretations of National Socialism (1922–1975)*, London, 1981.
Baird, J.W., *To Die for Germany. Heroes in the Nazi Pantheon*, Bloomingdale, 1990.
Barkai, A., *Nazi Economics. Ideology, Theory and Policy*, Oxford, 1990.
Broszat, M., *Die Machtergreifung. Der Aufstieg der NSDAP und die Zerstörung der Weimarer Republik*, Munich, 1984.
Carr, W., *Hitler. A Study in Personality and Politics*, London, 1978.
Childers, T., *The Nazi Voter. The Social Foundations of Fascism in Germany, 1919–1933*, Chapel Hill, 1983.
Falter, J.W., *Hitlers Wähler*, Munich, 1991.
Fischer, C., *The German Communists and the Rise of Nazism*, London, 1991.
Franke, V., *Der Aufstieg der NSDAP in Düsseldorf*, Essen, 1987.
Franz-Willing, G., *Krisenjahr der Hitlerbewegung, 1923*, Preussisch Oldendorf, 1975.
Franz-Willing, G., *Putsch und Verbotszeit der Hitlerbewegung. November 1923 bis Februar 1925*, Preussisch Oldendorf, 1977.
Giles, G.J., *Students and National Socialism in Germany*, Princeton, 1985.
Gordon, S., *Hitler, Germans and the 'Jewish Question'*, Princeton, 1984.
Gossweiler, K., *Kapital, Reichswehr und NSDAP 1919–1924*, Cologne, 1982.
Grill, J.H., *The Nazi Movement in Baden 1920–1945*, 2 vols, Chapel Hill, 1983.
Hambrecht, R., *Der Aufstieg der NSDAP in Mittel- und Oberfranken (1925–1933)*, Nuremberg, 1976.
Hamilton, R.F., *Who Voted for Hitler?*, Princeton, 1982.
Hayward, N. and Morris, D., *The First Nazi Town*, London, 1989.
Heinacher, P., *Der Aufstieg der NSDAP im Stadt- und Landkreis Flensburg (1919–1933)*, Flensburg, 1986.
Horn, W., *Der Marsch zur Machtergreifung. Die NSDAP bis 1933*, Königstein/Düsseldorf, 1980 (originally published in 1972).
Jäckel, E., *Hitler's World View*, Middleton, Connecticut, 1982.
Jäckel, E., *Hitler in History*, London, 1984.
Jablonsky, D., *The Nazi Party in Dissolution. Hitler and the Verbotszeit, 1923–1925*, London, 1989.
Kater, M.H., *The Nazi Party. A Social Profile of Members and Leaders, 1919–1945*, Oxford, 1983.
Koehl, R.L., *The Black Corps. The Structure and Power Struggles of the Nazi SS*, Madison, 1983.
Koshar, R., *Social Life, Local Politics and Nazism. Marburg 1880–1935*, Chapel Hill, 1985.
Kratzenberg, V., *Arbeiter auf dem Weg zu Hitler? Die Nationalsozialistische Betriebszellen-Organisation. Ihre Entstehung, ihre Programmatik, ihr Scheitern 1927–1934*, Frankfurt am Main, 1987.

Manstein, P., *Die Mitglieder und Wähler der NSDAP 1919–1933*, Frankfurt am Main and Berne, 1988.
Merkl, P., *Political Violence under the Swastika. 581 Early Nazis*, Princeton, 1975.
Mühlberger, D., *Hitler's Followers. Studies in the Sociology of the Nazi Movement*, London, 1991.
Paul, G., *Aufstand der Bilder. Die NS-Propaganda vor 1933*, Bonn, 1990.
Rempel, R., *Hitler's Children. The Hitler Youth and the SS*, Chapel Hill, 1989.
Rhodes, J.M., *The Hitler Movement. A Modern Millenarian Revolution*, Stanford, 1980.
Rietzler, R., *'Kampf in der Nordmark'. Das Aufkommen des Nationalsozialismus in Schleswig-Holstein (1919–1928)*, Neumünster, 1982.
Ruck, M., *Bollwerk gegen Hitler? Arbeiterschaft, Arbeiterbewegung und die Anfänge des Nationalsozialismus*, Cologne, 1988.
Speier, H., *German White Collar Workers and the Rise of Hitler*, New Haven, 1987.
Stachura, P.D., *Nazi Youth in the Weimar Republic*, Santa Barbara, 1975.
Stein, P., *Die NS-Gaupresse 1925–1933*, Munich, 1987.
Steinberg, M.S., *Sabres, Books and Brown Shirts. The German Students' Path to National Socialism, 1918–1935*, Chicago, 1977.
Stoakes, G., *Hitler and the Quest for World Dominion. Nazi Ideology and Foreign Policy in the 1920s*, Leamington Spa, 1986.
Stokes, L.D., *Kleinstadt und Nationalsozialismus. Ausgewählte Dokumente zur Geschichte von Eutin 1918–1945*, Neumünster, 1984.
Turner, H.A., *German Big Business and the Rise of Hitler*, New York, 1985.
Ziegler, H.F., *Nazi Germany's New Aristocracy. The SS Leadership, 1925–1939*, Princeton, 1990.

# *Index*

*Accumulation of Capital, The*, 121
Adenauer, Konrad, 7–8, 81, 95, 137
ADGB (Socialist trade unions), 10, 22, 79, 188, 189
'agrarian Bolshevism', 24, 54, 155, 169
Agrarian League, 102
*Alte Kämpfer*, 87
Altona riot, 130
Amann, Max, 8–9, 35
Americans, 9, 20, 32, 44, 148, 168, 173, 179
American–Mexican war, 130
anti-Semitism, 30, 39, 40, 41, 47, 50, 51, 57, 58, 60, 71, 76, 80, 87, 88, 113, 122, 135, 144, 145, 146, 162, 171, 173
    *See also* Jews
Arbeiterwohlfahrt, 97, 98
*Arbeitsgemeinschaft* (Communist), 32, 116
*Arbeitsgemeinschaft* (Socialist), 43, 67, 114
Arbeitsgemeinschaft Nord West, 171
Armistice, 23, 46, 195
army (pre-1918), 9, 10, 25, 31, 37, 38, 40, 42, 44, 46, 59, 62, 63, 78, 83, 86, 87, 131, 134, 144, 147, 176, 180
    *See also* Reichswehr
Artamanen, 30
Article 48, 24, 42, 83, 112, 114
Association for Germandom Abroad, 55
Association of Saxon Industrialists, 172
*Auf gut Deutsch*, 145
*Augsburger Zeitung*, 35

Baden, Prince Max of, 11, 20, 32, 46, 69, 149, 158, 195
Ballin, Albert, 26

Bamberg conference, 56, 171
banking crisis (1931), 7, 120, 121, 200
Barmat scandal, 11, 71
Barth, Emil, 9–10
Barth, Theodor, 21, 134
Basic Law, 81
Bassermann, Ernst, 172
Bauer, Gustav, 10–12, 23, 32, 46, 55, 126, 153, 158, 189, 196
Bäumer, Gertrud, 2, 12–13, 112
Bavarian Administrative Court, 101, 102
Bavarian Middle Party, 66
Bavaran People's Party (BVP), 44, 73, 101, 106, 112, 123, 147, 148, 169
Bayerische Motorenwerke (BMW), 59
Bayernwacht, 148
BDF (League of German Women's Associations), 12, 13
Bebel, August, 14, 42, 67, 114, 149, 182
Beer Hall putsch, 8, 16, 39, 48, 51, 55, 59, 87, 95, 101, 144, 146, 170, 173, 198
*Beigeordneter*, 7, 58, 95
Bell, Johannes, 126
Berg-Metallbank, 94
*Bergische Arbeiterstimme*, 37
*Berliner Tageblatt*, 109, 135
Berlin transport workers' strike (1932), 127, 177
Berlin Wall, 181
Berlin workers' strike (1918), 9, 17, 37, 42, 43
Bernstein, Aaron, 13
Bernstein, Eduard, 13–15

Bethmann-Hollweg, Chancellor Theobald von, 102, 135
Bielefeld Agreement, 165
Bismarck, Otto von, 14, 59
Black Reichswehr, 163, 198
*Blutmai*, 132, 180, 200
Boch-Galhaus family, 130
Böhm-Bawerk, 81
Bolsheviks, 22, 25, 62, 116, 118, 121, 129, 145, 146, 149, 163, 175, 180, 193
Bolz, Eugen, 15–16
Bouhler, Philip, 16–17
Boxer rebellion, 40
Brandler, Heinrich, 175, 177, 191
Brandt, Willy, 189
Braun, Otto, 17–18, 20, 65, 67, 71, 86, 91, 123, 165, 166, 197
Brauns, Heinrich, 18–19
Brauns Commission, 19
Brecht, Arnold, 19–20, 91, 109, 114, 166
Bredt, Johann Victor, 20–1
Breitscheid, Rudolf, 21–2, 179
*Bremer Bürgerzeitung*, 41, 52
Brest-Litovsk, Treaty, 69, 90
Briand, Aristide, 174, 199
Brockdorff-Rantzau, Ulrich Graf von, 22–3
Brüning, Heinrich, 2
  as Chancellor, 7, 19, 20, 21, 24–5, 27, 33, 34, 36, 54, 58, 63, 79, 83, 99, 100, 104, 108, 114, 125, 127, 130, 136, 147, 151, 154, 156, 160, 161, 169, 178, 179, 183, 184, 187, 200, 201
  early career, 23
  as leader of Centre Party, 97
  and Osthilfe, 155
  as Reich presidential candidate, 148
Brüning–Meyer compromise, 166, 189
Buch, Walter, 111
Buchenwald, 22, 71, 177
Bülow, Chancellor Bernhard von, 14
Bürgerliche Arbeitsgemeinschaft, 169
*Burgfrieden* policy, 165, 182, 193
Bund der Elektrizitäts-Versorgungs-Unternehmungen Deutschlands, 141

Bund zur Erneuerung des Reiches, 120

Catholic Church, 98, 99, 101
Catholic Labour International, 96
Catholic Peasant Leagues, 78
Centre Party, 2, 7, 15, 18, 23, 33, 34, 49, 50, 73, 77, 83, 86, 104, 107, 116, 122, 123, 126, 130, 136, 155, 168, 169, 185, 187
  in national government, 11, 17, 24, 26, 32, 46, 99, 122, 123, 150
  collapse of, 33, 97
  and separatism, 38
  and Reich presidency, 55, 147
  in Prussia, 65, 71, 76, 85, 91
  leadership of, 96, 98, 186, 199
  and NSDAP, 99, 148
*Chemnitzer Volksstimme*, 70, 128
China expedition, 40
Christian Democratic Party (CDU), 7, 137, 155
Christian German Trade Union League, 168
Christian National Coalition, 178
Christian National Peasants' and Agrarian People's Party, 151, 154, 178
Christian-Social Metalworkers' Union, 86
Chrisian Social movement, 71
Christian Social Union (CSU), 148, 169
Christian trade unions, 18, 23, 168, 179
Churchill, Winston, 129
Commercial College (Cologne), 124, 167
Committee of Investigation, 20
Communist International (Comintern), 25, 31, 50, 52, 82, 88, 115, 116, 127, 132, 143, 176, 177, 180, 190, 193
Concordat (1933), 99
Conservative People's Party (KVP), 90, 179, 184
Constitution Day, 138
Council of People's Representatives, 9, 10, 11, 22, 37, 41, 67, 82, 113, 114, 118, 119, 128, 135, 150, 188, 195
Criminal Code, 99, 100, 114, 138
Crispien, Artur, 25–6
Crown Prince, 163

Cuno, Wilhelm, 3, 26–7, 69, 79, 120, 197
Curtius, Julius, 27–8, 160

Dachau, 97, 102, 148
Dahlem, Franz, 28–9
Darmstadt Bank, 121
Darré, Richard Walter, 29–31
*Das Finanzkapital*, 81
*Das Freie Wort*, 71
*Das Gebot der Stunde*, 14, 67
*Das Kapital*, 81
David, Eduard, 32–3, 157
Dawes Plan, 69, 74, 77, 90, 107, 108, 123, 173, 198
DDP, *see* German Democratic Party
Decree for the Defence of the Constitution of the Republic, 68
De Gaulle, General Charles, 7
Democratic People's League, 80, 139, 140
Denazification, 9, 94, 131, 148
Depression, the Great, 7, 22, 24, 57, 63, 80, 83, 86, 87, 91, 96, 99, 107, 142, 161, 171, 177, 181, 200
*Der Angriff*, 57
*Der Deutsche*, 23, 168
*Der Deutscher Volkskurier*, 93
*Der Hauptfeind steht im eigenen Land*, 117
*Der Klassenkampf*, 116
*Der Sozialdemokrat*, 13
*Der Sozialist*, 21
*Der Tag*, 90
Dessauer, Friedrich, 33
Deutsche Bank, 74
*Deutsche Freiheit*, 167
*Deutsche Politik*, 80
Deutscher Bismarck-Orden, 110
Deutsche Hochschule für Politik, 80
Deutscher Kampfbund, 144
Deutscher Kampfbund zur Brechung der Zinsknechtschaft, 48
*Deutsche Wirtschaftszeitung*, 69
Deutschlandbund, 96, 155, 167
Deutschnationaler Handlungsgehilfenverband, 179

Deutschsoziale Partei, 110
Deutschvölkische Freiheitspartei, 39, 110, 154, 165
Deutsch-Völkischer Studentenbund, 110
*Die Deutsche Nation*, 80
*Die Frau*, 12, 13
Die Freie Jugend, 167
*Die Freiheit*, 78, 82
*Die Gesellschaft*, 82
*Die Gleichheit*, 97, 192, 193
*Die Glocke*, 70
*Die Hilfe*, 12, 45, 80
*Die Internationale*, 143, 175, 193
*Die Kreuzzeitung*, 90
*Die Neue Zeit*, 14, 81
*Die Rote Fahne*, 52, 122, 126, 127, 143
Dietrich, Hermann, 2, 34
Dietrich, Otto, 35
Dingeldey, Eduard, 35–6, 100, 160
Dinter, Artur, 146
Disarmament Law, 65, 105
Dittmann, Wilhelm, 37, 67
DNVP, *see* German National People's Party
Dönitz, Admiral Karl, 161
Dorten, Hans Adam, 38
*Dresdner Volkszeitung*, 61, 172
Drexler, Anton, 38–40, 48
Duesterberg, Abraham Selig, 41
Duesterberg, Theodor, 40–1
Düwell, Bernhard, 108
DVP, *see* German People's Party

*Early Diary* (Goebbels), 56
East Berlin rising, 132, 181
East Prussian Settlement Bank, 53
Ebert, Friedrich, 1, 27, 41–2, 55, 61, 62, 67, 72, 80, 83, 100, 113, 114, 150, 163, 169, 182, 190, 195, 196, 198
Ebert–Groener Pact, 62, 195
Economic Party, 20
Eckart, Dietrich, 145
Editors' Law, 35
Eher Verlag, 8
Ehrhardt Brigade, 103

Eichhorn, Erich, 85
Einwohnerwehr, *see* Home Guard
Eisenacher group, 37
Eisler, Elfriede, 50
Eisner, Clara, 192
Eisner, Kurt, 43–4, 195, 196
Emergency Decree (1931), 58
Enabling Bill, 15, 34, 36, 80, 97, 99, 167, 169, 183, 187
Engels, Friedrich, 14
Epp, Franz Ritter von, 44–5, 73, 148
*Erfüllungspolitik*, 23, 77, 89, 140, 173, 186, 197
Erfurt Programme, 14, 158
Erkelenz, Anton, 45–6
Erzberger, Matthias, 46–7, 74, 85, 186, 195, 197
Essen Programme, 168, 169
Esser, Hermann, 39
Evangelical Social Congress, 12
Eyck, Erich, 75, 99

Factory Councils Law, 11
Falkenhayn, General Erich von, 83
Fatherland Party, 39, 102
Feder, Gottfried, 47–9, 146
Federal Constitutional Court, 92
Federal Republic of Germany, 7, 53, 78, 79, 92, 98, 119, 137, 155
Federal Service Cross, 189
Federation of Christian Trade Unions in Germany, 168
Federation of German Democratic Trade Unions, 168
Fehrenbach, Konstantin, 3, 18, 49–50, 77, 106, 141, 159, 186, 196
Feldherrnhalle, 39, 48
Fellisch, Karl, 191
feminist movement, 12, 192
First Bavarian Foot Artillery, 16, 170
Fischer, Ruth, 2, 50–1, 177
Flag decree, 55, 112, 120
Foch, Marshal, 195
*For the Liberation of Women*, 192

Four Year Plan, 31, 60
First World War, 7–9, 11–12, 14, 16, 18, 22–3, 26–7, 29–30, 33, 35, 37–8, 40, 42–4, 47–9, 51–3, 58–64, 66–71, 73–5, 77–8, 80, 82, 84, 86–7, 89–90, 92, 94, 99, 102, 103, 104, 107, 108, 109, 110, 113–15, 117–18, 121, 124–5, 128, 130, 131, 136–9, 141, 142, 144, 147, 149, 154, 156–9, 161–2, 164–5, 167–8, 170, 172, 175, 178–80, 182–3, 188, 193
France, 7, 22, 23, 28, 30, 38, 65, 77, 78, 82, 97, 98, 173, 175, 179, 200
Franco–Prussian War, 83, 114
*Frankfurter Zeitung*, 43, 74
*Fränkischer Tagespost*, 43
*Fränkischer Volksfreund*, 167
*Fränkischer Volksverlag*, 48
Frauenschaft (Nazi), 13
Freedom Law, 151, 154, 178, 184
Free Conservative Party, 20, 76
Free Democratic Party, 34, 80, 92
Free Socialist Republic of Germany, 118
Free Workers' Committee, 39
*Freie Volkszeitung* (Göppingen), 174
*Freie Volkszeitung* (Königsberg), 25
Freikorps, 31, 44, 59, 61, 118, 129, 132, 156, 163, 165, 186, 190, 196
Freikorps Epp, 44, 144, 170
French Foreign Legion, 28
Frick, Wilhelm, 51–2, 165, 187
Friesland, Ernst, 50
Fröhlich, Paul, 52–3
Frontbann, 144
Führerkreis, 45
*Führerkult*, 56, 88

Gayl, Freiherr Wilhelm von, 53–4, 95
*Gemeinwirtschaft*, 158, 189
General Commission of German Trade Unions, 11, 157
Genoa Conference, 186, 197
George, Stefan, 80
German Academy of Administration, 89, 153
German Agricultural Workers' Union, 17

German–Austrian Customs Union, 28, 200
German Catholic Assembly, 73
German Communist Party (KPD), 31, 32, 30, 50, 52, 65, 79, 88, 89, 92, 93, 103, 107, 113, 116, 118, 122, 126, 127, 129, 130, 132, 142, 143, 162, 165, 173, 174, 175, 176, 177, 180, 181, 182, 186, 187, 190, 191, 192, 193, 195, 196, 197, 198
 and elections, 24
 and the NSDAP, 127, 132, 143, 175, 177, 180, 181
 and the SPD, 26, 132, 190, 191
 and the USPD, 37, 82, 108, 115, 116, 176, 193
German Communist Party-Opposition (KPD-Opposition), 52, 175, 183
German Conservative Association, 110
German Conservative Party, 90, 102, 110, 150
German Democratic Party (DDP), 2, 11, 12, 13, 17–18, 32, 34, 45, 54–5, 68–70, 75, 80, 91, 100, 105–6, 112, 135, 140, 150, 152, 153, 160, 169, 173, 181, 182, 187, 195
German Democratic Republic (DDR), 30, 63, 64, 89, 109, 131, 132, 180, 181
German Labour Delegation, 65
German Labour Front (DAF), 46
German Liberal People's Party, 27
German Industry and Trade Assembly, 69
German Metalworkers' Union, 9, 64, 92, 142, 164, 165, 188
German Municipal Assembly, 105, 120
German National League, *see* Deutschlandbund
German National People's Party (DNVP), 20, 28, 36, 40–1, 47, 49, 53–4, 69, 71, 74, 77, 89–90, 93–5, 99, 102, 104, 106, 110, 120, 150, 151, 153–4, 159–61, 164, 169, 173, 178–9, 184–5, 195, 199
German Peasants' Association, 78
*German People and Politics*, 135

German People's Party (DVP), 7, 14, 17, 26–8, 35–6, 45, 91, 95, 99, 100, 105–6, 120, 123–6, 141–2, 153–4, 160, 163, 169, 172–4, 178, 182, 191, 195
German–Polish Agreement, 153
German Red Cross, 55
German–Soviet Friendship Society, 187
German–Soviet war, 132
German State Party, 13, 27, 34, 36, 45, 76, 80, 91, 106, 112, 160
German Transport Workers' Union, 176
German Women's League, 12
German Woodworkers' Union, 37
German Workers' Party (DAP), 38, 39, 48, 87, 144, 145, 196
*Germania*, 130
Gessler, Otto, 54–6, 62, 69, 119, 163, 182, 199
Gestapo, 8, 22, 58, 64, 69, 82, 143, 172, 177
Gierke, Otto, 134
Gilbert, Parker, 107, 133
Glaubensbewegung Deutsche Christen, 111
*Gleichschaltung*, 51, 66
Goebbels, Joseph, 9, 35, 56–7, 119, 171, 172
Goerdeler, Carl, 16, 57–8, 69, 78, 119, 137, 155
Goering, Hermann, 17, 59–60, 119, 171, 172, 193
Goethe, Johann Wolfgang von, 12
Golke, Ruth, 50
Görlitz Programme, 14, 18
*Görlitzer Volkszeitung*, 125
Gradnauer, Georg, 60–1
Grand Coalition government, 2, 11, 24, 33, 34, 79, 82, 104, 106, 124–6, 133, 159–60, 165, 166, 169, 183, 187, 199, 200
Green Front, 78, 151
Groener, Wilhelm, 62–3, 156, 185, 199, 201
Grossdeutsche Freiheitsbewegung, 48
Grossdeutsche Volksgemeinschaft, 16
Grotewohl, Otto, 63–4, 132
Grzesinski, Albert, 64–6, 93, 167
Günther, Franz, 66–7

Günther, Hans, 51
Gutehoffnungshütte, 27

Haase, Hugo, 14, 25, 42, 67–8, 114
*Habilitationsschrift*, 20, 74, 75, 89, 99, 109, 124, 134, 137
Hague Conferences, 124, 159, 187, 200
Hamburg–American shipping company, 26, 27
*Hamburger Echo*, 52
Hamm, Eduard, 68–9
Handelshochschule (Berlin), 135
Hansa League, 172
Harrer, Karl, 39
Hartmann, Gustav, 168
Harzburg Front, 40, 93, 163, 164, 200
Hauptarchiv (NSDAP), 40
Haussmann, Conrad, 69–70
Heidelberg Conference and Programme, 11, 82
Hegel, Georg W.F., 139
Heilmann, Ernst, 70–1
Heim, Georg, 73
Heine, Wolfgang, 71–2, 157
Heinze, Rudolf, 3, 191
Held, Heinrich, 72–3, 147, 148
Helfferich, Karl, 46, 47, 74–5, 82
Hellpach, Willy, 75–6
Hergt, Oskar, 76–7
Hermes, Andreas, 77–8
Herrenklub, 130
Hertz, Paul, 78–9
Hertz Resolution, 79
Hess, Joseph, 71
Heuss, Theodor, 20, 79–81, 112
Hiertsiefer, Heinrich, 85–6
Hilferding, Rudolf, 79, 81–3, 116, 120, 124, 133
Himmler, Heinrich, 31, 134
Hindenburg, Paul von, 1, 7, 24, 28, 53, 54, 62, 83–4, 87, 95, 99, 112, 119, 123, 126, 130, 148, 151, 155–7, 160, 161, 169, 184, 185, 187, 199, 201
Hirsch-Duncker unions, 45, 168

Hirsch, Paul, 84–5
'*History of . . . German Municipal Law*', 134
Hitler, Adolf, 1, 8, 16, 20, 31, 35, 38–40, 44, 48, 51–2, 56–9, 63, 65–6, 73, 80, 84, 86–8, 101–4, 111, 121, 134, 144–6, 148, 154–5, 161–5, 167, 170–3, 183, 196–8, 201
    advent to power of, 19, 21, 24, 37, 41, 45, 60, 84, 99, 130, 131, 143, 157, 171, 179, 201
    and Hugenberg, 93, 94
    private finances of, 9
    and Reich presidency, 119
    trial of, 66, 102, 198
    and von Hindenburg, 84
*Hitlers Weg*, 80
Höchberg, Karl, 13
Hoernle, Edwin, 88–9
Hoetzsch, Otto, 89–90
Hoffmann, Johannes, 3, 68
Hohenzollerns, 135, 139
Höltermann, Karl, 93
Holy See, 99
Home Guard, 101, 110, 170, 187
Hoover moratorium, 28
Höpker-Aschoff, Hermann, 91–2
Hörsing, Friedrich Otto, 92–3
Hué, Otto, 157
Hugenberg, Alfred, 1, 54, 77, 90, 93–5, 151, 154, 173, 178, 184, 185, 199

Institute for Investigation of the Jewish Question, 146
International Bank, 124
International Brigade, 30
International Court, 153
International Institute of Agriculture, 89
International Labour Conference, 19
International Workers' Congress, 192
*Internationale Korrespondenz*, 71
*Internationale Presse-Korrespondenz*, 109
Internationale Rote Hilfe, 132
Inter-Parliamentary Union, 167
*Introduction to Legal Philosophy*, 137

*Introduction to the Study of Law*, 137
*Izvestia*, 160

Jarres, Karl, 95–6
Jews, 2, 7, 13, 32, 33, 34, 41, 43, 50, 51, 56, 58, 59, 60, 67, 70, 76, 78, 81, 84, 105, 111, 113, 115, 121, 122, 134, 135, 140, 152, 162, 172, 174, 192
Joos, Joseph, 33, 96–7
Jörns–Bornstein case, 116
Juchacz, Marie, 2, 97–8
*Jugendgerichtsgesetz*, 138
July Plot (1944), 16, 55, 58, 69, 119, 129, 134, 137, 148, 155
Jungdeutsche Orden, 45, 106
Junkers, 53, 54, 83, 102, 155, 156, 183

Kaas, Ludwig, 24, 96, 98–9, 147, 169, 199
Kahl, Wilhelm, 99–100
Kahr, Gustav von, 68, 100–2, 145, 198
*Kaiserreich*, 10, 49, 74, 84, 157, 159, 162, 173, 192
Kaiser Wilhelm, 62, 90, 119, 128, 135, 139, 149, 184, 185, 195
Kalle, Wilhelm, 124
Kampfbund für deutsche Kultur, 146
Kampfbund gegen den Faschismus, 143
Kampfverlag, 171
*Kampfzeit*, 16, 51, 59, 66, 170
Kant, Immanuel, 137
Kapp Putsch, 11, 20, 27, 44, 72, 76, 85, 100, 102–3, 104, 107, 113, 129, 138, 150, 153, 162, 165, 182, 183, 196
Kapp, Wilhelm, 102–3
*Kasseler Volksblatt*, 149
Kautsky, Karl, 14, 81, 114
Keil, Wilhelm, 103–5
Kellogg–Briand Pact, 174, 199
Kessler, Count Harry, 84
Ketteler, Bishop, 18
Keudall, Walther von, 3, 20, 113
Kirdorf, Emil, 35
Kirschmann, Emil, 98
Kleefeld, Käthe, 172

Koch-Weser, Erich, 91, 105–6, 112
Koenen, Wilhelm, 107–8
Köhler, Heinrich, 108–9
Köster, Adolf, 109–10
Kube, Wilhelm, 110–11
Külz, Wilhelm, 111–12

Landsberg, Otto, 113–14
Landsberg prison, 39, 87
Landbund, 31
Lange, Helene, 12
Lassalle, Ferdinand, 168
Lausanne Conference, 24, 131, 161, 201
Law of Hereditary Entailment, 31
Law for the Protection of the Republic, 19, 50, 65, 68, 101, 110, 138, 140, 184, 187, 197
Law for the Protection of Youth from Trashy and Erotic Literature, 12, 80, 112
League of Nations, 12, 21, 23, 61, 98, 137, 173, 184, 197, 199
Lebensborn, 13
Ledebour, Georg, 114–15
Legien, Carl, 182
Leipart, Theodor, 156
*Leipziger Volkszeitung*, 67
Lenin, V. I., 127, 175, 180, 193
Leuschner circle, 189
Levi, Paul, 29, 115–17, 193
Liberal Association, 100, 153, 160
Liberal Democratic Party, 112, 153
Liebknecht, Karl, 117–18, 122, 132, 192, 196
Liebknecht, Theodor, 115
Liebknecht, Wilhelm, 117
Liszt, Franz von, 137
Löbe, Paul, 2, 118–20, 160
Locarno Agreements, 90, 120, 123, 150, 160, 173, 184, 199
Loebell Committee, 95
Lohmann scandal, 55
London Conference, 49, 197
London Ultimatum, 70, 153, 186, 197
Ludendorff, Erich, 62, 83, 198

Lüders, Marie-Elizabeth, 2
Lueger, Karl, 87
Luftwaffe, 60
Luther, Hans, 7, 27, 106, 112, 120–1, 123, 150, 198, 200
Lüttwitz, General Walther von, 76, 103, 106
Luxemburg, Rosa, 2, 52, 115, 116, 117, 121–2, 132, 175, 192, 196

*Machtergreifung*, 77, 82, 143, 145, 167
March Action, 29, 92, 116, 175, 197
Magdeburg court case, 42, 80, 113
*Manifesto for Breaking of Interest Slavery*, 47
Manuilsky, Dimitri, 127
Marx, Karl, 14, 21, 81, 139, 192
Marx, Wilhelm, 3, 18, 69, 77, 95, 96, 107, 112, 122–4, 150, 151, 160, 187, 198
Marxism, 13, 14, 21, 31, 39, 40, 43, 52, 56, 60, 86, 88, 93, 101, 121, 128, 144, 149, 164, 169, 175, 178, 180, 192, 193
Marx–Engels Institute, 175
*Marx-Studien*, 81
Maslow, Arkady, 50, 127
*Maslows Offensive gegen den Leninismus*, 127
Mauthausen, 30
Mayr, Karl, 48
Mehring, Franz, 175, 192
*Mein Kampf*, 9, 87
Mendelssohn, Felix, 58
Merker, Paul, 29
*Michael, Ein deutsches Schicksal*, 56
*Mitteldeutsche Sonntagszeitung*, 32, 149
Moldenhauer, Paul, 124–5
Möllendorff, Wickard von, 188
Moltke, Helmuth von, 153
Müller, General Alfred, 191
Müller, Hermann, 2, 11, 33, 34, 77, 105, 106, 110, 124, 125–6, 133, 138, 158, 159, 160, 165, 183, 186, 189, 199
  see also, Grand Coalition
*Mythos des 20. Jahrhunderts*, 146

*Nation*, 134

National Agrarian League, 151
National Assembly, 11, 13, 14, 17, 18, 23, 31, 32, 34, 45, 49, 55, 70, 96, 97, 98, 100, 105, 108, 112, 113, 116, 118, 119, 122, 125, 135, 140, 150, 152, 165, 167, 168, 176, 182, 184, 185, 189, 195, 196
National Association of Catholic Labour Unions, 96
National Coal Council, 189
National Committee for a Free Germany, 89, 132, 181
National Economic Council, 189
National Front of German Estates, 184
National Liberals, 19, 34, 94, 100, 105, 152, 159, 172
National Social People's League, 39
National Socialism, 8, 13, 15, 25, 35, 51, 53, 56, 57, 59, 63, 66, 76, 97, 121, 127, 130, 132, 143, 146, 167, 170, 171, 175, 190
  see also, NSDAP
National Socialist Freedom Party, 51, 170
National Socialist Lawyers' Association, 66
*Nationalsozialistische Bibliothek*, 48
*Nationalsozialistische Briefe*, 56, 171
*Nationalsozialistische Monatshefte*, 146
National Youth Welfare Act, 12
National Workers' Council, 45
Nationaler Frauendienst, 12
*Nationalzeitung*, 35
Naumann, Friedrich, 12, 13, 45, 54, 80, 105, 139
Nazi Left, 56, 156, 171
*Neckar-Zeitung*, 80
Neo-Germania fraternity, 172
Neu Beginnen, 79
*Neue Gesellschaft*, 71, 118, 165
*Neue Kampffront*, 93
*Neue Presse*, 166
Neumann, Heinz, 126–8, 143, 193
New School for Social Research, 20
Nietzsche, Friedrich, 139, 192
Night of the Long Knives, 145, 172
  see also Röhm, Ernst
Nobel Peace Prize, 174, 199

*Norddeutsche Volksstimme*, 37
Nordic Ring, 31
Noske, Gustav, 14, 55, 69, 128–9, 182
November Revolution, 9, 10, 14, 17, 21, 28, 29, 31, 37, 41, 53, 61–3, 67, 69, 72, 83–5, 87, 90, 102, 113, 114, 117–18, 122, 126, 128, 135, 149, 156, 158, 165, 182
NSDAP (Nazi Party), 8, 16, 18, 21, 22, 24, 28, 30–41, 44, 48, 51–2, 56–62, 65, 66, 73, 80, 84, 86–8, 91, 93–101, 104, 109–11, 119, 127, 129–30, 134, 142–8, 154, 156, 164–5, 167, 169–71, 177, 179–81, 187, 193, 196–8, 200, 201
Nuremberg Military Tribunal, 52, 60, 131, 146, 162, 164

Old Prussian Union, 111
Organisation Consul, 47, 140
*Osteuropa*, 90
*Osthilfe*, 151, 154, 155, 169, 179
Ostmarkenverein, 89

Pan-Europa Union, 119
Pan-Germanism, 86, 162
Pan-German League, 89, 90, 94
Papen coup (July 1932), 18, 54, 64, 73, 86, 92, 130, 131, 133, 166, 183, 189, 201
Papen, Franz von, 2, 18, 41, 53, 54, 64, 66, 83, 91, 97, 99, 104, 130–1, 133, 137, 148, 156, 161, 185, 201
Paris Peace Conference, 23, 27, 54, 162, 167, 196
Parliamentary Council, 92, 119
Party programme (NSDAP), 39, 48, 87, 146, 171, 196
Patriotic Eastern Associations, 179
Peace Resolution (1917), 42, 46, 49, 56, 152
People's Court, 58, 78, 137
People's National Reich Association, 106
Pieck, Wilhelm, 131–3
Plebiscite, Schleswig, 110
Pocket battleship A, 116, 126
Poincaré, Raymond, 26, 186

Poland, 17, 32, 53, 61, 77, 78, 85, 89, 102, 113, 121, 153, 163, 173, 179, 187
Political Workers' Circle, 39
Pope, the, 98
Popitz, Johannes, 133–4
Popular Conservative Union, 178, 179
*Pour le Mérite*, 44, 59
Preuss, Hugo, 134–6
Progressive People's Party, 69, 135
Proletarian Hundreds, 190, 191
Prussian Constitutional Convention, 71, 72, 76, 90
Prussian House of Deputies, 17, 20, 84, 117, 122, 152
Prussian Mining Office, 108
Prussian State Assembly, 70, 76, 86
Prussian State Council, 7, 54, 95, 98, 119, 132
Prussian Upper House (Herrenhaus), 105, 159, 168
Prusso–Austrian war, 83
Pünder, Hermann, 136–7

Quakers, 167
*Querfront* policy, 142, 156, 171

Radbruch, Gustav, 137–9
Raiffeisenverband, 78
Rapallo, Treaty of, 23, 82, 90, 140, 163, 174, 187, 197
Rathenau, Walther, 1, 23, 61, 74, 80, 107, 110, 116, 119, 138, 139–40, 164, 186, 187, 188, 197
Raumer, Hans von, 141–2
Ravensbrück, 55
Red Army, 89, 132, 150, 156, 181
*Regensburger Anzeiger*, 73
*Regensburger Morgenblatt*, 73
Reich Association of German Newspaper Publishers, 9
Reich Association of the German Press, 35
Reich Association of German Technology, 48
Reich Colonial Office, 74

Reich Consular Service, 59
Reich Council for National Defence, 60
Reich Economic Council, 27
Reich Economic Council (NSDAP), 48
Reich Military Court, 117
Reich presidential elections
  in 1919, 42
  in 1925, 18, 73, 75, 83, 95, 123, 147, 176
  in 1932, 41, 84, 87, 148, 177, 201
Reich Press Chamber, 9
Reich Treasury, 11, 14, 26, 74, 124, 141, 152
Reichsabwicklungsamt, 64
Reichsbahn, 39
Reichsbank, 2, 74, 82, 91, 107, 120, 121, 123, 124, 133, 200
Reichsbanner Schwarz Rot Gold, 45, 92, 93, 96, 123, 165, 166, 183, 187, 198
Reichsbund der Höeren Beamten Deutschlands, 159
Reichskriegsflagge, 144
Reichskonferenz, 85
Reichslandbund, *see* National Agrarian League
Reichsnährstand, 31
Reichspartei des deutschen Mittelstands, 20, 21
Reichsrat, 20, 54, 60, 61
*Reichsreform*, 73, 85, 91, 105, 112
Reichstag elections, 11, 13, 15, 16, 18, 19, 21, 24, 33-4, 36-7, 44, 47-9, 53, 60, 61, 69, 75, 77, 87, 88, 99, 103, 104, 106, 110, 111, 115, 119, 127, 129, 138, 141, 144, 146, 155, 160, 170, 171, 176, 179, 180, 182-5, 196, 199, 200, 201
Reichsverband der Bismarck-Jugend, 110
Reichsverband der deutschen Industrie, 141
Reichswehr, 24, 26, 42, 44, 48, 55, 61-3, 83, 87-8, 101, 103, 113, 116, 119, 129, 144-5, 150, 155-6, 162-3, 165, 171, 190, 191, 195-6, 198
Reinhardt, Walter, 129
Remmele, Hermann, 127, 142-3
Rentenmark, 82, 120, 173, 198

Reparations, 8, 24, 26-8, 49, 69, 70, 74, 82, 107, 124, 126, 131, 133, 140, 141, 153, 158-9, 161, 173-4, 186-7, 196-8, 200, 201
Republican Democratic People's Party, 45
Republican Union, 187
Republikanische Soldatenwehr, 182
Revolutionary Shop Stewards' movement, 9, 10, 29
Revolutionary Trade Union Opposition (RGO), 29, 30
Revolutions of 1848, 70, 102
Rheinisch-Republikanische Volkspartei, 38
Rheinische Volksvereinigung, 38
*Rheinische Warte*, 38
*Rheinischer Herold*, 38
*Rheinische Zeitung*, 167
Rhenish separatism, 7, 8, 21, 38, 95, 167, 173, 198
Richthofen squadron, 59
Röhm, Ernst, 41, 60, 66, 102, 131, 143-5, 157
Rosenberg, Alfred, 145-7
Rotfrontkämpferbund (RFB), 93, 176, 181, 198, 200
Royal Palace, 118, 182
Ruhr industrial crisis (1928), 189, 199
Ruhr invasion (1923), 7, 8, 26, 38, 77, 95, 113, 173, 186, 191, 197, 198
Rupprecht, Crown Prince, 148
Russia, 10, 22, 23, 25, 67, 69, 83, 89, 90, 127, 145, 149, 160, 168
  *see also* Soviet Union
Russian Revolution (1905), 44, 59, 60, 63, 93, 130, 143-5, 148, 164-5, 167, 170, 201

Saalecker circle, 31
Saarland, 98, 167
Sachsenhausen, 22
*Sächsische Arbeiterzeitung*, 61
Sailors' revolt (1918), 69, 70, 113, 128, 195
Saxony, crisis of 1923, 61, 138, 159, 165, 167, 190-1, 198

Schacht, Hjalmar, 2, 74, 82, 121, 123, 124, 133, 157, 200
Schäffer, Fritz, 147–9
Scheidemann, Philipp, 11, 23, 46, 113, 118, 128, 135, 149–50, 152, 158, 188, 196
Scherl publishers, 94
Schiele, Martin, 2, 150–2
Schiffer, Eugen, 152–4
Schlange-Schöningen, Hans, 154–5
Schleicher, Kurt von, 1, 22, 63, 66, 83, 129, 142, 145, 155–7, 161, 171, 185, 201
Schmidt, Robert, 157–9
Scholz, Ernst, 36, 159–61
Schönerer, Georg von, 87
Schumacher, Kurt, 64
*Schwäbischer Tagwacht*, 25, 103, 104
Schwerin von Krosigk, Lutz Graf, 161
Second World War, 8, 13, 31, 35, 55, 57, 60, 64, 67, 78, 94, 97, 134, 146, 153, 179, 191
Seeckt, Hans von, 26, 55, 103, 156, 162–3, 199
Seldte, Franz, 40, 163–4
Sender, Toni, 2
Severing, Carl, 2, 17, 65, 72, 93, 129, 154, 164–6, 167, 189
Social Democratic Party (SPD), 2, 9, 10, 11, 14–17, 18, 21–2, 25, 29, 31, 32, 37, 42–3, 46, 52–3, 60–8, 70–2, 78–9, 81–2, 84–5, 88, 92–3, 97–8, 101–4, 108–10, 113–15, 117, 118, 121, 125, 128–9, 131, 137–9, 142, 149, 155–6, 159–60, 164, 166–7, 174, 176, 180–2, 188, 190–3
and congresses, 14, 104, 113, 119, 182, 189
in exile, 26, 79, 82, 167, 183
and KPD, 30, 42, 127, 132, 143, 176, 177, 190, 191, 198
in national government, 11, 18, 32, 46, 95, 106, 125, 126, 141, 150, 152, 159, 167, 182, 183, 185, 187, 195, 198
and NSDAP, 22

and party programmes, 14, 18, 82, 158
and pre-war revisionism, 13, 42, 43, 121, 125, 157, 165
in Prussia, 17–18, 64–5, 70–2, 84–5, 91, 93, 130, 131, 165, 166, 197
and Reich presidential elections, 18
toleration policy, 21, 24, 79, 127, 183
and USPD, 25, 37, 61, 79, 115, 116, 197
Social Education Institute, 12
Socialist International, 43, 183, 192, 193
Socialist League, 115
Socialist Unity Party (SED), 30, 64, 109, 112, 132, 181
Socialist Youth International, 117
Socialist Workers' Party (SAP), 52, 53, 115
Socialization, 70, 82, 108, 152, 158, 188
Socialization Commission, 82, 126, 140, 141
Society for Internal Colonization, 102
Sollmann, Wilhelm, 166–8
Somme, the, 164
Sonnenschein, Carl, 23
South German People's Party, 69
Soviet Republic (Munich, 1919), 43, 44, 52, 144, 170, 196
Soviet Union, 7, 56, 64, 82, 89, 90, 109, 132, 142, 143, 153, 163, 174, 175, 176, 180, 181, 187, 191, 193, 197, 199
*Sozialdemokratische Korrespondenz*, 121
*Sozialdemokratischer Pressedienst*, 167
*Sozialistische Monatshefte*, 71, 118, 188
*Sozialistische Politik und Wirtschaft*, 116
*Sozialistische Republik*, 30
Sozialrepublikanische Partei Deutschlands, 93
*Sozialstaat*, 18, 85, 86, 98, 161, 169, 188
Soziale Frauenschule, 12
Spa Conference, 49, 141, 196
Spanish Civil War, 181
Spartacists, 10, 29, 32, 42, 68, 85, 88, 114–18, 121–2, 131–2, 175, 182, 192, 193, 196
Special Court for Protection of the Republic, 50, 138

# Index

Spengler, Oswald, 139
SS, 9, 13, 17, 66, 134, 145, 146, 165, 172, 201
Staatsgerichtshof, 19, 86
Stahlhelm, 31, 40, 41, 65, 93, 163, 164, 179, 195
Stalin, Josef, 50, 88, 127, 143, 176, 177, 181, 193
Stalin Prize, 187
Stalingrad, 35
Stampfer, Friedrich, 157
Stegerwald, Adam, 23, 96, 151, 156, 168–70
Stinnes–Legien Pact, 140, 168, 195
Strasser, Gregor, 33, 48, 52, 56, 80, 145, 156, 170–2
Strasser, Otto, 56, 171
Stresemann, Gustav, 1, 55, 136, 151, 172–4, 200
    as Chancellor, 77, 95, 120, 123, 138, 141, 158, 159, 167, 169, 173, 190, 191, 198
    as foreign minister, 2, 23, 28, 77, 89, 90, 98, 120, 150, 160, 163, 173–4, 184, 199
    as party leader, 7, 36, 95, 100, 160, 172–4
Stritt, Marie, 12
Stroebel, Heinrich, 85
Study Group for German history books, 17
Süsskind, Heinrich, 127
Switzerland, 13, 14, 18, 22, 24, 26, 33, 72, 74, 82, 97, 115, 127

Tannenberg, battle of, 83
Tariffs Act, 151
*Tasks of International Social Democracy*, 121
Teusch, Christine, 2
Thalheimer, August, 174–6
Thälmann, Ernst, 127, 132, 143, 176–8, 180
Theresienstadt, 61
Third Reich, 7, 8, 9, 17, 28, 34, 46, 48, 51, 57–9, 76, 78, 80–1, 84, 88, 92, 94, 99, 104, 112, 120–1, 129, 131, 134, 137, 146, 153, 155, 161, 164, 166, 181, 183, 185, 189

Thule Society, 145,
Thyssen, Fritz, 35
Tietz, Luise, 2
Tirpitz, Admiral Alfred von, 102
Treaty of Berlin, 23, 90, 174, 199
Treviranus, Gottfried, 178–80
*Two Revolutions of 1917*, 127

Ulbricht, Walter, 30, 180–1
Ulitzka, Carl, 97
UFA (Universal Film), 94
unemployment insurance scheme, 79, 82, 123, 124, 125, 159, 126, 166, 189, 199
Union of Patriotic German Associations, 40
United Association of German Cooperatives, 78
United States, 20, 24, 25, 53, 79, 85, 98, 130, 167
Universities,
    Berlin, 80, 89, 99, 102, 110, 113, 120, 133, 134, 135, 150, 172
    Bonn, 23, 98
    Cologne, 24, 124
    Erlangen, 109
    Frankfurt, 33
    Freiburg im Breisgau, 35
    Freiburg (Switzerland), 33
    Geneva, 120
    Göttingen, 102
    Greifswald, 75
    Halle, 60
    Harvard, 24
    Heidelberg, 51, 56, 75, 115, 137, 138, 139
    Jena, 51
    Kiel, 120, 138
    Königsberg, 58, 67
    Leipzig, 19, 22, 75, 172
    Marburg, 20, 21
    Munich, 16, 21, 66, 68, 80, 101, 147
    Trier, 98
    Tübingen, 58, 102
    Vienna, 50

Upper Silesia, problem of, 61, 70, 92, 113, 140, 153, 163, 186, 197
USPD (Independent Social Democratic Party), 9, 10, 14, 21, 25, 28, 31, 32, 37, 43, 61, 63, 67, 68, 78, 79, 82, 85, 107, 113, 114, 115, 116, 118, 119, 121, 128, 132, 142, 176, 182, 188, 193, 195, 196, 197

Verband Nationalgesinnter Soldaten, 170
Verein zur Abwehr des Antisemitismus, 50, 113
Versailles, Treaty of, 11, 24, 26, 27, 32, 40, 46, 55, 62, 70, 74, 113, 126, 135, 144, 153, 158, 163, 173, 186, 196
Vichy authorities, 82
Völkischer Block, 39
Völkisch-Soziale Arbeitsgemeinschaft Gross-Berlins, 110, 111
Völkisch-Sozialer block, 170
Völkischer Akademikerverband, 110
*Völkischer Beobachter*, 8, 16, 44, 146
*Volksfreund*, 175
Volksmarinedivision (People's Naval Division), 10, 182
*Volkssozialismus*, 167
Volksverein für das Katholische Deutschland, 18, 122
*Volkswacht*, (Bielefeld), 165
*Volkswacht* (Breslau), 118
*Vorwärts*, 14, 28, 43, 61, 81, 109, 157

Walcher, Jakob, 88
War of Liberation, 41
Warmbold, Hermann, 2
Weber, Max, 139

Weimar Constitution, 11, 20, 24, 42, 46, 54, 55, 70, 83, 95, 100, 104, 105, 112, 135, 196
Wels, Otto, 181–3
Westarp, Kuno Graf von, 179, 183–5
*Westdeutscher Arbeiter-Zeitung*, 96
Wheeler-Bennett, John W., 156
White Book, 109
Wilson, Woodrow, 195
Windthorstbünde, 96
Wirth, Joseph, 11, 33, 61, 77, 110, 138, 140, 153, 158, 185–8, 197
Wissell, Rudolf, 2, 158, 188–90
Wittelsbach monarchy, 43, 73, 101, 148, 195
Wittorf scandal, 177, 180
Workers' and Soldiers' Councils, National Congress, 29, 114, 118, 122, 195
Working Committee of German Associations, 167
World Economic Conference, 151
WTB-Plan, 79, 169

Young Plan, 40, 90, 93, 124, 164, 174, 184, 187, 200
youth movement, 12, 63, 125, 142, 157, 180, 182, 192

Zeigner, Erich, 190–2
Zentralarbeitsgemeinschaft, 141, 142, 195
Zentralrat, 114
Zentralverband der Deutschen Elektrotechnischen Industrie, 141
Zetkin, Clara, 2, 97, 116, 127, 192–4
Zetkin, Ossip, 192
Zimmerwald conference, 114
Zionism, 14
Zörgiebel, Karl, 132